CONSIDERING EMMA GOLDMAN

NEXT WAVE:
NEW DIRECTIONS IN
WOMEN'S STUDIES

A series edited by Inderpal Grewal,
Caren Kaplan, and Robyn Wiegman

CONSIDERING
Emma Goldman

FEMINIST POLITICAL AMBIVALENCE
& THE IMAGINATIVE ARCHIVE

CLARE HEMMINGS

Duke University Press • Durham and London • 2018

© 2018 Duke University Press

Printed in the United States of America on acid-free paper ∞
Typeset in Arno Pro by Copperline Books

Library of Congress Cataloging-in-Publication Data
Names: Hemmings, Clare, author.
Title: Considering Emma Goldman : feminist political
ambivalence and the imaginative archive / Clare Hemmings.
Description: Durham : Duke University Press, 2018. | Series:
Next wave | Includes bibliographical references and index.
Identifiers: LCCN 2017027316 (print)
LCCN 2017041584 (ebook)
ISBN 9780822372257 (ebook)
ISBN 9780822369981 (hardcover : alk. paper)
ISBN 9780822370031 (pbk. : alk. paper)
Subjects: LCSH: Goldman, Emma, 1869–1940. | Women
anarchists—United States—Biography. | Feminist theory. |
Anarchism. | Women's rights.
Classification: LCC HX843.7.G65 (ebook) | LCC HX843.7.G65
H466 2018 (print) | DDC 335/.83092 [B] —dc23
LC record available at https://lccn.loc.gov/2017027316

Cover art: Illustration by Julienne Alexander

To the generous reader of the book

Contents

Contents

Acknowledgements

I am lucky enough to work in a context of enormous intellectual and emotional support: from friends and colleagues, and often from people who are both. Thanks are due first and foremost to those who listened to me gush or agonise at all stages of this project, or who read some or all of the manuscript: Rutvica Andrijasevic, Stephanie Berger, Tina Campt, John Chalcraft, Sonia Correa, Dasa Duhacek, Jo Eadie, Carrie Hamilton, David Hansen-Miller, Hilary Hinds, Hazel Johnstone, Amal Kabesh, Laleh Khalili, Ranjana Khanna, Julie Lindoe, Nicola Mai, Sonia Maluf, Kate Nash, Anne Phillips, Jane Rowley, Leticia Sabsay, Eva Skaerbaek, Jackie Stacey, Merl Storr, Alyosxa Tudor, Sadie Wearing, Robyn Wiegman, Michelle Wright. And to colleagues at the Department of Gender Studies and at the London School of Economics who always respond with enthusiasm to ideas I express, no matter how far away their own intellectual or political interests are from my own. These forms of recognition make daily life a pleasure and stand as a counter to the inflexible demands that institutions can otherwise make. A special thanks to all my PhD and MSc students, who often have no choice but to listen to me talking endlessly about queer feminist methodology, and who may now (perhaps) have some respite.

I want to thank all the people who listened to papers I presented, particularly in the early stages of this project, and to people who invited me to do so: I am thinking particularly of timely invitations from Srinivas Aravamudan, David Bell, Anne Berger, Richard Cleminson, Eric Fassin, Ruth Holiday, Eveline Kilian, Teresa Joaquim, Kaye Mitchell, Andrea Peto, Jan Radway, and Matthew Waites. These opportunities have helped me remember that I am not writing in a vacuum but with the hope that people might respond. Special thanks to Candace Falk at the Emma Goldman Papers Project for her generosity over several years, and to the archivists at Boston University Library for their interest in the Almeda Sperry letter-writing project. And lastly, my thanks to the members of "A Living Archive" project for the sense of queer anarchist engagement generated in such a short space of time.

Introduction

Emma Goldman was a really huge badass.

Sadly there are no surviving pictures of her riding a unicorn.

— HEXE, "ANARCHY, BDSM AND CONSENT-BASED CULTURE"

AMBIVALENT ARCHIVES

Emma Goldman (1869–1940), the larger-than-life anarchist activist and political thinker who has always inspired social movements and feminist thinking, continues to generate a hyperbolic critical response. According to Ally Fogg, writing in the *Guardian* in 2010, Goldman's relevance for contemporary politics is unequivocal, as she "tumbles through the ages like a snowball, gathering mass and momentum with each new appreciation." Vivian Gornick, her recent biographer, insists in the *Nation* that Goldman currently "occupies Wall Street" (2011b), while Maria Brettschneider (2013) and Bice Maiguashca (2014) situate her legacy as positively animating contemporary global justice movements. In a similar vein, Loretta Kensinger affirms Goldman's "ability to speak across time" (2007, 280), and Goldman is frequently cited as embodying the kind of radical spirit that is most needed in the present if the political and methodological deadlock between neoliberal and socialist forces is to be broken (Loizidou 2011). Judith Butler (2011) reflects on Goldman's value in a lecture at the New School in New York; Kathy Ferguson's (2011b) important full-length feminist engagement with Goldman's theoretical contributions was published in the same year, following an earlier edited collection on feminist interpretations of her work (Weiss and Kensinger 2007); and in 2014, "Revolutions," a special issue of *Feminist Review* (Andrijasevic, Hamilton, and Hemmings 2014), included discussion of Goldman's significance in four of the five full articles.[1] To some extent, this renewed interest in Goldman mirrors a renewed political and intellectual interest in anarchism more generally over the last ten or so years,[2] but unlike some of the rather dour anarchist comrades with whom Goldman overlapped—Alexander Berkman, Peter Kropotkin, Voltairine de Cleyre—it is Goldman's zeal, her ability to combine sexual and gendered politics with revolutionary international fervour, that is seized upon as essential for a contemporary radical political imagination.

The flavour of this critical and political engagement with Goldman is highly charged: it is by turns concerned to rescue Goldman from obscurity, delighted to have found the perfect heroine, and disparaging of her own myopia and inconsistency.[3] It is engaged, affectively saturated, and productive of its own passionate political desires. Thus, and typically, Kensinger is "thrilled" to come across Goldman (2007, 255), and Alice Wexler describes how Goldman "captured [her] imagination" (1992, 37). As Jason Wehling notes, Goldman's biographers find her by turns "amazing," "inspirational," or an "irritant," much as friends of Goldman's did during her lifetime (2007, 27). Those less seduced by Goldman's charm nevertheless tend to focus on her capacity to appeal, and on what they consider the unreasonable attachments that she generated—and continues to generate—in others (e.g., Herzog 2007; Solomon 1988). In more directly relational terms, Alix Kates Shulman insists that after decades of research proximity she can confidently assert that "we're a couple" (1984, 2), with all the ups and downs this suggests, foreshadowing Wexler's insistence that Goldman has taken up "permanent residence in my life" (1992, 49). In effect, then, the critical archive on Goldman (particularly, but by no means exclusively, feminist) is often marked by intimacy—the desire for it, the belief one has in it—and the disappointments that go along with investing too heavily in the significance of another. While engagement with Goldman's person and writing (her subjective archive) is central to this book, as I discuss later, so too is the engagement with her feminist interlocutors (her critical archive), as well as the theoretical archive that shapes the present.

The question of intimacy in the encounter with "the other," particularly the historical other, in research and biography is not uniquely produced by encounters with Goldman, of course. Joan Scott asks more generally how we might account for "our attraction to (or repulsion from) specific events, philosophies [or] figures" in history (2011, 147). Thinking relationally, as many feminist biographers and historians are apt to do, means that the "inmate relations" (Cook 1984, 398) or "flirtations" (400) that characterise this encounter are likely to be brought to the fore rather than denied. But they may still lead writers to "crystallize in their subjects unrealistic expectations about themselves and other[s]" (Ascher, DeSalvo, and Ruddick 1984, xxiii). In relation to Goldman, Wexler's account of the forms of identification and projection that attend the biographical process is the most direct, as she describes her fantasy substitution of Goldman for her own mother, and her mother's concomitant fight for her attention: in a rather extraordinary twist of fate, Wexler's mother dies on the same day as Goldman some forty years later (1992, 48). For Wexler, the point of tracking this process is both to foreground subjectivity in biographical research and also to show that this is helpful in making sense of Goldman's own "divided, conflicted subjectivity" (43).

Contemporary writers fascinated with Goldman are not alone in another way too. She has been consistently reinterpreted according to the mood of the time and the desires of the writer, as Oz Frankel (1996) has so thoroughly documented.[4] Indeed, Goldman herself was extremely sensitive to the importance of self-fashioning for a political and critical public and also was acutely aware of her own iconic status. As her devoted archivist Candace Falk tells us, Goldman took pains to transform her lectures into pieces of political theatre, employing a range of tactics—such as chaining herself to her podium, stuffing rags in her mouth to perform censorship, and so forth (2002, 13)—to make her political messages memorable.[5] She dramatised her politics and sensationalised her subjectivity as part of a highly developed strategy of promoting anarchism and herself as its advocate. The eloquent Christine Stansell describes Goldman's own person as embodying "both celebrity and politics, spectacle and radicalism, universality and self-aggrandizement" (2000, 121), noting further than such liveliness resulted in her being offered a place in vaudeville (an offer she refused), as well as making her a target for the American authorities who were extremely anxious about her popularity (138).[6] A range of writers, myself included, have embraced Goldman's enthusiasm and tenacity through characterising them as "passion" (Hemmings 2012b, 2014b; Rogness and Foust 2011),[7] yet this has also been a technique through which her contributions as a serious political theorist have been dismissed (see Weiss and Kensinger 2007).

The tension between a critical desire for Goldman and her own awareness and exploitation of this desire can be seen in the use of the diminutive to refer to her. The more attached to Goldman critics are, the more likely they are to want to demonstrate their intimacy with her through use of first name terms. Thus for Falk, Goldman is "feisty-edgy Emma" (2007, 43), and for Jamie Heckert while "Butler may have taught" us certain things (2012, 73) and "Rosenberg offers ... " contemporary anarchists certain insights, it is "Emma" who "has called us to be, to feel" (71). The special issue of *Social Anarchism* on Goldman is straightforwardly titled "It's All about Emma," and within its pages Kathryn Rosenfeld (2004–5) reflects on the importance for her and her friends of asking playfully "What would Emma do?" when faced with hard political or intellectual choices, while Sharon Presley (2004–5) takes up a "complex" Emma to rally a contemporary activist audience to be more daring. Other writers move more fluidly between "Emma" and "Goldman," as Cyril Greenland (2002) does in his funny and moving account of his childhood encounters with Goldman, Marie Stopes, and Margaret Sanger, and as Loizidou does in the acknowledgements to her edited collection on contemporary disobedience (2013, viii). Still others use the diminutive "Emma" in a familiar way to contrast with the sterner use of surnames for men, as John Ward does in his relentless counterposing of "Emma" and "Berkman" in his introduction to *Prison Memoirs of an Anarchist* (1970), and as Richard Drinnon and Anna Maria Drinnon do through their important collection of letters between these two comrades, *Nowhere at Home* (1975). Such a contrast draws on and reproduces a long history of diminishing women's achievements, marking "Emma" rather than "Berkman" as uncitable in the canon of political theory, and as less serious or challenging in her own time. It smacks of the long history of use of gendered diminutives—referring to women as "girls" or "pets"—and thoroughly domesticates the one thus described. But this is not something *other people* do, or that is the preserve only of thoughtless men or misogynists: as the preceding references quite clearly indicate, feminist and queer scholars also frame Goldman as a personal friend or confidante. And, indeed, in my own notes on her work and secondary sources I refer to Goldman variously as "Emma" or "EG," sometimes catching myself and inserting a more respectful "Goldman." The formal citation could be seen as marking an attempt, perhaps, to restore the distance that I otherwise find impossible to keep.

Importantly, Goldman also refers to *herself* as "E.G.," recognising the playful ways the contraction allows her to be exemplary or anonymous as well as informal. In a letter to Warren Starr Van Valkenburgh in 1916, Goldman notes that her friend may have difficulty getting his work on birth control published less because of its content and more because it "deals with E.G.," highlighting that she knows full well how she is framed for media and political community alike. As Falk notes, this serendipitous ability to make herself exemplary through her name facilitated Goldman's self-representation as "above conflict" too (2002, 17), as representative of anarchism rather than one among a range of its interpreters. Goldman often signed herself "E.G." in letters to friends (including to her lifelong friend and anarchist comrade, Alexander Berkman), clearly enjoying the pun (Drinnon and Drinnon 1975). Ferguson also reminds her readers that Goldman took the name "E. G. Smith" as a cover when she went underground after being associated with Leon Czolgosz's assassination of President William McKinley in 1901 (2011b, 300–305). So while our current critical and political attachments to Goldman are frequently demonstrated by a desire to suture ourselves to her), Goldman herself has often already anticipated that desire, playing with it, or mobilising it strategically to her own (or political) advantage. It is not just our own need for Goldman that catapults her across the ages to take her place as an exemplar of passionate radicalism, then, but her self-fashioning as an available figure in this dynamic.

I raise these intersubjective issues at the start of this book to foreground the dynamic nature of historical encounters and to flag the affective investments we all—critics and readers alike—have in a self-consciously charismatic figure such as Goldman. That relationship is never a neutral one, and this book centres Goldman as the point of attachment through which I explore several related aspects of contemporary feminist and queer historiography and politics. I argue that the uncertainty that characterises feminist and queer understandings of gender, race, and sexuality in the present is easily obscured through propositions of certainty about precisely these central concerns. In imagining that we know how to ameliorate gendered, racial, and sexual inequalities, or indeed what gender, race, and sexuality *are*, it is easy to miss the profound ambivalence about these terms and the inequalities or pleasures that cluster around them. That ambivalence is in fact fundamental to both the past and the present. It animates political struggles over and with precisely those objects we imagine we inherit as knowable, and it runs back and forth across time to challenge progress or loss narratives about where we come from and what political terrain we occupy now.[8] Attending to ambivalence as a continuous political and affective reality for those who want to intervene in gendered, raced, and sexual meanings and structures in order to ameliorate their harms shifts the nature of historical and contemporary inquiry. This approach refuses a political teleology that laments the loss of Left solidarity, for example, or one that straightforwardly celebrates an increasing integration of race within feminist or queer theory. It runs counter to a rights-based approach that characterises the twentieth century as one of increased recognition (or a lament about lack of recognition, or misrecognition), focusing attention instead on what is lost through a politics of certainty. What is gained from embracing a politics of ambivalence is a view of the past and present that centres both psychic and social aspects of inequality, the tenacity of our attachments to the objects that poison our lives, to paraphrase Lauren Berlant (2011), and an opportunity to engage in the struggle over what inequality is and how best to intervene to transform it. It tries to imagine inhabiting a reality as well as politics of ambivalence, and foregrounds the importance of affect as a guide to asking important political and theoretical questions. But if the past and present of feminist and queer politics are marked by ambivalence, then what tools do we need to take up in order to glimpse that past and make it fit for present purposes? How can political ambivalence be animated to ameliorate rather than increase inequality, and how will a critic or audience know the difference?[9]

Goldman is my guide in this project for several reasons that relate to the different archival contexts that frame her for a contemporary audience.[10] Firstly, there is the *subjective archive* of Goldman herself: her writing (published and unpublished); her letters to others and theirs to her; her actions and autobiography; the hopes and fears that trickle down to us in the tone of that contradictory archive and in its inevitable absences. Goldman was both a fervent and lifelong advocate of revolution—not a position we readily associate with ambivalence—and a person who struggled with all orthodoxies (including her own ideals). *Struggle* to articulate the unknown but to commit to it nevertheless could in fact be said to characterise her sexual politics as a whole. In this book, I bring forward the Goldman archive as a way of foregrounding these struggles over the meaning of key concepts we have inherited as ways of entering politics—gender, race, and sexuality—at one particular moment of their (revolutionary) articulation. In the process, I ask what it means to include Goldman in a feminist or queer history without wanting to clean her up first. And, of course, too, in the process, I hope to introduce Goldman's energetic theorising to a broader audience and through a particular lens.[11]

Secondly, I am interested in tracking the *critical archive* engaged with Goldman, as I have already begun to do in this introduction to the project. That archive forms itself through loops and folds, by turns uncovering Goldman, yet then burying her amid a sequence of affective and theoretical presumptions, or indeed forgetting her altogether. What do we learn about both Goldman's archive and the theoretical and political present when we attend to the critical archive as itself structured through ambivalence? Here I want to think through the question of historical inquiry and investment as an affective dynamic as well as a process of patient interrogation and investigation. My own and other critics' cleaving to or distance from Goldman's person or thought produces a rich archive to explore how we might manage our own ambivalence as well as hers. What we want to bring forward from Goldman's oeuvre or time and what we want to leave behind tell us something important about our present interests and political attachments. Central to this project, then, is a methodology that draws on my own and others' affective ambivalence as a way into thinking about the problems of the equally ambivalent political and theoretical present. I explore these aspects of methodology in more detail later, but for now I want to emphasise that understanding this process of engagement as an affective one recasts history (and historical research) as a dynamic that is alive, filled with political and personal yearning, and—importantly—not fully in this or any other writer's control. Goldman's subjective archive is not a dead set of texts that we deliberate over in the safety of our own time and space. Goldman jumps across that false distance to poke me, mock my presumptions, and fill me with longing. If the past and present are suffused with ambivalence, in other words, so too is the method of putting them in conversation with one another. My third archive, the *theoretical archive*, thus includes the set of presumptions and practices that frame what can be included as part of a feminist or queer project in the present. This archive includes understandings of what counts as "gender equality" (as well as how to achieve it), what "sexual politics" can or cannot include, and the place of "race" in a contemporary political imaginary. At heart it concerns the feminist and queer conversations that I see Goldman as speaking back to, intervening in, and at points radically reshaping. My access to this archive is of course fundamentally partial (since it is vast) and is enabled through my engagement with the critical Goldman archive as well as Goldman's own oeuvre. Attention to the critical archive gives me a sense of what it is that contemporary theorists—myself included—can bring forward or must leave to one side (or else not remain comfortable), and shifts our sense of the present to include its theoretical underbelly. What does the interplay between the visible and the buried of a contemporary terrain enable as part of a feminist politics of ambivalence going forward?

This project is thus not a great-person history with Goldman at its centre. It is not primarily an attempt to position Goldman as a lost foremother of a feminist or queer project that is necessarily the worse for ignoring her, although she most certainly did not like to be ignored. In that respect, I do not seek in this book to provide a full or final account of her life and work, or even of their foundational importance for contemporary theory and politics, although these aspects certainly have their moments in the book. But neither is Goldman an accidental choice, of course. It is her own *fervent ambivalence* about issues I hold dear in my own present, her consistent attention to questions of difference, and her failure to resolve the problematics that govern those questions that have drawn me to Goldman. So too it is her presence as a powerful figure in my own life (much as for Wexler), coming in and out of it at different moments, that makes me want to engage her in a conversation, the direction of which I am not fully able to anticipate. It is my feeling for Goldman and my enjoyment of her person and polemic that have opened up a range of theoretical and political questions for me about ambivalence at a variety of levels. It is in and through my attachment to her that I have come to imagine the past and present differently and to see that ambivalence might also be inhabited with "panache."[12]

My three archives—subjective, critical, and theoretical—are of course not always separate or separable. They interlock as we read Goldman's work and interpret what she says in ways that make sense for us in context. And they point us to another archive, the one that has yet to be written or read: the *imaginative archive*. As I detail later, this archive is extremely important in articulating a feminist politics of ambivalence, insofar as it foregrounds the gaps and fissures in the existing archives and positions the historian as a deeply serious writer and reader of fiction. That archive represents the straining to hear the voices that have never been heard, the attachments that cannot be given meaning, and the utopian desire for another future grounded in a different past. In this respect, my fourth archive might of course be said to be an anarchist, prefigurative one. It grapples with the relationship between the dead and the living in order to enact the future one wants to bring about in the present.[13] It prioritises subjective and collective responsibility to generate living alternatives to the deadening modes of representation we see around us. For me, this means that I have to take very seriously my conversation with Goldman not only in terms of how I represent her or engage her thinking for a contemporary audience but also in terms of how that representation contributes to what collaborators of mine have termed "the living archive."[14] Rather than provide a biographical sketch or account of Goldman's life as a preamble to my thinking with and through the "Goldman archives," I want instead to integrate my introduction of her to you into my fuller account of the book's ambitions. While perhaps frustrating for a reader not familiar with Goldman's life, writing, or politics, this approach is consistent with the book's interest in understanding the writing of history as a dynamic one, and the desire to know the other as animated by one's own location. I seek here to make those framings explicit rather than imagining a "neutral Goldman" I could present to you at the outset.[15]

FEMINIST ATTACHMENTS

A friend gave me a picture of Emma Goldman when I was seventeen years old, and in it she is only a few years older than I was then. The picture shows her meeting the camera's gaze face on, chin up slightly, hair pulled back, an uncomfortable-looking dress covering her slight frame. At the time I knew nothing of the importance of Goldman's image as part of how people tried to make sense of her; I was simply captivated by the mismatch between "anarchist" and "young woman" that the picture represented. I bought Goldman's autobiography, *Living My Life* (1931b, 1931c), and found out that this Jewish Russian woman had migrated to America when a teenager, moved to New York City as soon as she could escape her family and early marriage in upstate New York, and by her late twenties had become the "High Priestess of Anarchy" (*Chicago Inter Ocean* 1908, 284). I was in awe of this young woman who had travelled across America lecturing on anarchist revolution, minority creativity, sexual politics, and state violence, and whose refusal to misrepresent herself or her cause meant repeated prison terms. I felt her loss when her lifelong friend and comrade, Alexander Berkman, was imprisoned for his failed attempt on the life of Henry Clay Frick, and her fear when she was blamed for radicalising Leon Czolgosz, President McKinley's assassin (Goldman 1901). I entertained fantasies of refusing to recognise the authorities at the Church of England private school where I was a sixth-former, but knew I would not be able to sustain any such "revolution" beyond its initial frisson of transgression. Instead, I marvelled at Goldman's standoff with J. Edgar Hoover, broken only by her being stripped of citizenship and deported to a postrevolutionary Russia (Berkman and Goldman 1919). I appreciated the prescience of her critiques of the new Russian state authority, its violence and exclusion, and her disappointment at its failed postrevolutionary project, as well as the International Left's myopia (Goldman 1925b). In part, I relished this critique because it resonated with my own youthful 1980s, Thatcher-inspired anticommunism, in contrast to Alice Wexler, who is outraged by Goldman's perpetuation of the "'Bolshevik myth'" (1992, 44), writing from her own location as a frustrated American leftist in the same time period.[16]

Forced and chosen travels through Europe in the 1920s were by turns clear sources of frustration and pleasure for Goldman, as she struggled to find a place to belong: part of her remained forever attached to America, its newness perhaps mirroring her own youth and optimism while there.[17] The difficulties that Goldman experienced travelling across borders and her frequent disappointments in comrades (that pepper her autobiography and letters) were ameliorated by moments of intimacy and solidarity. She married Welsh miner James Colton for papers, her complicated friendship with Berkman remained strong, and she continued to pursue lust and love despite recurrent heartbreak. For a seventeen-year-old who dreamed of similar (literary and intimate, if not political) comradeship, what was not to like in this tale of thwarted ambitions and heroism? I later read in letters of her frequent illness and loneliness (Drinnon and Drinnon 1975), her misery after Berkman's death in the south of France (where she wrote her autobiography), and her doubts about the value of anarchist revolution. Despite viewing her as being on the wrong side of history and progress, I embraced what John Chalberg suggests is her "American individualism" (1991), agreeing with her sense that against the odds her life had indeed been "worth while" (Goldman 1933b). I too wanted a life filled with ups and downs, a heroic life, and I sighed with satisfaction at Goldman's autobiographical conclusion that she had lived hers "in bitter sorrow and ecstatic joy, in black despair and fervent hope. I had drunk the cup to the last drop" (1931c, 993).

But what truly caught me in Goldman's life and work, and that pulled me into reading *Anarchism and Other Essays* (1910) from start to finish one wet weekend, was the particular combination of her sexual politics and her disidentification from contemporary feminism. In alignment with my right-wing Thatcherite commitments, I was also rather virulently antifeminist myself at the time of this encounter, taking enormous pleasure in scoffing at attempts to give women or girls what I saw as "special attention." I was a perfect audience for Goldman's scathing indictments of both bourgeois femininity and dusty, censorious feminism (1910, particularly 167–211). Goldman reflected back to me my youthful interest in fashioning myself as an assertive subject, capable of anything, not to be cowed by norms as foolish as those that govern gender or sexuality. And of course, the ease with which I aligned her arguments and affect with my right-wing antifeminism is part of what alerted me more recently to the problematic nature of such attacks on the ills of femininity, as I discuss later.

When I was coming to the end of my last book some twenty-five years later, and was sifting through my mind for a new focus, Goldman kept coming back to me. I rummaged around to find that old image of her (that I had apparently never thrown away), and as I looked at it, I was captivated anew. We might say that I am now surely as invested in feminism as once I was hostile towards it. Yet that *captivation* echoes between these politically distinct selves to suggest something affectively common to both that has inaugurated this project. Both my younger and my older selves are suspicious of feminist projects that characterise women as in need of protection; both hold no truck with naturalised accounts of femininity or masculinity; both share an existentialist vision of a degendered human capacity that must surely lie at the heart of any real cultural and political transformation. My older self has come to align these critiques with both Left and feminist commitments, but I suspect that my younger self was more comfortable with the ambivalence of uncharted sexual and gendered territory.

The Goldman archive is overflowing with ambivalence about gender and sexuality, in ways that may initially come as a surprise. After all, this is Emma Goldman, who is unequivocal about the central role that sexual politics and the gendered division of labour and value play in the perpetuation of capitalist and militarist interests. Goldman spent her life foregrounding the inequalities attending and reinforcing women's subordinate role and was still making arguments about the importance of women as revolutionaries in her late sixties, when she was active in supporting the anarchist movement in Spain (Ackelsberg 2001; *Spain and the World* 1937). Goldman insisted that women's position in the family was a fundamental feature of how capitalism worked (rather than its lamentable side effect), emphasising the importance of the exploitation of their reproductive labour, as well as the impact of this tyranny on women as individuals. She was an early advocate of women's birth control, for which she was imprisoned (Goldman 1916b). Goldman railed against the ills of femininity that keep women locked into domestic servitude (1897a, 1911) and was forthright on the centrality of women's emancipation to social and political transformation (1906b). It was, in fact, precisely because Goldman wanted to centre women's freedom as essential for revolution that she was so critical of suffrage and the limits of efforts to gain the franchise (1917d). For Goldman, only women's fullest liberty would do, and she understood state-oriented recognition politics such as the claiming of the vote as a waste of revolutionary energy. In this she was not alone, of course: women's sexual and political freedom was consistently contrasted with the red herring of feminism or equality in a range of international anarchist movements (Hutchison 2001; Molyneux 1986).

The feminist critical archive has sought to rescue Goldman from this "splitting" at the heart of her revolutionary project on women by declaring that she is in fact a feminist, despite her resistance to the name. Feminist writers consistently claim her as such on the basis of these radical views of women's emancipation (Falk 2007; Kensinger 2007) and provide a series of caveats to reframe her antipathy to feminism as of her time and politics, rather than something to worry about too much in bringing her forward (Shulman 1982). Alternatively, feminist critics point to her own failed project of sexual freedom as a good example of all feminists' failure to achieve our ideals, citing her anxiety-producing level of devotion to male lovers (Marso 2003) and her lack of attention to divisions of domestic labour (Stansell 2000, 258) as aspects of her (still feminist) complexity that we can usefully learn from. Goldman's rather frequent unpleasantness to women is harder to integrate into this claiming of her as a feminist, though. While most feminist thinking includes a critique of femininity and of (some) women in their representation and reproduction of the status quo, Goldman is understood to take her judgements too far in this respect. She can be vitriolic towards women (representing them as stupid, vicious, petty, and corrupt), and—probably more importantly—she clearly takes great pleasure in her characterisation of bourgeois women as arch consumers and of women in general as responsible for many of men's failings (1931c, 556). As I explore in the next chapter, it is Goldman's enthusiastic antipathy towards femininity that signals her ambivalence about women's capacity to change in the subjective archive, while in the critical archive, it is the faltering desire for Goldman to be a feminist and the difficulties of succeeding in that endeavour that are instructive. In wanting Goldman to *be* a feminist in order to claim her as valuable to a feminist project, I will be suggesting that contemporary feminist theory seeks to mask its own ambivalence about precisely these same—and unresolved—questions about femininity and feminism.

Goldman's ambivalence about femininity resonates with the feminist archive's concerns, but her ambivalence about race and racism is harder for the archive to negotiate. If the feminist critical archive has been keen to claim Goldman as a feminist despite her strong disidentification from feminism, it stumbles when confronted with her aggressive characterisations of the ills of femininity, as I have suggested. In relationship to race and racism, feminists have noted with some dismay that Goldman "'misses race'" (Ferguson 2011b, 217–29), and to some extent they respond in a similar vein, ignoring the dilemmas that run through the subjective archive, claiming her instead as an intersectional heroine before her time. This is commonly achieved by focusing on her internationalism, Jewish identity, and community attachments (Reizenbaum 2005; Wexler 1992) and her focus on migration and antinationalism (Kennedy 1999), which certainly were strong features of Goldman's politics. Yet in the process of this reclamation effort, Goldman's reflections on race and racism, her attempts to integrate class and race analysis, her comparisons between anti-Semitic and antiblack violence in America (Goldman 1910, 69–78; Goldman 1927, in Drinnon and Drinnon 1975, 196), as well as her development of a "post-racial" model of kinship (Goldman between 1927 and 1930), receive less attention than I think they deserve. In wanting Goldman to be attentive to race and racism in ways that are familiar to contemporary feminist theorising, the critical archive deflects attention from the ways in which Goldman negotiates these questions in conflicting and conflicted ways. In the process, and as I argue more fully in chapter 2, that critical archive also protects a contemporary fantasy that questions of race and racism *can* be straightforwardly integrated as part of an intersectional analysis. In the attempt to present contemporary feminist theory both as attentive to race and as knowing what that attention should involve, the ongoing ambivalence about the relationship between race, class, gender, and sexuality in the theoretical archive is minimised if not directly repressed. As with attention to ambivalence about femininity and feminism, however, a more open approach to *what race is and means* might enable a politics more attuned to the continued uncertainty about the relationship between race and class, and point to ways in which a fuller analysis of sexual freedom challenges the nationalist and racialised understanding of "the family."

To give a little more detail of these threads here, and to flesh out our initial encounter with Goldman, we should note first that Goldman was indeed a practical and intuitive internationalist. She herself migrated or was exiled numerous times during her lifetime, and she had a trenchant critique of the relationship between nationalism, militarism, and capitalism, particularly insofar as these limited the possibilities for women to live full lives (1908b, 1915). She was thus a supporter of the Indian anticolonial movement (Elam 2013) and the Mexican Revolution (Falk 2012b) and worked towards "solidarity with anticolonial struggles in Africa and the Philippines" (Bertalen 2011, 225). Goldman was of course one of those anarchist migrants who became politicised after her move from Russia to the United States, and who was first educated in and then exiled to Europe (Goldman 1931b, 1931c). She fought to make anarchism a broader movement in the United States once she had converted to anarchism by lecturing in English rather than Yiddish or German as was the convention among New York anarchists in the 1880s and 1890s (Stansell 2000). She wrote to comrades and intimates all over the world no matter where she was living, and she participated in that vast network of transnational anarchist publication and translation that typified its vibrancy. As Falk thus notes, for Goldman "the crossing of national boundaries, so integral to Goldman's political vision was also critical to the long-term impact of her political work" (2005, 64). Goldman's border crossings and lack of belonging underwrite her challenges to patriotism and capitalism, as well as the gendered and sexual norms that secure them, and these skeins of her life resonate well with a feminist critical and theoretical archive that foregrounds a transnational feminist politics attentive to contemporary geopolitical complexity.

It is certainly true that Goldman, like many other European, Latin American, and American anarchists, was less clear on how to negotiate race politics. For Ferguson, Goldman's political commitments meant that "she was confident that class would always trump race in the production of social inequality" (2011b, 220), and for Falk, while Goldman had a clear analysis of lynching as "the most graphic and egregious expression of racist terrorism in the country," she did not theorise that horror as "the focus of her general critique" of state aggression (2012b, 12n33). Yet what interests me about this critical engagement is that this focus in Goldman is framed as self-evidently problematic, as clearly erroneous if not privileging race and racism. As a result of this critical "embarrassment" about how she "misses" race, a range of ways in which Goldman *does* explore how racism functions as a form of oppression are easily missed in turn. In wanting Goldman's attention to race to be familiar and privileged, the attention that she pays to lynching and her analysis of the concept of "slavery" are glossed over. And in turning to her critiques of nationalism, or the mobilisation of Jewish identity as an alternative, in framing her as an intersectional heroine ahead of her time (*despite* this inattention to race and racism), the very ways in which these approaches combine to provide a somewhat unexpected account of race and sexual freedom, or analysis of the relationship between anti-Semitic and anti-black violence, are also too easily overlooked.

In chapter 3 I explore the question—Goldman's and mine too—of sexual freedom as an antidote to a revolutionary theory and method that relies on the gendering of a public/private divide, and on the racialisation of reproduction and kinship. Goldman was among those early twentieth-century anarchists and socialists who understood sexual expression to be a "basic human right, a legitimate goal of the class struggle" (Snitow, Stansell, and Thompson 1983, 18). Indeed, Goldman's centring of sexual freedom at the heart of her revolutionary vision forms part of a long tradition of engagement with sexual politics on the Left, one that endeavours to make sense of how productive and reproductive labour come together and to identify the difference between sexual freedom and capitalist co-optation at both practical and theoretical levels. Goldman theorises the sexual division of labour not simply as a prior condition for production and thus capitalist exploitation but *as labour* (alienated and exploited, as is other labour in capitalism), and thus an integral part of economic production.[18] Through this analysis, Goldman links birth control issues, prostitution, and wholesale destruction of the poor in wartime and develops her strong arguments for love as the site of reclaimed value, creativity, and progressive possibility when returned into the hands of its workers: women. Goldman not only theorised sexual freedom, of course, but also practiced it through her life, refusing to be domestically tied to men or children, and struggling with the contradictions between feelings and politics that structure her bravery in this respect (Goldman 1931b, 1931c). Of particular interest to me are the ways in which Goldman's embrace of sexual freedom as both means towards and end of an anarchist utopia (L. Davis 2011) interrupts the temporal features that govern a more conventional rendering of the relationship of sexuality and capitalism, and suggests alternate ways of understanding and writing that history.

Goldman's investment in sexual freedom as revolutionary could be seen as a useful intervention in the long-standing political and critical opposition between "the cultural" and "the material," in this respect. Sexuality has consistently been associated with superficiality and "leisure" rather than the serious business of politics, a view that relies of course on the naturalisation of heterosexual family formations (Freccero 2012; Hennessy 2014; Parker 1993). It has been understood (as part of identity politics) as contributing to the fragmentation of the Left, and in academic terms as part of the "cultural turn" that has abandoned materiality.[19] As suggested, Goldman herself was extraordinarily clear that for women sexuality *is* labour, without which what is more properly thought of as "production" could have little purchase (1916c). She was convinced that there could be no real transformation of social or economic relations without a prior revaluation of sexual subjectivity for both men and women (*St. Louis Post-Dispatch* 1908) and was persuaded of the creative potential of noninstitutionalised sexual expression, including homosexuality, despite her own uncertain feelings on the question.[20] Goldman would certainly have had no truck with arguments that sexuality is "merely cultural" (Butler 1997; Fraser 1997), but she would also have wasted no time highlighting the many ways sexuality is intimately part of—rather than only a critique of—capitalism.[21] I can see her now (tumbling through time), arriving at a *Marxism Today* conference in East London and expressing her dumbfounded rage at the proposition that sexuality is not central to political economy, citing the history of continuous debate over these issues as coextensive with rather than fragmenting of anarchist and socialist fervour. I can see her travelling to a queer conference on the Eastern Seaboard (persuading all the other sea-bound passengers of the significance of anarchism by the time she arrived), thumping the platform in rage at the idea that sexuality could ever be separated from class analysis or nationalist interests, and cheering the interventions of queer Marxists. But I can also hear her laughing her head off en route to Amsterdam at the thought that homosexuality could paradoxically be reduced to its homonormative or homonationalist modes, insisting instead on the creative potential of all sexual feeling once truly free.[22]

The feminist critical archive on Goldman's understanding of sexual freedom is of course seduced by that centring of sexual politics as both means and end of utopia, and by Goldman's linking of nationalism, militarism, and control of women's bodies. Her support for and theorisation of prostitution as an effect of capitalism, migration, and repressed sex drives has pleased queer theorists too, as has her sometimes contradictory support for homosexual liberty. But so, too, that archive finds limits to this privileging of sexual freedom, representing it as too vague, on the one hand, and too excessively focused on love for men, on the other (Marso 2003, 306; Stansell 2000, 142). Bonnie Haaland (1993) perhaps goes furthest in this line of thinking, framing Goldman as a heterosexual essentialist because of her support for sexological and psychoanalytic understandings of sexuality, as well as her uncertain relationship to homosexuality. But a range of different thinkers celebrate Goldman's bold relationship to sexual freedom in her life and work, while also remaining dubious about her claiming of sexuality as the core of human nature, whatever its object choice (Day 2007, 110; Lumsden 2007, 45). It is important, I think, to consider the ways in which Goldman is interrogating the question of sexuality's relationship to capitalism and freedom at a point when sexuality as an identity is in the very process of being articulated. Goldman is forging her own theory of sexual freedom as a difficult and contested rather than *self-evident* position of critique or transformation. In addition, Goldman's complex engagement with sexual politics (in theory and in practice) poses an important challenge to assumptions about the nature of sexual identity and freedom in the present. As I explore in chapter 2, Goldman's support for birth control positions her in an ambivalent relationship to eugenics in her own time, and in chapter 3 her claiming of "nature" as central to sexual freedom returns us to concerns about racialisation, insofar as she links this to primitive drives. But so, too, Goldman's ambivalence about homosexuality (her own as well as other people's) moves us firmly away from both single-issue and identity politics that govern and limit contemporary understandings of sexual rights. As in my readings of subjective, critical, and theoretical archival ambivalence concerning femininity and feminism, and race and internationalism, my interest here is in the consequences of taking Goldman's sexual ambivalence seriously as politically and historiographically significant for queer feminist studies today.

The question of methodology is particularly central to my engagement with Goldman's (and the critical and theoretical archives') understanding of sexual freedom. On the one hand, I am advocating an approach that reads for ambivalence across these archives; on the other, I am aware that in relationship to sexual freedom in particular, that same question of ambivalence can easily be obscured. The clear emergence of sexual identities through the twentieth century and the contemporary foregrounding of rights over freedoms in political contexts actively work against reading for ambivalence. The task is thus a politically motivated one that starts from an interest in what is left out of the frame, and how to think from the (nonidentitarian) margins in the spirit of Goldman's own contradictory, anarchist interventions around sexual freedom. These questions of *how* to explore ambivalence in the interlocked set of archives I draw on throughout this book are central to the later chapters of the book, in particular. Moving on from the question of sexual freedom and "nature" in Goldman's work, I intervene in the question of how to *represent* a politics of ambivalence when its traces have effectively been erased. Drawing on the imaginative tactics of postcolonial writers and artists in particular, and as I explore more fully later, I write Goldman's sexual ambivalence into the archive where it does not currently exist.

Throughout this book I centre tensions in Goldman's thinking and in the critical and theoretical archives I am concerned with, rather than seeking to resolve them. I believe that it is more helpful to contemporary queer feminist theory to bring forward Goldman's ambivalence than to import the aspects of thinking and living that most clearly fit with the (often misplaced) certainties of the present. A sustained focus on ambivalence helps us to engage past politics and theory as complex or contradictory, and to foreground the importance of current complexity, despite our desire to have resolved both past and present paradoxes. For in relationship to the key areas raised thus far, feminist theory most certainly has not resolved the question of judgement of femininity or the relationship between feminism and its conflicted subjects; the relationship between race, migration, class, and gender in the present is less easily articulated than current intersectional approaches might perhaps have us believe; and yet faith in human nature remains central to political hope. From a deep engagement with her own thinking and its context, I want to bring forward Goldman theoretically, politically, and perhaps most importantly, methodologically. I want to engage her in order to disrupt the relationship between past and present, to challenge a critical certainty that there is a singular story that we can tell about how we got to where we (think we) are now. I want to read with and in tension with Goldman to allow her to shine, and I want to demonstrate that how we approach the past—and the throng that peoples it—raises a host of ethical and methodological questions about knowledge and politics. In addition, I want the reader to *feel* something: something that sparks an expanded sense of political thinking, perhaps, or a connection to past rebellion that lives in the imaginative present, a sense of possibility from sitting with the sounds of the dead one can never quite hear. For me, reading with Goldman these past few years has provoked at least some of these feelings; and it has additionally confirmed my sense that queer feminist thinking is always in process, never finally achieved, and never sutured to a singular political or intellectual trajectory.

DYNAMIC HISTORIES

If the subjective, critical, and theoretical archives I am engaged with here are ones that I am framing through their ambivalence, then I also need an appropriate approach to the work of teasing out that ambivalence, historically and contemporarily. For this reason, and because I also believe in the spirit of the engagement with Goldman herself, my methodology throughout the book is somewhat unorthodox. It centres the relationship between my own desires for a politics of ambivalence and Goldman's unresolved ambivalence on the issues sketched out in the previous section, and in that sense mirrors the dynamics that I have been teasing out between the different archives thus far. It considers my relationship to Goldman as an active one in which I attach to her through a yearning for a different past, present, and future than the ones I see writ large. That yearning positions me rather oddly in relation to the archive, of course, because part of that affective relationship to Goldman longs for and imagines the parts that are missing as much as it sits with those we have. It hopes against hope that there will indeed be surviving pictures of her riding a unicorn. And that yearning also positions me as engaging a lively, resistant Goldman who seems far from dead as I seek to represent aspects of her that continue to elude me.

I have presented several papers on this question of the affective motor of the historical dynamics I am interested in in this vein, and on several occasions historians in the room have found the exploration of my affectively saturated bonds disconcerting at best, or, on occasion, plainly outrageous. A common response to my interest in thinking about Goldman as inhabiting and generating ambivalences about sexual politics, for example, has been that this is not an acceptable historical approach, which should restrict itself to the available sexual terms and meanings circulating at the time. Certainly, I agree that contextualisation of Goldman's understanding of sexual freedom is extremely important, and have sought to ensure that my engagements with her theorisations and political efforts have situated her in her own context as far as possible. But I am also not a historian, and it is less Goldman's *time* that interests me than it is Goldman's fierce expressions of resistance to the *restrictions* of her time, and her optimism about a future that she brought into her own present without fully knowing its contours. I firmly believe—as Goldman did—that there are people in all times and places whose paths through the world and political or intersubjective imaginations allow them to exceed the historical contexts that they are nevertheless rooted in. Goldman was of the opinion that this was true of both Walt Whitman (Goldman n.d. [1991b]) and Mary Wollstonecraft (Wexler 1981), and I consider this to be true of Goldman herself. For me, Goldman's own commitments to an anarchist method of living the utopian future in the present, her centring of sexual politics as part of that revolutionary scrambling of time, and her inability to articulate her own desires in available terms produce a kind of excess of meaning that marks her presence in the world. What does it mean to "contextualise" such a figure, one who pushes and pushes against the boundaries of the known and knowable in her own time? It is a longing to trace that *excess* that motivates my interest in Goldman, and although I know that it is impossible to represent her sometimes inarticulate fervency, this increases rather than decreases my desire to do so. In this sense, then, my historiographic and political commitments are to exploring the resonance between invested parties, despite knowing that Goldman is dead, and despite knowing that my embodied desires to reanimate her fevered uncertainties may finally describe my own foolishness.

Such foolish yearning departs from earlier concerns of mine with resisting corrective histories of feminist theory and politics in *Why Stories Matter* (Hemmings 2011). I had thought—and in many ways still do—that to centre a key figure from the past as resolving the problematics of the present risks drawing a single teleological line from past to present in ways that tend to ignore what is excluded by or from that account. But in this project, I am less interested in the multiple pasts that an attention to feminist theory's exclusions reveals, and more in the continued desire for a corrective vision that motivates most radical history even when it is the object of critique. So I remain committed to telling stories otherwise, rather than only trying to tell different stories, as a way of interrupting singular histories and presents. But so, too, Goldman's *presence*, her resistance to interpretation, the difference of her thinking that cannot only be harnessed to my particular ends, stubbornly inserts itself into this project. I have a relationship with Goldman, a set of psychic and affective attachments to her that locate me in particular ways and that are not only one-sided. So while I want to tell a story of contemporary queer feminist theory with anarchist ambivalence about sexual, gendered, and race politics at its heart, I also want to do justice to the subjective archive in ways that refuse to abstract it from Goldman herself. Throughout this book, then, and as I explore more fully later, it is the *pull* of the corrective that draws me back into the past and present of queer feminism, that lures me into imagining and knowing something else. As Victoria Browne (2014) notes in her review of *Why Stories Matter*, this earlier work underestimated that pull. It is in returning to that question that my understanding of feminist historiography as a dynamic I am not fully in control of has emerged more fully. Without it, I argue, the future comes to seem as bleak as any singular past we may risk inheriting. As suggested, then, while this project is a long way from being "a great-person history," it remains one with Goldman's complex person at its heart.

The question of historical endeavour as political and intersubjective, as concerned with desire and fantasy, has long been a feature of feminist, lesbian and gay, queer, and postcolonial approaches to the past.[23] Here I want to think through some of these traditions as a way of fleshing out the concerns I have sketched here, and as a way of introducing a further set of reflections on attention to what *eludes* the historian's gaze as equally central to the dynamics of this project. As suggested earlier, a politicised history is always concerned with a desire for something different: a different legacy or a different future. Indeed, the longing for a past one can live with might be said to have inaugurated historical work within the crosscutting interdisciplinary fields of feminist, lesbian and gay, and postcolonial studies. The impulse is an extremely important one. It marks a difference between dominant characterisations of history and marginal subjects' own lives and meanings, and gives preferential value to the latter. As gay and lesbian historians John D'Emilio and Estelle Freedman point out in their introduction to the groundbreaking book *Intimate Matters* (1988), there is a political ethics at the heart of radical history that seeks to untangle dominant stories from the lives that are diminished in their telling. Counterhistories thus speak of survival rather than deviance, of community rather than isolation. Those lives—or our glimpsing of them—spur a political energy in the present, at its best enabling a continuity of intellectual and political effort that for feminist historian Maria Brettschneider looks to "our foremothers for how they might still assist us in the heady work before us today" (2013, 648). For postcolonial queer theorist Anjali Arondekar (2009), the colonial archive hides secrets that may not be straightforwardly visible but that lurk in the interstices of dominant tales, the echoes of which we might catch if we pay close enough attention, a position reminiscent of lesbian feminist historian Blanche Wiesen Cook's injunction to "listen carefully" to the people one is writing about, who "intrude on the privacy of my bath, join me in the ocean and the garden . . . tell me stories, give me feedback, disagree, suggest new sources" (1984, 398).

There is a certain awkwardness in naming these different historians "feminist," "postcolonial," "lesbian and gay," or "queer," particularly in terms of their overlaps. But I do so to highlight the specific (and, to some extent, distinct) histories that similar understandings of the importance of "the object" emerge from. What they share is the wish to make visible different threads of meaning that ripple back and forward through time. Such approaches are a question of methodology as much as of theoretical framing or political epistemology. Intervening in dominant history to change our understanding of the past and present requires attention to different sorts of evidence but also importantly the development of a sixth sense beyond eyes and ears for grasping the gaps. In this light, the radical scholar's task is at once archaeological (unearthing the hidden to change our view of the earth) and interventionist—retelling stories to allow for present living, in a process feminist literary historian Jane Marcus (1984) evocatively refers to as "invisible mending." It seeks truth but revels in inevitable creative openness as both means and end of politicised historical endeavour.

As I hope is already evident, the story of these traditions of radical history can be told as one of care as well as desire: it uncovers different sources and approaches to the truth and promotes a different set of values. But herein also lies the danger, as many scholars have pointed out. With reclamation projects that emerge from a particular political standpoint in the present (as I would argue all history does whether visible or not), the investment in the subjects and objects of inquiry is likely to be hyperbolic, making visible the stakes in the process but also potentially ignoring aspects of the past that do not so easily fit. The longing for a point of identification, a history that animates the present, can paradoxically overstate differences between dominant and resistant lives and experiences, for example, or overread through an identity politics transferred from the present to the past. The critique of such projective identifications has itself been a burning source of energy for radical history and has tended to focus either on the problems of decontextualisation, where figures from the past are wrenched out of their context in order to provide political fodder in the present, or on the problems of identity politics tout court. And, indeed, this has been a thread in my own argument in this introduction. Thus Joan Scott (1999) critiques a version of feminist history that seeks women who can be framed as feminist in the past irrespective of their own paradoxical circumstances much as I do here, arguing forcefully for the critical value of "gender history" over "women's history." Gayatri Spivak (1988) famously highlights the problems of a postcolonial desire for a precolonial subaltern voice because of its easy resonance with nationalist commitments in the present. And in respect of sexual history, Laura Doan notes the problems of mobilising identity as if past and present structures of sexual meaning were the same, advocating instead both careful use of historical example and attentive queer methodology over presumption (2013, ix). As such theorists have shown, desire for reclamation in radical historical projects is thus one fraught with the risk of flattening out the very lives and relationships one wishes to breathe life into, as one forges a path back and forward with one's eyes firmly set on the prize. And, indeed, as I have also argued, the temporality of such projects remains deadeningly linear, as the past becomes a repository for nostalgia in a dystopian account of inexorable loss, or for traces of hope made manifest in a utopian tale of eventual and inexorable progress (Hemmings 2011).

Yet as such thinkers also acknowledge but tend to de-emphasise, that drive to understand and represent the past through more than its dominant modes remains central as part of how we come to imagine a different present. All these scholars, myself included, act from a more or less tactical presumption that the relationship between the past and present could be understood differently, more fluidly, multiply, with different possible outcomes: in a sense, that is one of the central values of historical inquiry. Such faith in transformation and in tracing or imagining a past that can belong to a different future might be said to inaugurate any progressive historical project. Thus, even where unsettling refuses to reify a singular version of the past or present, the belief in alternate versions remains strong. This is, if you like, the paradox I hope to hold out as itself epistemologically and methodologically resonant through this book: that the pull of the corrective is necessary as a spur to a rooted political imagination, even at the moment of its displacement.[24] Certainly in respect of this book, while I hope to use Goldman's thinking and action as a way of unsettling queer feminist certainties in the present, I also necessarily privilege particular histories over a range of possible others in doing so: the obscured contributions of anarchist sexual politics; the lost traces of gendered critiques that distance themselves from named feminism; the long relationship between antinationalist struggles and the critique of the family form in Left social movements. While not necessarily linear in approach, such priorities nevertheless produce exclusions of emphasis. As Ferguson (2008) asks, for example, what difference would it make to contemporary political theory to foreground the ongoing histories of state and privatised violence in the suppression of social movements, an approach that becomes more visible when we take anarchism seriously? Or to restore to education theory the history of prefigurative knowledge production enabled by drawing a direct line between anarchist teacher Francisco Ferrer and epistemologist Michel Foucault? In my choice to prioritise *ambivalence* over other kinds of political knowledges and practices, histories that do not fit into these preoccupations are thus still likely to be sidelined, or will not be seen at all. Rather than seeking to include an ever richer, fuller range of threads in the hope of greater inclusion, however, my emphasis is on the dynamics that spur and emerge from my own theoretical and political preoccupations. In the process, my concern is precisely with the relationship between past and present, and past and present desires; with the inevitable partiality one encounters in the archive, and its often surprising resonance with our own lives.

In this approach I am influenced by a range of queer feminist historiographic work that intervenes both in questions of representation (of marginal subjects and meanings, and of the past in its complex relation to the present) and by suggesting different temporalities and relational modes of historical exploration. The challenge to linear progress narratives is particularly intense contemporarily in the evocative work on queer temporalities, for example, which seeks to shift the dominance of heteronormative, reproductive time. Writers such as Heather Love (2007) and Elizabeth Freeman (2010) move on from earlier theorists of temporal limitation and sexual alterity such as Teresa de Lauretis (1994) or Judith Roof (1996), challenging linearity by suturing queer moments together from the scrap heap of history to form an atemporal collage (with overlapping and frayed edges) rather than a seamless narrative of queer identification.[25] This important work tends to be seen as a departure from the long tradition of feminist theoretical reflections on time, but I think this underestimates the creative nature of the latter. This work has sought not only to provide an alternative tradition to that of a patriarchal history of "great events" but also to interrupt those triumphalist narratives in a range of ways.[26] I am thinking here of the work of feminist historian Luisa Passerini, for example, who reflects on the importance as well as the impossibility of generational thinking in her classic text *Autobiography of a Generation* (1996). In weaving together her own and activists' memories of 1968 in Italy, and connecting "personal and political testimony [with] . . . the scene of her psychoanalysis" (Baraitser 2012, 380), Passerini holds together contradictory voices that cannot be connected in a linear way.[27] Other feminist work on time has challenged a common fantasy that dominant time itself is in some way cleanly linear by focusing on the past as *always* radically unknowable (e.g., Felski 2002). Elizabeth Grosz's work on time as felt rather than objectively graspable (1995), and on the glimpses of other temporalities attention to that feltness generates (2004), brings us back to the interest in atemporality and dissonance that marks more recent queer historiography. Importantly for me here, too, is the way in which this call-and-response across feminist and queer concerns with temporality challenges an easy separation between feminist and queer theory and history. As Wiegman (2014) insists, a presumption that the two are separated in temporal as well as theoretical terms, with queer theory coming after and displacing feminist theory, is both inaccurate and also productive of a queer fantasy of its own privileged transgressive capacities.[28] Taking this relationship seriously, however, raises some difficult questions about how to represent the overlaps and differences between these traditions. My hope is that through the book as a whole the different and related ways in which I intend "feminist" and "queer" produce helpful resonances, even if what the terms denote remains less than clear. Across all this work, and what continues to appeal to me across its differences, it is the pull between the singular and the multiple, the corrective and the exploratory that enlivens historians' concerns with charting new political futures.

The doing of radical history is an affectively saturated process for all who attempt it. As demonstrated at the outset of this introduction, political desire shapes our view of people and events from the past in both evident and subtle ways. It is thus highly appropriate that much feminist, queer, and postcolonial historiography focuses as much on the role of the "historian" as on "history," or more precisely on the dynamic between subject and object. That attention is often as much on the "teller of tales" as it is on the historical context under consideration, and foregrounds the question of accountability for one's forays into the archives. This is hugely important, and a major site of consideration in this project, as we have seen. Building on this work, I can interrogate the assumptions we have about both the past and the present: pulling the rug from under the feet of the confident queer feminist writing subject, lifting her into the air to perform a series of cartwheels, not knowing where she will land. Yet of course we might also say that there is a rather glaring irony in such a burden of responsibility for knowing the (ambivalent) present resting on the very writing subject who is seeking to challenge its knowability. As I wrote in an earlier article, thinking through the dynamic of my engagement with Goldman, I have been struck by how the burden of that work of accountability rests paradoxically enough with the one caught most fully in its bright lights (Hemmings 2013, 338). My increased insecurity about a correct relationship to the history I am tracing (Serisier 2012, 253) is matched by my sense that the contours of the present are never fully knowable either.

As Elisabeth Young-Bruehl thoughtfully suggests, the fact that subjectivity is involved in the process of writing about someone else does not mean that the encounter can be reduced to the needs and desires of the writing subject (1998, 8). To return to the question of Goldman's own presence, then, the teller of tales is, I have found, never quite as in control of the stories she spins as she might hope. As I have indicated earlier, and want to underline here once again, Goldman herself is never only a figment of my imagination, moulded in my own image. She speaks back in the ways that those represented have a habit of doing: in her resistance that I feel in my belly, in the ways words or images will not bend to my interpretation, in the fervency of her own writing that seeps into mine, so that at times I feel more like a fraudulent medium than a queer feminist theorist.[29] Or too in strange moments of being drawn back to a fragment of text or an image, starting from an imaginative connection that makes me want to be faithful to Goldman no matter how far removed from her I am. Young-Bruehl again helpfully advocates what she rather beautifully calls a "biographical tenderness" (23) in writing about past figures, one that attends to the ways they escape our control as well as the ways they overtake us. I am pulled back not only to the way that the present shapes our engagement with the past but also to how the past is felt in the present, is profoundly unruly and disruptive of the political and intellectual certainties I might otherwise wish I could preserve.

Thinking through the past and present as intimately related and yet unknowable draws me to psychoanalysis, that method of treatment that asks its patients to reflect on their past and the analyst to take (that) history into account (Phillips 2012). Psychoanalysis, as many queer, feminist, and postcolonial scholars have explored, foregrounds emotion and intersubjectivity as significant ways of knowing, as challenges to objectivist perspectives of control and mastery (Mitchell 1974; Stacey 2013b). Further, and importantly for this book, a psychoanalytic approach to history privileges the ways the present contains the past (in both senses of the word)—an approach that has been fundamental to the development of postcolonial understandings of the present (Gilroy 2004; Khanna 2012)—and the radical unknowability of *both* past and present (Felman 1977; Wiegman 2012). Most significantly, perhaps, psychoanalytic approaches to history and knowledge open up the possibility of glimpsing ambivalence indirectly through its effects and affects, rather than entertaining fantasies of final knowledge in empiricist vein (Weed 2014, 10).[30]

Although this project does not take forward an exclusively psychoanalytic method, I have been strongly influenced by the rich work in psychoanalysis and history, particularly that which focuses on the question of fantasy in the dynamic between writer and historical figure.[31] As Leo Spitzer notes in his recent work with Marianne Hirsch, we need to "take into account . . . the apprehension and misapprehension of events—[that] complicates and restores a measure of contingency to history" (Hirsch and Spitzer 2013, 192). But to push still further, one might say that what I have been describing thus far as "history as (a) dynamic" should not be understood as straightforward transference of present concerns onto an imaginary past but rather as transference of a *fantasy present* onto an imaginary past one has designs on. What one knows about the present is always partial, related to what one remembers about the past and what one wants the future to look like. As Adam Phillips insists: "Memories always have a future in mind" (2005, 35), while for Susannah Radstone and Bill Schwarz "memory is active," making and remarking the relationship between past, present, and future (2010, 3). For postcolonial psychoanalytic scholar Ranjana Khanna (2003), there is then a battle in the present over which future will dominate, which is always to say, which past. Thus, to reframe my earlier argument in more psychoanalytic terms, imagining a seamless move from past to present always risks ignoring the violence that inheres in (making real) our fantasies (Rose 1996). In my desire to rescue the present as well as the past through Goldman, I risk importing ideas and theories that we hope will finally resolve the complicated problems of difference and inequality we live in; a more accountable position may be to sit with those difficulties a while and tease out what cannot quite be grasped.

Fantasy and temporality can never be disentangled in psychoanalysis: the present is always bound up with what is remembered, half remembered, or forgotten in a series of loops or folds. This framing of forgetting as "an active process . . . designed to protect the subject" (Sturken 1997, 8) is one reason I am drawn to psychoanalytic understandings of the relationship between repression and complex histories. Importantly for my purposes too, this understanding of the relationship between present and past allows for creative reconfiguration: we may inhabit more than one role—mother, daughter, neither—and are not simply doomed to repeat cycles of repetition or origin stories (Jacobus 1995). As Jacqueline Rose indicates so suggestively: "Fantasy is also a way of re-elaborating and therefore of partly recognizing the memory which is struggling, against the psychic odds, to be heard" (1996, 5).[32] What we obscure is, in this sense, surely as interesting for a queer feminist politics engaging Goldman as what we are delighted with. To consider history through memory's turns as well as reclamation's grasp in *Considering Emma Goldman*, then, is to foreground an understanding of the present as always containing multiple histories—visible and invisible—and our relationship to these histories as characterised by ambivalence rather than certainty (Berlant 2007).

But how can we address what hovers at the boundary between the known and the unknown in historical dynamics? How can we begin to think carefully about what we seem to want to forget? Can ambivalent knowledge ever truly be represented? There can be no direct access to the unconscious per se of course, but nevertheless in psychoanalysis the unknowable is insistent, speaks to us in narrative slips, half-remembered dreams, or, in Phillips's evocative phrasing, the moments "when two people forget themselves in each other's presence" (1996, 31). For some scholars, taking the unconscious seriously is less a question of evidence and more a question of methodology. Thus, Shoshana Felman (1977) advocates reading for ambivalence as a sign of the irresolution of conscious and unconscious forces, while Rose focuses on "moments when writing slips its moorings" such that otherwise precluded connections can be made (1998, 128). To turn to Scott again, she argues that the relationship that emerges between the historian and her subject can be read through disjuncture or incommensurability, through the "often chaotic interactions of past and present" (2012, 67), the misunderstandings of one another perhaps as well as the pleasure in forgetting the difference one from the other. Following Michel de Certeau, Scott suggests that we may be able to glimpse the workings of the unconscious through the uncanny, the irreducible dissonance of the historical encounter that no contextualisation can assuage: "that which historians know but must deny" (67). To return to Goldman, these psychoanalytic insights invite me to tease out what I know but must deny in my relationship to Goldman as I shuttle back and forth between past and present.

In an earlier section, "Feminist Attachments," I foregrounded the importance of ambivalence in the Goldman archives (subjective and critical), as well as in the theoretical and imaginative archives I am also concerned with. I asked what was ignored or denied in the claiming of Goldman as a feminist, as an intersectional foremother or queer interlocutor. What kinds of histories are reproduced, invented, or precluded in bringing Goldman forward in our own image? What slips outside of my grasp, or is easily framed as someone else's bad habit? And yet, what is it that I might want to push away, but which continues to insist, keeps on interrupting the neat narratives of self, theory, and politics I have a vested interest in? In methodological terms, it is my own affective response to the subjective archive that has opened up for me what I might know but (tend to) deny in relation to Goldman. I laughed uproariously at Goldman's viciousness to women when I first encountered it in her writing, sharing nasty laughter at women's manipulability and culpability for their own oppression. I have come to think of that pleasure as a way of letting my partner in crime carry the burden of our shared judgement of femininity; it lets me off the hook even as it binds me to Goldman. My initial response to Goldman's understanding of race and racism in her work was also highly affective. I shared the critical disappointment at her lack of sustained theorising of race politics and found a firmer footing in reframing her as a prophetic intersectional thinker instead. Yet something niggled at me, made me ashamed at my own displacement of race politics that seemed to mirror hers, even as I sought to distance myself from her in this regard. And finally, I wrestled for some time with my bodily glow at Goldman's sexual politics, her insistence on human capacity as generous rather than mean-spirited, trying to control that common joy by filtering her through a more sophisticated contemporary critical sieve. In so doing, the important temporality of Goldman's belief in human nature, a future orientation I was only able to glimpse when I gave in to that glow, eluded me. Much as one might apologise for a well-meaning but embarrassing relative in ways one later feels as a reciprocal humiliation, my own attempts to clean up Goldman could not be sustained: she kept jabbing at my ribs and stomach and in each case brought me back to her ambivalence as considerably more engaging than my own superficial certainties.

At this point in time, we have a veritable cornucopia of affect theories to draw on in validating bodily knowledge as an academic or political resource (Gregg and Selgworth 2010). My own position on affect has shifted over the years from one that was highly critical of the "affective turn" because of its consigning of feminist accounts of the body and feeling to the historical side-lines (Hemmings 2005), to one that is interested in affect as a source of knowl-edge that can take us in different directions to that provided by text or context (Hemmings 2011, 2012a). In line with Eve Sedgwick (2003), I am persuaded that attention to affect gives us a complex sense of the texture of life and has the capacity to transform both subject and object of knowledge in unexpected ways. Indeed, this is precisely my intention in thinking through affect as a way of foregrounding what might otherwise be forgotten in my relationship with Goldman. Where I still remain underwhelmed by "the affective turn" is at the point that theorists present it as running *counter to* the threads of social life that constrain and name (Massumi 2002), always interrupting and never consolidating, always excessive and never reductive. What affective purists might term my attachment to paranoid thinking, but which I prefer to think of as a healthy queer feminist suspicion of replacement orthodoxies, pushes me towards wanting a more restless theory of affect. Attention to affect most certainly provides a different way into the social, a way that might otherwise be overlooked; but for me, and where I depart, is that this attention is al-ways interpretative. For me, the question of affect remains one of knowledge: What does feeling allow us to know or preclude us from knowing? Such an approach leaves open the possibility that affect is as likely to consolidate the status quo as it is to disrupt it. In this, I am entirely persuaded by the careful

work of Lauren Berlant (2011) in mapping the role of affect—or intimate attachments—in securing a set of failing capitalist promises, by Sara Ahmed's
(2004) analysis of the ways in which affect sticks negatively to some subjects
and not others in line with historical and contemporary power relations, and
by Avtar Brah's (1999) work on affect as opening up imaginative possibilities
that challenge as well as reinforce racial and ethnic difference in ethnogra-
phy.[33] All three theorists value affect primarily for the ways in which it indexes
historical memory and power and sutures individuals and collectives to positions they otherwise might loathe to adhere to. All three theorists also—and
importantly—consider affect crucial as a way of imagining and feeling different histories, presents, and futures.

WRITING BACK

If the critical archive and my own attachments foreground the question of
affect as a central part of a feminist politics of ambivalence, then the same is
true of Goldman herself. As indicated earlier, Goldman's own engagement
with the world was marked through passionate attachments to both people
and ideas, above all other considerations. In reading Goldman dynamically, as
I hope to do, I am also drawn to her own engagements with others: in lectures,
in published and unpublished writing, in letters, and in others' representations of her. It is in her letters, in particular, that we see Goldman's struggles
with passion and politics, and that have also been most controversial. Letters
and fragments of lectures or ephemera in the subjective Goldman archive also
point me towards the role of fantasy and creativity not just in terms of role of
the writer but also in terms of historical methodology; not just what and how
we read and make sense of it but how we yearn for something more than the
gaps in the archive. A yearning for differences that make living better haunts
this project, but this is not only a question of finding lost traces or filling the
inevitable gaps that pepper any history that seeks to make ambivalence visible and readable. This is true of all searches for lost traces conducted from
a position of marginality, of course, but I am particularly concerned to think
through methods of articulating what Saidiya Hartman (2008) renders as
"speculative history" with respect to sexual politics and meaning in this project, because it is sexual freedom that is proposed as the antidote to external
and internal constraints in the Goldman archive.

Telling stories about sexual history that foreground freedom over identity,
or ambivalence over clear desire, will necessarily orient us towards different
sources: those that are less valued as part of the historical record (diaries,

letters, autobiographies, fragments, ephemera) and those that scramble the relation between the public and private in their expression of uncertainty or conflict. Feminist and lesbian historians have explored letters in particular as a space within which different concerns can be aired and the complexity of unrecognised feelings sorted through (Faderman 2000; Freedman 1998). For Margaretta Jolly (2008), it is of paramount importance that women's letters should not be thought of simply as offering a glimpse into a private or personal life, however, but rather as spaces of intersubjective and relational engagement, as arenas of self-making and practicing, and thus more properly as sites for the *negotiation* of public and private meanings. While inevitably the use of letters as evidence might raise anxieties in the historian (and reader) that we are mining writers' words not meant to be seen or reproduced, I see them, following Jolly, less as "spontaneous outpourings of the true self" and instead as a "literary genre [that] shows us there is something expressive, excessive about all writing" (2008, 7).

I have found letters to and from Goldman particularly productive in this respect, and attention to these is woven through the book as a whole. Letters already formed part of the public record for Goldman, who asked friends to send her letters they had received from her to help her reconstruct her life when writing her autobiography (Tamboukou 2012).[34] And as Stansell notes, Goldman was writing her own explicit letters at a time when there was a bohemian culture of people passing letters around as part of the refusal of sexual secrecy: "Free love involved sex, of course, but it also signified talking and writing about it, a lively discourse of sexual conversation and revelation" (2000, 274). In both chapter 1 and chapter 3, I read Goldman's sexually explicit, demanding, and occasionally self-debasing letters to her lover and tour manager Ben Reitman as a way she represented and worked through some of her ambivalences about sexual politics and personal passion.[35] In chapter 2, letters continue to play a dual role, evidencing both the transnational dimensions of anarchist collectivities and the importance of personal attachments in fostering new understandings of kinship not based on blood or nation. The anarchist movement during Goldman's time was extremely international, and revolutionaries wrote to each other as part of engaging in a politics of translation, seeking to build a coordinated revolution to reshape the word (Anderson 2005). In this context, too, many anarchists were exiled (or self-exiled) from their home contexts and retained connections to family, friends, and comrades through copious letter writing across borders that they themselves were unable to traverse (J. Cohn 2014). Goldman's letters to intimates demonstrate both more personal concerns (about health, love, the future of the movement) than we otherwise have access to and give us a clearer sense of her sticking points: they demonstrate profound ambivalence about homosexuality, for example, in ways that her few public statements do not. If we think of them as communicative testimony, letters can also reveal marginal history as a series of stutters and gaps in the archive. Letters may remain unanswered or be crossly returned, may reference other letters now lost, or present a partial and invested perspective that raises the spectre of their reception as we read them. Absence of reciprocation in love letters between women, for example, is evocative of a history of desire that is always open to interpretation; as Martha Vicinus reminds us, lesbian history "has always been characterised by a 'not knowing'" (1994, 57). With this in mind, then, my interest in letters in this project is as much on the creative process of reading the lack of responses, the imagination of letters and reciprocation that is not in the archive, as it is in the material evidence that surviving letters represent.

Taking the idea of what is missing forward in more general methodological terms, gaps within any marginal history might be said to be constitutive of that history, of its secrets and half-buried violences and pleasures. This is no real surprise, as we know there are archival consequences to the history of legal sanctions on homosexuality, on birth control, on miscegenation or prostitution. Much has been destroyed, and not only by outside forces, as people struggle to survive and protect themselves from harm or retain unstable privileges. As Avery Gordon writes: "We're haunted [by what] could have been and by the peculiar temporality of the shadowing of lost and better futures . . . sometimes as nostalgia, sometimes as regret, sometimes as a kind of critical urgency" (2011, 7). It is tempting indeed to want to fill these gaps, to find additional sources, and to write a counterhistory that displays alternative evidence for the skeptic. And in so doing, perhaps we also hope to displace those ghosts whose contours are impossible to delineate: now you see them, now you don't. But the history of what has been buried is not simply a direct representation of a *relief*; it is not a Rachel Whiteread sculpture that gives shape to the space within, outside, or around the substantive. It is not directly represented in the formal archive, and so must be sought in the interstices of the text and context (Spivak 1999). It is tempting of course to try and recover the past in a form that reflects our current position, or even directly stands in its difference as a marker of how far we have come or what we have lost. But in seeking to fill the gaps, we run the risk of plastering over the cracks of meaning and struggle that are not only a failure to come into recognition but also a legacy of the difficulty of struggle and meaning making. If we try to bring the buried truth of "'historic alternatives'" (Marcuse, in A. Gordon 2011, 7) into the present as part of a desired other legacy, we may ironically enough be enacting a representational violence of our own. As Gordon further explains, in hoping to rescue difference from the archive, we may end up less attuned to the ways that "abusive systems of power make themselves known and their impacts felt in everyday life, especially when they are supposedly over and done with" (2011, 2). While Gordon is talking here about the denial of the legacy of transatlantic slavery in a contemporary American political imaginary, her understanding of "haunting" remains more broadly relevant to an ethics and poetics of the dynamics of history (A. Gordon 2008). Her vision foregrounds the power relationships that make some memories traceable, while others are only barely perceptible: through a sixth sense, a frisson of fear, or the uncanny familiarity of new connection. Gordon's work has always asked us to think about the shape of the buried knowledges and bodies whose graves remain unmarked. Tempting though it surely is, then, my concern in this project is less with a search for lost sources and more with how we might read these archival gaps and half-grasped traces creatively. The shift is slight, but important, I think. It frames the ambivalent histories we inherit as ones that were *always likely to have been lost*. This acknowledgement of the significance of loss is not intended to leave open the wounds of history but to approach them from a different angle. It brings to the fore the significance of the historian, or teller of tales, in being able to register those traces through their contemporary resonance: in her affect, her dynamic with the archives she creates, and through the sense that there is something hovering that cannot quite ever be known.

My interest in an imaginative archive that seeks to tell the unsayable and imagine what cannot be retrieved leans heavily on a history of postcolonial theory and fiction. Writers in this tradition insist that stories can and must be retold from the position of these gaps and fissures, but not in order to mend or simply include. Most famously, Jean Rhys in *Wide Sargasso Sea* (1966) retells *Jane Eyre* from the standpoint of the "madwoman in the attic," and J. M. Coetzee (1986) reimagines Daniel Defoe's *Robinson Crusoe* from the perspective of Susan Barton, who joins Crusoe and the voiceless Friday on the infamous desert island, and whose experiences are distorted or erased by Defoe himself. More recently, Joan Anim-Addo (2008) rewrites Aphra Behn's tale of Oroonoko from the point of view of his otherwise untraceable lover. These writers eschew a search for innocent origins or even reparation; these are renditions of the violence of dominant narratives that leave space only for confusion or howls that fill the night air. And their protagonists have no time for identity or futurity. Theirs is a struggle to hold on, to reflect, and to survive. And while that struggle is always lost—both for them and for posterity—the ripples it makes continue to register at the level of *possibility*, if not reality.[36]

Postcolonial thinkers in this vein do not ask us to reverse history, or simply value the downtrodden or obscured. Instead, they focus on our practices of reading, of attention to one thing and not another; they invite us to read against the grain. Saidiya Hartman (2002), for example, starts from her sense of loss at the lack of stories of resistance to slavery in the archives. Surprised—and a little irritated by her own surprise—at the archival reflection of a dominant order (since resistance was routinely met with deathly obliteration), Hartman refuses to deny that historical violence, or accept what she encounters as the whole story. Instead, she embarks on a historical journey that begins from her desire for other traces of meaning beyond the deafening archival silence: if she wants evidence of solidarity in the face of annihilation, then she will have to imagine it. Hartman throws us into the uncertain hum of plausible alternatives by imagining moments of encounter and futurity between two girls killed on an Atlantic slave trade ship. The archive has no details of their—or any—relationship between slaves, reflecting the girls' status as cargo, so for Hartman their story can only be glimpsed as we "strain . . . against [the] archive" (2008, 11) in order to be able to "imagine what cannot be verified" (12). Hartman's narration of the violence and death of these two girls is shot through with her painful imagination of other possible moments of recognition and intimacy not as a way of mediating that pain but as a way of reorienting her, and our, historical sensibilities.

This idea of *speculative history* qua Hartman is reflected in artistic and academic practices of meaning making that splice together fragments from the archive—bits and pieces that cannot be catalogued, are undated, unmatched, nonsensical—with creative interventions. The work of Cheryl Dunye and Zoe Leonard in *The Fae Richards Photo Archive* and its companion piece, the fake documentary *The Watermelon Woman* (Dunye 1996),[37] are particularly good examples of the power of the imaginative archive. *The Fae Richards Photo Archive* brings together staged photographic images to chart the life of the fictional protagonist of the same name, from the early twentieth century onwards. The archive shows her stereotyped roles in films (hence she becomes known as the "Watermelon Woman"), her participation in the civil rights movement, and her struggles in between. Dunye's film enacts a further twist, in which Dunye herself plays an African American video store employee who is researching Richards's life and discovers a further lesbian (butch) reading of her (femme) desires. As Hartman does, so Dunye attributes her "falsification" of Richards's life story to the lack of any archival traces of this black femme starlet from the 1930s, commenting that *"The Watermelon Woman* came from the lack of any information about the lesbian and film history of African-American women. Since it wasn't happening, I invented it." Dunye-as-historian foregrounds the yearning of the contemporary queer subject for a past that she can claim, despite knowing that this will rely on fabrication of evidence. I prefer the term "speculative" to "falsified" here, however, precisely to highlight the believability of the narrative that eludes the historian's gaze, but which cannot not have been true.

My own aims in occupying the position of the imaginative historian are similar. I start from the letters that Goldman received from fellow anarchist activist and labour union organizer Almeda Sperry during 1912 and 1913. Sperry wrote a sequence of more than sixty seductive letters to Goldman, in which she depicts her frustration with small-town life and politics, her struggles with her husband, Fred, and her paid work for sex, as well as her desire for Goldman (which was temporarily reciprocated). There are no letters from Goldman to Sperry in the archive, and while I can entertain fantasies of their discovery in the attic of a distant relative of Sperry's, their loss is of course indicative. But as I read Sperry's letters to Goldman, I piece together their likely correspondence and enter a conversation between the two of them that reflects my own yearning for the letters that we do not have. In a fictional and political archival experiment, then, I write Goldman's letters to Sperry as chapter 4 of this book. In "A Longing for Letters," I use that reading dynamic as Dunye and Hartman do, as a springboard for imagining a past we do not have evidence of. I start from that yearning for those letters, both as a way of correcting assumptions about Goldman's heterosexuality—the critical archive tends to read *our* lack of evidence as *her* lack of desire—and as a way of imagining her pleasure and distance in relation to Sperry as filled with ambivalence. I start from the tension between wanting those letters and the knowledge that they not only have been lost but were, again, *always likely to have been lost.*

The letters I write back to Sperry seek to represent both aspects of her sexual politics that are part of the subjective archive, and aspects that elude us. I pore over Sperry's missives, taking in her frustration that Goldman has not written in ages, and her relief when she has received a letter. I can see that the letters were there, that Sperry received them, but only faint clues emerge as to what they might have contained: declarations of love and impatience; political diatribes; shared reading and frustration. I am interested both in the complexities of her own desire as we encounter it and in the parts that cannot so easily be confronted: her disgust as well as her pleasure, her fear as well as fierce courage and pride. The history I imagine is not one with identity at its heart but one that queers both the Goldman archive and the critical archive that longs for a safe and knowable history. I write back to Sperry the letters I imagine Goldman writing when I read the ones we have, and in so doing I foreground both our collective failure to find them and the importance of still imagining them there. I am not prepared to read Goldman only through the traces that remain; instead, I want to bring to life a sexual history in which her own ambivalence, same-sex passion and disgust, fear and bravery must have crafted the words she wrapped around Sperry's heart. I write Goldman's letters back to Sperry as a kind of memory work that focuses on my own yearning for a stronger trace of her appetite and anger, and that I know I will not find except imaginatively. I do not want to clean Goldman up, or reject her for her contradictions. I want to think with and through Goldman towards an ethics of representation and political ambivalence that starts from my own yearning for something that "cannot be verified" and from my gut feeling Goldman would have been tickled pink by my presumption.

one • Women and Revolution

REVOLUTIONARY CHALLENGES

Feminists across several generations have been seduced by Emma Goldman, and it is not hard to see why. Goldman not only centres women's experiences in her call for revolution; she also locates women at the heart of her analysis of capitalism at national and international levels. Refusing to push the harms women suffer to one side, she castigates her comrades for adding to their oppression and for their conservative discomfort with discussions of sexuality and the body. Goldman's important article "The Tragedy of Women's Emancipation" was published in the first issue of *Mother Earth* (Goldman's anarchist journal), and her comment that there are "internal tyrants, far more harmful to life and growth, such as ethical and social conventions" (1906b, 15) must surely have been meant as much for her anarchist comrades as it was for suffragists. She berated women for their failings, certainly, and aligned herself with those who thought bourgeois femininity a particular bar to revolution, but she also championed women's efforts to remake themselves and supported women's full participation in all spheres of life. Further, and to my mind particularly significant, Goldman inhabited her refusal of convention with unparalleled zeal. From the very beginning of her political career, Goldman occupied the anarchist stage with matchless fervency, horsewhipping Johann Most off the platform when he spoke against Berkman's failed attentat (1931b, 105), supporting prostitutes and homosexuals on the basis of her unwavering critique of morality, albeit in contradictory ways (Cook 1979a, 435–37; Greenway 2009a), and flinging herself into revolutionary struggles right up to the end of her life (Ackelsberg 2001; Porter 1983).[1] Yet while Goldman's life is marked by her insistence on the links between sexual politics and all other forms of oppression, to my mind it is not persuasive to claim her as a feminist foremother without first thinking more fully about several aspects of her ambivalence about women and the nature of their oppression and freedom.

For Goldman, women's social position marks them as dependent, vulnerable, duplicitous subjects. In line with many of her anarchist contemporaries, this means that women are seen as ill equipped for revolutionary activity, and their passivity and misery are framed as preventing men from participating as fully revolutionary subjects too (Gemie 1996). Far from sidelining women's needs, however, Goldman understood their situation as a central rather than peripheral concern for political transformation. She considered women, in their position as reproducers of social and human life, as occupying the boundary between the public and private spheres, and their subordination as essential to the maintenance of labour inequalities, as well as national and military interests (e.g., 1897b, 1913). For Goldman, women are terribly harmed by the institutions and practices they are forced into: marriage, frequent childbearing, prostitution, and economic vulnerability affect women in particularly horrific ways (1898b, 1909e, 1911, between 1927 and 1930). Goldman believed that when women act in accordance with their oppression, they reproduce the worst aspects of capitalism, reinforcing conservatism, nationalism, and class interests across the generations for whom they are largely responsible. At times, as we shall see, Goldman's acerbic critiques of women seem to veer into misogyny, particularly when she does little to disentangle the problem of femininity from those who carry its burden. Goldman's own life and words sit uncomfortably with accounts that seek to domesticate these critiques and revolutionary passions when they claim her as a feminist, however. Such reclamations tend to rely on a reframing of Goldman as less hostile to both feminism and women than she is. And yet, she not only is disparaging towards women (particularly bourgeois women) but also takes great pleasure in this attitude. She refuses to accept suffrage politics as emancipatory for women and develops an epistemology of qualitative value with respect to sexual freedom, arguing more generally against quantitative modes of counting equality. And she not only highlights the double standards regulated by a public/private divide but also seeks to challenge the idea of "the private" more fundamentally. In what follows, I explore Goldman's complex framing of women's oppression and her affectively charged focus on women's transformation. I focus on the ambivalences in her political imaginary with respect to women precisely because these highlight some important sticking points in understanding sexual politics and freedom both in Goldman's lifetime and in ours.

Goldman's refusal to spare women the full force of her rage is both disturbing for feminists and also a sign of her commitment to treating women the same as men: only then might they be able to take up the position of revolutionary subject. Her evaluations of femininity as coldly calculating are extremely consistent too. These enable her to make the links between individual accounting (relying on men's money) and the failure of an equality agenda that adds up gains rather than embracing human value. To want to bring forward Goldman *as a feminist* is thus perversely to erase the very political theory of sexual freedom that she develops: one dependent on the difference between her views of women and revolution and a feminist one. Her political ambivalence about women's role and person is, I argue, the very site of the development of a fresh and persuasive critique of a public/private divide, and the establishing of women's oppression as tethered to capitalist and militarist exploitation. Rather than claiming Goldman as a missing feminist foremother, then, I instead want to focus on her fundamental contributions to feminist history: contributions that depend precisely on her *critiques* of feminism. And I want to think with Goldman about the difference that her challenges to sexual and gendered norms make to how we understand the relationship between feminism and feminists in the present. I thus explore the usefulness of disarticulating feminism from a feminist subject not to undermine the former but to refocus on the content and claims that feminism can and should make. Grounding this inquiry first in the subjective archive, I then explore the role of the critical archive in domesticating the very insights that Goldman brings to a history of feminism and finally turn to the theoretical archive to suggest ways in which Goldman's judgement of women might be a helpful starting point for a renewed transformative agenda within feminism.

Before turning to the Goldman archive, let me put Goldman's work on women and transformation in some context. At the height of her notoriety in America—when she was dubbed the "High Priestess of Anarchy" (*Chicago Inter Ocean* 1908, 284)—Goldman participated in a scene of revolutionary fervour, in spaces saturated with reflections on the relationship between what we now call sexual politics and social change. Questions of gender and sexuality were rarely absent from the anarchist, socialist, and bohemian circles of turn-of-the-century America, and while never settled, these issues lay at the heart of political interrogation in ways that challenge our own contemporary sense that the Left was only later fragmented by the tangential concerns of feminist, sexual, and racial politics (Frost 2009, 74). Christine Stansell insists that the question of feminism itself was pivotal and not peripheral to the social, cultural, and political fermentation that characterised the modern age, noting in her preface to the 2009 edition of *American Moderns* that the bohemians "so often gave feminism pride of place in their longed-for democratic revival . . . [and] heralded the newest of New Women as heroines of a desirable modernity" (xi). As Kathy Ferguson has documented, Goldman's profound awareness of women's place in cementing and challenging social norms locates her as "very much of her time: her time and place were saturated with the bodies, voices, and ideas of many hundreds of radical women" (2011b, 251).[2] For Stansell, the dramatic changes in relationships between individuals and the social fabric that marked the era also produced considerable rage, such that "fear of immigrants, the black masses, and the labor movement blended with dislike of the New Woman" (2000, 31) to produce a reassertion of a conservative as well as radical masculinity.

Such retrenchment was not the preserve of the establishment alone. As such scholars also chart, the anxiety concerning women's changing position in the home or as part of revolutionary transformation produced a predictable backlash from within those very movements that prided themselves on openness and utopian commitment. While anarchists the world over greeted the new century with searing "critiques of male domination . . . [and] emphasized the oppressive and unnatural strictures of the institution of marriage, and the desirability of its prescribed remedy, free love" (Hutchison 2001, 532), real acceptance of women's changing role was rare. In part, this is because the fathers of anarchism either were silent on the matter or else positioned women's oppression as an unfortunate but secondary concern (Gemie 1996, 2001). Thus theorists such as Pierre-Joseph Proudhon, Martin Landauer, and Octave Mirbeau considered women to be more immoral than men because of their learned roles of vulnerability and sexual dependency in the family (J. Cohn 2010; Gemie 2001), while others—such as Mikhail Bakunin or Peter Kropotkin—remained disconcertingly silent on the question of women's particular oppression.[3] Proudhon certainly understands women's inferiority as bound to their subordination, but as Alex Prichard (2010) has explored, he depends on rather than challenges the public/private divide upon which that oppression relies in other aspects of his argument. For Proudhon, the domestic sphere needs to be retained so that men can be given the space to come home from their conditions of exploited labour to experience leisure or—more important—create the space for radical participation. In her witty "Anarchist Guide to . . . Feminism: The Emma Goldman Angle" (2014), Ruth Kinna imagines Goldman in a postdeath utopia considering the limits of Proudhon's understandings of democracy: "What niggled? Poor dear Proudhon was too much of a home man. . . . He failed to see that property worked in complex ways and that for women there was a double enslavement. . . . Proudhon's blindness made her shudder" (2014, 22).[4]

While men's absence of radicalism is consistently framed as a product of working conditions, then, women's absence of the same is much more easily bound to her person and understood as enduring. Woman's duplicity and cowardliness are naturalised such that her capacities as a potential as well as current autonomous subject are foreclosed. Not all anarchist writers agree with this assessment of femininity's flaws of course: Magno Espinosa insists on free love as a challenge to the marriage contract that binds women to their subordination, privileges bourgeois morality, and prevents female emancipation (Gemie 1996, 532), and he frames women's "character" as resulting from the current sexual division of labour in a vein more consistent with his broader critique of authority (531). And as David Porter argues, in many cases "emancipation of women was seen as a crucial part of overall social transformation" for anarchists, even if this was not viewed as an immediate priority (1983, 251). But for the most part, as Porter himself acknowledges in an otherwise positive gloss, anarchists rarely advocated a full-scale transformation of the domestic sphere, and "most frequently male anarchists retreated to cultural orthodoxy in their personal relationships with women" (251). In the meantime, women are directly blamed for their subservience and castigated for their bourgeois morality. As Jesse Cohn pertinently notes, within this complex "a newly 'unrestrained' female sexuality is made to bear the guilt for the demise of community" (2010, 418) and a bar to generational revolutionary capacity.

Goldman joined other radical women (and some men) in their scathing critiques of the patriarchal male thinking that caught women in a double bind of oppression and blame, both within and outside of the anarchist movement. With Crystal Eastman and Voltairine de Cleyre, Goldman (1911) portrayed the horrors and exploitations of marriage; with Max Eastman, Mabel Dodge

Luhan, and Louise Bryant, she promoted free love as a political as well as personal alternative (*St. Louis Post-Dispatch* 1908); with Margaret Sanger and Margaret Anderson, she analysed the links between the banning of family limitation and the creation of a reserve army of labour (Goldman 1916c); and with Henrik Ibsen, H. G. Wells, and Rebecca West, Goldman linked creativity and freedom of expression with utopianism (Goldman 1914b, 1928?a).[5] For these thinkers and activists, women's emancipation could not wait and was formulated as key to the success of a revolutionary agenda.[6] In articulating the links between lack of birth control and women's dependency, or between prostitution and marriage, the espousers of radical sexual politics challenged presumptions that women's position was natural or inevitable, and importantly also insisted that social transformation necessitated a shift in women's subjectivity now and not later. With increasing sexual and intellectual freedom, women would be able to join their male comrades in forging a new world free of oppression; without it, they would continue to hamper such efforts and remain caught in the horrors of femininity.

Thus, in contrast to sexual conservatives of all political persuasions who sought to retain the current familial structure or endorse women's natural role, radical women and men theorised sex roles in terms of socialisation in the strongest possible terms (Presley 2000). Women's position was understood as highly compromised, certainly: bourgeois women were castigated for investing in the temporary and superficial gains offered by marriage; prostitutes chastised for being seduced by consumerism; and mothers scolded for lack of care in relation to both men and children. But these familiar critiques were complemented by a twofold focus on the bodily consequences of oppression for women, and on their readiness for transformation: the new woman could not and would not wait. Along with others, then, and as Ferguson suggests, Goldman "gave a great deal of thought to the embodied conditions under which women struggle to birth and feed children, to have few children, to sell their labour, to love, to survive" (2011b, 251). In the first volume of her autobiography, Goldman foregrounds women's physical and emotional suffering in undergoing repeat and unwanted pregnancies (1931b, 185–86) and provides a human face to prostitution. In a much-quoted comment, Goldman insists: "Now that I had learned that women and children carried the heaviest burden of our ruthless economic system, I saw that it was mockery to expect them to wait until the social revolution arrives in order to right injustice" (187). One might be tempted to read Goldman's statement in 1908 that she intends to strive "until I die to break the shackles that make [women] the chattels of men" (*Chicago Inter Ocean* 1908, 286) as hyperbolic, but her promise is borne out by more than five decades of commitment to that freedom.

For those insisting that women's emancipation had to be central to a revolutionary imagination, this was no minor set of changes but involved a fundamental reconsideration of women's relationship to others and to the world. As Maxine Molyneux notes, anarchist women in Latin America not only highlighted how fed up they were with their ongoing domestic drudgery but also laid positive claim to their right to pleasure (1986, 126). Indeed, it was sexual freedom that took centre stage in the political imagination of women's freedom for many (Hustak 2012). For Goldman, emancipation would mean "woman's freedom . . . absolute sex equality" (*St. Louis Post-Dispatch* 1908), and she was heartened by what she saw as the increase of women's sexual independence in the first three decades of the twentieth century. Goldman celebrated the "flapper's" sexual freedom, for example, in the face of its characterisation as decadent or frivolous (*The Toronto Star* 1926), and she highlighted the importance of women's growing assertiveness after many of them had participated in "masculine" labour during the First World War (1926a).[7] An emphasis on sexual freedom within anarchist circles meant embracing struggles for women's access to birth control (which nicely combined individual freedom and critique of state restriction for anarchists), and Goldman was imprisoned for her reproductive freedom activism (Goldman 1916c). Indeed, during a period of intense public visibility in America, Goldman located birth control as a "most vital question" (1916b, 426), and the birth control movement as representing "the spiritual awakening of women throughout the world" (*New York Herald* 1916b).[8]

While embracing the sense that, as Charlotte Wilson put it, "'women who are awake to a consciousness of their human dignity have everything to gain, because they have nothing to lose, by a Social Revolution'" (cited in Greenway 2009b, 157), these revolutionaries did not adhere to feminism as a movement or set of interventions. In part this was because of the perceived bourgeois nature of feminism, and for anarchists of course, this was also because of its emphasis on the franchise, with its accompanying demand for state recognition. Goldman was scathing of the co-optation that arises from this need for recognition, and in particular of the nationalist fervour that some suffragists adopted and that made their ideas more palatable to the American political class (1917d). But, and as I detail further later, Goldman was also particularly critical of what she saw as the suffragist conceit concerning women's emotional or ethical advantage over men (1914d, 1917d, 1926a). Across her oeuvre, Goldman repeats both that she "'simply [does] not believe in the power of the ballot, either for man or woman,'" and that she takes "'exception to the statement of the suffragists that women are superior to men'" (*Brooklyn Eagle* 1916). Instead, Goldman argued strongly for the need for a more complete freedom from sex roles for women, insisting that while "the right to vote, equal civil rights, are all very good demands, true emancipation begins neither at the polls nor in courts" (1906b, 17). For Goldman, the morality of suffrage was as dangerous as the morality of religion or the state in terms of its hold over woman's soul, leading her to conclude that "woman is confronted with the necessity of emancipating herself from emancipation, if she really desires to be free" (10).

As I hope is clear, Goldman joins other radical women and men in centring the importance of women's freedom for (anarchist) revolution. While she certainly shares the prevalent radical view of women, particularly bourgeois women, as duplicitous and caught in the double bind of economic and interpersonal servitude, she does not consider this natural or inevitable. Quite to the contrary, in fact: it is precisely women's location at the intersection of public and private that means their emancipation is critical to fostering revolutionary conditions in the present. For Goldman, to leave sexual politics until after the revolution would be a grave mistake, since it is women's capitulation to consumerism and dominance that is passed on to a new generation of subservient souls. Thus, she writes passionately that "[if] we want to accomplish Anarchy, we must first have free women at least . . . unless we have free women, we cannot have free mothers, and if mothers are not free, we cannot expect the next generation to assist us" (1897a). Goldman's precise theorisation of women's reproductive role for the maintenance of capitalism constitutes a powerful intervention into our understanding of the public/private divide. For Goldman, the problem with women's association with the "private" is not the lack of recognition from the state or lack of opportunity to experience the same labour exploitation as men. The problem is, rather, that they are denied access to a public world of solidarity and organising. If women are to step out of their historical role and begin to participate fully in the development of a revolutionary imaginary, they will need to leave behind a world of special treatment and sly duplicity. They will need to leave the trappings of femininity and embrace a utopia that they are as responsible for bringing about as men are. In a sense, then, Goldman is not ambivalent about the future but has to bring all her ambivalence about women's contemporary role to bear on persuading them out of their contentment with what she sees as their sorry lot.

The Goldman archive identifies two main traps that tie women to capitalism and that mitigate their development of a revolutionary consciousness. The first is an astute assessment of marriage as snare for both women and men; the second is an account of women's reproductive and affective labour that underwrites the international capitalist military machine. In the first instance, family, sexual, and reproductive subservience, as well as financial dependence, characterise women's inferior status. Goldman considered marriage a site of direct violence for women not only because it is the basis of private property but also because it causes only "sorrow, misery, humiliation . . . tears and curses . . . agony and suffering" (1897a). This "private possession of one sex by the other" (1897a) gives men authority over women's bodies both legally and personally, meaning that love can never be free. As in much of her writing, Goldman lends her prose immediacy by foregrounding the direct impact of power on ordinary people's bodies and by castigating her audience for its attachment to corrupt and old-fashioned attitudes that are poorly attuned to contemporary political needs. Thus she insists that "marriage is a failure none but the very stupid will deny" (1911, 4), and that the fantasy that marriage protects women "is so revolting, such an outrage and insult on life, so degrading to human dignity, as to forever condemn this parasitic institution" (11).

The false "insurance pact" (4) that is marriage plunges a woman into ignorance, as she is encouraged to focus only on her appearance and is discouraged from engaging in depth with her partner in relation to anything "save his income" (6). Marriage is the perversion of love rather than its ideal form for Goldman, reflecting a substitution of economic bargaining for real intersubjective possibility. Within this institution, women are commodities to be exchanged, and their only currency is sex and attractiveness. The impact is on all women, though for Goldman it is bourgeois women who embody its worst aspects most completely because of their ability to become *wholly commodified* (between 1927 and 1930, 8). In an interesting set of reflections in her book *The White Slave Traffic* (1909e), Goldman also blames American consumerism for levels of prostitution among recent migrants, who are seduced by the possibility of superficial objects they can claim no other way. The driving force towards prostitution is the same as marriage, then: consumerist greed and not personal immorality. Marriage is thus prostitution not metaphorically but actually, with the difference being the number of men one sells one's body to, and the false morality that frames both practices (1913). Goldman elides the gap between marriage and prostitution by returning once more to the bodily and emotional impact of marriage on women, referring to it as "chattel slavery," as "horrid, humiliating and degrading... prostitution of the worst kind" (1897a).[9]

The impact of the corruption of love in marriage, then, is not only a question of economic freedom and the restriction of women to a private realm or a public shame. It shapes a woman's *very being* through subservience and passivity as she takes on the affects required to represent this ideal. To succeed as a woman, the double bind is of course that she must inhabit her objectification more and more fully, such that her very character is saturated with the most pernicious aspects of un-freedom. And it is here, in her descriptions of the impact of women's failure to challenge the institution of marriage, that Goldman most directly chastises them for their attachments. Thus, a married woman is condemned "to life-long dependency, to parasitism, to complete uselessness, individual as well as social" (1911, 4); she becomes a "nag," is "petty, quarrelsome, gossipy, unbearable," or "reckless in appearance, clumsy... dependent... cowardly, a weight and a bore" (10). Men do not fare well in Goldman's descriptions of marriage either, it should be noted, but while men are driven from their homes in search of unfettered comforts, women are the agent of that flight; and while a man may be "[robbed] of his birthright," and marriage "stunts his growth, poisons his body, keeps him in ignorance," for women there is no escape route. Marriage harms men but "makes a parasite of woman, an absolute dependent. It incapacitates her for life's struggles, annihilates her social consciousness, paralyzes her imagination, and then imposes its gracious protection" (1911, 11). Such prose reminds us, I think, of the critiques by other anarchists of women as captured ontologically as well as politically by the conditions of their own oppression. And it is in her framing of women as more particularly caught by domestic un-freedom that Goldman's profound ambivalence comes to light. Despite her own arguments to the contrary, then, woman's duplicity is precisely what makes her a woman, whereas men's enslavement *prevents* him being a man. Thus, while clearly wanting to liberate women from the traps they find themselves in, Goldman's florid characterisations of woman herself as ontologically rather than purely politically bound to her oppression risk ceding the terrain in ways that are reminiscent of Proudhon himself.

I return to this question of Goldman's judgement of women as a key component of her sexual politics, and one that may have effects other than simply resuturing "woman" to her unfortunate circumstances, later in this chapter, but for the moment let me turn to the second trap Goldman explores as what we might term the economics of sexuality in her archive. In a range of work, but particularly that focused on the sexual politics of militarisation, Goldman foregrounds reproduction as a key technique in sustaining capitalism's wars. For Goldman, the politics of women's sexuality are not only a question of domestic labour: they also constitute a link between the reproduction and maintenance of the social and political order. Women are both commodities themselves and also producers of the next generation of exploitable labour, within the twin evils of capitalism and militarism (1917a). Not only is women's experience of sex and love one of ignorant misery, then, but her reproductive labour is bound as part of what President Theodore Roosevelt saw as a national duty to provide offspring for the nation (Falk 2005, 70). Some of Goldman's most rousing analysis is produced as a critique of this abuse, as she appeals to her mostly working-class audiences who have direct experience of bodily violence of labour and know well which bodies are disposable in times of "peace" and war (1911, 3). While America prepares to enter the First World War, in a passage noteworthy for its visceral depiction of the role of reproduction in the maintenance of the military machine, Goldman spits:

> Capitalism . . . roars through its whistle and machine, "Send your children on to me, I will twist their bones; I will sap their blood, I will rob them of their bloom," for capitalism has an insatiable appetite. And through its destructive machinery, militarism, capitalism proclaims, "Send your sons on to me, I will drill and discipline them until all humanity has been ground out of them; until they become automatons ready to shoot and kill at the behest of their masters." Capitalism cannot do without militarism and since the masses of people furnish the material to be destroyed in the trenches and on the battlefield, capitalism must have a large race. (1916c, 468)

As in her writing on marriage, Goldman's prose is dripping with anger and reflective of the violence attending reproduction: from women's drudgery and ill health in childbearing, to the misery and pain of seeing one's children destroyed by labour or war or both. Importantly, women are uniquely situated both in bodily terms within capitalism and militarism, then, but also in terms of their role in reproducing generational capitulation to these economic and political structures. And this is of course why Goldman considers women's *sexual* emancipation all the more significant as part of a revolutionary vision.

As we can see, Goldman's intervention in a political field saturated with talk of and experimentation with gender and sexual roles underlines her strong focus on "bodies—pregnant bodies, laboring bodies, desiring bodies, prostituted bodies" (Ferguson 2011b, 250). It is partly this focus that leads her to refuse a delay in addressing the problems women face, since she is clear about the visceral harm that women continue to suffer: as she notes of marriage, it is not only the structure of it but "the thing, the thing itself . . . [that] is objectionable, hurtful and degrading" (1897a). As Linda Gordon notes, what marks Goldman out among her peers is that she "fused into a single ideology the many currents that mingled in American sex radicalism" (1979, 451) that were frequently held apart. We might also hypothesise that it is in this understanding of the interwoven aspects of oppression that Goldman also challenges a view of women's position as inevitable, or as simply tied to reproduction. Together, these insights oblige Goldman to develop a distinct understanding of the *temporality* of women's oppression (McKenzie and Stalbaum 2007), a view that allows her to move more fluidly between disparaging and championing women. This question of temporality relates to Goldman's sense of any meaningful revolutionary action as born of struggle (1927?), as located between personal and political action, between public and private spheres, distinctions that she challenges. For Goldman, revolution is ongoing, never-ending, and in line with her broader anarchist commitments, it is process based and prefigurative. As she notes: "'What I believe' is a process rather than a finality. Finalities are for gods and governments, not for the human intellect" (1920, 52). In relationship to women's transformation, then, the task is both an urgent and an ongoing one, a process of struggle to foreground the desire for happiness over that of financial gain, empathy over self-promotion.

For Goldman, women need to struggle within this broader temporal frame of revolutionary activity particularly hard because it is *their* lack of freedom that secures capitalism and militarism at the intersubjective level, *their* bodily acceptance that perpetuates passivity, and *their* lack of courage that keeps things as they are. On the one hand, then, women have nothing to lose from their true emancipation (because they have nothing real to hold onto now), but they also have to start from a uniquely demeaned position within capitalism because of their need to be "respectable." For Goldman, if woman can throw aside her role as "domestic drudge" (1926a) and refuse the pernicious respectability that keeps her chained to her own bodily and spiritual oppression, then she will be able to exercise more power than any man. If she can but turn her authority in reproducing social, national, and political norms into a matching revolutionary authority, then the walls of capitalism are sure to come tumbling down. But first she has to be roused to the task, and it is to this awakening that Goldman turns much of her energy with respect to women's emancipation. And this is why, in my view, Goldman's critique of women's acceptance of their current conditions is so frequently sharp, often vicious, as she seeks to prompt individual women to fill the "emptiness in [their] soul" (1906b, 16). In short, her ambivalence about women is also the source of her political commitment to their emancipation.

As we have seen, Goldman is particularly harsh on suffrage women (1914d), whom she sees as settling for too little, but in fact any woman can come in for the full force of her scorn. As Falk notes: "Goldman . . . took it as a duty to critique her sisters' political shortcomings" (2012b, 123). What riled Goldman most was feminine hypocrisy, which is unsurprising given her analysis of the ills of women's role and the necessity for risk at the heart of women's emancipation. Goldman insisted that women could not expect favourable treatment and was incensed when they used the duplicity of femininity to get what they wanted, all the while lamenting their lot (1912a, 1917d). To a great extent, this berating is all part of the Goldman performance—her published writings usually began as public lectures, and we can imagine her playing to the crowd, probably including voices of silly superficial women with no life of their own, or "dried-up" suffragists with no love in their lives—but to another extent, Goldman fervently believed that unless women were forced out of their torpor, then no revolution would be possible. As Martha Solomon observes, though with less appreciation than my own, Goldman's "platform style was deliberately aggressive and flamboyant as well. She baited and harangued her audience about their dullness and blindness in an effort to stimulate their thinking" (1988, 191). So we might say that, while Goldman remains unswerving in her support of women's full participation across her lifetime, her critiques of women often mirror rather closely those of her more straightforwardly misogynist comrades. As Solomon continues, Goldman's "broad and caustic attacks . . . left her audience with little psychological refuge" (192); other than the promise of utopia, Goldman offers women little incentive to take such a bold sets of risks.

Goldman's vision was future oriented, and part of her solution to the problem of women's oppression is a straightforward one. She advocated that women make their lives "simpler, but deeper and richer" (1914d, 27), and in doing so live lives free of consumerist attachments, lives of real value instead.

Women's emancipation should be joyful and generous, rather than blaming or restrictive, should be open to others and filled with possibilities (1906b). Goldman seeks to resolve some of her ambivalence about the role and capacities of women methodologically, it seems to me. She draws on her anarchist understanding of revolutionary temporality (prefiguration) in order to hold together women's complicity and their revolutionary significance. In the process, her central question is how women might become more fully human, might become fully revolutionary subjects like the best and bravest of men (1917a, 10). This will require considerable work, of course, but Goldman remains confident that the promise of freedom will propel women into acting in their real (long-term) rather than superficial (and immediate) interests. First, women need to transfer their allegiances away from the false promises offered them within capitalism. Fantasies of marriage will only result in misery in any event, as we have seen: with the abuse of a woman's body, the selling of her soul, and the annihilation of her children in work and war. Thus Goldman advocates a turnaround of the current situation in which a woman abandons her dreams of "moonlight and kisses, or laughter and tears" for "shopping tours and bargain counters" so that she can reap the real benefits of investing otherwise (1911, 8). Second, Goldman endorses women's rapprochement with men rather than a reversal of oppositional value. This is both a question of politics—Goldman supported women and men working together in ways that challenged sexual roles—and a question of methodology. She felt strongly that prioritising women separate from their relationships with men could not work in revolutionary terms. In this double move, Goldman differentiates herself quite clearly from the stereotyped picture of the suffragist, whom she portrays as misrepresenting women as having softer natures or superior judgement to men (*Brooklyn Eagle* 1916). For Goldman, a focus on women's purity easily slips into moralising, into a validation of "artificial stiffness and . . . narrow respectabilities" (1906b, 16). Indeed, she quite consistently trades in stereotypes of feminism as a foil to develop her own transformative agenda.

The issue of quality—as both a political goal and a way of getting there—is fundamental for Goldman. Across her oeuvre, Goldman is interested in the ways in which knowledge and power are constituted in part through a quantitative/qualitative difference, in which the first is privileged over the latter. For Goldman, quantification is the bedrock of authoritarianism, as people are subordinated to facts and figures and are reduced to "an example" of a broader set of trends. The real character of human life in all its difference and vitality is thus lost. In her 1920 update of her 1908 piece "What I Believe," Goldman firmly situates quantification not simply as the opposite of quality but as affectively bankrupt, as that which actively *precludes* generosity. Quantification is superficial and lends itself to commodification and privatisation in its inexorable drive for accumulation. A range of linked ills within capitalism—commodification, women's oppression, lack of creativity, militarism—have at their core the valuing of quantity over quality for Goldman, their replacement of real human values with greed and banal repetition. To move away from capitalism, Goldman believed—as did many anarchists—that quality needed to be emphasised over quantity in order to resist war, overpopulation, and alienation (the bedrocks of human exploitation). In her moving draft lecture "Why I Am an Anarchist," Goldman outlines the links between human freedom and a prioritisation of quality, noting that "the interest of the State is promoted by the number of its subjects; that of Society by the quality of its members" (1927?, 8). A focus on value, then, constitutes a challenge to the monochrome culture and lack of diversity necessary for authority to hold sway both in itself (as a utopian example of human life to be lived) and as a methodology to bring about a break in the chains of that authority, particularly for women.

This line of argument in Goldman is of course also firmly linked to her belief in individual capacity and creativity as more important than the easily manipulated masses. In "Minorities versus Majorities" (1910, 69–78), her most sustained engagement with the issue of quantity versus quality, Goldman argues that majorities will always be defined by their lowest common denominator, and that a view from this perspective will always reproduce tyranny (since the minority's views will never be respected: they are, in effect, disposable). She begins her polemic thus: "The multitude, the mass spirit, dominates everywhere, destroying quality. Our entire life—production, politics, and education—rests on quantity, on numbers" (69). The majority is superstitious (76), is content with partial political representation, silences difference and diversity, and applauds mediocrity (71–72). The question of creativity is very important in this analysis, since it is precisely individual creative action that is emblematic of the possibility of transformation in grim times. For Goldman, then, in line with her analysis of quality versus quantity, "The living, vital truth of social and economic well-being will become a reality only through the zeal, courage, the non-compromising determination of intelligent minorities, and not through the mass" (78). It would be easy, I think, to interpret Goldman as advocating a kind of individualism familiar to those of us living in the first decades of the twenty-first century, but this not an accurate rendition of her argument. As Berenice Carroll points out, in "placing 'human values' at the core . . . Goldman was moving beyond liberal notions of individual human rights" (2007, 151). Goldman's individual is not an isolated being but is connected to others through imagination and real engagement, both of which are essential to build solidarity.[10] Indeed, for Goldman, it is members of "the majority" that are more likely to act in their own personal interests, suffocating diversity and imagination. Goldman differs here from her friend and mentor Peter Kropotkin, who professed profound "distaste for individual autonomy" (McKenzie and Stalbaum 2007, 206). Instead, Goldman marks a distinction between "existing systems that promote false individuality (such as democracies)" and individuality that "[pushes] through these boundaries to a utopia of freedom and enlightenment" (212).[11]

Goldman extends her analysis of quantity versus quality and individuality versus individualism in her account of women's oppression and transformation. Indeed, it is here that her analysis of the detrimental impact of valuing the superficial over the deep comes into its own. In relation to marriage, we may remember that while Goldman is severely critical of the structural inequities that make women dependent on men, she is also fiercely disapproving of the means by which women reproduce this relation at both material and affective levels. Thus, she rails against the ways that women evaluate their husbands in terms of financial stability, asking not "whether the man has aroused her love, but rather . . . 'How much?'" he has a year (1911, 8). For Goldman, women's myopia means they mistake things for substance and confirm rather than challenge social norms. And in substituting a foolhardy belief in capitalist security as a way out of sexual oppression, women force men to work harder and harder to satisfy their greed. As Lori Jo Marso suggests, and in line with my argument here, a crucial part of Goldman's argument about women's emancipation is their recognition that "what [they] are taught to desire is that which also denies them their freedom" (2003, 308). Goldman's argument might thus be said to be a gendered extension of the Marcusian idea of "false needs" (explored by David Alderson in his recent book Sex, Needs and Queer Culture [2016]), in which people are taught to desire that which prevents them thriving.[12] We might say, indeed, that Goldman's early challenge to femininity as security—indeed, instead as "false insurance"—echoes forward through Marcuse and into Lauren Berlant's (2011) theorisation of "cruel optimism" with respect to intimate attachments that keep people locked into social and economic abjection.

The question of quality for women is also a practical matter. Goldman began her activism in an America where birth control was illegal and where she witnessed firsthand the toll on women's bodies and morale of unlimited pregnancies and child rearing. In vibrant prose Goldman laments the ills of having a "large brood of children, often many more than the weekly wage of the father could provide for, [since] each additional child was a curse.... The men were generally more resigned, but the women cried out against Heaven for inflicting such cruelty upon them" (1931b, 186). Goldman consistently lectured in favour of birth control, going to prison for her pains and drawing large audiences wanting practical information about avoiding multiple pregnancies. Of one of her many lectures on the topic in 1916 leading up to her arrest, a journalist notes that "many young girls were in the audience and they all listened eagerly to what the speakers had to say" (*New York Herald* 1916a). Goldman smuggled in methods of birth control from Europe, and she gave a series of lectures on the importance of family limitation to women's emancipation (Goldman 1916b, 1916c). But as in so much of her writing on women, Goldman's focus is as much on what women need to do—or are already doing—in order to change their lot as it is on what prevents them from doing so. She was rightly convinced that women wanted access to the means to control the number of children they had; she was "impressed ... by the fierce, blind struggle of the women of the poor against frequent pregnancies" (1931b, 185). Goldman endorsed an early eugenics movement's focus on quality of offspring, in what makes for quite uncomfortable reading from a contemporary feminist point of view. For example, as part of her argument about the political problems of quantification, Goldman asserts that "volitional breeding must take the place of accidental breeding, quality of offspring must take the place of blind numbers" (n.d. [1991a], 3), and in an enraged letter to her comrade and friend Max Nettlau, Goldman challenges his "male contention that women love to have broods of children," which serves to show her that "like the rest of your sex, you really know nothing about women" (1935, cited in Porter 1983, 254). For Goldman the issue of birth control was one related to a more general argument about value and revolution within which "humanity is not continued in this world by quantity, but by quality" (*Los Angeles Record* 1916). It is in this vein that she claims that if society were properly to support women's and children's needs, the question of birth control would cease to be an issue (Goldman 1935?b), and she was an enthusiastic supporter of alternative education and kinship arrangements (Goldman 1897b).[13] Although I would not want to minimise the dangers of eugenics arguments emerging out of Goldman's development of her quality arguments with respect to women and birth control, then, it is important to bear in mind that she never supported a eugenics view that privileged propagation as a mode of national or racial belonging, but rather as a route to women's freedom.[14]

Goldman insisted that with proper attention to their emancipation, the "quality of women's contribution to society would be equal to men's" (*St. Louis Post-Dispatch* 1908). While quality itself is—self-evidently—impossible to quantify, it does have certain characteristics that help us imagine what it might look like, as well as how to move towards it. For women to embrace quality, they must reject their sexual servitude, challenge the corruption of motherhood, move decisively away from consumerism, and open up to others in order to inhabit lives of depth and value. Considering Goldman's analysis seriously here is to think through the ways in which a dominant focus on "equality" in feminism may be to settle for—endorse even—the status quo, as I discuss more fully later. Goldman advocates nothing less than an overhaul of the present social, economic, and political system, starting with women's subjectivity, and this is challenging because it requires a full acknowledgement of women's failings (for her and us). Because marriage is so central to the maintenance of that interlocking system, one means to achieve a life of quality is to reject this in favour of free love, in terms of both the free association outside of religious and state sanction and the freedom of multiple relationships. Thus, for Goldman, sexual freedom is a key to unlocking women's real selves as well as a challenge to a central structure of capitalism (1911, 1913). In an early comment, Goldman defends sexual freedom against its rejection by other revolutionaries and insists that "anarchism not only teaches freedom in economic and political areas, but also in social and sexual life" (1897–98).[15]

Yet this emphasis on breaking out of social and sexual convention should not be taken to mean Goldman encouraged women to break free of men at the same time. Quite the opposite: for Goldman, "woman's freedom is closely allied with man's freedom" (1934?). She thought that women and men could only begin to establish true relations with one another once free of the shackles of institutional authority, but that without a renewed dynamic between women and men, social revolution could not be achieved. For Candace Falk, Goldman's emphasis on the importance of "harmonious relations between the sexes" is a metaphor "for social and political unity" (2003, 12). But in fact, Goldman's belief in the importance of generous, open association between men and women seems to me to be much more than a metaphor; indeed, it is more of a strategy and methodology for political transformation of the relationship between men and women so essential to revolution. The point of emancipation for Goldman is freedom rather than separation, and in many ways she conceived of that freedom as an opportunity to relate more closely to others, to meet them head-on. As indicated previously, encounters between men and women cannot proceed from a presumption of women's superiority but from the foregrounding of the recognition of others on their own terms. Only then will the existing filters of consumerism and quantitative judgement that foster women's dependency be finally lifted from their eyes. Goldman was as much influenced by Sigmund Freud as she was by Friedrich Engels in this understanding. She had snuck into Freud's classes while training as a midwife in Vienna (Haaland 1993, 132) and was impressed by his emphasis on authority lived at the level of the subject, as well as the unpredictability of the psyche.[16] This emphasis on the ambivalence of psychic formation is precisely what allows Goldman to understand the appeal for women of the conditions of their own oppression. Goldman locates the problem as one in which the traits they have been lauded for historically are those that have kept them imprisoned: "For centuries [woman] has been lulled into a trance by the songs of the troubadours who paid homage to her goodness, her sweetness, her selflessness, above all, her noble motherhood. And though she is beginning to appreciate that all this . . . has befogged her mind . . . she hates to give up the tribute laid . . . at her feet by sentimental moonshiners of the past" (1935?a). This excerpt is from a draft lecture defending August Strindberg against accusations of his antiwoman sentiments, and we can see the appeal for Goldman of reading Strindberg in this way: as highlighting rather than endorsing women's hypocrisy, a tactic that so precisely mirrors her own. For Goldman, women's emancipation "concerns itself with the complete human being, all the rights, of personality [sic] of the full grown woman" (n.d. [1991a], 5). There can be no room in such an analysis for petty grievances or for fantasies of moral rectitude attaching to women over men. Instead, Goldman's focus on relationality as one of the conditions of women's autonomy leads her to assert in absolute terms that "all loves do well to leave the doors of their love wide open" (1912?).

Goldman's views on the relations between women and men are complex. At some points she castigates men for their myopia, while at others she argues that women should become more like men so that they might be better able to express themselves and enlarge the scope of their knowledge (Goldman, in Wexler 1981, 118). My reading of Goldman across her oeuvre is that in fact neither men nor women currently inhabit the ideal of individuality and relationality; both men and women need to become more active, creative, and engaged. In this vein, Goldman endorses neither masculine nor (certainly) feminine traits but an active "vitality" that both men and women might possess. Indeed, Goldman diagnoses one of the effects of the First World War as a decrease in men's "grip on life," while women in the meantime have become more "virile . . . active, alive" (1926a). Reflecting further on "the devitalizing effect of the horrors of war on a great many men" (1926a), Goldman indicates that she finds women everywhere "'more vital than the men'" (*The Toronto Telegram* 1926). While never celebrating the effects of war, Goldman nevertheless relishes women's changed situation with respect to men, in part because it offers a glimmer of hope for new relationships between the sexes.

Goldman's revolutionary method for reuniting the sexes after centuries of strife relies on the substitution of positive for negative affect, in line with her prefigurative commitments (Ackelsberg 2012). Love is at the heart of Goldman's vision for women's emancipation. She privileges forgiveness and generosity between men and women (1906b, 9) over mutual antagonism and proclaims that "pettiness separates, breadth unites" (18). A woman must give in to the possibility of real joy rather than remaining caught in bitterness and its hollow triumphs. Only then will she be able to hear when the "voice of love is calling" in order to accept "life's greatest treasure, love for a man," without first counting the costs (15). It seems something of an understatement, then, for Falk to suggest that Goldman has a "perhaps idealized vision of the joyful harmony of the sexes" (2005, 48).[17] And it will no doubt not come as a surprise that Goldman's incitement to any woman to "abandon herself to the man of her choice, as the flowers abandon themselves to dew and light, in freedom, beauty, and ecstasy" (1913, 6), has met with some resistance from feminist and queer critics concerned about the emphatic heterosexuality of Goldman's revolutionary vision. As Ellen Dubois and Linda Gordon note in the broader context of free love discourse, the restriction of a revolutionary imagination to opposite-sex encounters further marginalises same-sex desire (1983, 18). And as Judy Greenway suggests, while in theory free love did not preclude homosexuality, in practice it was sanctioned, or "if mentioned at all, [it] was usually seen as an unfortunate medical condition" (2009b, 159). Thus we can already see some of the contradictions emerging out of Goldman's affective methodology for women's emancipation: an emphasis on quality over equality intersects with eugenics arguments, and a focus on generous openness to relations with men risks displacing issues of gendered hierarchy in intimate relationships, or reinforcing the widely shared anxiety among anarchists and more broadly about "the homosexual menace" (Cleminson 1998, 136). But so too we can already see that the hostility towards both femininity and feminism in the Goldman archive is essential in order for her own vision of qualitative sexual freedom to take centre stage. In what follows I explore feminist responses—including my own—to this ambivalence in the Goldman archive, asking what work the critical archive expects Goldman to perform on its behalf, and what this reveals about a contemporary feminist politics.

GOLDMAN'S "FEMINISM"

The feminist critical archive is by turns delighted and dismayed with Goldman, for reasons I hope are already reasonably apparent. She represents an assertive insistence on women's rights to pleasure and political engagement, and the strong links between women's oppression and capitalist and militarist misery. Yet as I explore in this section, feminist critical ambivalence about Goldman's politics and person often results in trying to claim her as a straightforward feminist heroine, whatever the difficulties caused by such an attempt. Critics thus seek to resolve both Goldman's and their own struggles with the nature of the public/private divide and with the problem of "femininity as duplicity" as well as passivity by positioning Goldman both as really feminist after all and as a failed—but thus human—revolutionary who cannot live up to her own ideals. In the process, the feminist archive tends to domesticate Goldman's brightest political insights, precisely through the desire to resolve her ambivalence about sexual politics, an ambivalence that is, however, the main strength of her contributions to that political history. In what follows, I track feminist critical engagement with Goldman's efforts to challenge a public/private divide, emphasising her own focus on reproductive labour as core to that process, and her refusal to let women off the hook for their participation in securing the naturalisation of the public/private divide she wills them to destroy.

I want first to sketch the ways in which Goldman has been cast as an ideal heroine for a broad range of feminists and queer theorists who claim her as helpful for challenging separate spheres (Alaimo 2000; Rogness and Foust 2011) or for foregrounding the relationship between psychic and social processes (Falk 2003; Kensinger 2007). Goldman's emphasis on sexual freedom as central to an analysis and transformation of existing hierarchical social structures and her efforts to see the importance of public acceptance of homosexuality have been linked to feminist and queer efforts to make visible those same concerns today (Heckert 2010; Marso 2003).[18] Others explore her ability to connect marriage, migration, and citizenship, focusing on the combined impact these forces have on women's bodies (Kennedy 1999; Shantz 2004), and take up her internationalism (Butler 2011; Kensinger 2007) or Jewishness as helpful for linking identity, space, and politics (Reizenbaum 2005). Indeed, Goldman's eclectic and multivalent approach to power seems particularly suited to the analysis of the complexities of the present and the development of appropriately sophisticated analytic tools. As Ferguson notes: "Goldman's anarchist feminism was ripe for intersectionality because she rejected hierarchy in thinking as well as in organizing social relationships" and refused "to identify a single cause as more basic than others" (2011b, 261). And along with David Porter, in his revised edition of *Vision on Fire* (2006, 251), Rogness and Foust ask whether contemporary social movements that centre these intersections might learn from Goldman's activism (2011, 163ff). In similar vein, Donna M. Kowal explores both Goldman's intersectional sensibilities (2016, 77) and her continued relevance for contemporary radical U.S. politics (123–29). In line with broader postanarchist scholarship, Goldman is sometimes claimed as a kind of pre-Deleuzian process queen, interested in the struggles of the everyday as a mode of "becoming minoritarian" (Ferguson 2011a), inhabiting her sphere as a "rhizomatic intellectual" (Blake 1997), and as uniquely able to highlight the links necessary for a contemporary sustainable politics.

The theorists I have cited are mostly quite recent (and I return to some of these discussions in more detail in subsequent chapters), but as Oz Frankel (1996) has documented, feminist and lesbian scholars such as Alix Kates Shulman (1982, 1984) or Blanche Wiesen Cook (1979a, 1984) were captivated by Goldman several decades earlier. It seems each generation discovers Goldman anew, happy to shape her words to a contemporary context, delighted by her vivacity and hoping she will resolve contemporary political questions in innovative ways. Thus, Alice Wexler situates her attachment to Goldman in the 1970s in relation to both the movement against the Vietnam War and the emerging feminist movement (1992, 37), and Shulman considers her a "radical feminist" before her time in her blending of concerns with the body and broader political issues (1982). While scholars and activists remain concerned about certain aspects of Goldman's thinking and action, her feminism is always finally reaffirmed, even if it is questioned or its limits traced. As Ferguson asserts, Goldman is credited with "bringing feminism to anarchism ... [by] weaving ... sex and gender into the mix" (2011b, 249), and Loretta Kensinger concludes her speculation on precisely this question by asserting that "there is, apparently, little doubt that Goldman is a feminist" (2007, 258). Kensinger's "apparently" suggests some scope for wondering further about that feminism, of course, but she herself ignores the queries she notes are raised by friends about whether one should call Goldman a feminist or not, concluding her piece by stating straightforwardly that her aim has been to provide "insights into [Goldman's] feminism . . . [that] still speak[s] to us today" (279). Kensinger's work is typical of the minority of critics who question Goldman's feminism at all, as we are only ever left temporarily in doubt as to whether "feminism" is the appropriate way of describing Goldman's particular interventions. And yet such certainty should be rather startling, surely, given that we know that Goldman herself not only disidentified from feminism but was actively hostile to many of its presumptions and proponents. Indeed, what does it mean that the critical feminist archive claims as feminist Goldman's arguments about women's emancipation that she herself articulates through their distinct *difference from* feminism?

Feminist scholars have been particularly intrigued by Goldman's handling of the public/private divide. While enthusiastic about her refusal to let women's reproductive labour remain unseen within anarchism, feminist scholars have been less impressed by what they see as her ignoring of the question of domestic labour. Molyneux (1986) and Elizabeth Quay Hutchison (2001) are both frustrated by Goldman's failure to consider child-rearing or domestic duties as central modes through which women's roles are naturalised, despite her otherwise trenchant critique of gender roles.[19] Stansell is a harsh commentator in this respect, too, noting that for Goldman and other anarchist women "the celebration of equality did not reach into the home. The iconographic power of feminism . . . was less suitable for the mundane spaces of everyday life, where meals were cooked, beds made, children dressed and sent to school" (2000, 258). Likewise, Linda Lumsden observes wryly that among revolutionaries the "possibility of a man pitching in goes unmentioned," and in respect of Goldman, she reads this as evidence of her blindness with respect to "patriarchal privilege" and "deeply entrenched . . . cultural beliefs about gender" (2007, 39). Some rather odd things are going on in these accounts. On the one hand, I feel confident that whatever Goldman's understanding of the relative importance of domestic labour, it makes little sense to describe her as ignorant of men's and women's roles, as Lumsden does here. Further, one might reflect that the question of domestic labour was primarily a concern for middle-class women who began to be paradoxically responsible for care in the home at the same time as gender roles were changing. Goldman herself and many of her associates were rarely settled in stable domestic environments, and, if they were, tended to be multiply packed into a small number of rooms. It was in exile in Saint-Tropez that Goldman first experienced the luxury of what we might think of as "domestic space" in her late fifties (funded primarily by Peggy Guggenheim and Edna St. Vincent Millay, so that she could write her autobiography), and she lived here on her own rather than with a partner to share (or otherwise) domestic chores.

My point here is not to wonder anew about whether who does domestic labour matters—of course it does—but to wonder about its critical role in respect of Goldman. The "oddness" that strikes me is perhaps a temporal one: first Goldman is claimed as a feminist, despite her own refusals of the term. She is then found wanting in this respect because of a lack of attention to sharing of domestic labour, such that we are asked to think further about how deeply her (assigned) feminist politics really went. Finally, she is reclaimed as a feminist despite these oversights: recast as a feminist figure who was blind to important critiques of power relations we now take for granted, or who was flawed in ways we can lament but also forgive her for. We may well wonder who did how much and for how long at home as part of a feminist account of the world, but there is surely a certain irony in expecting Goldman to foreground this issue when she writes so emphatically against "equality-as-stocktaking" as part of what is wrong with the modes of equality she dismisses. Importantly, too, while the feminist critical archive does explore the value of sexual freedom in Goldman as part of her broader challenge to a public/private divide (through its challenge to a production/reproduction opposition and presumptions about women as nurturing), there is a tendency to reaffirm naturalising presumptions about women in this work too. Women are unproblematically represented as more likely to be hurt in open relationships, for example, and Goldman's own decision not to have surgery that would have offered her an opportunity to have children is represented only as loss. Indeed, the feminist archive largely keeps question of "domestic" and "sexual" labour separate when discussing Goldman, paradoxically defusing the revolutionary experiment that sexual freedom might offer in reformulating the "private sphere" as a whole.

My suspicion is that the critique of Goldman both as feminist and as *not quite getting it right* in this particular way tells us something important about the contemporary feminist concerns of the writers and points to anxieties central to feminism itself. We want to claim Goldman as feminist, but if we do that without emphasising this particular oversight, then the feminism that we are left with is in fact not one easily recognised as "radical" (for Shulman or Marso), "socialist" (for Molyneux), or "intersectional" (for Ferguson). We can appreciate Goldman's emphasis on free love and revolution and on women's reinvention of themselves as feminist (because we recognise it) but are left pondering what feminism could possibly be without the detail of domestic equality as well. We could leave Goldman alone, of course, and suggest that this inattention means she cannot be claimed as feminist (in line with her own thinking on the matter), but this would also present problems. It would leave a focus on shared tasks and measurable difference as the primary feminist yardstick, repeating the opposition Goldman relishes between exciting sexual transformation and pedantic feminist accounting. One would expect most people to choose free love in preference to poring over the domestic spreadsheet, so instead of leaving either feminism or Goldman stranded, this "oddness" could be said to describe an attempt to unite these threads of women's emancipation in the critical archive. But in the process, of course, Goldman's own trenchant critiques of "equality" and her positioning of sexual rather than "domestic" labour as core to the maintenance of the private sphere and the gendered nature of capitalism are brushed to one side. Yet Goldman's "larger-than-life" persona, her refusal of the petty, is what has drawn feminists to her in the first place; a Goldman urging women in fervent tones to hand over the mop is hard to integrate into our enjoyment of her insistence that we radically transform ourselves and others.

If the preceding constitutes an overreading of what are frequently footnotes, I have come to this interpretation because of a related anxiety about Goldman's sexual politics expressed in the feminist critical archive. As discussed earlier, Goldman's advocacy of free love and complete sexual freedom for women throws its weight behind what she sees as the sacred union of men and women, a union currently fettered by marriage, but which could be glorious if liberated. The evident enthusiasm in Goldman's prose is rousing, and it is not surprising that a feminist theorist like Shulman was captivated by Goldman's insistence that women take "their destiny into their own hands," as Frankel notes (1996, 919). There is an intense investment here in Goldman as foreshadowing radical feminism, making the confrontation with Goldman's inevitable failure to live up to her own hyperbolic ideals particularly painful. If the opposite-sex delirium at the heart of Goldman's utopia makes feminists uneasy or queasy, then her inability to "exorcise ordinary feelings of jealousy, an emotion she counseled others to cast off" (Falk 2007, 49) seems to demonstrate a level of hypocrisy unforgivable in one so dedicated to consistency across word and deed. Although critics have wrestled with some examples of this tension in Goldman's autobiography, in which the context of "her own, agonizing struggles against . . . possessiveness" frames her "strongest denunciations of monogamy and sexual jealousy" (Frankel 1996, 925), most of the outrage at her inconsistency arises after Falk's discovery of Goldman's letters to her lover Ben Reitman in the 1980s.[20] The letters portray Goldman's desire for Reitman, her elation and disappointment, her obsessiveness, possessiveness, manipulation, and self-abasement, as well as her love of sex and politics intermingled.[21] As Stansell remarks there is little from this time outside of pornography that is as explicit as these letters (2000, 294),[22] and further that feminists have understandably been appalled and "fascinated by the great champion of women's freedom making a spectacle of herself before gamy Ben Reitman, a man on the make with any woman who crossed his path" (294). Suzanne Poirier (1988) is more cautious about the blame for Goldman's obsession lying so firmly with Reitman's debauched character, arguing that this popular dislike of him reflects conservative assumptions about the kind of sex a radical woman should have, as well as the kind of man she should be drawn to.[23]

There is much in the letters to tarnish Goldman in the eyes of those who had held her up as a heroine (Falk 2007, 49): her role-playing as "Mommy" (Frankel 1996, 926), her blind struggles within rather than against patriarchal values (Marso 2003, 306), and her capacity to be wholly captured by "uncontrollable passions" (Tamboukou 2012, 9). Goldman remains a feminist in even the most disappointed accounts of her subordination, but now she is represented as one who demonstrates for all of us the impossibility of ever fully extracting oneself from patriarchal demands. For Marso (2003), Goldman's imperfect desire is evidence of the problematically high expectations feminism places on women who continue to reside within the contradictions of patriarchal capitalism. For Ferguson, feminists should be wary of pointing to Goldman's inconsistencies as exceptional and should focus rather on the struggle between commitment and unruly desire that is always present in an attempt to live one's political ideals (2011b, 178–79). This argument mirrors that of Goldman's contemporary Max Eastman, who also describes her in terms of the "'desperate leap for the ideal'" she was bound to fall short of (cited in Wetzsteon 2002, 207). Such approaches foreground the distance between a utopian vision of sexual freedom at the heart of Goldman's work and life, and the necessary gap between this vision and any lived reality.[24] We can sympathise with Goldman's plight, moderate our vision of her as acerbic hero-ine, and be reassured that she is just like us: proposing an ideal she could never live up to, becoming entangled in badly judged love affairs, and demanding of others something she could only imagine rather than inhabit. It is this do-mestication of Goldman I want to resist, however, since once again it seems to return us to the quantifiable over the fantastic in ways that sit ill with what we know about her political temperament. All these approaches rely on a mode of forgiveness, one might say, that only makes sense if it follows an acceptance of that distance between ideal and action that is the site of Goldman's politics. Yet in claiming sexual freedom as a privileged site of transformation, I want to suggest, Goldman refuses to keep this distinction intact but instead takes up that shifting and uncomfortable terrain as precisely that of difficult revolu-tionary work. As Maria Tamboukou similarly suggests, Goldman seeks to find a way of "inhabiting multiple and uneven power positions vis-à-vis the be-loved" and grapples with "the asocial and anti-political aspects of love" (2012, 9). In resisting the quantification of both feeling and revolution, Goldman is drawn to sexual freedom not as a way of providing a blueprint for transform-ative action but as a site of contradiction generated by inhabiting the public/private divide. In wanting contradiction to *stand against* the ideal of sexual freedom, feminist accounts refuse the unpredictability and unresolved nature of that site, even as they also seek to recover Goldman as a (failed, but human) feminist heroine. They domesticate her heroism, it seems to me, identifying her efforts to live differently as ordinary and as failed because not "successful" in familiar terms. Sexual freedom, however, as Goldman knew very well, can-not be so contained, and it stands today—as it stood then—as a volatile site of uncertain promise, a place of inevitably flawed struggle for newness that may precisely be its political value and enduring appeal.

If Goldman's "errors" in respect of domestic labour and sexual obsession can be folded into a softly familiar feminism she would no doubt have balked at, this is much harder to achieve with respect to her antagonism towards other women. As we have seen, Goldman berates women for their acceptance of their lot (Solomon 1988) and insists that they deal with those "internal tyrants" (Shulman 1982, 245). In itself, asking women to shift their allegiance from patriarchy and its manners is not a problem for feminist critics, and in-deed is part of what makes Goldman appealing as a historical precursor to a contemporary feminist subject position. But it is Goldman's woman blaming and her impatience with women's refusals to take necessary action to change their circumstances (Shulman 1982, 248) that provide the particular sticking point for feminist authors. Not only is Goldman's bile understood as finding a misplaced object—women themselves, rather than the social structures that bind them or the men who gain from such strictures—she also appears to minimise the difficulties facing women in determining their own fates. Thus, and as Frankel notes, Goldman seems oblivious to "the limited options for women," despite her own difficulties in moving beyond "the miseries of her private life" (1996, 927). For Kensinger (2007) as well as Shulman and Wexler, expecting women to spontaneously transform their lives, be less concerned about financial security, walk out on husbands, take lovers, or resist convention perversely underestimates the challenges that change presents. Indeed, what Goldman frequently characterises as "'women's inhumanity to man'" (Kensinger 2007, 269) comes uncomfortably close to victim blaming and has "shocked and angered many feminists" (Shulman 1982, 250).

Goldman's language and tone in respect of women's failings do seem to run counter to any desire to claim her as a feminist. On the one hand, she has every sympathy with women's plight, while on the other she is at great pains to describe its pernicious impact on their character. Thus, for Goldman, woman's particular oppressive circumstances make her into a disagreeably petty and obsessive creature, one who nags or attacks men, is overly vain, and fills the air with "hysterical, sentimental rubbish" (1920). Her individuality is "stunted" (1920), and she cares only "for showy clothes and frivolity" (*New York Sun* 1901). Goldman is unwaveringly unpleasant about women's vanity, resisting the temptation to see this purely as a product of the separation of spheres, and analysing superficial femininity instead as perfectly aligned with capitalist and militarist interests. It is the duplicity of femininity that fills Goldman with horror and that serves as the momentum for her searing attacks on "emancipated" women who continue to support the idea of special privileges. In developing her tone of scathing vitriol, however, Goldman's analysis threatens to fall into a naturalising of women's role in her own right, as her critique becomes sutured to women's bodies. But as with the question of sexual freedom and the revaluation of "the private," to bracket out Goldman's judgement of women as not part of the feminism one wishes she could have espoused is to miss key aspects of her argument about transformation.[25] For Goldman's scathing attacks on women are one of the main ways in which she dismisses the (anarchist as well as mainstream) reification of the public/private divide, insisting as she does on the *social importance* of imagining women in helpless and corrupt terms. In simply finding Goldman's bile repellent, drawing a line between it and her potential take-up for feminism, we also lose one of the central insights the theoretical archive might need to hold at its centre: that femininity remains an unresolved problem, *is* indeed frequently conventional, grasping, self-serving, and superficial.

In thinking again about Goldman's vitriol, in not trying to bracket it out or excuse or domesticate it, I want to suggest that the problem with Goldman's thinking here is less the strength of her critique or its affect than the ways in which it slips back into ontological attachment to women. Partly, of course, this is because femininity does stick to women; thus the critique of femininity always also risks making a misogynist of the writer. But if we take Goldman's viciousness seriously, rather than being embarrassed, hurt, or enraged by it, we might be able to think again about the profound ambivalence within feminism about femininity. Just as the unpredictability of sexual freedom tells us something different about the public/private divide in feminist politics that is hard to get at if we frame it only as a failing, might Goldman's antagonism to women also start from an acknowledgement of femininity as both deeply flawed and transformable, and the feminist critic's own position as caught within these difficulties too?

"NOT A FEMINIST, BUT . . ."

It is not only other feminist critics who have taken up Goldman for their contemporary concerns, foregrounding their own political preoccupations in the process, of course. My own attachments to Goldman do similar work, as I explore her value for a feminist politics that centres sexual freedom as part of a challenge to the public/private divide and that does not shy away from judgement of femininity as active complicity with broader social and political forces. In this section, I sketch out the reasons why—in a commitment to my own political and theoretical archive—I consider Goldman's critique of quantification to be especially useful in addressing some continued issues in gender and sexual politics today. But I also explore more fully the reasons why I do not think claiming Goldman as a feminist is necessary, and indeed may be counterproductive, in bringing together economic and intersubjective understandings of how "gender" works and might thus be transformed. These theoretical and political concerns with bringing forward Goldman in the present mirror those of other theorists; my efforts are, to that extent, no better or worse than others'. But my hope is that in thinking from a starting point of what is commonly left out of the present archive, what power relations we "know but must deny" within feminism, the question of political ambivalence might be helpfully foregrounded.

We are in trying times, and "gender" does an extraordinary amount of work both to normalise and to challenge the politics of those times. While, on the one hand, it is commonplace to celebrate the successes of feminism in terms of an equality achieved in developed, Western nations (albeit with additional final touches still to be made),[26] on the other, we face a strong discourse of retraditionalisation of gender roles in the context of the financial crisis. As has long been the case, gender equality is thought to be all very well until there is job scarcity or a squeeze on public services,[27] at which point not only are women expected to pick up the care work and make ends meet (while not being so selfish as to consider their own paid labour as a priority), but they are also expected to bear the brunt of cuts in welfare provision (UNAIDS 2012; Womankind 2009). Even in the quantitative terms Goldman would not have approved of, global political and corporate participation of women is pitifully low, women's and men's experiences of violence remain unaddressed at both formal and informal levels, and indeed pay gaps across sectors endure.[28] And once we consider other modes through which power works, such a quantitative approach seems sorely lacking in its analytic and transformative capacity. Thus, for example, an increase in women's employment does not mean a concomitant decrease in their unpaid and caring labour but is likely to mean an increase in working (paid and unpaid) hours (Department of Economic and Social Affairs 2010, 98–103), and women are as likely to defend men's privilege as they are to challenge it, even when this runs counter to their own longer-term interests. For all the work on formal equality, the question of how to become subjects able and willing to transform our lives relationally in order to access that equality remains opaque. From a slightly different angle, the question of women's equality can also be used as a basis for deflecting critique onto others, with the trope of the culturally saturated patriarchally controlled racialised other finding its apex in the figure of the veiled Muslim woman. The "veiled woman" stands as evidence of both the differential times of modernity and as an anachronism that positions women's oppression as simultaneously firmly past and ever present. As many postcolonial feminist theorists have argued, such a dynamic relies on fantasies of a passive racialised other, waiting for her liberated sisters or brothers to release her from tyranny and into a freedom mirroring her own (emblematically Spivak 1988; Mohanty 1988).[29] So too it presumes that freedom can be read from an increasingly visible woman's body, an irony that is not missed on Joan Scott (2007) in her analysis of the patriarchal heteronormativity of such an argument. That slipping gaze of Western gender equality and its attendant certainties overlook the ways in which equality might need to be understood rather more broadly if we are to make sense of current power relations.

Thus we find ourselves one hundred years after Goldman's "Woman Suffrage" (1914d) in both a rather different and rather similar situation to the one she intervened within. There are no doubt more ways in which "gender" and "women's equality" are being mobilised as part of how global power relations are being managed, but the cynical use of "sexual equality" to endorse a clampdown on prostitution and migration in the name of protecting and liberating women would have been only too familiar to Goldman (Agustín 2007).[30] So too would the claims of women's superiority as an antidote to the financial crisis that ignore the ways gender underwrites the inequality necessary for the collapse in the first place (Perrons 2012; Prügl 2012); or the consistent use of the discourse of freeing women from Eastern tyrants as an alibi for war and profiteering. For Goldman, it would have come as no surprise that women's equality was so easily taken up as an alibi for war, since this was one of her particular bones of contention with a suffrage movement genuflecting to the militarist greed of the state as a mode of securing the vote. And while the heightened visibility of feminist activism recently (in the United Kingdom and globally) would have pleased Goldman, I suspect she would have been unfailingly critical of the strand that frames sexuality in terms of inevitable violence (and never in terms of freedom or pleasure) and would have balked at making gender inequality a singular (rather than complex, intersectional) issue.[31] Goldman helps me make sense of the contradictions inherent in a quest for women's emancipation and the different uses and take-ups of "equality" across the social, political, and interpersonal spectrum. Goldman would certainly have had little time for a postfeminist argument that equality has been achieved, and even less for the conservative occupation of the terrain of gender equality as though their policies did not contribute to women's impoverishment, but neither would she have tolerated the kinds of loss narratives that accompany feminist accounts of the recent past—nostalgia was never her genre. She would have balked at the generational logic underpinning both progress and loss narratives of feminist theory, both politically and personally: she embraced youthful innovation when she encountered it, and she refused to grow old gracefully.

Importantly, Goldman's analysis helps us make sense of our own complex contemporary terrain in two main ways: by remaining attentive to the ways in which a feminist analysis is never far from its mainstream or conservative sanction, and by highlighting the *predictability* of our predicament insofar as "quantity" has been privileged over "quality" in feminist political analysis. In the first case, I have turned to Goldman because of my own interest in teasing out the overlaps between feminist and conservative narratives about gender at the level of how feminist stories are told about what has been achieved and lost (Hemmings 2011). Goldman was ever alert to the similarities between feminist and nationalist narratives, as suggested, distancing herself from a duplicitous pro-war or a social purity agenda that reinforced class differences through its insistence on women's respectability and superior moral sense. She understood that wanting "the same" as men often meant wanting the same as a limited number of privileged bourgeois men, and she would have laughed at our "surprise" that such a focus did not transform personal relationships or social meanings of gender. Kimberlé Crenshaw (2011) makes a similar argument in relation to the investment in and representation of Hillary Clinton as a feminist. Crenshaw highlights that we can only think of Hillary Clinton as representing "gender equality" if we put other power relations to one side: Clinton's desire for "equality" is always bound to her expectation that her equal right is to access the same privileges as her white, elite husband (the former U.S. president). For Crenshaw, as for Goldman, and indeed for me, this model of equality is not only limited but also extremely problematic in its myopia and exclusions. Of course, Goldman might not have been able to anticipate the scale of global migration and its intersection with public/private divides, production, and reproduction, but she would not have been surprised by the ability of the richest to offset gender disparities by buying in "help" of a variety of kinds (Kilkey, Perrons, and Plomien 2013; Tronto 2002). Indeed, this would likely have formed part of her analysis of why a focus on gender on its own makes little sense, an analysis she would likely have extended to thinking through why and how "Reclaim the Night Marches" through racialised or poor neighbourhoods are counterproductive, even while supporting women's right to self-determination. In so many ways, then, Goldman heralds the importance of a healthy scepticism with respect to the circulation of *talk about* women's equality, and the need for both cross-issue solidarity and historicisation in order not to lose sight of the prize: sustainable transformation of human misery into human equality.

It is Goldman's impassioned emphasis on quality over quantity as bringing about real equality that appeals to me the most in my attempts to make sense of the world I live in. The tyranny of lies and disappointment that frames what it means to be a resistant subject in the "UK" following the referendum to leave the EU points us so surely back to Eve Sedgwick's (1990) wise insight that ignorance will always trump knowledge in a heteronormative and racist political economy of signs. Instead of hoping to find the final version of equality that can be counted, Sedgwick's (2003) queer view adopts Goldman's insistence that the question of equality is always finally a question of value over representation. How do we create and sustain contexts within which people can invest in different values? Why should they? For Goldman, this is a question of pointing to the false promises of capitalist rewards and highlighting the benefits investment in revolution will provide. Later in her life, once revolution had clearly disappointed, it was "living life" in all its complexity that still compelled her (1931b, 1931c). In her insistence on alternative value, Goldman reminds me of the limits to a political focus on formal redress or discrimination not only in terms of the difficulties of accessing those rights where they do exist but more fundamentally in terms of the misplaced expectation that such recognition would make women equal in the first place. Her focus on the importance of a transformation in *values* reframes emancipation in terms of relations with others and a responsibility to change oneself in order to desire a different world; it thus emphasises the politics of intersubjectivity, culture, and creativity as more likely than legal or policy interventions to effect genuine change. Is this a political sensibility we might be able to cultivate today?

Instead of being surprised at mainstream domestication of global equality agendas or at the psychic investments women of all ages have in the heteronormative status quo *despite* women's increased equality in other areas, Goldman asks us to see the links between an investment in superficial equality and the failure to imagine ourselves radically otherwise. Goldman's centring of quality in gender and sexual politics is not to be understood as a different— sequential or complementary—proposition, in truth. It offers a critique of the idea that equality itself can be anything other than an empty promise without first turning our expectations of what real equality would look like upside down. I am not suggesting here a pessimistic narrative of co-optation or loss in ways that mirror Nancy Fraser's (2013) proposals for reradicalisation in the face of feminist domestication: a different way forward but with eyes on the same prize. Such accounts ignore the plethora of different feminist (and nonfeminist) positions in favour of the telling of feminist history through its most dominant trends. And they generate powerful fantasies of being able to eliminate the danger of feminist co-optations, rather than a theory of accountability. Goldman is helpful in reminding us that even the most profound revolutions risk assimilation and ongoing violence, and I find it helpful to be reminded how challenging it is to recognise and inhabit the multiplicity and conflicts of interest that surround us.[32]

Goldman's argument about quality is properly interdisciplinary rather than multidisciplinary, requiring integration of object of inquiry and analysis and a move away from the single issue. It also requires understanding of the psychic or narrative dimensions of the economy, the historical and political context of creative arts, and the playful theatricality necessary to deliver a serious message. And as we have seen, it requires judgement of oneself and others. In this respect, to meet Goldman on her own terms we must change not only what we ourselves look and feel like but also what we imagine emancipation to be. Goldman's focus on quality takes her into the realm of sexual freedom as we know. This emphasis is not only a reorientation in terms of "what counts," though it certainly is that. It is also a vital challenge to assumptions about the subject and object of emancipation and about the nature and content of the public/private divide. Since sexual freedom will necessarily foreground the relational and intersubjective aspects of revolution, and since it is—and always will be—a site of struggle and ambivalence, where that freedom will take us is hard to predict. Countering equality with sexual freedom in its broadest sense moves us away not only from the fantasy that we can measure both the ills and the goods of human life so simply but also from the fantasy that the work will ever be completed. It centres power and anticipates difficulty and failure as part of the establishment of the ideal, rather than a sign of its loss.

Considering Goldman's work brings questions of women's emancipation to the foreground of analysis for me, as it does for other feminist scholars, then. Her vibrant refusal of convention and challenges to assumptions about women's behaviour across her oeuvre are extraordinarily appealing to my contemporary sensibilities about what is possible once restrictions on gendered character are lifted. Her focus on qualitative means to challenge a public/private split and her insistence on attending to complexity from a position of ambivalent fervour draw me to Goldman affectively as well as intellectually and politically. I have been less pulled into a desire to understand her as a feminist, though, mainly because of her own refusals of the term as well as the multiple ways she articulates her utopian vision with and against her feminist contemporaries. In my initial reading of Goldman's feminist enthusiasts and detractors, I became increasingly enraged as I encountered the description of her as a (heroic and then lacklustre) feminist over and over again. As discussed, her resistance to feminism noted, her engagement with questions of emancipation celebrated, her failings in this regard wrestled with and ultimately forgiven, Goldman has nevertheless been unambivalently described as a feminist even when this is the purported site of critical uncertainty and debate. In response, I have wanted to insist that she was not only certainly *not* a feminist, but that the feminist desire to claim her for a (reanimated, but superficial) contemporary feminism is little short of stale projection. But the more I have reflected on this problem, the more I too have been drawn back into what we might call a feminist loop: which practices and which subjects might we deem "feminist" enough to count in a history of "feminist intervention"? How can we think with sexual freedom as feminist practice without losing sight of sexual subordination? And within this, of course, while the question of self-naming is important, it is not the only issue that needs to be taken into account—after all, there are many self-proclaimed feminists I might not want to recognise, and there are many detractors whose words and deeds have contributed to a radical history of women's emancipation. Perhaps, I have subsequently wondered, the question of Goldman's feminism is less about whether she is or is not, can or cannot be so named, but one that might prompt a reevaluation of how we perceive or imagine feminism in the first place. Might we shift the point of entry slightly to invest less heavily in Goldman's own attachments, and more to think through what a feminism that includes Goldman without *her having to be rewritten as a feminist* might look like?

That my reflections on Goldman's feminism should take me here is not all that surprising. I have been thinking and writing over the last few years on issues related directly or indirectly to the nature of the relationship between subject and object of feminist theory (Hemmings 2011, 2012a), with a particular aim of interrupting feminist certainties in order to expand the range of possible ways of inhabiting feminism now and then. In "Affective Solidarity" (2012a) most particularly, I sought to explore the overstated nature of the difference between feminist and nonfeminist subjectivity, arguing that this difference could be said to be temporal rather than ontological or political. Thinking in terms of affect, I argued, allows us to consider the various kinds of judgements that subjects make about the conditions of possibility they live within, such that we might understand "unhappiness" or "disease" with uneven power relations as a mode of social critique in and of itself. Only a small number of subjects—and those not at all consistently—move from affective dissonance to political attachment, for all sorts of reasons. My aim here was not to dismiss the importance of a feminist subject position but to explore the effects that an investment in an absolute difference between this position and others results in. Feminists find it hard to discuss their ongoing attachments to norms or to have these validated as feminist; nonfeminists operate with a strong fantasy of what "being a feminist" entails; and these differences are affectively played out through shame and expectations that have little to do with political practice or community per se. My conclusions in this piece were that it might be helpful to focus on the shared dissonance-as-judgement that could be the basis of a nonidentitarian solidarity. My interest was, and remains, not in dismissing the political value of feminist attachments, and most certainly not the value of feminism itself, but in holding feminism's subject and object apart in order to widen the scope of ways that history frames us. The point here too was not to suggest feminism can be anything anyone wants it to be, or to imagine it somehow borderless, but to consider whether its borders are necessarily best thought of in terms of subjectivity and attachment rather than political judgement and activity.

Small wonder, then, that Goldman has piqued my interest as a companion in my quest to extend these reflections. She not only experiences the affective dissonance in respect of gendered and sexual oppression that I am interested in, but so too she wants to act on this to ameliorate it, open up broader possibilities for men and women, and insist on its significance for wider political change. That she does not do this *as a feminist* does not change the fact that she goes through these stages as part of what it means to her to act politically. Indeed, Goldman herself narrates her "coming to politics" precisely as a series of discomforts with social and gendered inequalities that she could not accept. In *Living My Life* in particular, Goldman describes the unbearable nature of witnessing injustice: from her radicalisation through the Haymarket Martyrs, to her outrage at being expected to behave "respectably" within the movement, Goldman's affect-as-judgement moves her into analysis and action and is a resource she returns to throughout her life (1931b). Goldman's insistence on the political importance of sexual freedom and on quality over quantity in bringing about women's emancipation allows me to think with her in order to trouble the assumption that a history of feminism must always be told through its feminist subjects (however they themselves identify). My reasons for wanting to bring in that trouble are themselves political: not simply to challenge a history of feminism for its own sake but to insist that it includes a much broader range of practices than might otherwise be appreciated, despite the fact that there are also limits to that appreciation. I take this approach not only because I am persuaded that the necessary suturing of "feminist" to "feminism" generates a more authoritarian feminism than the one I would like to inhabit (because of the gatekeeping that requires) but also because I know from my own life and the lives of people around me that "falling short" is always part of feminism rather than a sign of failure warranting forgiveness.[33] Ambivalence about gender inequality—how to negotiate its pleasures as well as its pains—has a long history within feminism that the suturing of ideal subject and object tends to obscure. But how are we to understand, rather than simply dismiss, the persistence of intersubjective gender inequalities and people's attachments to them, except through being subjects of ambivalence rather than fantastic certainty?

Reading with Goldman's rejection of feminism has also been productive in helping me make sense of my discomfort with a current mode through which that feminist/feminism relationship is secured: the feminist disdain for the speaker of the phrase "I'm not a feminist, but . . ." The grammar of this phrase expresses disidentification from the feminism that has given rise to changes one otherwise embraces (Williams and Wittig 1997) and is frequently the vehicle for the voicing of antagonism towards feminism through a series of stereotypes of both its aims and its subjects (McRobbie 2009). As Christina Scharff has explored in her empirical research with young British and German women—three-quarters of whom disidentified from feminism—there is a seeming paradox that arises from the fact that while "gender equality is a widely agreed upon value . . . feminism is unpopular" (2011b, 459). While I have no doubt that this phrase is very often a reflection of antifeminism, anxiety about being stereotyped, or conservative attachments including homophobia (since feminism and lesbianism remain indicators for each other as Scharff [2011b] further highlights), I want to hold open the possibility that this is not the fullest extent of the phrase's meanings. And, indeed, one of the surface interpretations the phrase delivers is the speaker's desire to separate a belief in equality from the necessity of being a feminist, and insofar as this separation needs to be represented at all, a simultaneous acknowledgement that it is in fact extremely hard to distinguish between "a person who supports feminist goals, but resists the label, and one who identifies as feminist" (Williams and Wittig 1997, 890). In other words, the *phrase itself* highlights a concomitant recognition of the history of women's emancipation and a resistance to inheriting it that is reiterated through its repetition. And, of course, it is precisely this proximity between subject and analysis that gives rise to concern in those for whom being a feminist is not an (appealing) option.

Zora Simic has proposed that one reason young women might disidentify from feminism is that they feel they lack "feminist competency" (2010, 76). In contrast to the apolitical passivity or capitalist co-optation Angela McRobbie (2004) identifies as key to young women's self-distancing, Simic diagnoses young women's anxiety as due to perceptions that they lack the qualifications to call themselves "feminist," as well as about being found wanting in the face of feminist expectations. The phrase may also, as several commentators have suggested, articulate a critique of perceived raced and classed narrowness of feminism and its presumed subject. Thus, drawing on Beverley Skeggs's work, Scharff describes her interviewees' desire for respectability as part of upward mobility (2011b, 460), resulting in their rejection of a feminist position they assume would require abandoning an already precarious femininity (2011a, 120). For Scharff, those with existing middle-class and white privilege felt they could take the risk of feminist identification more easily.[34] Such arguments about the bourgeois nature of feminism and the exclusive border patrolling of feminists would be ones Goldman would agree with, as would many of her contemporaries within the anarchism movement. In this sense, the "but" in "I'm not a feminist, but . . ." could be interpreted as a more active, deliberate critique than a passive acceptance of the horrors of contemporary sexualised culture and neoliberal values (Lumby 2011). Where Goldman would depart from this contemporary grammar is in its desire to retain femininity unchallenged as part of class mobility or raced respectability, rather than critiquing it as one mode through which those hierarchies are articulated and lived. Such framings are precisely why femininity needs to be rejected, for Goldman, rather than an understandable argument for leaving well enough alone.

What Goldman would have honed in on, however, is the rather smug tone of feminist dismissal of disidentification as evidence of the inexorable loss of politics more generally, and of young women's heightened attachments to their conditions of oppression. While I would not want to challenge the idea that disidentification from feminism is "prevalent among young women" (Scharff 2011b, 458), I do want to note that this disidentification is rather predictably widespread rather than age-delimited. Indeed, one thing that could be said to unite the majority of women *across generations* is their consistent rejection of and disidentification from feminism. As a political movement that (ambivalently and imperfectly) challenges the roots of femininity as heterosexist, classist, and racist, feminism seems perhaps to be the very definition of a minority pursuit. Yet as Jonathan Dean points out, even with repeated examples of ongoing *attachments* to feminism among young people contemporarily and the growth rather than demise of feminist social movements globally in the last ten or so years, "claims that young women are not feminist . . . are so entrenched in the feminist imagination that they remain largely untroubled even by empirical counter-examples" (2012, 316). My own reading of this overassociation of disidentification from feminism with *young women* is that it perpetuates a feminist loss narrative wherein we have moved from shared critique and feminist vibrancy to a present of political failure and antifeminist co-optation. That history has women radicalised in the 1970s or 1980s as its subjects, while young people can only be the subjects of contemporary political failures, whatever the evidence to the contrary. It (falsely) imagines a time that never was: when feminism was *not* a minority pursuit.

The conviction that the miserable present and its young subjects mirror each other perfectly is so strong that even young women's empowerment can *only* be read as disempowerment and co-optation, while older women's "choices" around femininity and ageing, for example, are rarely framed as a sign of a more general social and political apocalypse. Somewhat strangely, writers who oppose "'feminism' to . . . 'young women' and the 'popular culture' which defines and distorts their values" (Lumby 2011, 96) seem to be hanging around waiting for those same recalcitrant young people to "pick up the torch and carry on where 'we' left off," as Kathy Davis wryly notes (2007, 207). Thus, these errant daughters' "mothers" can be reassured that any reduced feminist political engagement on their part is both a sign of the times and something they/we are not responsible for. Further, the burden of feminist disidentification is then carried by the young and dumb, rather than by a series of marginal subjects who have not always seen themselves reflected back by the dominant subjects within feminist movements, as briefly noted earlier. The trenchant critiques of dominant feminism from black and lesbian/ queer feminists, for example, do not have to be engaged with in this fantasy of inexorable loss with young women as the duped dismissers of a feminism otherwise unchanged. As Dean (2009) explores, such a move comes at a high price, since it sidelines current political engagements, stereotypes a range of "postfeminisms" as a uniform set of beliefs, and reduces the productive nature of debate across meanings and histories of feminism itself.

Is it possible instead to think of disidentification as the result of a complex set of negotiations all gendered subjects make and that cannot always be resolved? Disidentification from feminism that retains a critique of gender relations might, in this reading, highlight the proximity as well as opposition between "feminism" and "nonfeminism." Or where it is articulated as direct antifeminism or misogyny, might the grammar of that "but" also reveal an anxiety about capitulation as much as a firm attachment to femininity's ills? Reading with Goldman as a way into contemporary gender and sexual problematics foregrounds for me the political importance of a history of ambivalence. A range of divergent subjects may feel uncomfortable with social constraints on women but also feel discomfort about sets of expectations that feminism itself generates. They may derive pleasure from aspects of femininity that arise within a history of inequality, while being keen to see improved conditions for women. The vexed "but" of our contemporary gendered lives might, following Goldman, be a useful place to reside indeed *precisely because* it reveals the mixed feelings that structure a relationship to feminism for the vast majority of subjects. Instead of seeking to transform resistant subjects into feminist subjects, we could do worse than interrogate that grammar for what it reveals about a history of uncertainty at the heart of feminist history.

AFFECT AND JUDGEMENT

Goldman's "but" draws her back inexorably to the problems of gendered oppression, negotiation, and transformation she was exorcised by. But she also risks the "but" referencing a conservative rather than generous gender critique or indeed outright misogyny. In affective terms, I have found Goldman's bile in respect of women both repellent and appealing, perhaps in equal measure. It is repellent as it repeats and reinforces sexist characterisations of women, even as it wants to create an opening for a different way of being. It is appealing because it reminds me of a key insight of feminism—that femininity is indeed an unresolved problematic that functions differently to masculinity. Successful (or emphasised) femininity does not give straightforward access to authority, financial reward, or heterosexual stability, as Raewyn Connell (and, before her, Sigmund Freud) reminded us some time ago (Connell 1995; Connell and Messerschmidt 2005; Freud 1931). Its success is dependent on the embrace of subordination—perfect passivity—that Goldman and I find so obnoxious, and our joint certainty that this is a characteristic of "other women" heightens the sense of outrage at its evident ills. I find it appealing for another reason too, which is that Goldman's harsh judgement of femininity allows me to appreciate her critique and strongly identify with it, while not having to claim it directly for myself. The judgement—particularly the direct viciousness—takes place somewhere else and is authored by someone else, even as I take a guilty pleasure in the nature of the attack. As I suggested in my introduction, I can experience the pleasurable affect of (another's) judgement while not risking an interrogation of my own vexed relationship to femininity. Even more rewarding, I can remain the kind of feminist who is inclusive, open to parodic resignifications of femininity, and nonjudgemental of women's choices (a good feminist indeed), while also enjoying Goldman's attacks both as accurate and as "not mine." Yet feminism must surely include some judgement of actions or structures as running counter to full equality, else it is nothing at all. And the uneasy "but" in a disidentification with feminism highlights the ways in which affect itself can be such a judgement, though of feminism as much as of social patterns of gendered oppression.

To return to an analysis of my discomfort rather than my comfort with Goldman's attacks on femininity, this seems to reside primarily in the slip from her judgements about practices to judgements about subjects. The problem in Goldman, to my mind, is not the critique or the vitriol but the ways that her judgement becomes a way of finally knowing her object as failed and failing, rather than as grappling in an ongoing way with the same difficulties that she does, and that we do. At one level, and as Kensinger points out, Goldman's tone seems to understate the force of the social in ways that are at the very least "jarring" (2007, 280) and "[lose] sight of the intensity and depth of these vital structural realities" (271). How women behave is read both back and forward such that their futures resemble their pasts: only a radical break can save them, but since their characters are so weak, how is it possible for them to become other than who they currently are? Rather bizarrely, then, the force of the social becomes transformed more into something like a failure of will. Yet, as most of us know from experience, sometimes it may be possible to act in accordance with the onto-epistemological dissonance that precedes countersocial action, but many times it is not. In other words, in her own (or our) judgements of women themselves as lacking, Goldman assumes—and surely falsely—that all women who act in accordance with capitalist femininity have failed to make judgements in their own right.

In her reductive reading of women's character, Goldman seems further to miss the moments women take up the resources available to them in ways that are not only coextensive with duplicity, even when they most resemble it. Ironically, given her own love of performance and style, Goldman does not consider the hyperbolic nature of femininity in action; nor does she pay very much attention to different subject positions that struggle to be recognised as inhabiting femininity at all (raced, classed, sexual). We know from psychoanalysis that femininity-as-lack lies at the heart of subjectivity (Freud 1931, 1933; Lacan 1991) and from many feminist critiques that this white heteronormative origin story takes phallic sexuality and masculine gender as normative (Irigaray 1973; Rose 1983). But to seek to rescue women wholesale from normative femininity, to turn them into something entirely other, we underplay the significance of that lack in the formation of both the subject and their social context.[35] For most women, their relationship to femininity is by definition ambivalent, since they have learned to take themselves as an object, combining the masculinity of the gaze with the femininity of subordinate embodiment. Laura Mulvey's (1989) work on the gaze is formative here, as she argues that the possession of the gaze is always masculine, making transvestites of women who look. My own suspicion is that all gendered subjectivity is ambivalent (rather than split as such), as one learns one's place in the world through a dual valuation of being objectified and objectifying, but also through never meeting the requirements of femininity as symbolic (even if one meets its structural expectations of race, class, and sexuality; and even more so if one does not). The hyperbolic performance of femininity that Goldman is so critical towards might thus also be read as overstated or compensatory, or even as "camp" or what Joan Riviere (1986) theorised as masquerade.[36] Rather than as a reflection of interior attachment or profound truth, the excesses of femininity (or femininity as excess) might better be seen, in line with Goldman's own thought and experiences, as an imperfect way of negotiating that ambivalence at the heart of gender. Yet in failing to consider any difference between action and ontology in the performance of femininity, Goldman's vision of feminine possibility becomes overly brittle.

Goldman is not alone in setting impossible standards for women. Her berating of women for failing to challenge their own subordination at the most profound level makes clear the dynamic inherent in all political judgement of course. But so too my own response to Goldman's viciousness reminds me of the fundamental ambivalence of femininity insofar as it describes the impossibility, and yet the fact, of being that failed subject and object at the same time. It reminds me too of the inherent risk involved in feminism: a risk of judgement attaching to nonfeminist subjects as radically distinct from feminist subjects. Instead, we might assume that all gendered subjects participate in this risk and crack open the suturing of a subject's actions to an impossible, but important, ideal. We might, for example, want to insist on the importance of judgement as part of the challenging of oppression and normativity, but start from the assumption that this is not something happening to one side, or opposite. We might want thus, via my reading of the risks Goldman took and my responses to those risks, to imagine judgement as a relational accountability that allows for an evaluation of practices without an assumption that these "make the person," or that we know what particular actions mean for an individual (even if we want to interrogate their effects). If we assume we are continually struggling with the ambivalence of gender and its relationship to subjectivity and embodiment, as well as its relationship to the possibilities of transformation in our own lives, then we might be clearer about the presumptions and displacements inherent in expecting others to identify in our own image. This is not really a question of being more "forgiving" of others and hoping for the same treatment back (since, as I have been arguing, "forgiveness" delimits feminist terrain in no uncertain terms), but a recognition of political struggle as ongoing, never finished, and a history of feminism as one peopled by those engaged in the struggle over gendered and other meanings and possibilities whatever their identification. Without the generosity Goldman advocates, there is no accountability, and there is certainly little joy.

two • Race and Internationalism

THE BORDERS OF AMBIVALENCE

If Goldman remains conflicted about gender and sexual politics, then this is even more the case with respect to her engagement with race and racism. Feminist scholars in the Goldman critical archive can go along with her excoriations of femininity to some extent, but they are less able to make a similar inclusive gesture of "forgiveness" with respect to her lack of attention to race, and still less when she is identified as racist.[1] Goldman has been understood as "'insensitive' to racism" (Gurstein 2002, 68; see also Drinnon and Drinnon 1975, xi), and her broader arguments theorised as weaker because, as Linda Lumsden suggests, she "failed to recognize racism as anything more than a symptom of capitalism" (2010, 233). In many ways, this position reflects what critics see as a broader anarchist limitation whereby race has been inadequately explored independently from class. Thus, it has been noted that while Goldman was outspoken in her opposition to lynching and other forms of racialised violence, she was more concerned to track the historical and contemporary realities of capitalism, militarism, or male domination than racist oppression. Kathy Ferguson narrates her view thus: for Goldman "racial differences . . . were facts not histories. She was confident that class would always trump race in the production of social inequality" (2011b, 220).

In what I partly read as anxiety about her handling of race politics, feminist theorists tend instead to focus on what they typify as Goldman's intersectionality, as well as her own embodiment and experiences as a Jewish migrant to America. Goldman is thus heralded as—and indeed was—a great internationalist. As outlined in my introduction, Goldman systematically analysed militarism and nationalism as twin evils reinforcing capitalism; corresponded with revolutionaries in India, Mexico, and the Philippines; and travelled throughout Europe (most notably Spain in the 1930s) to foster links with other international anarchists and to support insurrection. Further, Goldman formed part of a community of Jewish migrant revolutionaries in New York, and she was subjected to anti-Semitism in terms of how she was represented in the press as well as by other revolutionaries (Blake 1997; Kowal 2016, 90–95). Yet as I explore throughout this chapter, the feminist critical desire to deflect or sometimes simply to ignore Goldman's race politics has two unfortunate effects. In the first instance, it ignores the particular ways in which Goldman does think carefully about race and racism, albeit in ways that are conflicted and less in line with a contemporary understanding of their significance. As suggested in Lumsden's view that Goldman "failed" in not theorising race independently of class, there is a marked tendency to assume that we already know the best way of understanding race and racism, and that Goldman's own ways of doing so fall short of that standard (and thus are barely worth tracking). As with desires to claim Goldman as a feminist, however, the critical archive does her a disservice in this regard. In wanting Goldman's views on race and racism to better reflect our own, and in negotiating their disappointment when faced with that failure, critics turn away from some very interesting interventions that remain relevant for understanding both racism and nationalism.

It is certainly the case that Goldman did not privilege "race" as a historical category of analysis, but she did reflect on the relationship between different forms of slavery and on the relationship between types and extent of violence affecting black and white workers and black and Jewish targets. In addition, Goldman explores her commitment to sexual freedom as a way of challenging links between biological understandings of "race" and nationalism. As I hope to show in what follows, Goldman's critique of the family as a strong component of both capitalist production and militarist aggression helps her develop a theory of *race as kinship* whose day has passed (between 1927 and 1930). In intriguing ways, Goldman starts from an expansive understanding of the familial in order to think through a cosmopolitan challenge to patriotic identifications. Ironically, then, we might say that the feminist critical archive's stupefaction at the ways in which Goldman "'misses race'" (Ferguson 2011b, 217–18) results in it missing precisely the interesting and important ways in which she opens up less familiar ways of thinking about race and racism. In trying to claim Goldman in familiar terms — and, in particular here, by focusing on her Jewish and migrant status as the *alternative* yet parallel focus on race politics — the feminist critical archive rather oddly sets up what I think of as its second problematic effect: it overinvests in the differences between race politics and internationalism. In seeking to rescue Goldman from her own (and our?) racist anarchist context *in spite* of her inattention to race, the overlaps she struggles to articulate between different forms of nationalist or race-based violence are buried. Thus, ironically, it is once more Goldman herself who carries the burden of a contemporary critical feminist desire to move beyond the muddy terrain of uncertainty that typifies race politics and internationalism as well as gender.

This chapter first explores Goldman's subjective archive in terms of her antinationalism and sexual politics, with a particular focus on masculinity. It tracks the ways that Goldman links family limitation to international struggle, and the particular ways in which she understands both slavery and lynching. I foreground Goldman's ambivalence on questions of race and racism, her struggles to make sense of race oppression and its relationship to "other" modes of vile authority. I then move to provide more detail of the feminist critical framing of Goldman as concomitantly "race-blind" *and* an internationalist and suggest several ways in which we might think again about this opposition. I focus here on the modes through which Goldman herself was set up as a racialised character in the journalistic obsession with her femininity and embodiment, suggesting that it is as important to consider how linked fields of power frame Goldman, even as she herself might struggle to connect these fully. Finally, I explore how further consideration of Goldman's own compromises around attachment and intimacy, in the form of her late marriage to Welsh miner James Colton, might open up the relationship between challenges to kinship and nationalism in important ways.

Before looking at the Goldman archive on race and internationalism, I want first to situate her views within the anarchist context Goldman participated in. While the theoretical canon of modern anarchism tends to reinforce its European roots and cite a trail of dead white men from Proudhon onwards (Evren 2012), this is a profoundly inaccurate representation of the intellectual and political life of what was an exceptionally vibrant international movement that called for revolutionary change at all levels of life. In part, of course, an expansive international sensibility is essential to an anarchist challenge not only to nationalism but to all forms of top-down authority. Thus, Goldman joined her fellow anarchists in positing both intersubjective and international transformation as antidotes to capitalist and militarist domination: at the personal level, one could change relationships to others; at the transnational level, one could reinforce the importance of political upheaval in multiple sites at the same time. So while prefiguration might be methodologically most embedded in the local, its practices of resistance, as Jesse Cohn insists, have always had global aspirations (2014, 22). For Benedict Anderson, the exceptional popularity of anarchism at the end of the nineteenth century was a global phenomenon, with movements and writers agitating impatiently for total revolution across the world. As he further notes of this extraordinary period of anarchist political fomentation: "This world was unique in the zigzag of insurrectionary explosions in the metropole and in the colonies" (2005, 81). In one sense, then, anarchist internationalism was straightforwardly tactical, with an advocacy of cyclical and spontaneous moments of advance and retreat that would be harder for authorities to track than established organisations with identifiable headquarters and ringleaders (Turcato 2007).[2]

For a range of contemporary scholars, anarchism's internationalism does not only pertain to where movements were located or of its openness to a global perspective, but also to issues of migration and mobility. Indeed, this is where the intersubjective and the transnational aspects of anarchist theory and practice come together. Anarchists wrote thousands upon thousands of letters that crisscrossed the globe, travelled far and wide to speak and share experiences and strategies, and importantly too, of course, were frequently exiled because of their revolutionary attachments. The international anarchist network was thus a kind of home in its own right, one that challenged and compensated for revolutionaries' sense of exile. In the process, texts travelled too, were translated and passed back and forth, and those producing them also often wrote from a position of dislocation rather than belonging. For Anderson again, this means that when we come across anarchist intellectuals and activists we encounter "Italians in Argentina, New Jersey, France, and the Basque homeland; Puerto Ricans and Cubans in Haiti, the United States,

France, and the Philippines; Spaniards in Cuba, France, Brazil, and the Philippines; Russians in Paris; Filipinos in Belgium, Austria, Japan, France, Hong Kong, and Britain; Japanese in Mexico, San Francisco, and Manila; Germans in London and Oceania; Chinese in the Philippines and Japan; Frenchmen in Argentina, Spain, and Ethiopia. And so on" (2005, 5).[3] In this sense, anarchist thought was ever dynamic and mobile, translated and engaged in multiple spaces and at different times, adapting its liveliness as it travelled.[4] J. Daniel Elam (2013) provides a lovely example of this process at an intellectual level in his discussion of the take-up of Goldman's work in India by decolonial revolutionaries, arguing that despite her abandoned plans to visit India, Goldman took root in Indian anticolonial consciousness through the translation and circulation of her texts. Cohn remarks that these patterns of transnational affiliation and exchange should not be seen simply as emerging global networks through which existing anarchist theories from Europe were imported into local contexts, however. Rather, "As anarchist ideas travelled from France to China, from China to Korea, from Russia to Brazil, from Germany to the U.S." (2014, 22), they changed and formed themselves anew and should be seen as generative rather than iterative.

Unsurprisingly, anarchists were also directly engaged in or at minimum highly supportive of a range of decolonial movements, most notably in India and the Caribbean (Shaffer 2011, 12). Anarchists were committed to regional as well as local and international organising, as suggested by Goldman's exhausting travels across the United States in the first decades of the twentieth century, during which she sought to connect anarchist and social movements for transformation. Yet, as Süreyyya Evren (2012) notes, early twentieth-century anarchist approaches to coloniality tended to remain superficial, precisely because these resistance movements were understood primarily in opportunist terms rather than as wholly valuable in and of themselves. So while certainly sympathetic to the oppression that colonised people experienced, European and American anarchism often failed to provide an adequate theory of coloniality as a distinct structure of dominance rather than as a particularly unpleasant version of international class oppression. Further, anarchists tended to privilege these decolonial struggles, with their insurrectionist intentions, over more localised race politics, such as African American struggles against racist violence and for state recognition. Partly this can be attributed to the revolutionary rather than reformist commitments of anarchists, as Kathy Ferguson has suggested (2011b, 229). But in this privileging of a particular politics, anarchists were less than fully equipped to make connections between capitalism and racism other than through understanding the latter as a particularly egregious example of the former. One consequence of this is that black radicals—of whom there were a large number—were largely absent from anarchist circles (Stansell 2000, 68), and when they did participate in these, they frequently found themselves fetishized and their oppression metaphorised (Lumsden 2010). As we will see, this issue of the relationship between race and class oppressions, as well as different forms of slavery and violence, runs through the Goldman archive too.

In my view, anarchism's largely forgotten vibrant and international past provides some pointers for a fuller attention to race and racism (both locally and transnationally) going forward. In some ways, we might see the misplaced understanding of anarchism's theoretical history as Euro-American as a more general problem of a largely obliterated political history tout court: the canon is what remains of a political memory of anarchism. My experience from presenting papers on Goldman these last few years is that for scholars and activists not focused on anarchism, its onetime historical preeminence in the late nineteenth century, when, as Anderson again notes, it "was the dominant element in the self-consciously internationalist Left" (2005, 2), quite frequently comes as a surprise. Indeed, we might say that anarchism has been marked by spectacular political failure far more than any other popular social movement has been. From the failed attempts to make assassinations count, to the inability to generate sufficient resistance to the First World War (on which issue anarchists were split), to the crushing of the anarchist movement in 1930s Spain, and even to the unsustainability of a contemporary Occupy movement, anarchists appear always to be on the losing side of history. For Walter Benjamin (1940), of course, history always reflects the victor, but in the case of anarchism those losses might be said to displace even the shadow of a memory of its ascendency, precisely as Marxist materialism has become both the dominant Left perspective and the way of evaluating other claims.[5] Yet for Evren and Cohn at least, anarchism's place *beyond* the margins of history is precisely what makes it so epistemologically significant.[6] And in drawing out the transnational and global character of those forgotten histories, they argue that we need to attend not to documented political successes and writings still in print but to patterns of exile, association, and engagement that challenge linear and national histories of resistance and require engagement with different kinds of sources. A transnational anarchist epistemology might thus seek both to uncover that which has been erased politically and historically (which in archival terms links social movements with questions of sexual politics and antiracism), and to pay attention to the political traces of erasure as a powerful reminder of the ghostly presence of the forgotten at both macro and micro levels.

Maia Ramnath is in sympathy with this approach, arguing that its epistemic marginality from the history of revolutionary endeavour, the failure that typifies its every effort across three centuries, also makes anarchism well suited to decolonial intellectual and political work. To remember anarchist history is to remember that there have been powerful alternatives to class struggle and solidarity, traditions that themselves "did not sufficiently address the fundamental global structures of imperialism, or the realities of racism and colonization" (2011, 30). It is to remember both an-other history to that of Marxist-inflected postcolonial nationalism and an-other anarchist history to that represented by its theoretical canon. Methodologically speaking, if it is indeed the intersubjective and transnational associations that compensate for the inevitability of anarchist political disappointments (J. Cohn 2014, 16–23), then these must also be the focus of political and intellectual effort in building solidarity.[7] Paraphrasing Gustav Landauer, Cohn insists that if "we can await nothing from 'external conditions,' we must demand everything for ourselves, from within" (2014, 19). For Cohn this radical approach requires a refusal of borders at a range of levels—material, psychic, intersubjective—and the transformation of knowledge through creative processes that scramble both what we know and how we know it. In no uncertain terms, he claims that "as a massively transnational, migratory phenomenon, the anarchist movement fails to comply with the compartmentalization of knowledge" (22). It is in this spirit that I hope attention to Goldman's thinking about race and internationalism might contribute to my broader project here on the problems of subject/object relations in historical knowledge production, and the importance of struggle over historical and contemporary political meanings. In particular, I hope to show that Goldman's approach, while remaining limited in its account of race and racism, opens up ways of thinking beyond identity about the relationships between different modes and scales of oppression. As suggested earlier, the critical desire to separate out and leave behind "race blindness" in Goldman, or to claim her as *nevertheless* international or ethnically and culturally marginal tends to reproduce a distinction between race and antinationalism in ways that strangely obscure Goldman's own concerns with the former. I want to sit with the difficulties of Goldman's negotiation of race and racism and consider their implications for her broader understanding of the links between sexual politics and political transformation.

Goldman herself was a strong anarchist internationalist. At an intuitive level she dismissed national borders, particularly insofar as they related to political attachment and to a sense of belonging. Goldman was consistent in her belief that "there is nothing for any sane man to defend in the culture of his particular country" (1914c) and considered nationality to be a "mere accident of birth."[8] Goldman was one of the many anarchist migrants who became politicised after her move from Russia to the United States, and who was first educated in and then exiled to Europe (Goldman 1931b, 1931c). Cyril Greenland (2002) insists that Goldman was at home anywhere: an attitude no doubt in part fostered as a result of her multiple experiences of migration. She fought to make anarchism a broader movement in the United States once she had converted to anarchism by lecturing in English rather than Yiddish or German as was the convention among New York anarchists at the time. She wrote to comrades and intimates all over the world no matter where she was living and participated in that vast network of transnational anarchist publication and translation that typified the movement's vibrancy, as suggested earlier. Goldman's expansive view of home was not only a question of experience and empathy, however. As Candace Falk notes, for Goldman "the crossing of national boundaries, so integral to Goldman's political vision, was also critical to the long-term impact of her political work" (2005, 64). Indeed, Goldman's internationalism was central to her critique of capitalism as a "worldwide economic system" (Falk 2007, 43), and she developed a series of linked arguments about the importance of antinationalism in thinking about a global anarchist approach to revolution.[9]

Importantly for our understanding of the Goldman archive on antinationalism, she supported transnational revolutionary movements and took a resolutely international approach to disrupting capitalism and the authoritarian role of the state. Goldman was a staunch supporter of the Mexican Revolution (Falk 2005, 2012b) and worked towards "solidarity with anti-colonial struggles in Africa and the Philippines" (Bertalen 2011, 225). But unlike many of her comrades, Goldman did not separate out her critiques of patriotism-bolstered capitalism and the sexual subordination of women (1908b, 1915). For Kate Rogness and Christina Foust, this ability to connect sexual politics to global politics comes from her specific "standpoint . . . [as] an immigrant and a laborer" (2011, 153) and as a woman. Goldman experienced firsthand the problems of citizenship's connection to marriage and was considerably more vulnerable as a woman in exile than she had expected. As a result, and as I discuss later, she was forced to marry for papers despite her resistance to having to do so. Goldman's own border crossings and confrontations with misrecognition (of her person, origins, and politics) confirmed for her the ways in which these processes bolster sexual and gendered norms and are themselves shot through with hypocritical double standards. Goldman's negotiation of these borders highlights both their gendered nature and her own difficulties surviving as a woman, rather than only as a revolutionary.

Goldman's experience-inflected understanding of the sexual politics of international borders and global power relations translates directly into her key analyses and informs the links she makes among the different strands of social and political subordination she was concerned with. So, for example, in her critique of the discourse on *The White Slave Traffic* (1909e), Goldman "knits together the practices of capitalism, immigration, family structures, and religious authority to explain prostitution" (Ferguson 2011b, 261), never prioritising a single thread in her efforts to provide a holistic analysis worthy of the women whose lives were consistently devastated by the conditions of their trade. And in her challenges to the necessity of American military action in the run-up to the First World War, Goldman's arguments are particularly effective when she connects capitalist, religious, and patriarchal interests as fuelling what she terms the "war mania" (Goldman 1917a). Firmly identifying the people who gain from war as mining their patriarchal as well as capitalist interests, she writes: "Out of international carnage they have made billions; out of the misery of the people and the agony of women and children, the American financiers and industrial magnates have coined huge fortunes" (1917a, 6). For any real progress to be made against these related rather than singular structures of oppression, Goldman insists that "all narrow, stifling national prejudices should be eradicated" (7). In this respect, Goldman continues in her commitment to a prefigurative politics that sees individual and intersubjective belief and transformation to lie at the heart of broader transformation. Here, challenging women's reproductive role as bearers of the next generation is absolutely central to interrupting the mechanisms of capitalist and militarist accumulation.

But the Goldman archive does not only point us towards the relationship between capitalism, militarism, and women's role. The devastation wrecked upon young men in wartime is Goldman's starting point for her important argument that we need to *invert* the masculine value placed on military service and patriotism. In a striking set of assertions that reframe conventional understandings of masculinity and manhood as sutured to patriotism and aggression, Goldman seeks to resignify masculinity and manhood for revolutionaries as emerging precisely from *challenging* nationalism. Real masculinity and real maleness are not the opposite of femininity or femaleness but instead might be expressed through a transformative orientation towards the other: for Goldman, maleness could and should be expansive, creative, and transgressive of national and internal restrictions. Goldman achieves this reframing in a number of ways. In the first place, and crucially, she demetaphorises the bloody cruelty of wartime violence that results from narrow patriotism. She points to the tragically ironic difference between "patriotic forgeries of history to prepare the young generation for 'the protection of national honor'" (1917a, 8) and the reality of "bleeding to death for the crooked transactions of a gang of legalized, cowardly thieves" (8–9). And she castigates the "'brave boy' who goes to offer himself in battle while his father slaves and sweats at home and his sister sells herself in the streets" (*San Francisco Cell* 1898, 332). Goldman's second tactic is to contrast this "'brave boy'" with the men she believes exhibit real courage of revolutionary conviction. Thus, for Goldman, manhood is not demonstrated by warmongering but by its refusal, and she feminises soldiers instead as living lives "of slavish submission, vice, and perversion" (1908b, 10). A man who previously resisted militarism but who later supports war once it is declared is cast as a "weakling" (1917b, 2), while the "young man who out of a keen sincerity and idealism refuses to take arms in a cause [in] which he does not believe is stronger" than state-sanctioned terror (6). Standing against the current understanding "of patriotism, and its terrific cost to every country" (1931b, 428), Goldman advances real manhood as requiring "greater courage" (n.d. [1991b]) than capitulation to the "war mania." For Goldman, then, the soldier is a "poor, deluded victim of superstition and ignorance" (1908b, 10), and a man can only act freely "as long as he does not wear the uniform" (1917a, 10). In short, patriotism "[degrades] manhood" (10), while those who retain their independence also retain their self-respect (12).[10] For Goldman, only "human brotherhood and solidarity will clear the horizon from the terrible red streak of war and destruction" (1920), and this will necessarily be based in solidarity beyond arbitrary national borders or false capitalist alliances.

Importantly, what we might begin to call Goldman's theorisation of a *cosmopolitan revolutionary masculinity* is articulated as much against the hyperbolic macho performances within anarchist movements as it is against the dumb masculinity of the "patriotic hero."[11] Goldman's challenges to aggressive masculinity are laid out in her autobiography (1931b, 1931c), and she was a supporter of homosexual creativity and liberty.[12] Goldman was thus often at odds with dominant anarchist views on men's and women's roles and the binary characteristics that defined masculine and feminine behaviour. The use of inversion as a tactic to disrupt the traditionally gendered underpinnings of nationalism does risk reaffirming the very oppositions that are the target of her critique, however. Indeed, portraying soldiers as feminised and therefore weak rather than manly in their misguided courage draws on the same static gendered oppositions she otherwise refutes. To give some more examples: in her rage-fuelled obituary for Lenin, Goldman states that he chose "to unmake the Revolution, to emasculate it . . . to destroy its substance" (1924), rendering Bolshevism as unmanly rather than heroic, superficial rather than revolutionary in rather stereotyped gendered terms. And when feeling abandoned by her comrades after Leon Czolgosz's assassination of President William McKinley, Goldman writes that she is "kept busy regretting the fact that so many even in the radical ranks have lost their manhood and womanhood at the sight of Government and Power let loose" (1901, 480). In both cases, the manliness that Goldman regrets the loss of appears more conventional than transformative, her tone uncharacteristically bitter rather than playful in its complaint. At points, then, Goldman's reversals feel less like a resignification of masculinity and maleness and more a reassertion of their importance in familiar form. Yet in the earlier comment on the cowardice of radicals, of course, "womanhood" has also failed in its convictions, suggestive of a more open revolutionary partnership in which "real women and men" are equally resistant to false promises and gendered affects. Thus we might say that despite lapsing into stereotypes, Goldman did begin to articulate a link between a transformed masculinity and a critique of nationalism in compelling ways: in her focus on the material reality of war and on the importance of internationalism as part of a sexual political counter to affective and embodied oppositions.

Goldman's complicated relationship to family limitation and to the eugenics movement is harder to integrate into her internationalist anarchist critique of nationalism, I think. As discussed in chapter 1, birth control was high on Goldman's agenda in the first two decades of the new century in particular, and she once described it as "the most dominant issue of modern times" (1916c, 471).[13] Goldman's position on birth control was of course consistent with her endorsement of women's bodily autonomy as an essential feature of their ultimate emancipation. So too it chimed with her views on the link between repeated child rearing and the necessity for vast numbers of disposable workers and soldiers. She writes that women are encouraged to "[bring] hapless children into the world only to [see them] ground into dust by the wheel of capitalism and . . . torn into shreds in trenches and battlefield [*sic*]" (470). For Goldman, the correlation is straightforward: "Capitalism cannot do without militarism and since the masses of people furnish the material to be destroyed in the trenches and on the battlefield, capitalism must have a large race" (468). She thus advocates a withdrawal of that labour, which is both better for women individually and ultimately more likely to hasten revolution through the privileging of quality over quantity.[14] To continue this reading, Goldman advocates family limitation as the precise method to realise the qualitative methodology she sees as essential for bringing about an international revolution: if they are not too busy producing cannon fodder or exploited workers, women will come to value their time too, and be more likely to emancipate themselves.

As was the case for many commentators at the time, however, Goldman's arguments about birth control bring her in line with a eugenics discourse that we are now likely to shy away from. As discussed briefly in the last chapter, Goldman's case for "volitional breeding" over "accidental breeding," and her emphasis on "quality of offspring" taking "the place of blind numbers" (n.d. [1991a]) are explicitly placed in the context of "the new eugenics movement . . . whose principles are one with that phase of the woman movement [*sic*] which seeks to liberate and empower the mother in women" (3). Further, Goldman uses a eugenic language of a "diseased race" that is likely to result from "indiscriminate breeding" (1910, 171), and of a general decline in human quality perpetuated by "the overworked and underfed masses" and their "incessant breeding . . . of defective, crippled and unfortunate children" (1916c, 469). For Goldman, the "production of a race of sickly, feeble, decrepit, wretched human beings" diminishes the likelihood of there being a new revolutionary generation who have "the strength [and] . . . moral courage to throw off the yoke of poverty and slavery" (1911, 13). Here is the language of dissipation so familiar from a more general eugenics discourse, in which a nation's human "stock" is depleted by careless reproduction that values quantity above all else and that risks moral and physical degeneracy over refinement and improvement.

Goldman was developing her own arguments about family limitation in a context of broader anxiety among the American and European middle classes that they would be left behind in a new "modern era" within which traditional upstanding masculinity was contested on all sides by bohemians, "the modern

woman," and the relocations caused by mass immigration and internal migration within the United States (Stansell 2000, 30–31). Christine Stansell makes
this argument particularly clearly when she argues that birth control and free
love advocacy were inevitably and invariably coupled with eugenics precisely
because of the ways this aligned with an emphasis on "men of quality" over
"the black masses, and the [tumultuous] labor movement" (31). Making a still
stronger intervention, Carla Hustak (2012) suggests that this anxiety (only
made worse by the crisis in men's "nerves" following the First World War)
was a strong motivating factor behind white middle-class support for free
love, when coupled with renewed responsibility for controlling fertility. For
Hustak, powerful literary and philosophical couples like the Russells and the
Shaws felt compelled to participate in the new cult of "free love" or else be left
behind in the premodern while "the primitives" took the radical centre stage.[15]
As part of her insightful argument, Hustak takes such middle-class couples
to task for their duplicitous appearance of openness as a central technique
through which they consolidated their privilege, mirroring Stansell's position
that birth control and free love movements in which women were given only
limited freedom were thus easily co-opted to "restore traditional hierarchies"
(31).[16] Such arguments are highly persuasive, placing a large question mark
over the "freedom" part of "sexual freedom" and contextualising it in terms of
fear of loss of old privileges in the face of sexual, classed, and raced transitions.
I am less persuaded by Hustak's explicit (and Stansell's implicit) invoking of
Goldman in the same narrative breath as these middle-class intellectuals or
even bohemians, however. Goldman had no elite power base to secure, and
her own belonging even to radical bohemian groups was always conditional
on knowing when to draw the line (which she mostly did not). Goldman's
classed, migrant, and sexual location and embodiment meant that she had
very different investments than the middle-class radicals who were making
similar arguments about family limitation as she was.

To extend this analysis, we might also point to where the question of quality and value lies for different proponents of a eugenic discourse. In Goldman's expositions on the subject, while she most certainly does relish her
descriptions of feckless reproduction in ways that might make us profoundly
uneasy, she also keeps her eye firmly on the situation of women above all
other concerns. Thus, she insists that children should be born of love rather
than obligation or downright misery (1911), and she argues that women would
be naturally inclined to have fewer children if they were able to control their
bodies and choose their partners. With full economic and intersubjective in-

dependence of the kind she spent her life advocating for, Goldman believed that women would only want children they could give attention to, rather than reproducing for the purpose of security or in the hope of improving their class position (1911). We might say that Goldman's focus on quality over quantity, while at one level chiming only too well with discourses and practices of the most repellent population control, is firmly focused on the quality of interaction *between mother and child*, rather than primarily on the "quality" of children themselves. Qualitative value attaches much more firmly to women in general than it does to children throughout Goldman's birth control discourse. Thus, in an unpublished lecture, "The Passing of the Family," she writes that in future women "will consider one fine woman worth four generations of mere quantity. They will consider one fine woman worth more than a brood of commonplace offspring" (between 1927 and 1930). In this same—and rather revealing—draft lecture, Goldman insists that women should be encouraged to "leave the family group to get our breath," a position that situates birth control firmly outside of kinship and inheritance structures, and thus much more firmly in line with her class analysis and materialist critique of capital. For Goldman, the primary value of birth control is its capacity to increase women's sexual and economic freedom, rather than as a means to "perpetuate the race" in established familial, classed, or raced terms (between 1927 and 1930). Goldman's position on family limitation could be read as part of her cosmopolitan antinationalism as easily as it could be read in opposition to it, then. Goldman refuses to endorse a woman's role as homemaker or mere producer of children, and she also refuses to "[proclaim] birth-control as the only panacea for all social ills" (1931c, 591).[17] Rather strikingly, too, Goldman believes that women are more inclined than men to commit "race suicide," particularly where they have to decide between "delight" and the pain of repeat pregnancies and child-rearing duties (between 1927 and 1930), suggesting a rather different picture to that of the nationalist and class-based interests more familiar in eugenics. Instead, Goldman's focus is on the variety of ways in which women's autonomy can be secured so that they can participate fully in an international revolutionary movement, rather than in order that they can preserve the status of a privileged few within a narrowly defined nationalist agenda.

To stay with her lecture notes, Goldman's final page of this unpublished draft confirms this sense of a birth control agenda linked to a changing understanding of the family and of kinship. It is a passage worth quoting at some length, as it is here that Goldman articulates her imagination of cosmopolitan

kinship most clearly and challenges the concept of "race" as tethered to immediate kin and nation. She writes that in the ideal future:

> We shall regard other people's children as we regard our own, other
> people's parents and other peoples' [sic] brothers and sisters as our
> own. "Home, sweet home" ties may appear beautiful to-day. But as our
> ideals socialize they will seem narrow, crude, savagely isolated and cold
> and confining.... We shall need larger distributing centers for our big-
> ger affections. We shall open up our hearts and entertain non-relatives
> with kinsmen, strangers with life-long intimates. We shall live easily,
> affectionately among whosoever happens to be our neighbors. And we
> shall feel toward them as the people of old felt toward the clan, as we
> of to-day feel toward our next of kin. What is now provided us in the
> lesser measure and the lower degree by the little loving home circle
> we shall then receive in the fuller measure and the loftier degree of the
> community many, the community any, of the large tenderness and op-
> portunity of the wide, wide world. An expanded clan or family feeling
> if yu [sic] will. But the old family group is gone. The representative
> types live as personal units. And they will thereby betoken the rise of
> the individual and a completer expression than ever of racial solidarity.
> (between 1927 and 1930, 10)

In this rather extraordinary passage, Goldman theorises the family quite
clearly as an anachronistic structure producing a false allegiance to "our
next of kin." The need to abandon this familial nostalgia is framed both as
a logical consequence of critiquing class and inheritance and as a reflection
of an international commitment to broader affections. For Goldman, those
larger attachments will also serve as their own reward, as she reassures her
audience that "we shall live easily, affectionately" and "receive in the fuller
measure ... the large tenderness and opportunity of the wide, wide world."
Birth control and its freedoms will thus allow for entirely different affiliations as well as fewer children, but importantly those affections will be *both*
close and expansive, as we are hospitable to "strangers" and "life-long intimates" at the same time. Against the remnants of contemporary kinship,
then, Goldman imagines the best of proximity together with the best of
undetermined encounters and expansive horizons. Goldman's harmonious
vision is one that witnesses "a more perfect socialization of the individual
and a completer expression than ever of racial solidarity" (10). This is not
the "racial solidarity" of a narrow group or class, clearly, but a human sol-

idarity that takes in the "wide, wide world" as part of an imagined future global kinship. In her challenges to restrictions on women's ability to control their own fertility, then, Goldman explores the key role that reproduction has in securing capitalist nationalism. But even more important for our exploration here, Goldman's free parents can also throw off the arbitrary yoke of "race" in order to identify with communities and individuals beyond their immediate purview. Internationalism can thus be realised through sexual freedom and the challenge to reproductive necessity as much as through transnational organising and broader political solidarity.

Goldman's approach to birth control certainly draws on a deeply unpleasant view of disability and a stereotyped set of representations of the "breeding masses," as we have seen. It chimes with a eugenic linking of population management and racism that makes it hard to celebrate as a central part of Goldman's internationalism from a present viewpoint. But thinking in more detail about "race" and antinationalism in Goldman, we can also see that her understanding of "quality" in birth control remains resolutely focused on the well-being of the mother and her relationship with her child or children. Neither is Goldman's support for sexual freedom a method to ensure the consolidation of race or class interests in a hierarchical order, as Hustak suggests was the case for some contemporary white, middle-class proponents of freer sexual practices. I want to suggest that in Goldman's case, a familiar eugenic unpleasantness in representing "degeneracy" coexists with a different understanding of race politics: one that emphasises the emergence of free individuals in a resolutely antinationalist vision of kinship; one that centres "race suicide" in eugenic terms as no bad thing in the face of corrupt class and nationalist interests. We might say, then, along with Ferguson, that for Goldman the project was less to recognise race or even racism in its own right than to "reach past those to an ideal of universal human liberation" (2011b, 239). "Race" for Goldman has value only when it is conceived of as the "Human Race." For that global sensibility to be attained, Goldman urges men and women to refrain from spawning unwanted dependents, since this will prevent them from creating the conditions under which they will be able to take up that universal human position. Instead, Goldman's liberated men and women of the future will be fully available to open up to others within and outside of psychic and national borders. Goldman's vision is thus ambivalently located between a degraded, stereotyped vision of human value and that of a global kinship based in postfamilial, postnational solidarity. My larger methodological point here is that we can only access the parts of her arguments that develop a transnational "human solidarity" that uncouples race from kinship and nation if we read with and through rather turn away from her eugenic othering.

Goldman's antinationalist arguments might be said to chime with Paul Gilroy's in *Against Race* (2000) at certain points and in certain ways. For Gilroy, any fundamental challenge to racism will have to move beyond racial difference, since the latter is rooted in nationalist and violent colonial histories. Goldman's push away from racialised identifications in the form of kinship and nationalism resonates with this view, as it does with the necessary global or transnational sensibility that it brings into the frame. One difficulty that arises with this approach, however, is that the resolution of "race" and racist oppression is primarily imagined through a *shift in scale* to an international perspective. This is, perhaps, one reason why Goldman's attention to African American politics while she lived in the United States was rather cursory compared with her engagements with other modes of oppression.[18] While understandable in terms of her own revolutionary methodology, Goldman's focus then also means that her understanding of marriage or women's specific burden remains filtered through whiteness. As a result, and as Falk notes, Goldman pays no attention to the particular forms of violence that black women face because of racism as well as patriarchy, or to the ways in which "the family" is *already* shifting within the national context because of patterns of migration and segregation that impact what we think of as the household. Michelle Wright's work in *The Physics of Blackness* (2015) is instructive here, in that she argues that to take account of black women's marginalisation, one cannot move "beyond" race without first addressing violence within social movements and epistemic communities. Wright proposes a broader transnational epistemology to make sense of the relationship between gender, race, and migration, one that does not presume a heteronormative family structure or a masculine "head of household." Wright's perspective, much like Goldman's in her allusion to enjoyment of proximity as well as of distance, does not presume that the problems of race and racism can and should be resolved through attention to the national or the international but through a combination of the two. While Goldman's desire to foreground women's emancipation centres the international, her brief vision of "non-relatives" coexisting with "kinsmen" suggests more integrated ways forward that I will return to later in this chapter.

METAPHORICAL SLAVERY AND RACIST VIOLENCE

While scholars have appreciated Goldman's internationalism and antination-alist arguments in ways that chime with my own, they have remained troubled by her lack of detailed attention to race and racism, particularly while in the United States. As Falk notes, while she was concerned with violence directed at black people (as she was with violence against all oppressed people), Goldman's engagement with racism was "uncharacteristically brief" (2012b, 40). For Falk, while Goldman had a clear analysis of lynching as "the most graphic and egregious expression of racist terrorism in the country," her approach was limited in that she did not theorise that horror as "the focus of her general critique" of state aggression (12n33). And, as Ferguson indicates, and as I suggested at the beginning of this chapter, Goldman empathised with the black American condition but did not use black experience as the starting point for a more systematic critique, as she did with anti-Semitism (2011b, 224). While Stansell (2000) and earlier Richard Drinnon and Anna Maria Drinnon (1975) lament Goldman's seeming lack of awareness of race, Ferguson interprets Goldman's inattention not as race *blindness* or racism but as a sign that "she simply did not think [racial identities] were particularly important politically" (2011b, 228). Ferguson's insight here certainly chimes with my own analysis of Goldman's investment in internationalism and the importance of birth control, as discussed earlier. And since Goldman saw racism as nationally bound in terms of its operations, "she did not give racism a history, as she did patriarchy, Christianity, capitalism, or empire" (238). While Ferguson frames this lack of history as a lament that weakens Goldman's understanding of race and racism, it could also be theorised more positively as part of her international methodology, as suggested previously.

Yet as both Falk and Ferguson—who have written the most extensively on race and racism in Goldman's work—insist, her decentring of racism does not take place within the utopian context that she craves, other than imaginatively. What we might call Goldman's cosmopolitan imaginary takes place within the political context of an anarchist movement that reproduced as well as challenged the racial segregation that marked the contemporary United States at the time she resided there (and indeed still does).[19] Prevailing social as well as political segregation and exclusion meant there were few black anarchists to challenge the pervasive whiteness of the anarchist movement; and the focus on the "ideal of universal human liberation" (Ferguson 2011b, 239) did not take account of who was thought of as fully human in a context of racial hierarchy in the first place. Goldman lectured in parts of cities where, while people from "an array of ethnic and class lines" came to hear her, black people would not have gone (Falk 2012b, 17). So although she made sense of this for herself in terms of minimising risks of violence towards black people in the event of police raids, the opportunities for black engagement with her work, or her development of revolutionary theory that took black history and experience seriously, remained limited. Goldman revisited "her relationship to the South and the race issue in America" in later life and came to "regret this gap in her lifelong advocacy of freedom" (Falk 2012b, 41). Goldman demonstrates particular ambivalence about race and racism insofar as she attempts to represent the direct violence that black people experience yet consistently lapses into metaphorisation when wanting to make a larger political point. On the one hand, Goldman has moments where she seems to understand that the violence black people experience needs an independent analysis; on the other hand, she gravitates towards and returns to the metaphorisation that her raced location enables and makes routine. So too, Goldman veers between stereotypical representation of black—particularly African American—people, on the one hand, and her instinctive political empathy for those targeted by authority, on the other.

The most notorious example of this ahistorical as well as depoliticising response comes in her account of racial division in prison on Blackwell's Island. Goldman comments on what she reads as the matron's preferential treatment of black over white inmates as follows: "While I see no difference in races, I think all shuld [sic] be regarded as human beings. The most depraved, ignorant repulsive black woman is sure of a warm reception from this head matron and is placed above the most intelligent white woman. . . . They abuse, insult and even beat their white sisters in misery" (1894, 195). Describing the same context in her autobiography, Goldman provides a fuller account of what she sees as racialised inequity in a passage worth quoting at some length. Having noticed some missing eggs that she was responsible for distributing to sick inmates, Goldman observes that the matron

> felt a violent dislike of everyone not Anglo-Saxon. Her special targets were the Irish and the Jews, against whom she discriminated habitually . . . the missing portions had been given by this head matron to two husky Negro prisoners. That also did not surprise me. I knew she had a special fondness for the coloured inmates. She rarely punished them and often gave them unusual privileges. In return her favourites

would spy on the other prisoners, even on those of their own colour who were too decent to be bribed. I myself never had any prejudice against coloured people; in fact, I felt deeply for them because they were being treated like slaves in America. But I hated discrimination. The idea that sick people, white or coloured, should be robbed of their rations to feed healthy persons outraged my sense of justice, but I was powerless to do anything in the matter. (1931b, 138)

At one level, the passage reads as a straightforward description of what were no doubt endemic manipulations of implicit and explicit hierarchies by those in authority in prison. Yet as Ferguson remarks, Goldman's comment that the black inmates were "being treated like slaves" deflects rather than highlights any "recognition that only thirty-five years before, they actually had been slaves. 'Slavery' was not a simile in this context" (2011b, 220). We might note too that the language Goldman uses in both passages is far from neutral. The "depraved, ignorant repulsive black woman" is contrasted with "the most intelligent white woman" in ways that affirm stereotypical descriptions of black and white people in general, such that the juxtaposition is jarring as a rhetorical device; the thieving black favourites are "husky Negros" rather than themselves part of the discriminated-against group of non-Anglo-Saxons Goldman says she wishes to defend. Goldman thus segregates in her own right those who are unfairly marginalised by ethnicity and religion as well as migration (Irish and Jewish inmates) and those she sees as gaining from the matron's viciousness (black inmates). What she does not consider is that there may be different ways in which racism works to divide and rule. As a result, Goldman is ill equipped to recognise that there are different stakes in toeing a line for black and other subjects (despite her acknowledgements elsewhere of the specific brutality meted out to black subjects).[20] Goldman is further "dumbfounded" by her friend John Swinton's challenge to her representation of prison as prejudicial (in which he raises similar points to those I have just touched on). In continued defence of her commentary, Goldman insists that she "had pointed out the discrimination practised between sick and starved white women and Negro favourites. I should have protested as much had coloured women been robbed of their rations" (1931b, 154–55). Again Goldman appears blithely myopic in her analysis of how race and racism work to inflect difference in a context such as prison.[21] Goldman's comments appear perversely naive—and are indeed racist—as she seems to accept these differences of treatment at face value rather than interrogating their history. In seeking to make "difference" neutral Goldman makes use of language that reinforces rather than challenges the representational aspects of that history.

It is Goldman's careless racist stereotyping in a passage such as the one quoted that makes feminist critics anxious, as might be expected. But rather than grappling with her complex and often contradictory understandings of race and racism across her work, critics tend to insist that she ignores these issues, or—as I discuss more fully later—they position her as attentive to *other structures* of ethnic and religious oppression as a more positive alternative.[22] While never considering "race" to be a key analytic for unpicking the interlocking structures of oppression she was concerned with, Goldman did address race and racism in a variety of ways. The primary ways she does so are first through her conception of slavery as both practice and metaphor and second through several discussions of the horror of lynching. As was the case for many anarchist thinkers at the time, Goldman consistently takes up "slavery" as a general term to indicate oppression and the helpless condition of the masses. As in all her thinking, Goldman links the situation of women with that of broader oppression: in part, she achieves this through her representation of *marriage as slavery*. While noting that slavery as a formal institution has been abolished, Goldman contends that women's lot within marriage is an equally profound unfreedom within which they are slaves to their husbands. A married woman "has sold her self into chattel slavery during her life, for a home or title," making her a legal prostitute who—worse still—exercises no choices over her sexual or economic life (1897a). Marriage is a context of slavery in a variety of ways for Goldman, of course. Women are slaves to men within marriage in that they are bodily and economically bound, but they are also slaves to their own bodies in their lack of control over their own reproduction (1916c). The absence of birth control makes women slaves to their bodies, then, but also renders them utterly subservient to capitalism in the process. Slaves themselves, women also *produce* slaves for capitalist exploitation as workers, and for slaughter as cannon fodder in wartime. As Goldman acerbically points out: "You cannot have militarism with free born men; you must have slaves, automatons, machines, obedient disciplined creatures, who will move, act, shoot and kill at the command of their superiors" (1915, 335). For Goldman, discipline and restraint (of soldiers, workers, and children, as well as of women) inevitably lead to "slavery, submission, poverty, all misery [and] all social iniquities" (1910, 165). For Goldman, then, we might say that "slavery" is *both* a metaphor—in that she is aware that the oppressive conditions that she loathes are not identical to the historical institution of slavery itself—and also a more direct description of both women's condition and that of the masses.

The difference between metaphor and analytic description seems to rely on the question of "voluntary slavery" in Goldman. In contexts where women are forced into marriage and multiple childbirths, or men are forced into military servitude, Goldman uses "slavery" as her chosen descriptive term. Yet in contexts where workers are blindly "doing things at the bidding of others" 1900, 384), when they work as "voluntary slaves" (1928?a), this is used as a metaphor designed to spur a more revolutionary relationship to economic and social conditions. In effect, Goldman metaphorises slavery as a means to castigate workers, to shame them out of their compliance. She marks the difference in an early address as follows: "With Ruskin I can say: 'There are two kinds of slaves—one are scourged to their work by the whip; others by their ignorance; some are bought with money, otherwise with praise (or promises of chocolate?)[.] Again, it matters not what kind of work slaves do; some are set to digging fields, others graves; some press the juices out of vines, some the blood of men, but it is slavery just the same'" (1900, 387–88). Here Goldman baits her audience by accusing them, via Ruskin, of selling their freedom through obliviousness or for promises of superficial sweet rewards, urging them to replace false consumer fantasies with a strong dose of revolutionary reality. For Goldman, the masses are held in slavery from without and within, in ways that perpetuate "poverty and disease" (1909d, 450) and prevent the development of autonomy necessary for lasting change. In terms of sexual politics, women would cease to be slaves to patriarchy, religious authority, capitalism, or militarism if they could but control their sexuality. In making this connection, Goldman foregrounds the material realities of women's reproduction and the importance of sexual freedom for revolutionary change once more. Real slavery could be avoided—as her once friend Margaret Sanger put it—by "'refusing to populate the earth with slaves'" (cited in L. Gordon 1979, 460), both by withdrawal of labour in the context of production and by "'refusing to supply the market with children'" (460).

This interplay between depiction and metaphor in relation to race and racism is not confined to her political use of "slavery." In her use of the term "lynching," Goldman also moves between figuring it as something that happens to particular black bodies in America and as a term that can be applied to different experiences of systematic and applied violence. Goldman deplores lynching as a particularly egregious act of violence, as an atrocity visited on black people who are also "tortured and burned by infuriated crowds [in the South] without a hand being raised or a word said for their protection" (1900, 386). Goldman's understanding of lynching is that it is a ghastly example of mob violence, a position in clear alignment with her broader concerns about the awful tyrannies of majorities, as discussed in the previous chapter (1910, 69–78). Goldman's longest set of reflections on lynching form part of her 1907 address to the anarchist congress in Amsterdam, where she describes "the position of the American negro" as "sad and deplorable in the extreme" (in Falk 2012b, 42n158). Goldman identifies violence against black men in particular as a daily practice, calling attention once more to the "brutal spectacle of so-called 'mob justice': the hanging or burning of a colored man" (42n158). And here too, Goldman seems to be articulating the beginnings of a material analysis of racism, that situates it both in relation to the particular "persecution, suffering and injustice" black people are subjected to and in terms of the lack of equality between white and black people, "socially, politically or economically—notwithstanding his alleged constitutional rights" (42n158). She continues unequivocally: "Legally and theoretically, black slavery has been abolished; in reality, however, the negro is as much a slave now as in antebellum days, and even more ostracized socially and exploited economically" (42n158).

Yet Goldman also metaphorises lynching by using it to refer to mob violence against the oppressed more generally. For example, she portrays the betrayal of and violence against striking workers that was routine as lynching and locates it as part of the "vicious mob brutality" (Falk 2012b, 120) that resulted in attacks on individual anarchists and socialists, such as that on Ben Reitman in San Diego in 1912.[23] As Lumsden (2010) indicates, one of the problems with portraying striking workers or the individual revolutionary as "lynched" is that it takes for granted that the historical structures of racism are either parallel to or subsumed within capitalism: all bodily attacks are equivalent. Further, Lumsden notices that in the anarchist cartoons that do portray workers as "lynched," the images consistently invert the real racial dynamics of these practices. Thus the bosses are represented as "primitive" or animalistic in ways that align with more widespread racist representations of black people, while the bodies of the "lynched" workers are both white and subordinate.[24] Following Lumsden, then, the extension of the metaphor of lynching to include a broader range of forms of violence against the oppressed risks deflecting it as a specifically racialised practice enacted on black bodies (through generalisation) and becomes a precise mode through which the history of racism may be representationally reversed. Indeed, this tactic of inversion (through general application of lynching as a metaphor) resonates with Goldman's in her depiction of black inmates as privileged in racial terms, as discussed previously.[25]

As I have flagged, a number of feminist scholars attentive to Goldman's antinationalism but anxious about her more uncertain engagement with race and racism have described her revolutionary politics as "intersectional." Some of this work claims Goldman's rejection of hierarchies of categorical analysis and her embodied theorising of the links between migration, gender, and labour as intersectional in ways that predate the inception of this critical tool (Kowal 2016, 77; Rogness and Foust 2011, 153); other work has centred Goldman's Jewishness as the wellspring of her intersectional and international sensibility, a position giving rise to her own experience of multiple oppressions as an immigrant, a Jew, and a woman (Blake 1997; Redding 1995, 8). There is a particular structure to these representations of Goldman as Jewish: her inattention to race and racism is flagged as regrettable; the writer moves swiftly to indicate that this was largely a contextual oversight (a sign of the times); her Jewishness or international solidarity provides one avenue through which she might be more appropriately engaged with, or even redeemed. Importantly, race and racism are typically not returned to once this sequence has begun. Goldman's location as Jewish is thus not simply one point of engagement like any other but is taken up to offset her perceived inattention to race and racism. Thus, for Falk again, Goldman's status as "a Russian Jewish immigrant who identified with other eastern European immigrants" cannot "excuse her oblivion to the racism against others" (2012b, 41), but that status means that "she too experienced racial prejudice, but never with the same intensity as African Americans in the United States" (41). While acknowledging a difference of "intensity ... [of] racial prejudice," Falk ensures Goldman both carries the burden of that difference and negotiates what becomes their combined moderation of "oblivion to racism." Falk joins Alice Wexler (1992) and Marilyn Reizenbaum (2005) in their centring of Goldman's Jewish embodiment both as central to her understanding of exclusion and as an alternative point of identification for contemporary Jewish feminist scholars.[26] Other scholars frame Goldman's experience as providing the basis for her instinctive critique of techniques through which migrants were considered "alien" (Kennedy 1999), her Jewishness providing an embodied link between the "foreignness" of both the immigrant and the anarchist (Redding 1995, 8).[27]

I mentioned the dangers of proposing Goldman as an intersectional heroine at the beginning of this chapter, particularly when this is cited as an "alternative" to her perceived lack of focus on American race politics, and here I draw together my reasons for being suspicious of this move. In one way, of course, it is an important aspect of the stories that we tell about Goldman: she was indeed a Jewish migrant who drew on that experience as a way to link multiple oppressions and their impact on particular bodies. And as I detail later, Goldman herself was depicted in the media as a gendered, classed, and ethnic (or racialised) pariah; this was an essential part of how she was demonised and her threat to decent society both amplified and contained. But such critical engagements perform other work as well, particularly when enthusiastically taken up in the face of confusion or embarrassment about Goldman's own deflections. In the first instance, and as I have flagged, discussion of Goldman as an intersectional heroine or a Jewish revolutionary ahead of her time is not simply descriptive. In the feminist critical archive, Goldman's migrant experience and racialisation come to stand in for attention to race and racism, and in that sense displace rather than grapple with their complexities. Goldman's lack of engagement with race and racism can be lamented, then, but the critical desire for that focus can also remain at the level of fantasy. This grammar of what we might call an "intersectional alibi" proposes Jewishness or intersectional attention as *equivalent to* attention to blackness, but in fact it also substitutes the one for the other in the process, a point Alyosxa Tudor (2017) underlines as part of how "migratism"—their term—works. Even where, as in Falk's account given earlier, the violence experienced by Jewish migrants is represented as of a lesser degree, the slip from the black body to the Jewish body continues to conflate the two. It suggests that if the oppression *were* of the same level, that the substitute would be absolute, and thus repeats the lack of historicisation of the structure of racism that critics find deplorable in Goldman herself.

Such conflation chimes oddly with a contemporary theoretical archive on intersectionality as well. Black feminist critics as disciplinarily diverse as Kimberlé Crenshaw (1991), Avtar Brah and Ann Phoenix (2004), and Nira Yuval-Davis (2006) take up intersectionality for two main reasons. First, they do so to highlight the "problems of difference" that attend multiple oppressions and to explore the best way of taking account of those differences in theory, in law, and in political culture. But secondly, and as Robyn Wiegman (2012) points out is a frequently forgotten central premise, intersectional theorising proposes that we start from the subordinated experience of black womanhood rather than *any difference* one might want to bring to the fore. In both respects, I would say, it is hard to claim Goldman as an "intersectional" precursor in any meaningful way. While Goldman's analyses are certainly concerned to link the multiple oppressive structures and their impact on particular bodies, Goldman does not start from the question of misrecognition and violence against the bodies most marginal within an authoritarian economy of difference; nor is she interested in using "marginal contradictions" as a way of increasing rights or recognition within a legal, political, or social realm. And since Goldman's aim is to eradicate difference as well as its worst effects, her uncertainty about the significance of black oppression can also be thus resolved at both a theoretical and a political level. In her arguments against patriotism, for example, Goldman's horror at the vision of young men's dead bodies lying strewn across the battlefield (1906a) enables her to link the ills of patriotic education and masculine pride that result in devastating loss. Similarly, the problem with what she terms the "patriotic cholera" (1914a) is its contagious nature, its capacity to devastate the natural resources—again, young men's bodies—that could otherwise be liberated through a more revolutionary education and future. Not only does Goldman start from young men's bodies to make her claims, her primary concern is to use any outrage she can generate as a springboard not for increased rights or recognition for young men in wartime but for proposing a cosmopolitan belonging that "[asserts] kinship with all countries" (1917b, 5). Goldman is certainly interested in how different and multiple oppressions reinforce one another and act to shape bodies and their role in the world. But her analysis is also underwritten by a deep humanism that starts from any and all oppressed individuals and whose goal is—as I have said, but I think it is worth reiterating here—the *eradication of difference* as the starting point of a new communitarianism. In that sense, unless we want to extend the theorisation of "intersectionality" to a point of pure description over analysis, it seems to me that it is neither accurate nor particularly useful to incorporate Goldman into the concept's history.

The feminist critical archive's claiming of Goldman in this way also works to reproduce rather than counter Goldman's own erasures of race and racism, in particular ways. Claiming Jewishness as a distinct non-Anglo position (along with Irishness) as uniquely subordinated in the prison context of Blackwell's Island, discussed earlier, works against a thorough account of black women's negotiations of oppression. It operates as a defence against consideration of the complexity of legacies of slavery and the targeting of blackness in this context, and it further pathologises black female subjectivity. In other words, it is through the privileging of nonblack otherness *as racialised and subordinate* that Goldman mobilises her most notoriously racist discourse. At the very least this should give us pause. It seems perverse, then, for feminist critics to jump to claim Goldman as Jewish and migrant as a way of excusing her inattention to race and racism, since it redoubles this mode of *comparison as displacement*, which is part of how racism is being mobilised. If we return to the earlier discussion of generalising the practice of lynching to refer to bodily violence against oppressed workers as well as black victims, we can see that the desire for equivalence reorders power hierarchies in a similar way. Here, as Lumsden (2010) highlights, it is the generalisation of lynching that allows for a reversal in which white (or migrant) workers are rendered subservient to specifically racialised bosses. Such a move reposi- tions blackness as threatening and authoritative in ways familiar to us from Frantz Fanon's (1991) articulation of the psychic displacement of rage onto the black body and away from the structural and psychic desires of the white subject to annihilate the black other.[28] In not attending to the specific mecha- nisms through which race and racism are managed in Goldman's writing and a broader anarchist context, the feminist critical archive risks instantiating the erasures that it seeks to excuse its heroine for. In taking up its tactic of deflection, it misses (and thereby repeats) the ways in which this is a central mechanism through which race and racism are obscured and naturalised. As a result, there is little attention to the complicated relationship between different modes of racialisation and demonisation that both connect Jewish and black experience and simultaneously function to keep them apart. And in reality we are no closer to a consideration of what would need to shift in Goldman's account of sexual politics to address the specific experiences of oppression that black women face (in prison or elsewhere), or indeed their specific hopes and strategies for liberation.

Finally, here I want to suggest that the feminist critical archive's preference for a substitution of Jewish and migrant embodiment and sensibilities for at- tention to race and racism in the American context rather ironically prevents us exploring some interesting ways in which Goldman herself attempts to theorise the relationship between these oppressions in more depth. While for the most part Goldman's account of lynching takes the form outlined earlier—namely, pointing to its particular horror but also thinking about its conceptual value for a broader account of targeted violence against the oppressed—there are moments in her discussion where she seeks to link black and Jewish experiences of violence in suggestive rather than reproduc- tive ways. If, in her Amsterdam address of 1907, Goldman makes the familiar comparison between black experience and the "brutal treatment of the Jews" (in Falk 2012b, 42n158), by 1927 she is more circumspect, writing to her life-long friend Ben Capes that she considers "the position of the Negro in America" to be "much more terrible . . . than that of Jews anywhere in the world" (Goldman 1927 in Drinnon and Drinnon 1975, 196). In an important analysis of the parallel, Goldman goes on to note: "Of course there are pogroms and persecution of Jews going on all the time, still it is not so constant and so brutal as that of the Negro. And the whole world is outraged when something particularly wanton takes place. Witness the amount of publicity given the hazing of the Jewish interns in the hospital in New York. But the cruelty to the Negro goes on and on and no one gets particularly excited even" (196).

Interestingly, Goldman refuses any straightforward comparison between Jewish and black experiences of violence, pointing instead to different histories and contexts through which we might understand both forms of violence. For Goldman, the difference between these experiences is one of consistency, on the one hand, and the reception of the depth of that harm, on the other. Here, then, there is a sense in Goldman's writing of the question of *perception* as fundamental to how racist violence works, an important point that might usefully have been integrated into a fuller account of the relationship between forms of racial and ethnic othering in her own work. Goldman never does extend her thinking on this comparison, however, only making occasional gestures to the significance of the overlaps between different modes of racialisation and violence, or between hatred of immigrants and of black people born in America.

There are glimpses of where Goldman might perhaps have gone with her analysis had she focused her attention more fully on race and racism, rather than reproducing the deflections and comparisons that enabled a blunt equivalence inattentive to the historical and material realities giving rise to specific forms of difference. In a more thoroughly intersectional vein, Goldman's interest in sexual politics as a revolutionary method might have been deepened and extended had she explored what Ellen Dubois and Linda Gordon (1983) theorise as the consistent efforts among black women's movements in the early twentieth century to understand black women's slavery as a specific, racialised form of prostitution, for example.[29] Or we might push Goldman's theorisation of sexual freedom to include a more historically located sense of changing postslavery family forms in the United States, as well as an integration of a critique of miscegenation legislation and culture into her linking of marriage, reproduction, and nationalism. Such incorporation would not necessarily have led Goldman to privilege race and racism over other forms of analysis in her work—and nor, I think, should that be an expectation. But such attention would have enabled her to secure her own links between the structures of marriage, nationalism, and capitalist greed more rather than less effectively, in line with her existing argument.

As suggested in my analysis thus far, there are points in Goldman's work where she gives signs of insight into the limits of a comparative account of racism that only seeks equivalence. In her brief mention of the *commonalities and differences* between Jewish and black experience of historical and contemporary violence, their shared experience of divergent authorial attempts to obliterate them at both collective and individual levels, Goldman might have begun to explore the complex interactions between migrant and settled, religious and secular racialised histories and structures. In the next section, I try to run with these possibilities to evaluate racialised, gendered, and classed representations of Goldman in the press coverage that was obsessed with her at the height of her notoriety. In addition, I explore how Goldman's encouragement of women revolutionaries to commit "race suicide" in the development of transnational solidarity might be more carefully theorised within her own life and thinking in relation to a more expanded—but also more circumspect and strategic—understanding of universal kinship.

RACE, REPRESENTATION, AND KINSHIP

In this section I explore ways in which the productive threads I have already identified in Goldman's thinking about race and internationalism might be brought to the fore. In the first case, I return to the question of Goldman's ambivalent linkages between Jewish and black American experiences of violence (collective and individual), to continue the work on the limits and importance of comparison between forms of racialised violence. As we have seen, Goldman took up comparison both as a means to erase black oppression as distinctive and also to examine more fully the differences and similarities across forms of racism. In these latter reflections, Goldman identified a key issue that I want to probe further here: that of representation in perpetuating fantasies of racist violence against black people as of a lower level and gravity than was the case. In her acknowledgement that part of the horror of "the cruelty to the Negro [that] goes on and on" is that "no one gets particularly excited even" (Goldman 1927 in Drinnon and Drinnon 1975, 196), Goldman identifies the question of reception as key in a frame of racist representation. Goldman likely had in mind the ways in which racism functions through and is perpetuated by the media, and the powerful role of perception in generating affective response. In what follows I hone in on an intimate sphere of representation for Goldman too: depictions of her in the American media that are intended to heighten American middle-class anxiety about anarchist terror and that link race, class, and gender in a pathologising discourse. The aim in tracking these representations is to pull out ways in which the journalistic obsession with Goldman depicts her through an interlocking set of markers of difference that reinforce but also work to displace one another. In this sense, then, I am interested in showing how Goldman herself was subject to the similar modes of displacement in order to at once marginalise and contain her that were used to minimise the structural hierarchies framing black American experience. If Goldman "'missed race,'" or more accurately missed how racism was made to disappear (including through her own discourse), then it is instructive to consider ways in which similar techniques were applied to her. My approach here is not intended to draw an *equivalence* between Goldman's experience of being represented and the black American experience (of representation or of violence), but to suggest that there may be shared *methods* through which both experiences are fetishised and minimised. Newspaper reporting portrayed Goldman in ways that secured the representational links between foreignness and political violence, for example, but also simultaneously reduced that threat through a focus on her femininity. It is precisely through a consideration of the gendering of Goldman's representation in the press that I hope to suggest a comparative methodology that presumes displacement as well as equivalence as a key technique of racism.

In the second "experiment," I return to the question of universal kinship so central to Goldman's challenge to nationalism. Here I discuss Goldman's postexile compromises with respect to marriage after her American citizenship had been stripped from her. Despite having spent her young adult life berating others for their instrumental marriages of convenience, a more mature Goldman acted strategically to enable the continuation of her political activity in ways that suggest a shift in position (at least with respect to her personal experiences of mobility). Certainly, the media was delighted with Goldman's apparent change of heart, seeing it as an opportunity to bait her as a hypocrite and to frame her as increasingly benign as she aged. More generously, we could read this as a sign that Goldman was—at least in this respect—able to consider political compromise under certain circumstances and was less rigid in her views on strategic manipulation of legislation in order to secure, for example, the right to travel across borders. It is paradoxical, of course, that citizenship via kinship is the mode through which Goldman is able to secure her continued international activity. It appears that despite her desire for an expanded universal familial sensibility that Goldman herself is trapped in the confines of a rigid national form. Yet in fact, such a straightforward critique diminishes the importance of the relationship between Goldman and the man who conferred citizenship on her—James Colton, a British miner and anarchist. Their relationship, as I hope to show, is neither fully reducible to the kinship form nor entirely separate from the affections and attachments that Goldman advocates in her discussion of universal kinship in "The Passing of the Family" (between 1927 and 1930). It is precisely this combination of the proximate and distant that we might want to take forward as the basis of Goldman's renewed cosmopolitan sensibility towards the end of her life.

Goldman was a consistent presence in newspapers, particularly in her early adult years in America. Journalists conducted frequent interviews with her (e.g., *New York Sun* 1901; Thompson 1909; *The World* 1920), raising paper sales through the publication of her controversial views and details of how she looked, and titillating a public fascinated with the "High Priestess of Anarchy" (*Chicago Inter Ocean* 1908). Even those journalists politically favourable to Goldman, such as Guido Bruno, who interviewed Goldman in prison in 1917, continued to focus on her appearance: her "large and deep blue [eyes], always smiling, full of mirth and kindness, of energy and self-confidence" (1917, 61).[30] Goldman relished the attention to a large extent, engaging in theatrics that would appeal to the press, as mentioned in the introduction, and taking every opportunity to express her political views to a wider public. Falk argues that "the young, attractive Goldman's mix of sexuality and aggression terrified not only those wary of anarchism but also those accustomed to relegating women to the background of political debate" (2005, 9), such that the force of her personality and embodiment opened up the public sphere in ways hitherto unknown for women. At the height of her popularity, Goldman routinely gave lectures to thousands in her audience, as many drawn to listen to her because of her notoriety as because of her anarchist sentiments. Yet Goldman was not always in control of her own representation, of course: editors exploited that public terror to boost sales, and journalists developed ways of talking about her that fuelled the imaginative links between terrorism, immigration, and anarchism and minimised or amplified that same threat.

Journalists who spoke to Goldman appeared convinced that they would find the truth of her political deviancy in her body. They engaged in detailed examinations of her form overall, but in particular of her face: her mouth, hair, eyes, brow, complexion, and the shape of her head were all subject to intense and often contradictory scrutiny. Thus in an early article, the description of Goldman shifts from a dismissive but innocuous "she seemed rather pretty" (*New York World* 1892, 112) to a comment on her cheeks as "slightly sunken," and thence to all-out viciousness: "As she turned her head the tendons bulged out into scrawniness, and blotches here and there added to the sharp disappointment one met with after leaving the upper part of her face" (112). Finally, in a comment directly mocking the "prettiness" attributed to her smile, the author describes it instead as "lips wreathed into lines that were uglier than when her face was in repose" (112). Goldman's appearance is here not only a disappointment the journalist clearly relishes but, importantly, also a sign of her deviousness: she initially appears attractive, but closer inspection reveals her looks to be positively diabolic, in line with her anarchist sentiments. Such invasive assessment of Goldman's looks reminds us perhaps not only of the prurient interest in stars by the media but also of the empirical turn in criminology and the emerging racial and sexual sciences characterising Goldman's own time. And, indeed, Goldman finds herself portrayed in the *Phrenological Journal and Science of Health* in familiar ways that are worth quoting at some length: "The back head is rather long, showing friendship, domestic attachment and love of the opposite sex. There is considerable width just over the ears at destructiveness and appetite for food. . . . The facial signs of destructiveness and alimentiveness are very pronounced in the form of the mouth, and it is chiefly in the mouth and eyes that we may detect the signs of quality and temperament which account for the woman's disposition to attack the present social fabric" (1895, 215). As Sander Gilman (1992) has so brilliantly taught us, bodily signs of deviance may well index more than one social or biological failing, producing on the one hand a heightened anxiety that we will not be able to read the difference and on the other a certainty that *difference itself* will nevertheless be visible, if only one knows where—and how closely—to look.[31] Here greed and aggression are identified in Goldman's mouth and ears, while her eyes, ears, and mouth reveal her destructiveness (mentioned twice) and lack of care for convention. Lasciviousness, greed, and a violent disposition, as we know, are attributes that attach to and serve as signs for a range of antisocial subjects: prostitutes, the working classes, the Irish, and people of African descent, as well as anarchists and Jews. The brilliance of phrenology is that it only needs to highlight the signs, and the conventional imagination will make the links, helped along by the emerging racialised sciences and social sciences (Gilroy 1998).[32] While we might want to insist that a whole variety of forms of bodily "evidence" of deviance in depictions of Goldman are indirectly racialised, there are particular moments in which her Jewish or Eastern European origins are more directly laid bare for the voracious reader. In "Talk with Emma Goldman" for the *New York Sun*, for example, we begin with the familiar need for a "second glance" at Goldman to register her "determined chin and firm mouth" (1901, 5). Once Goldman's superficial attractiveness has lost its appeal, this investigative journalist is able to detect "the mouth of a worker and the eyes of an enthusiast. Her face is quiet, but it is the face of a Slav" (5). Goldman's status as an Eastern interloper having been established, the reader needs no further convincing that "no one would think of calling the woman handsome" (5). Her racial origins as Slav show themselves in her face; her "determined chin and firm mouth" read back so the reader can be reassured that her true character would always reveal itself to the attentive viewer.

Goldman's appearance is also pored over for signs of her working-class, peasant roots. Thus, we hear that "Miss Goldman is a small woman, of the type termed 'shapeless,' who dresses in a manner not calculated to impart charm and whose face has the glow of health, although extremely plain" (*Spokesman-Review* 1908, 323). Goldman is healthy and strong but no beauty, her dowdy appearance underlined by the fact that "she carried a large, old-fashioned handbag full of newspaper clippings . . . and looked more like a farmer's wife on a shopping tour than a bombthrower" (9). Far from being seduced by Goldman's fiery personality and rhetoric, the reader is mockingly comforted by her unworldliness. As if to underline this very point, the journalist imagines that Goldman "blushed like a girl" (6) when asked about marriage: a very unlikely response from our free love advocate but an important journalistic consolation to the reader of her staged naïveté in the face of a modern world. This rhetorical contrasting of the journalist's and the reader's joint expectations that what they will see in an encounter with Goldman is a "fire-eating virago breathing death and vengeance to rulers," with the reality of an aging woman "with the clear, healthy complexion of a girl of fifteen . . . rather short and just a little stout" (*Globe and Commerce* 1911?) is a consistent tactic in her representation. Less seductive than staid, less beguiling than stubborn, Goldman's features and dimensions titillate and soothe in equal measure, precisely because of the ways in which they are classed, raced, and gendered as an attempt to make her threat readable and ordinary.[33]

Thus we see that the media-fuelled anxieties about bomb-throwing anarchists led by a charismatically fiendish Goldman are alleviated almost as soon as they are generated by a consistent gendered domestication of that threat. While the preceding examples hope to find femininity but instead find evidence of a racialised European peasant morphology, a related representational tactic embellishes her ordinary femininity to reassure the reader in a different way. Utilising the time-honoured tactic of juxtaposition (one Goldman herself was also rather fond of), journalists contrast the knowledge of Goldman's anarchist fervour with careful descriptions of her as "pretty" and "neatly clad" (Goldman 1897b, 9), or describe her as "a little woman, with a complexion that many of her sisters with less unpopular ideas might envy" (*Providence Evening Bulletin* 1897, 283). As well as providing a space for reassuring the reader that Goldman's ideas are not as popular as they might imagine, such comparisons suggest a "neat" containment of that (minimal) threat through the emphasis on order rather than chaos. That dynamic is made particularly explicit in the following portrayal of Goldman at the time of her arrest in 1901: dressed "in a jaunty white sailor hat, white waist, blue skirt, belt and necktie" the "anarchist queen . . . looks anything but bloodthirsty" (*New York World* 1901, 1). Such representations highlight the specific modes through which the racialised and classed threat of anarchism is both heightened and diminished. Her complexion is surprisingly enviable (not ruddy or rough, as it is elsewhere), and she is small and neat, well dressed, and even "jaunty," rather than over-bearing, out-of-control, or too intellectual.[34] Femininity here brings Goldman back into the acceptable social world from her position of "other"; it does considerable work to offset the classed and racialised threats otherwise firmly associated with her. Emphasis on Goldman's femininity is not simply a question of juxtaposition or compensation, however. It is also the primary mode through which she is categorically dismissed. Thus, in one account, "Miss Goldman gave a little nod of her head to emphasize her words, and quite a pretty head it was, crowned with soft brown hair, combed with a bang and brushed to one side" (*St. Louis Post-Dispatch* 1897, 290). Here, Goldman's threat is minimised in the typical way, but she is also explicitly condescended to, so that the reader can participate in a sexist discourse (of the kind where women do not need to trouble their pretty little heads) that frames her views as not needing to be taken seriously in the first place.

In articles that are broadly sympathetic to anarchist politics, such as one from the *Toronto Star Weekly*, journalists may draw on equivalent oppositions in more knowing fashion. The author has invited Goldman to a social evening and notes that she is not the "wild-eyed woman of streaming hair, disheveled dress, shrieking words, [or] fighting fists" of the public's imagination but instead "a dormant volcano at least, peaceful, picturesque and altogether beneficently fitting into our quiet home atmosphere" (1926). Here, the contrast is exaggerated to mock both the fantastic vision of a witchlike harridan and the entirely tame woman of the domestic sphere so central to mainstream representations of Goldman.[35] Similarly, in his interview with Goldman for the *New York Times Magazine*, Charles Thompson directly implicates the representational tactics of other journalists, noting that they "describe her with unnecessary emphasis as a 'Russian Jewess'" (1909, 437). Yet Thompson too uses his readers' and his own stereotyped expectations of what that "emphasis" might mean as his point of departure, continuing in an approving tone that "there is so little of either the Russian or the Jewess about her looks. . . . A high, broad brow, clear, earnest eyes, a frank and honest face, a firm mouth that has elements of sweetness and nobility in it" (437). Positively appraising Goldman's looks at some length, Thompson waxes lyrical about her "eyes, which are large and fine, [and which] have the curious combination of brilliancy and softness—rare, that, in eyes of blue and gray," despite noting that "she would not like to have her looks made the subject of even a paragraph" (437). Thus, even those more positive accounts of Goldman's appearance invest heavily in its significance: it will tell us the truth of her character by confirming or belying the baseness of her Eastern and Jewish origins, or the elevation of the whiteness implied by these contrasts.

The obsession with Goldman's looks serves a range of functions, then. For one, it demonstrates the belief that political or social deviance could be read in bodily signs, and serves to underline or dismiss Goldman as a specific threat on that basis. Accounts of Goldman's appearance highlight the interlocking modes through which contemporary political upheaval and chaos are racialised and classed as an immigrant threat, but so too they suggest a range of ways in which gender is mobilised to confirm or undermine that threat. The endless focus on Goldman's appropriately or inappropriately gendered characteristics is an integral part of how she is racialised and classed, in other words, as well as how her person and politics are diminished. Gendering here is a discursive and representational method of erasure and deflection that situates femininity itself as white, middle class, and domestic. The aggression that typifies this field of representation should not be underestimated. The reduction of Goldman to her appearance combines with the violence of racist and classist stereotyping as an attempt to ridicule her person and obliterate the threat she posed. Such gendered belittling easily turns to aggression if its terms are refused, as Goldman no doubt knew only too well. In an article for the *Los Angeles Times*, one journalist takes this confluence of gendered and racialised dismissals to their logical conclusion, accusing Goldman of being a "tease" in her stated preference for America over Russia and noting that "she reminds one of those women whose eyes say yes when their lips say no" (1925). This rape fantasy is, I think, implicit in much of the obsessive dissection of Goldman's body. Her own experience of gendered and sexualised racialisation—as a working-class Jewish immigrant woman—may have been part of why Goldman sought to generalise racialised violence to include a broad range of positions, and why she was not always attentive to the differences among forms of violence and their particular histories. The violence of Goldman's representation in the press, however, highlights very clearly how one cluster of associations (here around femininity) can work effectively to diminish and undermine others (of race and class). It is clear in these complex representations of Goldman in the media that racialisation and its *gendered inflections* are key to fantasies of national insecurity and thus perhaps also key to exposing and challenging the same. An analysis of Goldman's experience of being "put into discourse" might shine a spotlight on ways in which other racialised and classed subjects also consistently fell (and fall still) outside of normative femininity, without needing to make those experiences of oppression equivalent. In methodological terms, considering Goldman's representation in the media in this way might also offer a model for comparative accounts of race and racism that presume neither sameness nor absolute distinction. It foregrounds the importance of looking at representation (narrative, visual, and political) in terms of the work that citation of a particular characteristic is doing at a given moment. It shifts the question from "What is race? Or class? Or gender?" to one that seeks to understand the work that taking up race, or here very strongly gender, does to other categories of experience and analysis in the maintenance of authority.

The U.S. government knew the threat that Goldman posed to national security very well indeed and would no doubt have approved of (and actively promoted) media efforts to portray her as devious, foreign, and violent. So too it would have approved of the same attempts to diminish that threat through a gendered discourse. In the fashioning of an emerging American identity, it was crucial that the "rugged individualism" of the nation be sutured to capitalist accumulation and exploitation of natural and human resources rather than resistance to authority or progressive utopianism (Day 2007).[36] This became increasingly important the more Goldman began to fashion herself *as an American*, appealing to the imagined universal values of this modern nation and positioning herself and anarchism itself as at the centre of a new patriotism with a more open set of relational values.[37] The U.S. government became more and more determined to find some way of neutralising the danger that Goldman (and other anarchists) represented as she became an increasingly popular orator, and in light of the wave of international—and particularly Russian—revolutionary fervour that threatened to spill over into America. Indeed, the director of the newly formed Federal Bureau of Investigation, J. Edgar Hoover, had Goldman followed everywhere, hoping to identify criminal behaviour at every turn (Silvestri 1969).[38] While Goldman travelled across the United States encouraging insurrection, government officials put equivalent energy into permanently curtailing the activities of Hoover's nemesis as part of national security. But multiple arrests and continuous police and media harassment were not enough to stem the rising tide of Goldman's influence. As the lust for war increased among those in authority, Goldman's (and other anarchists') threat to the order of things became more and more intolerable. In the end, classed, racialised, and gendered demonisation of Goldman fell short of requirements: she had to be cast out of citizenship altogether, exiled along with her lifelong comrade Alexander Berkman.[39]

In her piece "A Woman without a Country" (1909f), Goldman discusses the lengths federal agents went to in order to strip her of her American citizenship, and the vulnerability that women face when only ever considered citizens through marriage. Goldman was twice married to Jacob Kersner, and although he had died before Goldman's trial in 1917, his citizenship was posthumously revoked. This meant Goldman could be retrospectively positioned as without citizenship, as a current and prior alien whose claims to remain in or return to the United States could now be framed as baseless and dishonest (Goldman 1909f; Kennedy 1999, 51). The irony of having her own citizenship and rights revoked via a relationship that had long had no meaning for her was not lost on Goldman, who saw it as further evidence of the different positions of men and women in relation to nation and nationalism. Goldman faced a stark choice when finding herself without papers: remain undocumented and be prevented from crossing borders at every turn, or marry a legal citizen of a country that could facilitate her mobility. Goldman resolved her dilemma by marrying James Colton—a Welsh miner and a labour activist—in 1925, despite the compromise that this entailed. In what follows, I explore this decision in terms of both the shifts it indicates in Goldman's thinking about marriage and the strategic negotiation of power that moves her away from a revolutionary sensibility and more towards the "reformist" attitude that she otherwise deplored. But so too, I try to think through Goldman and Colton's attachment in terms of its importance for an empathetic theory of race, gender, and migration, deriving from their gentle reshaping of the kinship form.

Journalists were of course delighted with Goldman's apparent change of heart in marrying Colton, reading it as a pleasing defeat of her radicalism in the face of more resolute conservative gendered and national values (Frankel 1996, 912). Thus Gene Cohn writes for the *Stanford Advocate* under the title "Emma Goldman, Former Queen of Agitation, Found to Be Tamed" (1926), and the headline in the *Rochester Times-Union* gleefully confirms that "Emma Goldman, Marries" despite her not having "Changed Views" (1926), while "Emma's Love Views" from the NEA *Service* (1926) reports her hypocrisy with knowing relish. Cohn in particular takes great pleasure in outlining the different ways in which a post-Russia Goldman has mellowed, exemplified by her "staid acceptance of marriage" (1926). His article is accompanied by "before and after" images in which the postmarriage ones have a softer aspect, and Goldman is represented as more feminine in appearance: she is smaller in the second and sports a more formal, conservative hairstyle. Once again, femininity carries the burden of making or unmaking radicalism.[40] Goldman acknowledged that her decision to marry Colton needed some commentary. After all, it was she who had described marriage some twenty-eight years previously as the basis of private property and the cause of great "sorrow, misery, humiliation . . . tears and curses . . . agony and suffering" (1897a). At that time, Goldman understood marriage straightforwardly as the "private possession of one sex by the other" (1897a) and as giving men authority over women's bodies both legally and personally. Importantly, too, Goldman had spent considerable energy vilifying marriage not only as a corrupt institution that fosters conservatism and works against anarchist and socialist political interests but also as a self-evident "failure none but the very stupid will deny" (1911, 4). As I detailed at some length in chapter 1, those women who marry for protection are not only unwise but also duplicitous for Goldman, participating in "this parasitic institution" (11) in ways that degrade them and mark their own lack of courage and independence. Indeed, as we have seen, Goldman pours scorn on her weak-minded audience who attach to corrupt and old-fashioned values such as marriage, willing them to reject the necessity of dependency and challenging women to put their energies elsewhere or risk losing their souls. And in defending her decision to marry Colton, Goldman certainly continues to make a structural argument, highlighting that her critique of marriage as an institution does little to alter its power to curtail women's mobility (1926b) and making a distinction between condemnation of its form and acknowledgement of its necessity (*Emma Goldman Scrapbook* 1933).

Yet there appears to be a distinct shift in Goldman's representation of marriage as an institution at this time, one that positions her as investing rather heavily in the very public/private divide whose horrors she had earlier been at pains to expose or even ridicule. Thus in the wake of her marriage to Colton, Goldman is reported as insisting that the "union of two people is an entirely private affair" and that those who undertake it might well "go through with the process in the same spirit as one takes out a passport or secures a visa—to obtain breathing space and to protect the privacy of human personality" (NEA *Service* 1926). In a similar vein, Cohn cites Goldman as justifying her marriage in strategic terms: she continues to oppose marriage but "admits the custom protects one from interference and from peeping toms" (1926). Further, and with a more familiar fighting spirit, Cohn reports her as asserting that her marriage is of little consequence and is no indication of changed views on her part: "'Since the State pokes its nose into private lives it becomes more comfortable to make the gesture than not. The ceremony can never make any difference in two lives'" (1926). In effect, then, Goldman makes a double defence of her decision to marry Colton. On the one hand, it is a strategic choice that enables her to escape journalistic and governmental scrutiny; she is able to travel as a married woman and thus retain her independence and privacy in a range of ways. Yet on the other hand, and presumably in full knowledge of her own prior critique of women marrying tactically and for their own advantage, she presents the decision as justified "if for love and not merely maintenance" (*The Spectator* 1927). Marriage can be justified after all, then, if it remains about private affections (Goldman 1926b). In this dual framing of marriage as "private," then, Goldman attempts to reposition her decision as defensible when concerned to protect an intersubjective intimacy *from the state*, rather than as an institution developed *by the state* as part of the control of women within a nationalist structure. Already here, then, in this early defence, we see the two strands of thinking I am concerned with as central to Goldman's rethinking of the kinship form: a strategic framing to protect the vulnerable from state sanction, on the one hand; a centring of love and intimacy as the only legitimate basis for that protection, on the other.

In the second volume of *Living My Life* (1931c), Goldman has more space and autonomy to outline her thinking on her marriage outside of the journalistic fascination with the same. She notes with amusement that "the papers were lurid with the news that romance still lived in this crassly materialistic world: Emma Goldman and James Colton, a southern Welsh miner, had rediscovered their mutual affection after twenty-five years and had joined their lives in matrimony. The immigration authorities were reported to have stated that there was no intention of interfering with my presence in Canada as long as I 'did not advocate bombs'" (1931c, 987). Here Goldman takes a more straightforwardly ironic tone, situating her sudden and resurgent "romance" as an antidote to capitalist materialism. Earlier in her text, Goldman cites the experience of other radicals, such as Rosa Luxemburg, who married while in exile to facilitate their mobility, and she notes her new amenability to the possibility of marriage "in order to gain a foothold now in some corner of the world" (957). Thus she firmly situates her union as a strategic manipulation of marriage as an institution that requires a *performance of romance* not rooted in the reality of her relationship to Colton. Yet the personal nature of Goldman's affection for Colton is very much present in these reflections, as she notes that he is "sixty-five" and "still compelled to slave in the mines for his daily bread" (974), and that she "married the old rebel James Colton" to do as most British people do, namely, to facilitate leaving to "escape their country's climate" (981). Goldman only ever spoke gently and with fondness for Colton: he was a long-standing friend whose well-being she was invested in and whose presence in the world she treasured. Perhaps, after all, it is not so far-fetched to think of this in terms of "mutual affection" or "romance," in light of Goldman's views on the expansiveness of both concepts. Could Goldman's marriage for citizenship purposes be part of, rather than only opposed to, her understanding of sexual freedom as part of international solidarity?

In their correspondence, Goldman and Colton exchange letters and cards that demonstrate an attachment that goes well beyond political expediency. Certainly, part of their correspondence includes Goldman's pragmatic request for "a letter saying you do not object to my going [to Canada], I may need that at the boarder [sic]" (June 22, 1926), and there is no sense that they had a sexually intimate relationship at any point (and Goldman would not have been coy about this). But so too Goldman's letters to Colton give voice to their mutual care and concern for each other's emotional and physical health, and their plots and plans for her to come and give lectures in support of the striking miners in South Wales (November 15, 1915). In return, Colton gives sympathy and support when Goldman most needs it. In several letters to Colton, Goldman remarks on his sickness and her hopes for his speedy recovery, as well as revealing her own struggles with ill health. In 1925, for example, Goldman writes encouragingly to Colton: "I am so glad you are better, dear Jim. I hope you will keep fit from now on. The winter must be more trying in your work than the summer. Take care of yourself, dear friend" (November 4, 1925), and in 1932, she replies to a letter from him, remarking: "I received your note saying you had been ill, I meant to write to you—but I have been racing from town to town, speaking every night. I arrived here too ill to stand on my feet, but pulled through three meetings, then I was forced to take to my bed" (March 1, 1932). Over their more than ten years of correspondence, until Colton's death in 1936, the friends talk candidly of their weakness and illness in the face of the grueling demands of mining and anarchist organising, and yet also of the importance of holding fast to their shared ideals. "It is a slow grind, and so discouraging," Goldman writes in November 1925, "I don't know. I cling to hope, that is all one can do" (November 4, 1925). Goldman and Colton have barely two pennies to rub together, but they continue to believe in the solidarity of the working poor to "pitch together" to support those even less fortunate than they are (November 4, 1925). Most sweetly, Goldman establishes a wedding anniversary tradition of sending Colton one pound so that he can take a day away from the toil of work each year. In this gesture, and in the warmth of her writing, Goldman marks her relationship to Colton as precious. "My dear Jim," she writes to him from St. Tropez:

> Forgive my slackness in replying to your dear letter. . . . I have as a matter of fact cut down on my letters. I have asked my friends to be satisfied with postcards for a while. But it is different with you my dear comrade. . . . Another five days and it will be a year that you have taken the anxiety from me as to where I might find some safety. I shall always remember that dear friend. I want you to have a little holiday on the 27th especially as it falls on a Sunday. For that I enclose a pound. I wish I could make it a hundred times as much. (June 22, 1926)

Interestingly, this is the same letter in which Goldman asks Colton to write an endorsement to facilitate her border crossing into Canada, further framing the request through care and thoughtfulness, as well as necessity.

In their last, and particularly poignant, exchange, Colton writes of his sorrow on hearing of Berkman's death. "My Dear Dear Emmy," he says, "I am writing this from a very sick bed where I have been confined over 4 weeks" (August? 1936). Colton's letter is hard to read and covered with ink pools where he has not been able to move the pen fast enough across the page, yet he has been compelled to write because his suffering is "nothing like what grieving [unclear] is and I hasten to extend to you my deepest sympathy . . . in your awful predicament to loose [sic] such a brave comrade as Alexander Berkman." Colton notes that "these few lines have taken me some trouble" and that family are on their way to see him; he dies soon afterwards. He never receives the letter that Goldman sends him in reply, which once again includes one pound: this time she has sent it to help with what she hopes will be his swift recovery. She writes:

> Jimmy Dear . . . It makes me most unhappy that I cannot do more for you in your present illness. But the long illness of my old pal and the expense of laying him to rest has completely sapped me out. My dear, my dear it is cruel to have worked for an ideal all ones [sic] life only to be ill and helpless in our old age, and so frightfully poor. My heart goes out to you my dear staunch comrade. But what is sympathy and solidarity when we can do nothing to make life easier for our comrades. (August 5, 1936)

In this last heartbreaking and heartbroken letter to her dear friend, Goldman tells him exactly how she now feels without Berkman to share her life: "There is nothing I can say about myself. The bottom has been knocked out from under me with the untimely end of our great and wonderful comrade. It is no small battle to go on living without him. Everything seems empty and futile. But will have to continue the struggle for Sasha and myself" (August 5, 1936). Even in the midst of such desperation, Goldman goes on to express her disappointment in English radicals and the "light in the present European darkness" of "the heroic struggle of the workers in Spain" (August 5, 1936). Soon after, Goldman began working as international advocate for the Confederation Nacional de Trabajo (Federation of Spanish Anarcho-Syndicalist Unions) as part of her support for the anarchist movement during the Spanish Civil War; images from these last years show sorrow etched deep into her face (Porter 1983, photo inserts between 178 and 179).

These few surviving letters between Goldman and Colton clearly indicate that their marriage was one that was undertaken for strategic reasons: Goldman needed British citizenship in order to access the mobility necessary for her to advocate for international revolution. The particular form that it took was compromised and necessitated by circumstances rather than being freely chosen, that much is true. Yet their friendship is also embedded in shared political contexts and networks of association, and the circumstances of its perpetuation produce a dynamic that subverts its expediency. We may recall Ferguson's (2011b) argument that Goldman did not sufficiently explore the political value of reform, resting in her conviction that all social transformation should and would involve overturning existing institutions and political structures. For Ferguson, this is a missed opportunity for Goldman, preventing her from developing empathy for black American experience of racism and from creating links of real solidarity with any cause that she saw as flawed in that rather harsh light. Yet here, in her relationship with Colton, Goldman is able to strengthen her understanding of the importance of cross-border intimacy from *within* a loathed institution. One might even say that her capacity to connect with Colton relied upon rather than subverted the strategic manipulation of the current system of marriage. She would not have sent the annual gift of memory and thanks were they not married; and she might not have entrusted Colton with the depth of her pain and grief had they not established their bond through this complicity. Even through such a tentative overreading, I want to suggest that this relationship could have given Goldman a glimpse of the ways in which compromise can sometimes deepen rather than only ever weaken political and personal attachment, raising important questions about the best ways of ensuring lasting solidarity in a world bent on self-destruction. The narrative and affect of Goldman's relationship to Colton was never simply a shadow relationship, a sham, but one resonant with the prefigurative potential of international affection and connection that Goldman wanted to bring about in the future.

Goldman and Colton's relationship was one based in genuine care and respect. They attempted as best they could to support one another in times of trouble: marrying to enable mobility; speaking to raise money and provide support; establishing traditions to provide brief respite from poverty and exploitation; and opening up a space for the other to express his or her pain, grief, and continued belief in human solidarity. While theirs was not a romantic relationship in any traditional sense, to represent their friendship as anything other than intimate would be a great injustice to its sweetness. We know of course that Goldman valued connections to others well beyond her sexual relationships with them, as her abiding loyalty towards Berkman attests. And we know further that that she grasped sexual freedom as an expansive practice to challenge limited understandings of kinship as a prop of capitalism and nationalism. As discussed earlier, Goldman saw a future for kinship based in solidarity beyond "race as nation," her understanding of kinship including kin as well as strangers. Here, Goldman extends this to foreground empathy and loyalty as central to this understanding of universal kinship. In this reading of her politics and of their exchange of letters, Goldman's marriage to Colton might best be thought of as part of further extension of a transnational vision of kinship from within the constraints and proximities of marriage, rather than only in opposition to them.

Throughout this chapter, I have been concerned with the different ways in which Goldman explores questions of race and internationalism in her life and work. While privileging class hierarchy over racism as a structuring form of authority in her own analysis, she is nevertheless concerned to think through the different forms of violence and oppression black people faced. While her ambivalence about race results in slips, deflections, and metaphorisations that prevent Goldman giving racism a distinct history and theorising specific instances of oppression from that perspective, Goldman was also a firm advocate of an inclusive freedom beyond difference. While at points this presents problems for her, in that she takes up blunt comparisons that mitigate a full analysis of racism, she remains a lifelong advocate of international solidarity beyond the confines of nation and "race" in its biologically determinant form. Goldman's concerns with women's reproductive role as part of how capitalism and militarism maintain themselves return us to the importance of gender in securing violence and the fantasy of national security. Further, and most important perhaps, her commitment to an expanded understanding of race—one not tethered to nation or kinship and not belonging to particular identities—emerges as a central part of Goldman's visionary sexual politics.

In contemporary Europe, the Left remains baffled as to how it is that racism comes to carry such a heavy compensatory burden in a context of generational unemployment and the crushing disappointments of austerity. Its response either accepts the terms of that racism and anti-immigrant feeling or refuses its logic as simply misguided. Following Goldman, we might hazard that part of what is happening is the attachment to the next level or scale of kinship in light of changing family fortunes. Racism based in race identifications provides solace in the face of both the withdrawal of work and the collapse of welfare, and in the face of attachments to immediate kin (or local context) failing to mediate the worst effects of disenfranchisement. In part this account draws on the work of Lauren Berlant (2007, 2011), whose understanding of "cruel optimism" suggests that we invest more heavily in those structures of intimate attachment that do us the most harm in this contemporary economic and political climate. Berlant is extremely helpful in this analysis, but perhaps Goldman sheds more light on the ways in which, when the cruelty of those optimisms based in immediate attachment also fail (when those in power have no interest in keeping everyone on board with the neoliberal project, for example), then "race" affiliations as the basis for kinship come into their own. Racism, in this account, might be a form of displaced investment in kinship; nationalism, in this account, might actually be the necessary affective response to the real threat of localised obliteration. Both may be essential to the endurance of a white sense of self in the face of generational disappointment. Drawing on Berlant on intimacy and late capitalist attachment, then, and assuming (as I do) that Gilroy (2004) is certainly right that "postcolonial melancholia" allows for a white nostalgia about past European "greatness" whose violence has yet to be mourned, the conditions for this racist nationalism are firmly in place. Following Goldman is helpful both for making sense of how and why this happens and also for providing a sketch of ways that we need to challenge "race" itself as a "melancholic fetish" underwriting nationalism. Goldman's proposition of human solidarity in an expanded understanding of kinship recentres the relationship between sexual politics and antiracist politics in ways that are both uncomfortable and provocative. But it is only by delving into Goldman's ambivalence around race and racism that we will be able to grasp hold of the significance of a refashioned intimacy as Goldman's ambivalent gift.

three · Sexual Politics and Sexual Freedom

PROPOSING SEXUAL FREEDOM

For Emma Goldman, control of women's reproduction is absolutely central to the maintenance of capitalism, militarism, and religious authoritarianism. As I have been charting in this book thus far, Goldman theorises the problems of femininity and existing kinship structures as crucial to her materialist analysis of power. For Goldman, women's bodies and their overassociation with the private realm underwrite unequal divisions of labour; women work physically and emotionally in that realm for free and are thus the most fully exploited of labourers. Women's position provides an original template for hierarchy among human beings—children learn authority within the family— and gives space for men to enter the workplace as exploiters or exploited. And further, while in this materialist analysis woman's labour in the home is not directly mined for profit, her subordination is a core component of the structure of economic production. So too, and here Goldman's analysis is at its fullest, we might think of women's reproduction in terms of the production of raw materials for capitalism and for militarism. A new generation of workers and soldiers requires that women continue to perform their reproductive labour; indeed, if they did not, the wheels of the capitalist and militarist machine would grind to a squealing halt. Thus, Goldman theorises the sexual division of labour not simply as a prior condition for production and full oppression under capitalism but *as labour* in and of itself. Women's reproductive and affective labour meets the definition of both exploitation and alienation; a woman's relationship to her own life and the children she produces can never be fully real and filled with joy until this process is taken back into her own hands. This is, as we have seen, the substance of Goldman's argument concerning birth control: that the relationship between mother and child depends on her ability to make a free choice and to limit the number of children that she has. And, as we have also seen through her scathing critiques of femininity, the very means through which a woman maintains her position in the private sphere are rooted in affective falsehood. Bourgeois femininity in itself is an affective relationship to men governed by greed and duplicity, rather than generosity and honesty, and one that must be wholly rejected if the conditions of women's oppression are to be transformed.

In this sequence of compelling arguments, Goldman links birth control issues, prostitution, and wholesale destruction of the poor in wartime (among other forms of violence and degradation) precisely through her foregrounding of women's experience of reproductive control and affective alienation within capitalism. Starting from this analysis of the ills of femininity, Goldman develops her passionate arguments for the social and political—as well as intersubjective—significance of challenging sexual oppression, and of claiming love as the site of real value and freedom. For Goldman, returning "sex" to the hands of its most exploited workers—women—will yield more than individual and relational pleasures, though it will also most certainly do that. It will allow for the expansion of love as a site of creative and progressive possibility and will provide a model for collective process and solidarity. If we recall Goldman's argument about *universal kinship* in her essay "The Passing of the Family" (between 1927 and 1930), the radical possibilities of intimate attachments were framed as limitless, but rooted in proximity. Refusing the strictures of reproductive constraint offers new ways of engaging others and importantly propels us beyond the deadening nationalism of this archaic form. For Goldman, then, the capacity of sexual freedom to disrupt power relations reaches well beyond the family and relationships between men and women. It offers an embodied, heartfelt way of investing in international solidarity over the false promises of attachments derived from classed and raced interests and hierarchies. Not surprisingly, then, for Goldman sexual freedom is a right that all human beings have and a "legitimate goal of the class struggle" (Snitow, Stansell, and Thompson 1983, 18); in Goldman's eyes, the demand for that right should be at the heart of any movement for social transformation.

Goldman's insights here locate her firmly within her own context, since a range of men and women were making similar arguments about the importance of transformed relationships between men and women as part of revolutionary endeavour. But so too, Goldman's fervent belief in sexual freedom's capacities to transform more than their immediate sphere echoes across time to resonate with a range of more contemporary feminist and queer accounts of the same set of interlocking problems. Marxist feminists, radical feminists, and lesbian and gay and queer theorists have all told a rich, compelling story of the relationship between sexuality and capitalism. For all these theorists, sexual and gendered norms and controls harness women and minorities to a damaging yoke of affective duty. And, as they have made plain, albeit in different ways, capitalism and nationalism are dependent on reproductive as well as productive labour. So too such approaches have grappled, and continue to grapple, with the importance of a renewed sexual politics from below and explored the extent to which sexual and gendered meanings might be resignified outside of deadening capitalism and nationalist modes. Writers as varied as radical feminist Shulamith Firestone (1970), Marxist feminist Gayle Rubin (1975, 1984), queer feminist theorist Judith Butler (1997, 2008), and postcolonial feminist scholar Jasbir K. Puar (2007) have all engaged the damage done by existing models of kinship and reproduction. And so too they have each—in various ways that I will come back to—explored the limits of claiming an "innocent" sexual freedom or identity as a sustainable, transformative alternative to those models. Indeed, perhaps one of the central ironies within a history of sexual politics in its dominant rights form is its tethering to fantasies of progress in a context of increasing "national security" and demonisation of the Islamic, black, and/or migrant Other.

Leticia Sabsay (2016) insists that contemporary queer theorists would do well to look beyond liberal, rights-based models in order to articulate and inhabit an expansive sexual freedom. For Sabsay, the problem of individual rights or identity politics is that they limit the frames through which we might imagine that freedom, and further, that they sidestep interrogation of the ways in which Western fantasies of democratic freedom rely on sexual regulation (including in identity forms) at their dubious heart (2016, xx). Sabsay's approach resonates back to Goldman's, whose work and life fundamentally resisted the tethering of desire and freedom to identity or rights. While supportive of the individual right to freedom from state interference or privatised violence, Goldman would not have supported the political development of a rights agenda as a solution to sexual oppression. Not only does such an understanding limit the potential for engaging others, but it tends to the kind of single-issue politics Goldman balked at. But Goldman's embrace of sexual freedom as both means and expression of anarchist utopia (see L. Davis 2011) also offers a radical challenge to the ways in which we tell the story of sexuality and capitalism in the first place. As I explore more fully in the rest of this chapter, Goldman's propositions for sexual freedom force us not only to reconsider its role in the history of Left politics and political economy but also to narrate the history of sexuality as something other than an increase of rights or the inevitable corruptions of identity. Her energetic insistence on sexual freedom as prefigurative method rather than as singular end point or aim resonates results in contradictory claims about the capacities of desire to overcome capitalist repression in ways that remind me of later approaches such as Herbert Marcuse's.[1] While contemporary theorists of sexuality and capitalism tend to paint a picture of progress or loss, of improved recognition or heightened co-optation, of playful transformation or ongoing commodification, the question of *what has happened* to sexuality in the last 150 years remains largely agreed upon.[2] We might think about increased freedom for sexual minorities or the growing significance of sexual identity in late capitalism in different ways (as having good or bad effects, or both), but that history is nevertheless understood to be a shared one: critiqued and lamented, certainly; framed as contested in its own right, rarely. Returning to Goldman's interrogations of sexuality as a form of labour that stultifies love delivers us into a scene of struggle over these meanings and relationships during the very period that identity and sex become thought together.[3]

Perhaps even more important, Goldman's own struggles to articulate sexual freedom and the contradictory relationship to that freedom that punctuated her own life raise questions about the nature of sexual storytelling itself. Goldman's enthusiasm for sexual freedom always threatens to be excessive: too linked to a spiritual understanding of nature for the contemporary tastes of feminist critics, for example; and while supporting homosexual rights to self-determination as we would expect, Goldman remained ambivalent in how far she was prepared to embrace homosexuality as part of a transformative sexual methodology. To return to a series of historiographic questions raised in the introduction to this book, this chapter explores how we tell a story of sexual politics that recognises the importance of a history of sexual marginality but does not slip into a reification of that marginality. How might we represent (or at least skirt around the edges of) Goldman's desiring ambivalence when we are unlikely to find very much evidence of its contested nature in the pages of the sexual archive? How, in other words, might we bring into knowledge those pieces of history that have been quite actively hidden from the dominant gaze, that have been organised through a public/private divide the archive is bound to reproduce.[4] In this chapter more than any other, then, I turn to the stories we tell about sexual freedom and how best to achieve it. By "we" here I mean Goldman's own writings and experiments, the feminist and queer critical archive concerned with Goldman's propositions, and the theoretical and political archive that engages questions of sexual progress and loss. And here too, I turn to the *imaginative archive* more fully than I have done thus far in this project in order to grapple with ways of representing a complex, ambivalent sexual history without losing the incisive capacities of a minority standpoint. The structure of this chapter is somewhat different from prior chapters, in that I engage the critical and theoretical archives as I explore three different aspects of Goldman's own reflections. Firstly, I continue my discussion of Goldman's intervention on the question of women's reproductive labour *as labour* as well as her claiming of sexual freedom as revolutionary. I use Goldman's subjective archive here as a way of engaging the theoretical archive that continues to keep sexuality distinct from other aspects of economic life. Following Nancy Fraser in the 1990s, debates continue to position sexuality as cultural rather than economic, even while it may (or may not) be thought of in materialist terms. This opposition has of course been consistently contested, but in that most writers also continue to think about sexuality in terms of identity or rights, the question of "how far homosexual recognition has come" remains at the centre of these debates. For Goldman, of course, women's reproductive imperatives as well as homosexual oppression are signs of the horror of kinship contracts, but her vision of sexual freedom is one with the unknown and unknowable nature of sexual connection at its heart. This intervention, I will suggest, allows for an approach that brings feminist and queer theorising about the nature of sexual politics together and also opens up a sense of the sexual history we are presumed to have inherited.

Secondly, I explore Goldman's understanding of the importance of "sexual nature" in more depth, concentrating on her defense of prostitution in *The White Slave Traffic* (1909e), her sexually charged letters to Ben Reitman (her lover and tour manager while in America), and her conflicted accounts of the significance of motherhood for women. Goldman's arguments about sexual freedom from reproduction and repression have delighted and dismayed writers in the feminist critical archive. On the one hand, her passion and commitment to a new form fit well with a more recent feminist insistence on the importance of sexual politics as central to broader social and political transformation; the feminist axiom "the personal is political" could easily have been Goldman's. But Goldman's claiming of sexual drives as natural and opposite-sex passion as elemental or even spiritual produces a profound discomfort in those same critics. Yet as I explore here, this critical anxiety produces and is based on a misreading of what it is that Goldman intends by her focus on "nature." Once again, I am particularly interested in the temporal nature of Goldman's interventions. How does her prefigurative understanding of nature—as always to come and always a process of ongoing struggle—challenge more contemporary expectations that claiming "nature" invariably falls into damned essentialist determinism or racist or sexist biologism.

Finally, I chart Goldman's unsettled relationship to homosexuality in what remains of her scant writings on the subject. Goldman was exploring questions of sexual freedom at the same time that "homosexuality" as an available category was becoming more established. While Goldman remained resolute in her public defence of homosexual creativity as well as the right to freedom from persecution (in her support of Oscar Wilde, for example), we know that she was also profoundly ambivalent about homosexuality. On the one hand, she did of course refuse any single-issue politics on anarchist principle; on the other, her distaste for homosexuals is revealed at points as a *distinct difference* in her treatment of the range of possible sexual freedoms central to revolution. Crucially, what we also know about Goldman is that she had intense, desiring, intimate relationships with other women, and in particular with Almeda Sperry, her anarchist activist comrade, who wrote her more than sixty love letters between 1911 and 1912. Although we do not have Goldman's replies, the content and nature of Sperry's missives make clear that this was a sexual relationship, albeit one doomed from its inception. How do we make sense of these competing relationships to homosexuality in the Goldman archive? Is there a way of being able to account for her ambivalence without wanting to resolve it "one way" or "the other" as though we could finally know how she really felt or rescue her from her desiring struggles?

The question of methodology is also central to the development of my arguments about sexual politics in this chapter, as it was in the previous two. In arguing against a progressive (utopian or dystopian) view of the history of sexuality and capitalism's entanglements, I am advocating an approach that reads for ambivalence both in the Goldman archive and also in historical and contemporary accounts of that relationship. This perspective is less about a promotion of radical discontinuity between past and present as such, but rather one that starts from an assumption that at any given moment more than one history of sexual meaning is likely to be in play. The task is thus genealogical in the sense that I am interested in the different histories that pertain to Goldman's engagement with sexual politics—both capitalist and revolutionary—and to our own (Foucault 1972, 1980). This Foucauldian approach may risk overinvesting in the contradictions that mark sexual politics instead of the dominant strands that endure, but that risk seems appropriate to the task. I am not, for example, suggesting that a story of ambivalence is a more real alternative history to the progressive or dystopian ones I want to trouble, but proposing such stories as interruptive of historical and contemporary certainties about the relationship between sexuality and capitalism (and the revolutionary attempt to transform it) in the first place. The task is thus a politically motivated one that starts from an interest in what is left out of the frame, and how to think from the (nonidentitarian) margins in the spirit of Goldman's own contradictory, anarchist interventions. In this sense, I am in agreement with Jenny Alexander's (2011) insistence that consideration of *Prison Memoirs of an Anarchist* (1912), by Goldman's comrade Alexander Berkman, with its sweetly tentative explorations of passionate attachments to other prisoners, would not only alter who we think is included in a history of homosexuality but also challenge how we conceive of sexuality and its role in the social world more generally.[5]

Much as we may wish we could, we cannot fill the gaps in the archive with the straightforward truth of sexual freedom. Indeed, the desire to do so may itself constitute a kind of violence that seeks to plaster over the cracks of meaning and struggle that typify how sexuality is lived as contradiction. To seek to fill the gaps with a recognisable image of present identity is, for Martha Vicinus (1994) and Laura Doan (2013), an example of wish fulfilment: a fantasy that we can travel across time to find our resemblance in the past, and have our hearts healed by finding individuals and relationships that reassure us we do not have to make everything anew. And yet of course that yearning to fill the noisy absence of recognition is, as I discussed at the outset of this project, the contradictory impulse that inaugurates the possibility of telling stories about another sexual past at all. With this sensibility in mind, then, I turn in the final section of this chapter to the seductive and sexually explicit letters sent from Sperry to Goldman, in which Sperry graphically depicts her own and their shared sexual pleasure. How can we read sexual history through a one-sided correspondence? How might we negotiate the tension between a necessary yearning to discover or recover Goldman's replies, on the one hand, and the knowledge that they were always likely to have been lost or destroyed, a tension I want to claim is a central part of the history of sexual politics? The letters themselves chart a relationship of common politics and uneven passions, reference Goldman as an imagined and real interlocutor, and demonstrate the fictional nature of all sexual history in their intense representations of longing, pride, desire, and desperation. And as I read them, I am drawn into a conversation that I observe, take sides in, and even fabricate (along with Sperry). One might say, then, that Goldman does in fact linger within and between the lines, through references to her letters that we do not have but that were clearly sent, through Sperry's responses to the real and imagined Goldman, and through a reader's own fictional investment in their relationship. Reading these letters thus highlights for me the inevitable complicity of the outsider in delving into sexual politics, and I explore ways of writing that knowledge of a wholly partial ignorance back into the frame.

SEXUAL FREEDOM BEYOND CAPITALISM

Goldman considered the capitalist system to be anathema to real sexual freedom. Capitalism tethers sex to profit, creating the bankrupt institution of marriage and condemning women to routine reproduction for capitalist ends. This system ties women to men and exploits their labour both by not compensating them for it and by claiming the fruits of that sexual labour—children—as fodder for the factory or battlefield. Children of working-class women are disposable, their lives only of value in terms of other people's profit and profiteering (1913, 1916c). As Linnie Blake notes of Goldman, she believed that the "state's transmutation of sensual relations . . . echoed the market economy's transformations of social relations into lack-based commodities" (1997, 48). Marriage and the relentlessness of reproductive sexual labour keep women subordinate to men as a class, we might say, but also keep them tethered to particular men. They do not have property in their own person, are not in control of their labour, and do not reap any rewards for their physically demanding work. This combination of general oppression as women and particular oppression within marriage makes resistance exceptionally difficult (Goldman 1911), since they face both destitution and loss of their already compromised status *as women*. This is particularly the case for women who turn to prostitution, but in Goldman's view the anxiety about loss of dubious feminine privileges runs deep and is a central part of how women come to invest in their own oppression. And this is of course why she insists that women's emancipation can only come from within. For Goldman, and as discussed more fully in chapter 1, such oppression is an intolerable ill in its own right (1897a, 1931b), making countless women's (and men's) lives deeply unpleasant. It pits them against one another and creates inward-looking, miserable households that cannot see beyond their noses. The control of women's sexual labour, then, runs directly counter to conditions that enable solidarity: for Goldman, as we have seen, the "passing of the family" (between 1927 and 1930) is a necessary condition for revolution.

Goldman is particularly disgusted by the sexual servitude of women because of her embrace of love as the greatest source of joy and connection to others. The horror of women's lack of sexual autonomy—particularly, but not only, with respect to reproduction—lies in the reduction of their life force and passion to mechanistic repetition. The moral and economic strictures on sexual association are, for Goldman, veritable "crime[s] against humanity," binding "love as an infinite source of energy, passion, and strength, to the state and capitalist economy" (1908b, 1). At an intersubjective as well as structural level, then, what makes women's sexual servitude particularly unpleasant is the way in which it forces women (and men) to invest in the *appearance* of desire, its superficial trappings and hollow discourse. Instead, women (and men) should be free to experience the full force of love's beauty.[6] Goldman is clear what needs to happen in order to challenge the reduced state of things. A woman must refuse her role as a sexual labourer, as a subordinate sexual drudge, and claim her birthright—sexual freedom—instead; only then will she be able to "[assert] herself as a personality and not as a sex commodity" (1914d, 27). The sexual revolution will come from passion rather than asceticism, from embracing pleasure rather than reducing it to its empty bourgeois form. In this respect, Goldman seizes upon *passion* as a revolutionary methodology, a revaluation of that which lies outside of capitalist co-optation of human attachment. In Goldman's eyes, such an approach not only will provide a deep challenge to the exploitation of human resources necessary for nationalism and militarism as well as capitalism (1908b) but also will transform human relationships at the deepest level (1934?).

Goldman was not alone in her privileging of sexual freedom as revolutionary but joined a host of contemporaries concerned to link changing gendered and sexual possibilities to the rising tide of revolutionary fervour in the early twentieth century. Thus, for Ellen Dubois and Linda Gordon, Goldman formed part of a growing community of women—Crystal Eastman, Elizabeth Gurley Flynn, Louise Bryant, and Margaret Sanger among them—who "asserted a woman's right to be sexual. They slept with men without marrying. They took multiple lovers. They became single mothers" (1983, 18). And Ginger Frost notes that for socialists, the argument that "the capitalist system required monogamy in order to secure male property rights" was ubiquitous, as was the belief that "under communism, such property in women would no longer be necessary" (2009, 76). This was a time of experimentation, of exhilaration at the radical political and personal opportunities opened up by refusing authoritarian sexual morality.[7] In both her critique of the dominant socialist and anarchist perceptions that women should wait until after the revolution for their liberation, and her articulation of sexual freedom as a real and necessary alternative to the family form, Goldman can be thought of as participating in the exciting and messy sexual politics that typified her era. Resolutely nonidentitarian, always linked to a radical understanding of sexuality's capacity to disrupt capitalism, anarchist and socialist sexual freedom was positioned as a catalyst to a utopian but unknowable future (Greenway 2011). As Jamie Heckert and Richard Cleminson suggest, the widespread exploration of different models of sexuality among American radicals in the early twentieth century should be understood less as a precursor to a late twentieth-century sexual tolerance and more as part of an alternative sexual history that had (and has) yet to be told (2011b, 2–4). The centrality of sexual freedom to radical anarchist and socialist experiments in utopian living was not uniformly welcomed, of course. Dell Floyd's disparaging comment is not unusual, for example: he quips that anarchists have "left the industrial field more and more and have entered into other kinds of propaganda. They have especially 'gone in for kissing games'" (1913, 58–59).

Acknowledging that "it took grit, bravado, and ingenuity for a young woman to fashion a life different from her mother's" (2000, xiii), Christine Stansell remains cautious in her celebration of changing sexual roles for women in the American bohemian context she explores. For Stansell, sexual freedom confirmed a political "faith in women's power to undo sexual oppression by changing themselves" (2000, xii) but also made women vulnerable to exploitation, social ostracism, and personal hurt (see also Frost 2009). And, indeed, while Goldman remained optimistic about the possibilities of sexual freedom throughout her lifetime, she was just as consistently brought up against its most brutal limits in her own relationships. Yet for Goldman, it is precisely the connection between sexual freedom and personal turmoil that makes the former so valuable in political terms. Passion, as Laurence Davis (2014) has also noted in the context of anarchist utopianism, has the capacity to take you somewhere you did not expect, and thus sexual feeling constitutes a kind of knowledge of the future that otherwise remains opaque.[8] The pleasures and traumas of connecting to others in hitherto unexplored ways, the sheer unpredictability of sexual freedom, are exactly its value for Goldman.

I want now to turn to considering the theoretical archive that is engaged with similar questions to Goldman about the relationship between sexuality and revolution. Rosemary Hennessy is a key thinker in this regard and has long puzzled over the question of why it is that there is such a long and "well-established convention of segregating the history of sexuality from the history of capitalism" (2000, 54).[9] Hennessy notes quite rightly that even for those Marxist and socialist theorists who do consider the "sexual division of labour" important to understanding production (41), it is still the latter realm that remains privileged. The presumption is that they are separate spheres (that the public/private divide really does describe two different arenas of experience) and that change in relations of production will bring about the collapse of hierarchy in the sexual sphere. For Hennessy, as for Goldman, there is a long tradition of dismissing the very idea that the sexual division of labour might actually *inaugurate* other divisions of labour. And further, part of the maintenance of this hierarchical distinction of spheres is performative; it is brought about through repeated raised eyebrows or rolled eyes at an insistence of their mutually reinforcing relevance (54). For Andrew Parker (1993)—a most insightful writer on these connections—that denial points firmly to the need to hold apart sex and labour, to ensure that men's relationships with one another within (and as commentators upon) the productive realm remain resolutely heterosexual.[10] For Parker, it is not only the modern gendered division of labour that is secured through men's anxieties about their relationships with one another but also the relationship between "serious" and "frivolous" work: thus neither theatrical labour nor sex work qualifies as "production," ostensibly because no material goods are produced. But as Parker highlights, that very definition of "production" already has "sex" in mind in a range of ways, linking it to "culture" and leisure in order not to have to account for its more fundamental role. Production is thus sutured to the making of goods and their subsequent circulation as objects of exchange from the outset, rather than to what we call "social reproduction." The point here is that the terms are a discursive and material construction, rather than an inevitability, and one that already has heteronormativity in mind. Parker's analysis is helpful, I think, not only in challenging how we conceive of the origins of materialist analysis but also in providing a history of the association of homosexuality with superficiality, theatricality, and promiscuity as well as with femininity and what we now call "affective labour" (Hardt 1999). For Parker and Hennessy, as for Goldman before them, we have a doubled problem then: the Marxist analysis of relations of production itself and the critical take-up of Marxism by contemporary critics who reproduce its own displacement of sexual and creative labour in their hyperbolic performances of heterosexual masculinity.[11] Interestingly, Goldman was not only concerned to theorise women's reproductive labour and the hypocrisies of condemnations of prostitution but also engaged with fiction and theatre; for Parker these are interlinked realms that form soft shadows around the bright lights of production framed through heteronormative denial.

Of course, since Marxist feminists entered the critical and political scene, there have been a range of ways in which the relationship between sexuality and capitalism has been more attentively theorised. Thinkers in this broad tradition highlight not just the relationship between production and reproduction but importantly the nature of that separation as a hierarchical one in which the "sexual division of labour" is actively obscured (Hochschild 1989). In ways explicitly or implicitly reminiscent of Goldman, Marxist feminists provide an account of the relationship between kinship and the capitalist economy, insisting that not to pay attention to sexual labour reinforces masculine production as more exploitative and thus resistance in the workplace as self-evidently more challenging to capitalist structure and function. In her recent book *The Problem with Work* (2011), Kathi Weeks questions the nature and acceptance of "work" itself within late capitalism, as well as its gendered nature. For Weeks, the privileging of the narrow field of "production" in all our lives haunts the capacity of the Left to resist contemporary capitalism. This tendency to elide women's conditions of oppression was discussed in chapter 1 as part of how the hierarchy of revolutionary urgency was maintained among anarchist thinkers. What anarchism was unable to face directly, it seems, was the importance of unrecognised caring (rather than simply reproductive) labour not just for capitalism to tick along uninterrupted but also for creating conditions of leisure for political association and revolutionary fermentation *among men*. To combine Goldman with Parker and Eve Sedgwick (1985), then, we might say that the sidelining of the sexual division of labour is one way in which the public sphere remains not only a world of men but also a homosocial world. For Sedgwick, indeed, it is a heterosexual/homosexual divide that inaugurates the public/private divide (more even than a male/female one), since this is governed by ambivalent secrecy and partial visibility: the "epistemology of the closet" (1990), as she later famously termed it. Desire between men, for Sedgwick, is both denied and essential, and it is that ambivalence that requires the naturalisation of women's labour, on the one hand, and the demonisation of same-sex desire, on the other.

Goldman's proposition of sexual freedom as the solution to the production/reproduction divide and its impact on women also resonates with feminist, lesbian and gay, and queer theory. If, as Goldman suggested, kinship structures and reproductive sexuality are a fundamental part of the fabric of capitalism and militarism, then nonreproductive but also importantly nonheterosexual expressions of desire must surely be located outside of those structures. We might think, for example, of radical feminist Shulamith Firestone, who makes a similar set of moves to Goldman in her extraordinary book *The Dialectic of Sex* (1970). Firestone squarely identifies reproductive sexuality as the central problem for women and insists that there will be no "feminist revolution" (the book's subtitle) until sexual pleasure and reproduction are finally uncoupled. A revolutionary sexual politics for Firestone must include freeing bodies themselves from the tyrannies of sex and blunt nature, and so for her that revolution will rely on new reproductive technologies (the extent of whose influence she could only have guessed at in 1970). For Goldman too, of course, birth control was key to women's freedom, although the nature of reproductive technology was rather more rudimentary in her time. For the optimistic Firestone, separating reproduction and sexual pleasure will allow women to become men's equals, but while Goldman would certainly have approved of the sentiment, she would also have been suspicious of any solution that turns away from women's bodies.[12]

Gay liberation theorists too, such as Mario Mieli (1980), seize the opportunities opened up by a feminist exposure of the sexual politics of capitalism to position homosexual desire as radical *in its own right*. If capital accumulation relies on a reproductive logic, refusing to participate in happy families and refusing to reproduce as a (gay) man also offers a challenge to capitalism.[13] Like other gay and lesbian theorists, Mieli extends the purview of sexual subordination to include homosexuals as well as women; both interrupt capitalist temporality and reveal the problematic naturalisation of gender, sex, and sexuality.[14] For Mieli, sexual liberation starts from disavowed homosexuality as a means of creating solidarity with women in the challenge to capitalist lies that disadvantage all marginal people within patriarchy (1980, 21–52). Goldman seemed to grasp some elements of this intervention in her affirmation of homosexual creativity and support for individuals in the face of persecution, though she did not extend her account of sexual freedom systematically to include nonheterosexual pleasure and community as part of her vision of an altered form, an issue I explore more fully in later sections of this chapter.

The combination of critique of women's sexual labour and celebration of the radical potential of sexual freedom in the theoretical archive is perhaps best exemplified in the work of Monique Wittig, who insists on the radical outsider status of lesbians to the extent that they famously "are not women" (1980, 32). In an irony that anticipates queer theory's love of linguistic and cultural intervention, Wittig subverts the usually homophobic characterisation of lesbians as "not women," presenting this as a bid for freedom rather than cause for shame. Importantly in the context of Goldman's materialist analysis, what makes a woman into a "woman" for Wittig is her provision of unpaid sexual and domestic services for men (or a particular man); lesbians are thus "not women" in that they are already free from the *labour* of sexual oppression. Wittig's declaration can be seen as the logical extension of a tradition of materialist analysis that sees women's sexual subordination as essential for the functioning of capitalism. Wittig's rather wonderful contribution is to insist that "woman" is a *heterosexual woman* not because of desire but because of her participation in the domestic economy; importantly, this means that a lesbian is not *doubly oppressed* by sexuality and gender but rather already free from that economy's strictures. If she is subject to punishment for this transgression, it is because she—like the striking worker who withdraws "his" labour—refuses to perform the requisite work that is part of "her" naturalised role.[15] Judith Butler famously extends Wittig's argument in *Gender Trouble* (1990), arguing that "gender" itself and the categories "man" and "woman" should be thought of as effects of what she terms the "heterosexual matrix," rather than its origins. Though she is often critiqued for her nonmaterialist analysis (see Hennessy 2014), Butler's sense that nonnormative gender performativity challenges a system of meaning can also be understood to derive from these earlier Marxist feminist and radical positions on what lies outside of the *sexual division of labour*.

To view nonfamilial or nonheterosexual sexuality as a mode of psychic or social transgression of a prior or enduring capitalism is, however, as many commentators have pointed out, somewhat ahistorical. While there is a tacit acceptance of gay and lesbian experience as *outside of* twentieth-century capitalism in much of the preceding work, historians of sexuality chart a rather different relationship between them. John D'Emilio's foundational work "Capitalism and Gay Identity" (1983) challenges any easy separation of gay and lesbian identity developments from the emergence of modern capitalism, as he explores ways in which the "expansion of capital and the spread of wage labor" are "most directly linked to the appearance of a collective gay life" (102). Homosexual possibilities for men and women are sutured to the development of more open markets for D'Emilio and cannot thus be seen as a necessary or straightforward challenge to the repressions on which capitalism is built. The increased entry of women into the labour force allows them to be folded into new capitalist formations more generally, of course, and generates the possibility of new desiring subjects: in particular, the new spaces opened up by gendered segregation of waged labour allow women to encounter and thus desire each other in both public and privatised contexts outside of the home. Further, and as a range of feminist, gay, and lesbian and queer theorists have pointed out, the increasing numbers of women in the workforce or the increased recognition of homosexual subjectivities and communities in developed capitalist economies can be historicised as one engine of capitalism's growth and spread, as central to rather than a transgression of its modern forms. The theorists who take up this history suggest that we track both old and new forms of sexuality's entanglement with capital and, in particular, focus less on the ways in which sexual identities "at the margins" challenge the status quo, and more on the ways in which they also confirm it or provide new ways through which markets can assert themselves internationally as well as nationally.[16] Although Goldman was not in a position to make this kind of critique (which has the benefit of hindsight), her anarchist suspicion of identity politics and "special status" accorded to particular subjects rings loud and clear as an early warning. Goldman was alert to the ease with which sexuality could be commodified and resisted what she saw as the potential for fetishisation of all identities. It would not have surprised her that newly emerging sexual identities in her context would be so fully folded into capitalism's voracity over time, nor that it would move beyond the need for reproductive servility in women and rugged heterosexuality in men as these roles shifted and markets expanded.[17]

Importantly, for a range of contemporary commentators the question of women's sexual labour needs to be historicised more precisely to take account of its location within the international political economy of colonialism. In decolonial materialist spirit, Carla Freccero and Hennessy extend D'Emilio's argument to explore the racialised as well as gendered and sexual character of shifts in waged labour and the family at the turn of the twentieth century. As discussed in the previous chapter, Goldman never did push her own linking of nationalism and the family form far enough to precipitate a historical account of racism, even though she was supportive of decolonial struggles. For Freccero (2012), however, the colonial roots of capitalism are precisely what create the ideal conditions for a surplus of *racialised* labour that can underwrite the production/reproduction nexus as the gendered division of labour changes. While it remains (white) women who continue to *manage* the sexual division of labour in late modern capitalist households, the labour itself does not have to be performed by them (Hennessy 2000, 65–66). Indeed, the low wages for black or migrant women doing other women's domestic or caring labour contemporarily (and, indeed, reproductive labour if we consider the global reproductive tourism industry) allow for some women to enter the labour market and change their familial position, while other women are not considered properly gendered or sexual subjects in the first place (Himmelweit and Plomien 2014).[18] In Freccero's analysis, it is the *obscured* colonial foundations of capitalism that allow for the unequal sexual division of labour in the household to continue even when its economic basis has been all but obliterated. If the heterosexual family continues as an affective unit within a capitalism that appears to have moved beyond its necessity, as D'Emilio suggests (1983, 103), for Hennessy and Freccero this is because of the ways in which the intertwined structures of colonial inequality and gendering have already been naturalised. While Goldman could see the ways in which Marxist analysis obscured the sexual foundations of capitalism, here Freccero points firmly to what Goldman's account obscures in turn: the colonial history of gendered kinship that will enable some women's emerging freedom to be privileged at the expense of others'.

The focus on colonial power as the missing link in terms of how sexuality and capitalism are sutured, and how that tie is narrated in the critical and historical archive, has been very usefully extended in work concerned with commodification and sexual citizenship. Thus, Dennis Altman (1996) has explored the growth of gay identity as a commodity that can be both bought (or brought into) in urban, developed centres and also exported as part of the circulation of international goods and services from the centre to the periphery. For Altman, the international market in gay identity works in more than one direction: for Western gay tourists to be able travel to "exotic" places while remaining certain of their identity and community; and as a point of identification for those whose geographic and/or political locations position them as "behind" in sexual rights terms. To buy (into) gayness is thus a way of reaffirming power relations between regions and nations, even as it appears to proffer a universal mode of identification that goes beyond borders.[19] Indeed, the increasing role that sexual rights in identity mode have had over the last thirty or so years cements the association of homosexuality in particular—though less so other forms of nonfamilial sexual liberty—with global capitalism, and capitalism with social democracy as against cultural tyranny.

By now, most readers will I suspect be familiar with the term "homonationalism," which Jasbir K. Puar (2007) coined as a way to depict the peculiar role of gay identity as the mediator between two imaginaries: a secular West with its promotion of sexual and gender equality, and an Islamic East with its (continued) patriarchal and homophobic attachments.[20] Such chains of association set the conditions for entry into "the modern" and ensure that only certain histories and expressions of sexual politics can be folded into this regime of identity recognition: struggles for recognition of sex work or freedom from sexual violence of all kinds, for example, are harder to fit into such an oppositional progress narrative, a feature that would certainly have alerted Goldman to its limits. It would be easy to understand gay identity's entanglement with global capitalism as an unfortunate co-optation made easier by the increasing importance of sexual rights in mediating international hierarchies, but this would be to ignore the ways in which the conditions of homosexual visibility have always been underwritten through national and global mobility and power. As Leticia Sabsay (2012, 2014) has pertinently noted, the conditions of possibility for homonationalism are already present in the historical and contemporary conditions of possibility for homosexual recognition—for her, sexual and gendered citizenship—in the first place. For Sabsay and others, to ignore the complex intertwined history of sexuality and international capitalism can only contribute to the reification of sexual identity central to its material workings contemporarily, with the continuing effect of effacing relations of class, gender, and race.

These historical and interpretative twists and turns would make Goldman laugh out loud, I suspect. As Rofel points out, the Left has always been "suspicious of attention to desire and pleasure" (2012, 185) and may now gain a perverse satisfaction from being able to point to homosexual identity as part of the problem rather than part of the solution, as always already a capitalist trick of the light. We can now be advised to return to material relations of production (cleansed of the distractions of sexual freedom) with a clear conscience;

after all, who would want to be associated with sexual and gender politics that have become part of the policing of borders? A focus on sexuality always appears to be on the side of political co-optation in fact; we might recall the critiques of queer and poststructuralist feminist theorists in the 1990s and beyond, from materialists advocating a return from the excesses of the cultural turn. Thus sociologist of sexuality Steven Seidman blames queer theorists for ceding the terrain of sexual politics with their focus on abstraction and linguistic play, and asks that they move away from the "preoccupation with self and representations characteristic of identity politics" (1993, 137). Hennessy makes a similar plea in her recent chapter "Thinking Sex Materially" (2014), and Debra Curtis urges a shift of the gaze from "sexual subjectivity" to "the desire produced in the market" (2004, 95). In one way, such calls echo my endorsement of material historical analyses that track continuities with respect to the relationship between sexuality, capitalism, and colonialism. Queer theory has indeed developed a strong thread of analysis that foregrounds transgression and alternative subjectivities in ways that designate queer theorists the inheritors of early gay liberationist or radical feminist approaches to capitalism as repressive and (nonreproductive, nonmarital) sexuality as freeing.[21] But in a curious twist of fate, it is in fact queer theory that has been the site of the most renewed attention to the materiality of sexual politics within global capitalism more recently (e.g., Rosenberg and Villarejo 2012). Indeed, it is within recent queer work on what we might broadly characterise as *political economy* that the problems of sexual identity and sexual rights as entangled with historical and contemporary forms of racist and colonial violence are most fully worked through. Given this, I find it hard to shake the feeling that the continued association of queer theory and politics with individualism and superficiality, no matter what queer theorists *actually theorise*, reflects a more profound investment in continuing to hold materiality (as economic) and sexuality (as cultural) apart. To return to Parker's analysis of the inaugural scene of determining "production" (1993), sexuality thus becomes reassociated with the triviality he identifies as central to the carving out of Marxist theories of production, whatever its own claims to an expanded terrain.

Lisa Duggan's (2003) work on "homonormativity" has been particularly helpful for me in working through the problem of separating sexuality and capitalism in the critical archive. Along with many of the theorists discussed earlier, Duggan situates sexual identity at the heart of the market, as a central driver of the fantasy of Western progress, and identifies the particular work championing sexual and gender equality does to obscure the exploitation and violence at the heart of (old and new) capitalism. Yet, importantly, Duggan also foregrounds the dangers of a critical reproduction of the very dynamics under the spotlight, not least an acceptance of the terms of the debate in which production belongs to (particular kinds of) labour, and reproduction (or its challenge) to a private or cultural realm. Thus sexuality appears to be claimed as economic by Marxist theorists only when it is taken up as a neoliberal alibi, and not when women are doing all the domestic labour, or when gay and lesbian people are subject to economic disadvantage.[22] For Duggan, one of the results of this *critical repetition* is the disproportionate burden carried by gays and lesbians in relationship to both consumerism and unequal global power relations. In characterising gays and lesbians as the "new women" in terms of their role in signifying the modern,[23] the continued importance of heteronormative regulation of national and international borders can easily disappear from view. In the process, the ongoing and uneven inequalities that gays and lesbians face in a range of global, regional, national, and local contexts can be overstated in favour of a vision of homosexual identity as entirely subsumed within its dominant capitalist entanglements. For Gavin Brown (2012), such absolutism risks erasing the complexities of queer lives as they are really lived, reifying the "homonormative gay figure" as representative of queerness more generally in ways that we would do well to challenge.[24] But so too such commodification might point to the importance of Goldman's insistence that we explore more carefully the relationships among the varied but linked sexual oppressions of prostitutes, married women, and homosexuals rather than circling around and around the privileged figures of a queer critical archive.

Duggan's challenge is taken up in a different but related way by Rofel, who argues that in work on desire that retains a distinction between production and culture, capitalism itself is positioned as a "universal, uniform totality" (2012, 187) rather than as variegated and subject to change. For Rofel, then, it is not only the meanings of sexuality that are limited by the existing terms of debate. As Peter Jackson (2009) insists, characterisations of the relationship between sexuality and capitalism—including those set out to resist its most normative forms—tend to assume a preeminent, all-powerful "West" from which meaning and history flow forth, ignoring regional flows of sexual meaning that have little or nothing to do with modern capitalism. The question of the relationship between capitalism and sexuality is thus fraught with difficulties, not least perhaps the inevitable risk of reinstantiating oppositions and teleologies one may be highly invested in challenging. I find myself returning to Parker's point about the terms of the debate themselves, and our too easy acceptance of these parameters.[25] For Goldman, as for Parker, the narrative of a production/reproduction opposition is complex: it tells a particular, naturalised story of separate spheres, and it also accepts the presumption that pleasure and production are innately opposed. In this sense, Goldman's sexual freedom both promises to disrupt a public/private divide and also leaves "pleasure" intact as that which cannot be folded into profit. This is in itself a pleasing naïveté: as the title of Hennessy's book *Profit and Pleasure* (2000) suggests, however, it is not only identities that are subject to commodification but pleasure itself. For Parker we would need to focus on the history of pleasure as that which haunts capitalism to have any idea of what sexual freedom might be (or be able to do).

Hennessy (2000) and Eng (2010) have rightly suggested that a continued focus on sexual identity can only underscore that history and prevent us thinking more expansively about desires in and of capitalism. Well aware of the pitfalls of the sexual-capitalist entanglement, Hennessy and Eng, as well as Puar (2007, 204), propose a shift to *affect over identity* as a way of developing nonindividualistic accounts of "'revolutionary love'" (Hennessy 2000, 220), ones less amenable to co-optation by global capitalism. Perhaps this is what Goldman had in mind; after all, it is love that resides at the centre of her revolutionary sexual vision. And, indeed, if identity is the favoured mode of capitalism's vicious alibis, it makes perfect sense not to continue to invest in it. A focus on affect also chimes well with Goldman's emphasis on "passion" as a significant revolutionary methodology and promises to value precisely those queer lives and experiences Brown identifies as obscured by a focus on normative identities. So too a focus on affect as an alternative entry point to what we might know about capitalism and sexuality resonates with my own efforts to value other methodologies and sources of knowledge in the recognition of past and present political complexity and ambivalence. But to imagine affect as outside of the history it seeks to escape has another effect: it rather easily accepts the story of the relationship between capitalism and sexuality in its dominant historical and critical modes, even as it proposes ways and means of moving on. Along with Freccero (2012), I want to insist that this story is a setup, a circular narrative in which shifting relations of production always inaugurate what we think of as modern gender and sexual subjectivities, leaving us with "no choice" but to abandon the overdetermination of identity and move on. Instead of proposing a way out, Freccero—like Parker—invites us back to the scene of "origin" inverting the authoring capacities of feminist and Marxist epistemologies to insist "that commodity exchange in Marx takes its form from the exchange of women" rather than the other way around (2012, 53).

To be fair, Freccero's argument is less a contest over "which came first" and more a questioning of our certainty about how struggles over the questions of production and commodity exchange have been resolved. Her challenge to us is to explore the multiple ways in which "queer desires . . . animate the scene of capital" (54), rather than accepting a narrative within which homosexuality only becomes a condition of possibility through the formal organisation of labour in a changing capitalist sphere. As Parker quips, while Marxism has resisted thinking sexuality, "sexuality . . . nevertheless thinks Marx" (1993, 23). In proposing a return to the "scene of origin," Freccero not only suggests an alternate ordering through time but also reorganises the authorial relations of that order. In asking us to think again about the historical emergence of desire, Freccero invites us to engage what Lauren Berlant (2011) might call the intimate life of capitalism not as a part of the design of an escape route from the entanglements of capitalism and sexuality but as a way of reimagining the stories we tell about that relationship in the first place. In the next section, I return us to thinking with and through sexuality in the Goldman archive, seeking to queer the scene of sexual repression and sexual freedom through attention to her own excavations of "sexuality and revolution" as similarly a question of struggle rather than resolution.

STRUGGLES OVER NATURE

Goldman inhabited sexual freedom as a site of possibility from within the heart of her anarchist belief in "the complete material and psychological re-generation of human individuality" (1907, 245). As discussed in chapter 1 with respect to her argument in "Minorities versus Majorities" (1910, 69–78), Goldman saw the relationship between the individual and the group as mutually constitutive, but she also privileged the former over the latter as the best site for immediate change. As she elaborates for one of the many journalists desperate to talk to her to secure paper sales in the first decade of the twentieth century: "'First, the individual instinct, standing for self-expression; second, the social instinct, which inspires collective and social life. These instincts in their latent condition are never antagonistic to each other'" (*Chicago Daily Journal* 1908, 291). The creative capacity for transformation flows, for Goldman, from the inside outwards, such that it is imperative that a human being's life should be "a true mirror of nature, a conscious following of the only real necessity, the inner natural necessity . . . no longer held in subjugation to an outer artificial counterfeit—an arbitrary power" (1927?, 9). In developing her particular understanding of "nature," Goldman drew both on revolutionary theories and on psychoanalytic understandings of the importance of drives and the unconscious workings of the mind, foregrounding individual instinct as both natural and powerfully transformative.[26]

Goldman's framing of sexual freedom combines existing anarchist and socialist commitments to free love with a psychological belief in the damage wrought by sexual repression. Thus, for Goldman, when religious moral forces condemn any sexual expression that does not have "sanction from the church," they "[commit] great crimes against the human race" in general and women in particular (*The Toronto Daily Star* 1935). Since it is woman's sexual energy that is the specific target for moral and religious restriction, it is *their* nature more than men's that is most compromised by social prescription. In this light Goldman asks rhetorically whether there can be "anything more outrageous than the idea that a healthy, grown woman, full of life and passion, must deny nature's demand, must subdue her most intense craving, undermine her health and break her spirit, must stunt her vision, abstain from the depth and glory of sex experience until a 'good' man comes along to take her unto himself as a wife" (1911, 7). If the problem of sexual freedom is one of capitalist and patriarchal repression, then attention to that which seeks to find expression is a pertinent revolutionary avenue of exploration, of course, and one that has had considerable influence on theorists such as Marcuse and Mieli, as discussed earlier. For Goldman, absolute freedom demands full emancipation of women, as we know, and most particularly it requires "[listening] to the voice of her nature, whether it call for life's greatest treasure, love for a man, or her most glorious privilege, the right to give birth to a child" (1906b, 15). Woman's nature, then, is both her stolen birthright and something for her to reclaim as part of the means and end of revolutionary endeavour.

As Goldman circles around this question of "nature," particularly women's nature, in all her arguments about sexual freedom, it is perhaps not surprising that her embrace of the concept has raised eyebrows from a range of feminist commentators. Feminist writers have been utterly seduced by Goldman's foregrounding of sexual politics as the linchpin of political revolution but also dismayed by what they perceive to be the reinforcement of essentialist conceptions of womanhood that are part of the problem. A focus on women's nature is thought both to privilege relations between men and women (rather than homosexuality or other modes of sexual freedom) and to draw on a potentially essentialising understanding of the body, and has been roundly critiqued in the queer feminist critical archive more generally.[27] And this is also true of the feminist critical archive that reads Goldman's sexual politics. Thus, as Alix Kates Shulman notes, while Goldman was highly critical of any contemporaries who invoked traditional femininity in order to persuade those in authority that recognition of women would not fundamentally challenge the existing political order of things, "she herself quite clearly mobilised her own understanding of 'women's nature'" (1982, 253) as a powerful force for positive change. And in her reading of *Mother Earth*, Linda Lumsden (2007) dismisses what she sees as Goldman's fatal biological determinism and compares this to an unreconstructed contemporary ecofeminism.[28] In a similar vein, Janet Day underscores Goldman's insistence on the importance of "a positive opinion of human nature," the expression of which is "under the right circumstances ... conducive to positive relations with others" (2007, 110), a position Day remains highly sceptical of. In relation to the links between Goldman's "gender essentialism" and her too fervent affirmation of "heterosexist norms" (Marso 2003, 306), theorists remain cautious in the face of her lauding of free sex between men and women as the most glorious revolutionary feeling. For Stansell, Goldman's "interest in free love [was] always conceived as heterosexual" (2000, 142), and it is this conflation that makes her vulnerable to abuse by men "on the make" (294) such as Reitman. Bonnie Haaland provides us with the most sustained critique of Goldman's heterosexual essentialism in her important text *Emma Goldman: Sexuality and the Impurity of the State* (1993). As discussed in the introduction, Haaland reads Goldman's sexual politics through a resolutely constructivist lens, finding her embrace of psychoanalytic and sexological views highly problematic in and of themselves (because of their own presumed reliance on essentialist understandings of gender and the body), and ultimately dismissing Goldman's passion for sexual freedom as part of her "limited heterosexist vision" (1993, 144). For Haaland, Goldman's articulation of sexuality as "a driving instinctual force" (117) constitutes a self-evident barrier to a more inclusive sexual politics, and she laments Goldman's failure to more fully explore "the possibility of emancipation in same-sex relationships" (144).

In marked contrast, there is a range of writers in the critical archive who claim Goldman as a heroine of anarchist sexual possibility beyond identity politics. But for the most part, this reclamation is only achieved through ignoring or bracketing out that same "problem" of nature in Goldman's assertion of the value of sexual freedom. Thus, queer advocates tend to foreground

Goldman's sexual antiauthoritarianism in order to herald Goldman as variously a polyamorous heroine (Heckert 2010; Levine 2012), a queer anarchist who challenged sexual conventions ahead of her time (Conrad 2012; Daring et al. 2012), and one who may be helpful for thinking through queer as well as anarchist understandings of consent and play (Shepard 2010).[29] Those feminist or queer theorists less concerned about the question of nature in Goldman tend to foreground her emphasis on process rather than essence, reflecting the considerable influence of Deleuze and Guattari on post-anarchist thinking (e.g., Ince 2012; Maiguashca 2014). Blake, citing Alice Wexler, makes a connection between deterritorialising politics and Goldman's view of "desire as contiguous with natural and social activity, a creative energy which itself was the only 'inspiring, elevating basis for a new race, a new world' (Wexler 1984, 93)" (Blake 1997, 48).[30] Such approaches reflect my own interest in reading "sexual nature" in Goldman as a politically charged and emergent state, rather than a fixed origin, and so I am in many ways more sympathetic to this kind of reclamation than I am to the dismissal of her prefigurative approach in light of the spectre of damned essence. But such queer or poststructuralist feminist approaches are also so keen to avoid any whiff of essentialism themselves that they usually ignore the question of "nature" altogether. The framing of Goldman through a deterritorialising lens does not explore different ways in which "nature" is significant in her thinking, but subsumes the texture of her thinking to a theoretical approach that is privileged over her own complexity. Theorists wanting to claim a Deleuzian understanding of process, then, prioritise Goldman's migrant and sexual crisscrossings but pay little to no attention to what is happening in her ecstatic missives to Reitman or her lauding of motherhood as the greatest natural state a woman can take up.

Let us consider Goldman's heartfelt arguments on prostitution as an example of what is lost when reading her views on sexual freedom in this way. In her best-known essay on the topic—*The White Slave Traffic* (1909e)—Goldman exposes the hypocritical sexual morality surrounding prostitution and insists that the real difference between it and marriage is a question of numbers and control: "To the moralist prostitution does not consist so much in the fact that the woman sells her body, but rather than she sells it to many" (1909e, 348). For Goldman, prostitution needs to be framed through an economic analysis and its primary cause shouted from the rooftops: "Exploitation, of course: that merciless Moloch of capitalism that fattens on underpaid labor" (344). Yet this is by no means the only cause for Goldman, for whom the lack of knowledge about sex for young women, combined with the lack of avenues to express their natural sexual overexcitement, is also bound to lead them astray. Nor of course is abstinence the answer because this simply leads to the repression of those same natural urges. While Goldman fully supports prostitutes (considering sex for money to be honest at least, unlike marriage [1911]),[31] she nevertheless considers the conditions of prostitution loathsome not only because of their economic and intersubjective violence but also because of their perversion of the *beauty of desire*, the transformation of it into a commodity to be exchanged on the market. To ameliorate the worst ills of the profession, then, Goldman advocates both economic revolution (1909e, 351) and—very importantly—sexual freedom, because the latter would mean women's desires could be more naturally fulfilled through free encounters with loved others, and would prevent their being drawn into prostitution because of repressed sexual urges.

In a range of ways, then, *The White Slave Traffic* is a good example of a text that seems to speak directly to the concerns of the queer feminist critical archive. Goldman not only aligns herself firmly with sex workers (through supporting their person, if not their trade) and positions the problem as a thoroughly economic one but also condemns the scapegoating of recent immigrants as a particularly scandalous authoritarian displacement tactic. And, indeed, this is the way that I have read and presented her arguments thus far. Goldman's argument is twofold here: she highlights the misuse of statistics to give a false impression that the problem of prostitution is effectively an immigrant problem, and she empathises with those recent arrivals turning to prostitution after being blinded by the light of American consumerism (349). Yet her insistence that as long as women have few outlets to bring their "oversexed condition to a climax" (348), they will turn to the corrupt conditions of prostitution to satisfy their natural but repressed need for sex has received less comment. We could critique Goldman here for her sexual essentialism concerning drives, or we could ignore it and focus instead on the more familiar intersectional economic approach, but if we do so we also sideline her detailed theorisation of "sexual freedom" as essential to revolution *precisely because* it unrepresses women's instincts, making their sexual labour considerably more difficult to co-opt. When scholars such as Martha Solomon (1988, 186) and Candace Falk (2003, 12) indicate that Goldman's understanding of sexual freedom is too vague to provide a genuine platform for change, they ignore those practical solutions that she does envisage, perhaps because they are hard to fit into a familiar agenda. In the case of prostitution, Goldman carefully lays out that better sex education, free birth control, and fewer sanctions on sex before marriage would ameliorate the worst harms of the profession. That does not seem particularly vague to me, though it does sounds like a hard as well as specific set of solutions to take on board.

Goldman's views on natural sexual urges as she articulates them in *The White Slave Traffic* are worth taking seriously for another reason. The feminist and queer theoretical archive on prostitution and sex work is a particularly oppositional one. Writers and activists are usually "for or against" abolition or decriminalisation; selling sex is either a fundamental expression of women's oppression or an expression of choice; and paid sex is read either as wholesale commodification and marketisation or as ordinary employment that needs regulation and unionisation. These views tend to be mutually exclusive in this field of critical and political investigation. While my own view on the topic has shifted from one that privileged agency in a sex-positive context to one that situates the sex trade in relationship to "national security" and the need to support vulnerable workers in an unsafe trade, this has never felt entirely right. I have never been fully able to accept that the antidote to the worst ills of this industry would be straightforwardly "regulation" (even if in the hands of its workers), or that there is nothing particular to sex, such that the harm caused by its commodification or exploitation as part of the market is genuinely likely to be experienced by women as simply equivalent to other labour-related harms. Goldman's interventions here are helpful because she returns us to some earlier concerns within the feminist and lesbian "sex wars," namely, those that consider sexual oppression of women to be horrific in a range of spheres, including *both marriage and prostitution*. Goldman's argument in *The White Slave Traffic* is thus less about claiming those who have sex for money as particularly agentic or as particularly coerced. Rather, for Goldman, sexual oppression is universal, as is the need to challenge it at more than a superficial level. This analysis is complemented by her insistence that the answer to sexual hierarchy, commodification of sexual relations, and sexual violence and intimidation of all kinds (including enforced childbearing) is not to advocate for *better conditions* (though this would no doubt be better than nothing) or to pit choice against subordination as though they were similar types of evidence but to posit a more radical vision entirely. For Goldman, all commodification of sexuality is a horror and a terror; arguing about equivalent horrors and terrors elsewhere is not a transformative argument in this sense, though it may help to shift the moral sanctioning that surrounds paid sex.

While I do not share Goldman's views that if women and girls were free to express their natural sexual desires they would never turn to sex for pay, or that the industry itself would disappear, I do think her views raise questions about sexual experience and freedom that are often missing from the debates about prostitution as a practice and industry and the "sex wars" more broadly.[32] For Goldman, all women want sex, and they have a right to its pleasures. They have a sex drive equivalent to men's and a vitality that needs expressing or ill health and social decay will be the result. The problem with paid sex is not that it is morally or politically wrong, or that it represents the worst aspects of women's oppression; the problem with it is that it prevents full expression of love and thus an experience of revolutionary solidarity in the here and now. In this sense Goldman's challenge in *The White Slave Traffic*—via her insistence on the importance of women's sexual drives—is to sexual and social misery in general rather than the particular sexual and social misery of those who sell sex.

To keep focused on the question of nature as central to Goldman's understanding of sexual freedom also brings us back to the obscured colonial nature of sexual politics that I discussed earlier via Hennessy and Freccero. Indeed, one of the more troubling aspects of Goldman's revolutionary theory is the way in which it frames sexual freedom as a *primitive* as well as natural instinct. In this context, Goldman's solution to the ills of sexual oppression for women has been critiqued for its reliance on a vision of sexual nature that reproduces the racialised oppositions between "traditional" and "modern" that are so key to the power relations both within and between nation-states. In particular, critics have pointed to the ways in which Goldman unreflexively invested in Reitman's appeal as an authentic working-class figure and a racialised "hobo" whose sexuality was never settled (Falk 2005; Ferguson 2011b; Stansell 2000, 296).[33] From feminist and queer perspectives, the problem with nature and instinct as the ground of sexual freedom is its essentialism, and Goldman does nothing to allay concerns about the racist or classist basis of "essence" here. Indeed, to return to *The White Slave Traffic* argument, if "natural urges" for Goldman are also primitive ones, then this needs full accounting for by the critical archive that is otherwise so delighted with her embrace of sexual freedom. But to say that Goldman employs a racist understanding of nature and drives should not be a reason for turning away from a fuller engagement with her arguments, but at minimum to suggest that this additional analysis should be folded into an account of her complex arguments. While Goldman exposes the patriarchal interests in scapegoating immigration as a central cause of prostitution, then, she also reinforces a racist, essentialist grounding of desire: these are the very contradictions that require our critical and political attention and that also guided her more direct engagements with race and racism discussed in the previous chapter. The critical anxiety about (other people's?) racism means it is easier to ignore Goldman's arguments about nature than it is to grapple with the complexities of sexual freedom that we inherit. Yet so too, that anxiety tends to lead to thinking of Goldman's vision of sexual freedom as more determined and determinist than it always is. As I have already argued briefly in chapter 1, nature in Goldman is not fixed or conceived of as a starting point from which change arises, but rather as that which emerges *from struggle* as part of how one imagines a utopian future in the present.

To return to Goldman's relationship with Ben Reitman, for so long the object of her "primitive urges," her letters most certainly do represent a hard-to-take self-abasement at points and a sexual obsessiveness that is vulnerable to conventional gendered interpretations. Yet the direct and unabashed sexual expression in these letters is in itself something to be treasured as a rare example of active, uncompromising female lust, whatever its target and its dangers. For Goldman, it is in experiencing the intensity of that desire that her political commitments are given life. She writes: "Hoboo, Treasure Hoboo, Now, that I have tasted the invigorating breeze of your primitive, untrammeled nature, I feel the narrowness of family even more. . . . Joy or sorrow, delight or pain, I want to share everything with my precious boy, may I not? . . . I am too restless to reason now. Not too restless to love you, love you intensely and passionately. . . . Write soon. . . . Above all, write me, if you love me, as much as ever" (1908a, 334). By turns generous and whiny, explicit and coy, engaging and embarrassing, Goldman's letters to Reitman also demonstrate her fervency that any man she cannot resist—including Reitman—must embrace her worldview as well as her; when this does not happen, she rails against such offence: "I cannot reconcile my established belief in the power of love, (a belief much deeper in my system, than even the belief in freedom) with the realization of how little love done for you" (1909b, 440). The letters reflect Goldman's point of view, of course: failings tend to attach to Reitman, wounded pride and generosity to Goldman herself. This is of course one of the representational modes of the desperate love letter.[34] Only at her lowest moments does Goldman doubt her politics on the basis of her love, and this is clearly the cause of considerable pain:

> What you call love, is an insatiable monster, that saps loves [*sic*] blood and then kicks it into the cold. Your love excludes giving . . . Your love

takes and takes and when it can take no more, it thrusts love aside . . . as if love had never existed. . . .

Meetings, free speech, ME [*Mother Earth*] are nothing to me now, if my love my life, my peace my very soul is to be mutilated. . . . This may also account [*sic*] why I . . . could crouch on her knees and beg and plead with you. Yes, I believed in your love, or rather I believed too much in the power of my love to teach you. (1909c, 464–65)

Hard to read though such self-berating and belittling may be, Goldman never rests in her self-abasement for long. Indeed, in matters of the heart, where it does not prove possible for her to align politics and nature, Goldman is at least as likely to prioritise the former as the latter. And as Falk notes in respect of her relationship to Reitman, "Goldman's personal trials and tribulations in the realm of love might have been the experiences that sharpened her attunement to the political dimensions of sexual desire" (2012b, 25). While certainly not always succeeding, Goldman sought to *politicise* nature. Stacy Alaimo suggests that Goldman went so far as to imagine we could "naturalize a revolutionary vision of a just society and to forge an insurgent, not reproductive, identity for women" (2000, 93). Goldman's experiments in living and loving were part of how she grappled with and sought to bring about this revolutionary vision. That these experiments were as likely to reproduce gendered, sexual, and racial norms as to challenge them is hardly surprising. What *is* remarkable is her refusal to allow political and intersubjective experiments to be held apart in her imagination of a new world.

Alaimo is particularly helpful in putting Goldman's explorations in context, pointing out that "nature, in the early twentieth century, was a highly politicized space—both the ground for demarcating the contentious claims of the body politic and the site for asserting that women's bodies are themselves political" (87). Thus, for Alaimo "nature" should be understood as a complex concept that was as consistently imagined "as a utopian space" (88) or as a "force for social change" as it was envisioned as a "menacing [drive] denying women freedom, agency, and self-determination" (87). Alaimo's analysis emerges from her detailed reading of nature as it blossoms within Goldman's journal *Mother Earth*, suggesting that much of the dynamism of her political thinking is a result of the movement between revolutionary commitment and everyday experimentation. Chris Rossdale considers "radical subjectivity" in Goldman's oeuvre to be a "ceaselessly mobile" concept, "never resting, always creating, and never arriving" (2015, 129), and one might well make the same argument about her understanding of "nature." For Goldman, human nature—while essential to the possibility of transformation—is currently corrupt to the core, a memory and a hope rather than a reality, something to be *achieved* through political effort, not something that one can start from or straightforwardly draw upon. As we saw in chapter 1, "woman's nature" in particular has been so tainted by bourgeois superficiality and the displacement of value by bankrupt economics that a woman needs to emancipate herself first before her true nature can even be glimpsed. Goldman's vision is of course fundamentally prefigurative, in the sense that it combines an anarchist critique of authority with a process-based method for transformation (living now, as one would hope to live then).[35] This is a long way from a poststructuralist or purely psychoanalytic understanding of process: for Goldman sexual nature is a privileged site for transformation that capitalism never quite succeeds in repressing. But neither is it a preexisting resource to be uncovered. True sexual nature needs to be both believed in and brought about; the process of turning drives into freedom is an active one that promises to *make nature* anew.[36]

Sexual freedom is a site of everyday struggle for Goldman, as we have seen in terms of her turbulent relationship with Reitman, and as becomes evident when we consider her ambivalent relationship to motherhood. There can be no doubt that Goldman elevated motherhood to an exalted position, celebrating "the mother courage, the mother greatness, the maternal instinct" (between 1927 and 1930, 3), even considering it woman's "deepest function" (1912b) under the right—which is to say, free—conditions. Goldman believed motherhood to be a pinnacle of achievement for women and particularly important from a revolutionary perspective, since the cause will prevail only with generational education based in and on alternative values (1897a). While motherhood is natural and instinctual, the miserable conditions under which a woman finds herself the "incessant breeder of hapless children" (1913, 3), however, make contemporary motherhood into nothing short of a sickening parody. For Goldman, while "the Earth Spirit is motherhood carrying the race in its womb," it is precisely that "flame of life" that "[lures] the moth . . . to destruction" (1935?a). In this respect it was extremely important to Goldman that motherhood be regarded both as resulting from that natural spirit and as a dangerous desire that could (and often should) be refused.[37] Thus while Falk reads Goldman as vacillating "between exalting and demeaning childbirth and motherhood" (2005, 33), I am more persuaded by Ferguson's parsing of this "instinctive urge" as "a powerful predisposition that could nonetheless be resisted" (2011b, 165). While Goldman lauded the mother instinct, she was also clear that not all women felt that pull, writing to Max Nettlau that she has "known quite a number of women, feminine to the last degree, who nevertheless lack that supposed-to-be inborn trait of motherhood or longing for the child" (1935, 186). As with Goldman's understanding of the sexual urge, the pull of motherhood is made most meaningful not in its essential, original form but when women claim their "rights to control [its] conditions" (Kensinger 2007, 268).

Goldman knew about these dilemmas firsthand, from her own experience of male lovers trying to persuade her to have children, and battled to reconcile the appeal of an enduring home life and her conviction that this would make a full political life impossible (1931c, 580). Faced with a medical condition that prevented her having children without an operation (Falk 2005, 31–32), Goldman decided against it on the basis that "strife and not peace" would be her lot in life, thus leaving "no room for a child" (1931b, 187). Both Ed Brady and Reitman eventually had children with other women, and Goldman felt the hurt in each case as a doubled one: that of being abandoned for a more lasting attachment, and that of being reminded of the sacrifice that her own difficult choices engendered (1931c, 613). She empathised with other women's difficult domestic circumstances but resisted being pulled by "that blind, dumb force" into a predictable female lifecycle that "[wastes] woman's youth and strength" and makes her "a burden to herself and to those to whom she has given birth" in old age (1931b, 340). In the face of her abandonment, while Goldman felt "deeply grieved and humiliated at the same time," she also narrates her decision in her autobiography as a political choice that she stood by and did not regret (187). In a further recasting of motherhood, Goldman held apart the desire have a child and the desire to raise one, insisting that a mothering urge might "embrace all children" (1933a) whether related by blood or not. In this sense, some forty years before Firestone's (1970) excitement about new reproductive technologies, Goldman sought to interrupt the overdetermined connection between a mother's body and child rearing, a reflection more broadly of her commitment to children's independence and to the ethical value of raising children collectively.[38] In her analysis of the range of representations of "motherhood" in Goldman's autobiography, Heather Ostman highlights its appearance as variously "'natural essence'" (2009, 63), the cause of unnecessary suffering, the site of woman's martyrdom or authority, and a social demand that can be repudiated. For Ostman as for me, Goldman's invocation of motherhood is consistently strategic, by turns challenging and confirming convention, always mobilised in service to the political point she is making.

Sexual freedom, then, is most certainly underpinned by a privileging of human nature for Goldman. Indeed, without that belief in the psychic as well as social basis of human life, it is hard to imagine her commitment to sexual freedom—in women, among lovers, for mothers—making sense. While sexual urges are natural, their constraint or repression by institutional authority and morality (particularly in marriage and child rearing) is hypocritical and ultimately ineffective. If we could but harness those drives that are strong enough to lead women into prostitution, if the harmful and hypocritical sexual moralities governing women and men could be abandoned, then other ways of relating to each other would inevitably emerge and a pure revolutionary sexual nature might emerge as a result. Goldman's emphasis on nature is disconcerting to a contemporary readership because it raises the spectre of exclusionary essentialisms; indeed, theorists are at considerable pains to point this out, or to ignore her "natural urges" altogether for fear of reproducing them. But if we accuse or avert our eyes without further attention, I believe that we miss two important aspects of Goldman's thinking that remain relevant in the present. Firstly, we risk laying claim to her international or intersectional political thinking as mediating rather than being entangled with more conservative racialised and classed presumptions and tropes, somewhat ironically ignoring the complexities of her essentialism in order to ensure being beyond it as critics. And secondly, we miss the particular *character* and *temporality* of Goldman's belief in nature. In highlighting sexual freedom as a dense site of struggle, Goldman opens up a different temporality to human nature: as emerging *from* political effort rather than underwriting or preceding that effort (or its lack). Goldman's foregrounding of woman's nature in her vision of sexual freedom keeps us located within gendered, raced, and sexual experimentation rather that removing us from the messy business of political struggle.

SEXUAL FREEDOM AND HOMOSEXUAL AMBIVALENCE

I return now to the question of Goldman's ambivalent relationship to homosexuality, exploring its potential significance both for how we see Goldman's struggles with sexual freedom and for how this might shape our own critical and historical engagements with sexual meaning. Unsurprisingly, the Goldman archive is filled with gaps about her personal and political position on homosexuality. We know that Goldman lectured on homosexuality, but only the front pages of these polemics remain; she had intense attachments to women and a passionate relationship with Sperry, though the archival evidence is scant; and she championed homosexuality as a principle of individual liberty within sexual freedom but was not always consistent in that support. These conflicted traces are important in their own right of course, providing a glimpse into the seams below the surface of Goldman's text. Clues are few, and those we have do not always paint a positive portrait of Goldman, yet piecing these together provides clarity on both her own views and those of her time. At the height of Goldman's development of her ideas on sexual freedom, homosexuality was publicly and privately vilified. Thus, while there was plenty of same-sex sexual experimentation among the urban bohemians, "their own silences about homosexuality make it hard for us to uncover this aspect of their sexual lives" (Dubois and Gordon 1983, 18). And in relation to women, this is still harder to track, given what Blanche Wiesen Cook rightly asserts as the "historical denial of lesbianism" (1979b) even within homosexual representation or public culture. In this context, Goldman's "addresses on homosexuality" would most certainly have been understood—along with her broader claiming of sexual freedom—as disreputable, and it is not at all surprising that these are no longer to be found. Much may have been destroyed, since the social and moral as well as legal sanctions against homosexuality would not have been easy to challenge, even for someone as unconventional as Goldman. We might want to match this doubled denial—in the archive and in the historian—with a doubled queer desire for echoes and whispers; replacing concrete traces with our own yearning for them, as discussed in my introduction. As lesbian and queer theorists from Lillian Faderman (1991) to Ann Cvetkovich (2003) have emphasised, reading between and below the lines of dominant sexual history is a method akin to how queer people read sexuality in the world: reading desire against the grain in one's interpretation of others; using all six senses to verify what lurks just out of sight.[39]

Goldman appreciated the importance of homosexuality for sexual freedom, linking the "social ostracism of the invert" (1931c, 556) to other forms of moral condemnation she found repugnant. She is most well known in this respect for speaking out against the conviction of Oscar Wilde (Cook 1979a, 435; Liesegang 2012) at a time when this was not at all fashionable, later lamenting the "cruel injustice and hypocrisy of the very society which sent [Wilde] to his doom" in a letter to sexologist Magnus Hirschfeld (1923?). Reflecting back on her hopes that she would meet Wilde in Paris, Goldman writes in her autobiography that she "had pleaded his case against . . . miserable hypocrites" (1931b, 269) and further notes with some satisfaction that her speaking "without reservation on such a tabooed subject" had "scandalized" friends (269).[40] Goldman's defence of Wilde reflects her more general support for individual choice in respect of sexuality and her belief in sexual experimentation as a route to liberation. As Loretta Kensinger explains: "She sees a connection between liberation and sexual freedom not only for women . . . her discussion of responses to her lectures on homosexuality confirms the seriousness with which she treated the issues of sexual freedom for all people" (2007, 263).

Goldman certainly did fight against intolerance wherever she found it and was often the first to come to the aid of those directly experiencing injustice. But her interest in homosexuality was more than a reflection of a general sentiment: she saw homosexual persecution as a particularly unpleasant example of repression of sexual expression and made considerable efforts to reframe same-sex desire as wholly natural. Thus in her unpublished notes for her lectures on Walt Whitman she laments ignorant attempts to cover up his "sex variation" by otherwise "enlightened people" and provides a no-nonsense account of "the love of girls for girls, or girls for their favourite woman-teachers, and that of boys and boys and their favourite male teachers" as "a common occurrence" (n.d. [1991b]). Elsewhere, Goldman asserts that "economic inadequacy does not stamp out heterosexual urges any more than the enactment of a punitive law can destroy homosexual impulses" (1935?b), and she railed against the branding of "men . . . who in their sex psychology divert from the so called normal and who are branded by our social and ethical stupidity as degenerates" (1925a, 1).[41] But further than this, Goldman considered homosexuals to be naturally creative and able to inhabit a future world of equality in the present through peculiarly imaginative means. In this sense, Goldman is making a case for the *specialness* of homosexuality within her broader framing of its naturalness. Thus in the same letter to Hirschfeld in which she defends Wilde, Goldman writes of "Urnings or Bi-Sexuals" that "I have found them far above the average in intelligence, ability, sensitiveness and charm" (1923?). This certainly reflects her view of both Whitman and Wilde, in whose work she saw the development of "the beautiful ideal" that "stressed the creative capacity of the reader, providing a literary training ground for self-emancipation from hierarchy" (Robbins 2015, 81). Goldman's sympathy for homosexual men was further strengthened by her deep friendship with Alexander Berkman, who, as we have seen, expresses his own same-sex erotic attachments in his *Prison Memoirs of an Anarchist* (1912).

Yet, as Greenway pertinently notes: "Emma Goldman—who did as much as anyone to make it possible to speak publicly about homosexuality—could be strikingly contradictory" (2009a, 112). Goldman had close friendships with lesbians, notably Margaret Anderson and Ellen Kennan, the editors of the *Little Review* (Cook 1979a, 432; Falk 2012b, 151), and yet she was scathing of her friend, colleague, and Berkman's ex-lover Eleanor Fitzgerald's embrace of desire for women, writing in no uncertain terms: "'Really, the Lesbians are a crazy lot. Their antagonism to the male is almost a disease with them. I simply can't bear such narrowness'" (cited in Faderman 1991, 14). Goldman had "cautiously intimate relationships with women throughout her life" (Garber 1995, 125), making a hard-to-interpret passionate friend of Kate O'Hare when they were both in prison (Haaland 1993, 175), writing copious letters to female friends and fellow activists throughout her lifetime,[42] and reflecting on the changing nature of her relationship with Margaret Sanger as "expressive of my previous theoretical interest in sex variation" (1929?, 14).[43] Yet she also considered there to be "nothing duller in all the world than exclusive gatherings of men or of women" (1931b, 397), and she drew on vicious stereotypes to characterise homosexual men as vain or laughably effeminate. Despite her own framing of homosexuals as particularly—even uniquely—creative, then, Goldman also criticises what she views as their self-involvement, dislikes what she read as their "misguided attempts to claim notable individuals for their 'creed'" (Greenway 2009a, 112–13), and shares an unpleasant joke with Havelock Ellis about homosexuals' self-proclaimed superiority that together they dubbed "homoservility" (Ellis 1924).

Nowhere is Goldman's ambivalence about homosexuality more evident than in her defence of Louise Michel, one of her anarchist revolutionary mentors. In 1923, Goldman wrote a twelve-page letter to Hirschfeld, thanking him for agreeing to publish her argument against Levetzow's accusation that Michel was a lesbian in his book *The Red Virgin*. As Greenway notes once more, the letter repeatedly insists that while Goldman is very much in favour of homosexual freedom, she cannot condone this characterisation of Michel (2009, 112–13). While critics tend to read the letter as proof of Goldman's own defensiveness and perhaps too her desire to distance herself from similar accusations (Cook 1979a, 437; Haaland 1993, 170), Goldman does in fact make quite a persuasive argument about the sexual politics involved in reading Michel in this way, a point taken up by Ellis (1924) in his support for her letter. Goldman writes that she is sick of the tendency to read every woman who is not a "charmer of man, the bearer of children . . . the general cook and bottle-washer" as a lesbian (1923?, 3). She directly challenges the presumption that a woman who eschews femininity, cares little for her appearance, and exhibits great courage should be assumed to be a lesbian solely on that basis (4–6). For Goldman, continuing to associate these traits with men is both old-fashioned and irrational. Not all nonconformists can be claimed as homosexual, Goldman argues, and she convincingly frames Levetzow's desire to do so as absurd. But as Cook rightly notes, in her defence, Goldman "bring[s] forth every imaginable argument" (4) as to why Michel is *not* a lesbian, to the point where the twelve tightly argued pages come to constitute a kind of excess of certainty about how to read gender and embodiment in their own right. Goldman's own femininity was consistently scrutinised in the press, as we have seen in previous chapters, which may partly account for the forcefulness of her response about the readings of Michel's lesbianism through her "inappropriate" gender and embodiment. Yet in the letter's fervour, one might say that Goldman not only wants Michel not to be read as a lesbian but also wants it *not to be possible* to read her as one. And to achieve this, Goldman has to "prove Louise Michel as she really was, an exceptional woman . . . a complete woman, free from the prejudice and the tradition which for centuries have held women in bondage," putting together a depressing argument that tacitly holds womanhood and lesbianism apart (12). As Cook further suggests: "It appears that, in Goldman's mind, to be a lesbian was an absolute right, and nothing nasty about it. But it was also to be rendered somehow less a woman" (1979a, 437). Goldman thus spends considerable time identifying areas that confirm rather than undermine Michel's womanhood: her comradely need for other women's companionship, her motherly love (1923?, 9) and her sympathy towards animals (11) among them. This is not an early Wittigian argument championing lesbian existence as outside of female gendering, or a new materialist challenge to Michel's critics' anthropomorphism. In defending Michel against Levetzow's reductive interpretation by insisting on Michel's specific and rather conservative feminine traits as tethering her to heterosexual womanhood, Goldman firmly reassociates masculinity with lesbians in a sequence of reductive moves of her own.

Goldman's ambivalence towards homosexuality has been interpreted in a variety of ways by the critical archive, as one might expect. Her closeness to other women, hints at experience of same-sex desire, and her hyperbolic "defence" of Michel have led to speculation about the extent of what she herself may have been hiding. Only C. Brid Nicholson (2010) makes the rather wild claim that Goldman was really a lesbian, while Falk (2012b) and Garber (1995, 75) both explore the possibility of her being more properly thought of as bisexual. For Falk, "bisexuality, so forcefully affirmed by polyamorous anarchists of the day, was nonetheless relatively hidden" (2012b, 125). Yet despite this acknowledgement of the politics of sexual recognition and the implications of this for what is likely to be visible in the archive, Falk insists that Goldman's relationships with women were self-evidently "*overridden* by her profound sexual and emotional longings for men" (125, my emphasis). Other commentators, Lillian Faderman among them, have suggested instead that Goldman's desire for women should not be overinterpreted in identity terms, writing that "women did not necessarily perceive themselves as lesbians because they lived such experiences" (1991, 34), though she too bases her assessment of Goldman on the visible binary tracks in the archive. Thus Faderman comes to her conclusion not as a critique of identity politics but because she cannot contemplate anyone who expressed such caustic characterisations of lesbians as being themselves a lesbian. In so doing, Faderman preserves the category of lesbian as one marked only by visibility or closeting and never by uncertainty or contradiction.

Goldman's ambivalence about same-sex desire, particularly among women, her knowledge that sexual freedom should be defended, her instinctive rejection of what we would now think of as a combination of identity politics and historical reclamation, but also her pull towards and recoil from actual instances of same-sex attraction as well as her own anxieties about representation, may help us read the strongest indication of same-sex desire within the Goldman archive: her letters from Almeda Sperry. During 1912 and sporadically during 1913, Sperry—a labour activist, witty raconteur, and self-proclaimed alcoholic who sometimes had sex for money—wrote Goldman more than sixty, often very long, hilarious, provocative, smutty, over-the-top, and deeply disturbing letters that document her activist activity, her loneliness and critiques of small-town life and sexual morality, her money woes, her relationship difficulties with men and women, her unrepentant love of drink and cigarettes, and her paranoia. As Howard Zinn tells us: "Almeda Sperry's letters to Emma are remarkable for their passionate declarations of affections, their intense social consciousness, their insights into the life of a woman struggling to survive" (2012, n.p.). Sperry's letters weave together fantasy and memory; describe her desires for women and men, as well as her dislike of the men she has sex with for money; analyse the failings of anarchist, socialist, and conservative writers and men she has met (including Reitman); and return us to her obsessive difficulties with drink and relationships. But the primary critical interest in them is their explicit desire for Goldman.

Let me give an initial taste of Sperry's writing. Fairly early in their correspondence, she confesses: "Dearest . . . I have just awakened and find that I am thinking of you; it is always so—sometimes I curse you for dominating me and I say 'God damn her—I will rid myself of her.' Sometimes I have so great a passion that . . . I am compelled to plunge into a cold bath about four times a day" (April? 8?, 1912).[44] Sperry is straightforward about her passion and Goldman's hold over her, ensuring her friend knows that she is the first thing Sperry thinks of when she wakes and the last thing she thinks of before she turns in: "Well, I'll smoke a few more cigarettes and dream of you before I turn in. I like to think of you from the first glimpse I ever had of you. Tonight I approach you with reverence" (August 24, 1912?). While her desire is fervent, Sperry is also playful, at least in the beginning, teasing Goldman with talk of other women's lust, writing that her friend "Florence . . . oozes sex. . . . She tells me that she shakes with desire for intercourse" (April 20, 1912), and leaving her with promises of what is to come: "I think I have said enuf wild things to you—I'd better save some until I see you" (August 24, 1912).[45] And Sperry is also entertaining, particularly in her depictions of men, dismissing Max Stirner by noting, "I'm sure he had piles, his writing is so strained!" (December 12, 1912?), and insisting: "O, how I love men—not" (October 11, 1912). So too many of her missives are filled with enthusiasm for the labour movement, anarchism, and the theatre: she says with a touch of irony, "If I could go to a good show every night . . . I'd be kind to everybody!" (August 1, 1912).[46]

Although there are no surviving reciprocal letters from Goldman, it is clear that she did write in turn, both from direct comments on her letters in Sperry's—for example, and typically: "Dearest: It is awfully kind of you to write me when you need a rest" (between July and August? 1912)—and from explicit responses to Goldman's comments or queries in Sperry's letters, such as "I note where you say that love should not mean worship" (August 24, 1912). Indeed, Sperry's letters read as an ongoing conversation with Goldman, both real and imagined. Neither of these two larger-than-life women suffered fools gladly, and they shared a vicious sense of humour and lack of respect for authority; importantly, in many ways Goldman was the more sexually naive of the two. As their correspondence builds momentum over the spring of 1912, Sperry tells Goldman more intimate details about her life with her violent and gambling-addicted husband, Fred, the necessity for her to take clients to survive, and her inner experiences of turmoil and misery, as well as her increasing attachment to Goldman, writing: "I am a savage, Emma, a wild wild savage. . . . And it is the untamed part of me that loves you" (August 8, 1912?). After a protracted back-and-forth about arrangements, the two meet in early September in New York and have sex.[47] Sperry's letters become nostalgic for particular rather than generalised intimacy after they meet, and she is by turns romantic and sexually direct in her writing in the months that follow. Yet even at the height of Sperry and Goldman's passion for each other, desire for other people—men and women—is woven through the letters, in ways that make later critical framing of Sperry as Goldman's more straightforwardly lesbian suitor rather suspect in its own right.

While savouring her newfound intimacy with Goldman, Sperry becomes increasingly desperate to claim her as her own. In the same famous letter where she expresses dismay that she "cannot escape" Goldman's "love juice," Sperry expresses her "yearning to possess you at all times" and confesses: "At times my hatred of you is greater than my love. I hate that your interests are myriad" (between September 5 and 30, 1912). Of course, such is the intensity of many relationships at their lusty inception, but the floridly violent imagery in Sperry's letters swiftly becomes the norm. Sperry dreams Goldman is a rose she bites the heart out of and "crush[es] with [her] heel" (October 17, 1912), and threatens that when she does not hear from Goldman, she wishes she "were a giant with thirty league boots. I would stride to where you are . . . strike you in the mouth. . . . And then—and then—I kiss your feet and ask forgiveness" (October 21, 1912). When Goldman does not write, or does not write enough, Sperry falls into despair, writing loose-lipped prose that is sometimes incoherent and always self-abasing in the face of a love she craves: "I've simply got to see you before you start out west. I won't annoy you, dear, I only want to look at you" (December 12, 1912). While Goldman and Sperry do continue to communicate, Sperry moves in and out of jealousy and in and out of drink-fuelled mania and is unable to curb the tide of her demands. By early 1913 the relationship seems in irrevocable decline, despite Sperry's claim as late as August of that year that "whiskey has lost its charm" and that "I will woo you all over again" (August 1913).

According to Jonathan Ned Katz (1976, 524), Goldman saved the letters and returned them to Sperry. Feminist and lesbian and gay historians in particular have been delighted with their wild, explicit tone and content since Alix Kates Shulman discovered them and Katz published a selection of them in *Gay American History* (1976). They have been reproduced or analysed since not only as evidence of Sperry's desires but also for what they may or may not tell us about Goldman's desires. Lori Jo Marso (2003, 318) and Haaland (1993, 174) consider this correspondence an indication that Goldman's otherwise thoroughly opposite-sex-oriented desires may have been more fluid than there is direct evidence to support. Cook—ever cautious—understands the letters as complicating what we know about "Goldman's attitude towards lesbianism" (1979a, 436), noting that "it is impossible to know the significance of this correspondence in her life" (436), while Faderman is clear that "although she had held another woman to her 'unconfined bosom' and shared her 'love juice' with her," Goldman should not be thought of as a lesbian (1991, 34). For Faderman, as well as being too critical of lesbians as I mentioned earlier, Goldman also remained too fond of men to be so reclaimed. I concur with these sentiments about Goldman's lack of identity attachments, though not with Garber's reasoning that this is because of a lack of explicit mention of the affair elsewhere (1995, 75),[48] nor with Faderman's assumptions that she simply falls short of self-evident criteria. Goldman saw sexual freedom as distinct from identity. More curious, perhaps, are the efforts to shape reception of Sperry herself. Jenny Alexander claims Sperry most directly as a lesbian (2011, 27), but while other commentators are less hasty, the selection of which of her letters to publish reflects a more general pull towards this reclamation. Thus the erotic letters, and in particular those that reference "love juice," are more consistently reproduced than those in which Sperry threatens to cut Goldman's flesh open with a sharp blade. While with the exception of Alexander in relation to Sperry, and C. Brid Nicholson in relation to Goldman, neither woman is *routinely* claimed as lesbian (because of their attachments to men and consistently scathing attitudes towards women), these choices suggest that they are nevertheless being buffed and polished for a familiar progress narrative of bisexual if not lesbian history. The possibility that Goldman might have been a somewhat manipulative dabbler, for example, or someone either genuinely conflicted or truly disingenuous about her desire—or both—is never considered; she either is not really interested in women or is interested but repressed. And we never encounter a debate about whether Sperry might have stood a chance of a longer-term sexual relationship with Goldman but thwarted this possibility because in the end drink and a pauper's pride were her main masters.

My own investments come from the pleasure I take in pinning my hopes for an alternative history of sexual freedom, one without identity at its inauguration, on the missing side of a hard-to-read (Sperry tended to scrawl, particularly in late-night missives) two-year correspondence that resists being put in proper date order. To yearn for Sperry and Goldman's correspondence in all its complexity allows me to centre Goldman's struggles within sexual freedom as part of a history of revolutionary thinking and being, in which love and lust are dynamic forces that cut through and across politics. Reading between the lines, imagining these remarkable women's passion for each other on and off the page, is to face their mutual conflict, distraction, punishment, dedication, loyalty, and directionless fervour—both for each other and for all sorts of others in their lives. This affect-laden encounter (that we only partially have) is glorious! It is part of a sexual history made stale if we try to clean it up. Goldman's uncertainty and Sperry's mania, as well as their desire, should be read *with rather than against* Goldman's ambivalent support of homosexuals as part of the sexual history that we inherit. And, indeed, Sperry's correspondence is no less opaque because we have it than Goldman's because we do not; they are opaque in different ways. As I read Sperry's chaotic missives, I am drawn in by the many levels of fantasy that they represent: fantasies about Goldman and her motives, fantasies about sex they did and did not have, and fantasies about her own past and future possibilities. They draw me in and ask me to participate in this conversation; or perhaps they don't and I am an unwanted interloper trying to get in on the action. Either way, one of the privileges of being alive and reading their present and absent historical legacy is that it is harder for them to interrupt *my* reading practice.

So I empathise with Sperry's longings and her struggles not to drink too much again tonight, not to write another begging letter to its mute recipient, her struggles simply to survive. And I take great pleasure in her humour, her commitment to labour politics, and her refusal to be cowed by conventions despite recurring shame. I encourage and warn Sperry in turn, hoping the outcome will be different this time. I can hear Goldman's pleasure on receiving Sperry's flirtations and feel her flush at the memory of their time together; I can hear her laughing at Sperry's apt critiques of society and manners, her gift for ventriloquism, and feel her concern at her friend's unhappiness. I share Goldman's horror at Sperry's violence, or so I believe, while trying to distance myself from her likely second thoughts about it all (Sperry's mania providing a perfect alibi for distance). I open another letter in trepidation at which Almeda I might find inside: the one who tickles Emma all sorts of colours or the one who tips herself into madness; the one who holds fast to what she knows or the one who tries to corner Emma in ways I know she will never tolerate. I want to stop her from writing another time this same day, or this same week, and hold onto a little bit of mystery so that Emma can learn to miss her, but she never does hold back. And once silence cloaks even Almeda's passion, I am left the frustrated voyeur with a partial account of an unclear relationship I have no business interfering with. But still I yearn for what is missing in this fragmentary sexual archive, and see that yearning as central to telling sexual history differently, even as it implicates me in ways I might prefer to override. But when I read Sperry's letters, I cannot help but imagine what Goldman would have written or said in turn, and I am a consistent misanthropic voice from off-stage, precisely because I know where this all ends. I want to piece together the exchange they had, and fill the gaps in this lost history even though I know this is an impossibility. But so too I want to make visible my own desire for this couple: a desire not to diminish their passion because it does not fit a proper narrative of sexual rights or identity; a desire to sit with them both while they try to work out their differences, even though I know that will never happen; and a desire to show that their passions were not necessarily limited by the promiscuity of their affection for each other.

And so, in the next chapter, I write Goldman's missing letters into the botched sequencing of hard-to-place letters from Sperry, following the correspondence we have, imagining the words we do not. As discuss in my introduction, I create an imaginative archive that starts from loss and frustration: my own as well as Sperry's. That these are letters that reflect my own concerns, my own imaginative limits and possibilities as I read Sperry's, is evident. Indeed, it showcases the necessity of the active longing of a third party in generating sexual histories that cannot be told. There is nothing innocent in this. Yearning for sexual freedom writ large in a past that will not be able to give me that—except in snatches—I hope to animate the importance of sexual and gendered entanglement and experimentation in a contemporary context that seeks to reduce, marginalise, or calcify its political potency. These are my contemporary concerns, and I read and write my way into their correspondence with this in mind. My fictional letters to Sperry (whose letters are in turn dripping with fantasy) seek, then, to transform our failure to find them into an opportunity to enter into a historical dialogue that refuses settled meanings in the relationship between sexuality and politics, that instead foregrounds concerns about the relationship of intimacy to both capitalism and revolution. I appreciate that this is quite some presumption on my part, especially since it may of course have been Goldman herself who destroyed her letters (sent back to her perhaps by a furious Sperry, covered in wine splotches and bile). It is indeed possible that this remarkable, heroic woman who went to prison, endured poverty, sickness, and exile, may not have been able to risk this. But the letters are not Goldman's, of course, they are mine; they represent *my yearning* for a different sexual history: one that struggles to make sexual freedom a reality and knows it will fail; one that knows that the politics of that failure are probably more important than a fantasy of sexual certainty.

four · A Longing for Letters

Goldman to Sperry, Chicago, March 1, 1912:

Dearest Almeda: Your letter cheered me no end. It is my best hope that whatever small efforts I make that they will inspire others to take up the cause of Anarchism. I spend so much time battling with the socialists over marriage and the theater. Did you know that they mock me for showing women's lot as it is, but I suppose this is to be expected in those who gain from the oppression of others. . . . Did you hear our own Teddy? He used to think as I did, but I fear he likes power too much. How do you survive in your small town with the small minds of America? You should move to New York or Pittsburgh, 'Meda. What fun we'd have chasing away the demons!

I feel a kinship with you that is rare these days—comrades can promise so much but so often disappoint. And our talk of love as the key to everything means so much to me. Oh, I have such trouble with love—I have always wanted men with poetic souls and fire in their bellies but have always wanted them to feel with me the divine cleansing power of love. Love to wash away the petty jealousies of ordinary life, but not to deceive. . . . Tell me, Almeda, and I hope you do not think me too direct—you may as well know me as I am!—have you ever loved so deeply and so passionately that you find yourself standing at the edge of a cliff, knowing that to throw yourself over is certain death but leaning over to feel the salty wind in your hair?

Your loving friend, Emma

I am sending you four copies of my book. If you do sell any, send money to me in Minneapolis or Denver.

Sperry to Goldman, New Kensington, March 4, 1912:

My own Dear—my cherry-blossom—my moon-beam shimmering on a dark pool at night—my mountain so calm, so serene—my drop of dew hidden in the heart of a wild rose: I do not know whether I have loved deeply and passionately or not; if you mean have I ever loved a man I will frankly say that I never saw a man. I have seen bipeds who pose as men but I never saw a man. No, I have never loved any man. I seem to exact too much. The men are lying pups and all they are after is sex. . . .[1]

Sperry to Goldman, New Kensington, March 5, 1912:

Honeybug: Don't pay any attention to those socialists—their time is short. Rooseveldt's latest speech? It seems that he has adopted the socialist platform in its entirety. The people will bite again. I admire him for being an astute politician. Now, if you weren't so darn honest you would learn how to be crafty and get strings on people. . . . The socialists here have started a paper and want me to be editor. Well, I'll not do it. . . . New Kensington is not so much a mental prison that you think it is. I have been here two and a half years and have done some good . . . I have gotten the principal of the Arnold school to have lectures on sex delivered to his pupils; the kids up there used to laugh at a woman in a family way but now they revere them. . . .

I haven't been able to do much with the New Kensington school. There is such a damn lot of christians in this town. The other day one of the teachers in the New K. school went to see a friend of mine and deliberately knelt down and started to pray. I say, "No quarter" for such people and I gave my friend a raking over the coals for not putting that stinking, virtuous, old maid out. . . .

Lovingly, A.

Goldman to Sperry, Minneapolis?, March 20?, 1912:

Dearest Almeda, you flatter me too much. I'd like to say stop, but I like it! It's true I have no guile in me, but that is for impatience more than a right attitude. If you knew me better you wouldn't think me calm or innocent as a dew drop, dear (heavens!), but I treasure your faith in me, I really do. You are right to expect everything from love if not from sex, and although I have had great passions in my life, they have also been the source of great disappointment. We must never stop trying, though, Almeda!

I am exhausted and sick with lecturing. Ben is such support and makes all the arrangements, carrying me along with his showmanship and enthusiasm, but I find it hard to match his zeal at times. But then the crowds of people who want so much to find another way of living, and who are at the end of what they can stand with the capitalist lies and the hunger and misery, they make me ashamed at my own lack of strength and I feel their energy coursing through me. Then I can give all of myself to my speech and to the crowd. Ah, Almeda, sometimes I seem to become one with the people then and forget myself altogether. I wish I could look out and see your loving face in the crowd—you should hear for yourself our shared disgust at the christian buzzards that pick at dead meat while blaming others for their greed.

Perhaps in the summer after my lecture tour we could take a holiday together.

Yours, as you know, Emmy.

Sperry to Goldman, New Kensington, April? 8?, 1912:

Dearest: It is A.M. I have just awakened and find that I am thinking of you; it is always so—sometimes I curse you . . . Sometimes I have so great a passion to see you . . . that I am compelled to plunge into a cold bath about four times in one day . . .

I am rather happy too—at that—I have taken a "shine" to my sweet-heart—he does not drink but don't care how much I consume; the result is that I do not care to drink while with him. I have never cared so much for a man before and he is the sweetest thing—barring yourself—in the world to me—he doesn't criticize nor vivisect me and the result is that I think a mighty heap of him. . . .

Emmy, the fun I'm having! In the summer, after I see you, I'm going to some drowsy little town in Canada and just dress in a house dress and fish (I do not eat fish—bah!) and swim and ride horse-back.

My eyes are not well again—it is on account of the approach of warm weather—and I fall over . . . and go bumping into New Kensington swine, in other words, the citizens.

I would like to open an artery at one of your wrists and drink some of your warm blood.

With deepest love, A.

Goldman to Sperry, Denver, April 16, 1912:

'Meda mine, I arrived several days ago in Denver after a hellish time running from place to place. I have barely had time to write my nightly lectures, and so writing letters to the cherished guardian of my heart has had to wait. But I have been thinking of you, and hoping you are still enjoying the flush of your new love. We must seize what delights we can in this world. Denver has embraced the cause it seems, and I am surrounded by radical women comrades full of stories of "Man's Inhumanity to Man." When I think on what women suffer and how men barely even know the half of it—it makes me shake with rage.

Good news: I have been asked to teach a course on the plays I love so much and their importance for the people, so I am to stay here longer than planned. It is such a relief to be in one place for more than a few days, and I'll have the chance to rest my legs and head.

My goodness, Almeda, what would your sisters say if they heard your talk of blood sucking. I confess I find your words quite delicious, though I am fond of my life's blood too. Such a gothic imagination! Ben is quite put out that he didn't think of vampirism to seduce me.

Your Em.

Sperry to Goldman, New Kensington, April 20, 1912?:

Dearest: I have just finished reading your article upon Christianity and it is masterly; how I envy you your sameness of expression. I could never give my thots upon that subject in such a dignified manner—all I can do when I think of that subject is to curse and rave and use the rottenest language possible....

In the daytime I loaf a good deal in Florence's office—there all the radicals drop in from time to time.... I met a woman there who edits an Italian newspaper; she has a pleasing personality and is so brainy and is an anarchist....

Florence ... lives with her uncle, is a girl of nineteen who is as mature looking as a woman of 45. She is a mixture of French and Irish and is the most unconventional creature I have ever met ... She has the prettiest mouth I ever saw. She said "Almeda, you could drink 'til hell froze over for all I care, only you are ruining yourself and besides your breath isn't nice." So we made a bargain—I'm to stop drinking and she will stop using crude language—very vulgar language ... She tells me that she shakes with desire for intercourse but is afraid of "getting in" wrong—that is, having a baby. I am not telling you this for gossip. I'm only describing Florence. I said to her, "Insidious poison, how did I ever become acquainted with you?" and she said, "I flirted with you."...

Florence never tires of hearing about you—she would like to meet you. I told her if she ever talks to you like she does to me sometimes I'd break her jaw....

I'm to write a review of Berkman's book for the P.F. Press. After all this I.W.W. business is over, I'll write my heart out for them. We're just simply turning this town inside out. Run me out, hey? Not 'til I get damn good and ready.

And I aint dead yet and aint done for, either.

Love. A.

... Enclosed find a love letter from a man who means it—a letter to me. Poor soul! I mean the man.

Sperry to Goldman, New Kensington, April 30, 1912:

Honey-bug: It seems to me, dear heart, a long time since I have heard from you. I love you—love you—love you—to me you are most beautiful.

I was talking to that anarchist woman who runs an Italian newspaper. To my great surprise she said, "Emma Goldman is no good. She works only for the money—you can ask any of the American comrades in the movement in Pittsburg and they will tell you she is no good—she stays wid a tousand men!" I said, "And what would be the difference, madame, providing she loved the thousand men!" She opened her eyes. Her husband is an I.W.W. man. She has lost his love. He is just now in jail. She says she does not care to love a man any more—she only wants to make men suffer.

But Emmy, I don't see why she says such things of you—how can she possibly think such things when she ought to know how you have spent your energy.

I thought all people who called themselves anarchists were broad minded but I find that there is much jealousy in their ranks and I am sorry.

O, Emmy, I'm not much good but I sure have faith in you.

Love A

Goldman to Sperry (postcard), San Francisco, May 25, 1912:

'Meda, you worry too much when you don't hear from me—you are ever in my heart. Don't you know that once I love, it is forever. The San Diego incident has changed Ben—he will not let me near him. Your Emmy. x

Sperry to Goldman, Arnold, June? 1912:

Dearest: It was so very dear of you to write me that postal—it is so very dear of you to support my soul with the wine of your affection.

I am out in the country again. While I am worn out with the violence of living, harried and persecuted by ignorant people of New Kensington. I miss my cigarettes and my bath tub—miss them so much that I am not affected by remembrance of the fact that that town brings out the subtle twisted ways of me. . . .

Not a great while ago a man and woman were tarred and feathered ...
they lifted her garments up and made her [indecipherable] while they
applied hot tar—the men who did it are all Christians. ...

Lovingly Almeda.

Sperry to Goldman, Arnold, June? 1912?:

I wish I had the comfort of your dear presence just now. How good
you've been to me—good even when I'm in ugly, jealous moods. I am
awfully hungry, dear, to stroke your arms and face and neck. Ah, dear
heart, how very grateful I am to you for telling me I will never lose you.
If only I could do something big for you, Honey-bug.

I imprint a slow kiss upon your mouth.
Almeda.

Goldman to Sperry, Seattle, June 18, 1912:

Meda mine, you cannot know how much I wish you were here with
me at this moment. Your letters keep me going and as you know, I am
exhausted. The constant struggles with the police—and this a country
of free speech: ha!—the fear of threats to kill me, but the cowards never
act in the end. I am to return to Denver in a few days to speak on modern
drama, the curse of patriotism and the promise of family limitation:
the thread is Anarchism of course, that one belief in the power of the
individual over the tyrannies of "fortune" and despotism. I cannot wait
to return to New York in July—despite the weather that has me sweating
like a donkey! Sasha tells me the house is all in order and mama is waiting
to greet me with open arms.

'Meda, you are a breath of fresh air in my life. I would like so much to
be near you, and wonder if perhaps you haven't bewitched me with your
tales of life and longing. There is enough misery in this world without
our adding to it, and I wish my dush would understand as you do the
need to grab hold of life, wring it to the last drop, whatever we face the
morning after. I wonder when we might drain a few glasses together again
and talk till the sun rises.

Until then I smile at the thought of
that slow kiss—Em.

Goldman to Sperry, Denver, June 28?, 1912:

My own Almeda . . . It appears the new eugenics movement has yet to appeal to the people of Denver, but they remain rapt by talk of "Marriage and Love"!

The old battler Voltairine died a week ago, and it was best for her really. She was a stick in my back, but I sure do need some of her strength now to help me fight on.

I tell you, I have only now begun with San Diego. Ben has become more and more distant. As the weeks go by I am more and more convinced that the scars left behind are more than physical ones for both of us. He continues to refuse to talk of it and recoils from me. It fuels my bitterness over every hurt I have endured and not taken out on him. I know this is selfish, but I feel I can tell you whatever is in my heart and you won't think the worse of me for it. Is that true, Meda dear? Can I unwrap myself before you?

> I think of you every day, sweet girl.
>
> Em. X

Sperry to Goldman, Parnassus, between July and August 1912:

Dearest: Have been thinking of you constantly lately. I am wondering how soon you will be home and if you will be too fatigued to allow me to come to see you. I know I don't deserve it but think what a wonderful being I would have to be to deserve anything so delightful. . . .

My husband has not written to me since he went to E. Pittsburg the last time. I have been hoping that he is weaned away from me . . . It used to be that I liked to have him fondle me—liked to have him rub my nude body and kiss my bosom—liked to get in bed with him and love by the hour—liked to lie upon him full length with all my clothes off but now I chill with horror if he offers to love me as I have taught him. . . .

If Fred would be satisfied to live by himself I would beat it to New York this fall. . . . I wish my head were lying on your bosom just now, Honeybug. I am so lonely . . . I wish you and I were sitting out on the porch of your country place. Everything would be quiet wouldn't it—and you and I wouldn't speak—we wouldn't need to. And neither one of us would be lonely for I love you.

A

Sperry to Goldman, East Pittsburgh, July 14, 1912:

Dearest Emmy: In a weak moment, when my rheumatics had the upper hand, I sent you a postal begging you to write.

Dear, I am so pleased when you say, "I tell you, I have only now begun with San Diego." You could not have said anything else—if you had, then I would think senility had begun its work upon you.

Every visit you make in every town has its far reaching results; your work may seem to be thrown away at first but it never is. . . .

The 27th is your birthday, isn't it? Yesterday was mine—34. Gee! Climbing up some. Life is short. I think that since I have met you. I could stand 100 yrs of life if you were in the world. . . . You are always uppermost in my mind.

Love, A

Goldman to Sperry, New York, July 23, 1912:

Sweet Almeda: I am home! So many months of traveling, so much pain and so much accomplished—I feel as though I have lived a full decade of life in just these short months. New York is a hive of activity and Mother Earth is in the best shape it ever has been. I knew Sasha would enjoy not having me peering over his shoulder all the time!

I would write more to you, dear, but there are people in and out all the time—sometimes I feel they would suck the very marrow from my bones in the name of revolution! I am so so tired and cannot imagine ever feeling truly lively. All the travel has taken its physical toll, and I have had this bursting headache that sleep alone will be able to cure. . . . Yet I get so little of it.

You too seem to have lost some of your vigor, 'Meda, and the sparkle of your stories has slipped to the side. Courage! I miss your teasing pen and the way your words make me long to see you again. Write to me, 'Meda, and remind me why I love you.

Emmy x.

Sperry to Goldman, New Kensington, between July and August? 1912:

Dearest: It is awfully kind of you to write when you need a rest and should be doing nothing but relaxing yourself. Please do not ever feel that you cannot keep pace with me as far as correspondence goes—I do not expect you to—your time is too valuable to humanity. I would be content with just one line from you about once a month. Indeed, I marvel that you pay any attention to me at all. . . . I certainly have not done anything constructive enuf in the world to justify your wasting any time upon me.

I meant to write you the other night but there were so many damned noises about that I couldn't. The Episcopalians were having a choir practice and their blatant base sounded like a fog horn. Down the street a way an Italian family has a phonograph . . . next door a boy of sixteen is "learning" the violin and his caterwauling is enuf to raise the dead . . . a couple of doors away from that is a bake shop that sends out stinks all day long. Now, I know that these are some of the insignificant things that I should not notice but I cannot help it. I am willing to die for humanity but I am not willing to smell stinks, hear blatant noises, nor wear dirty clothing for humanity. . . .

. . . I must see you before the first of September as I am coming back here to perfect myself in stenography in September. Then, when I have mastered stenography I am going to where I can see you often.

Sperry to Goldman, New Kensington, July 27, 1912:

Dearest: —

The reason that I have been reticent with you lately was because I have been ashamed of myself and did not want to tell you what I was doing; you see, I went on that trip with Newton. Newton is a Carnegie steel man whom I have known since panic times. Fred and I were living in Braddock at the time and the larger was pretty empty—in fact I helped clean out a flat for a peck of potatoes and some onions and some cabbage and I also did several ironings. Then I said to myself, "Any body who works like this is a darned fool." So I got a friend of mine to introduce me to Newt, who had nothing to do during the panic but walk the streets and spend his money. . . . So I've had Newt ever since . . . and when he asked me to take a trip with him this summer I hated to kill the goose that lays the golden eggs for god knows that Fred don't make enuf to keep me in cigarettes and magazines. So I went on the trip and I never had a more miserable time in all my life . . . I must say I am more disgusted with men than I ever was and if I ever give Fred up it will have to be a "cookoo" that gets me next time. . . .

How will the 26th of August suit you for me to come to see you—that is, if you would like to meet me after telling you all this? I don't care—I'll be darned if I go hungry for anybody. . . . So Newt sent me up $5 a week. Poor thing! he likes me and I do him—for his money. . . .

I cannot understand myself with Fred. I know, that he has murderous instincts. I know that when he wants to lacerate my soul that he talks in a lacivious Michigan lumber-camp strain that makes me tremble with horror. I know also, that I have saved him from the penetentiary twice since I have been married and that I have seen him thru the hospital twice. I know that he is selfish and that he lives like a nigger from day to day, never thinking of the morrow and that whenever he gets into any difficulty he looks for me to get him out. . . .

Write to me, dear, I need it. Let me know when it is your pleasure to have me come to see you. I want to touch you—I want to see whether you really have substance or whether you are merely one of my dreams.

Lovingly A

Goldman to Sperry, New York, August 2?, 1912:

My very own 'Meda, you have burrowed right into my heart. I would never want you to be anything but plain with me—that is part of how we meet each other, is it not?—straight on. I am not shocked by your sex with Newt for money, for god knows we all have to get by as best we can in this rotten world. And what you do is more honest than the women who bleed men dry and pretend they love the husbands they hate! I am curious though, 'Meda dearest, how you feel about the men you have sex with. Do you have romantic feelings for them even though the exchange is clear, or do you cut yourself off from the possibility of love? As you know I fall in love with every man I lust for and am too soft inside and out to keep my distance. It has caused me such grief I wish my body and soul were made of tougher stuff.

You have talked of leaving Fred, of your lack of passion, and of his crippling sickness and need of you. But you will never leave him, 'Meda, because you and he are peas in a pod, and besides, how would you brave life in New Kensington without Fred, even if his absences grow longer? No 'Meda, you speak one thing but do another, though I wish you would leave him when I hear from comrades of his violent temper and his lack of care for who sees him do what and where. He is not worthy of you, but what man is!

I kiss your sweet face and hands and prize you for the brave and lusty woman you are!

Emma.

Have you ever heard the American negro W. E. B. Du Bois lecture? I did just yesterday and have rarely seen such presence. Now that is a man, unlike your bloodsucking, good-for-nothing husband!

Sperry to Goldman, New Kensington, August 8, 1912?:

My sweet dear: I just received your letter and am in bed answering it . . . . When a woman makes up her mind . . . she must wear a mental shield over her bosom else her life would be terrible. One becomes used to it and forgets after each incident; that is the only way to do — to cultivate a forgetting memory. I once started to count on my fingers how many men I had been with and when I reached my last finger I cut the counting out. I was appalled at that number. I know you could never do a thing like that and that is one reason I like you — you are so strong — and yet so comprehensive.

I have absolutely no reciprocation as far as passion is concerned for a man who pays me for sex. So bent is such a man for self gratification that he seldom bothers to find out whether the woman responds or not and if he does want response he can easily be "bluffed." Nearly all men try to buy love — if they don't do it by marrying they do it otherwise and that is why I have such a contempt for men. Love should be worship but love seems to be with most people — ejaculation. I fear I never will love any man. I've seen too much and I am no fool.

Possibly you are right about my not leaving Fred. Perhaps I will have him somewhere in the background always. Habit is even stronger than love and it is nice to sleep with someone so that when a person wakes up in the middle of the night why one can touch the other person and not feel so alone. And then, too, in the winter time—when the wind howls. My word! If I were alone then, I'd ask the nearest male who had any kind of health to sleep with me just for the sake of his animal warmth. . . . But as far as violence is concerned, violence don't hold me to anyone. It is the sweet part of Fred I had hold me—and the fact that we have been thru strikes, pains and hunger and sickness together. The time he went to cut my throat I kicked him in the abdomen and he forgot about wanting to slit my neck. You can ask my mother if she ever got a whimper out of me when she beat me . . .

I am a savage Emma, a wild wild savage. . . . And it is the untamed part of me that loves you because you don't want to put leading strings on it. If you did I would tell you that you are a liar and your book is a lie. And it is the wild part of me that would be unabashed in showing its love for you in front of a multitude or in a crowded room. My eyes would sparkle with love—they would follow you about and love to gaze on you always. . . .

God! God! God! God!

A.

Sperry to Goldman, Parnassus, August? 1912:

Dearest: They didn't have a meeting on the streets after all last Sunday so I didn't get put in jail and I am glad. . . .

I have a sister Anna; all one gets in her house is Jesus Christ and culture. One day a friend of mine, who I hadn't seen for years, was hunting me up and she asked my sister Anna's husband where I was and he said, "What do you want her Almeda for? Has she done anything criminal" I'd criminal him if I had him in some wild county. I'd make him forswear his God. Do you know what that skunk did? He bought a mortgage from some man—cheap; the man did not like to foreclose the mortgage for the mortgage was a widow-woman with children. That skunk sold that woman out. And then I'm a criminal . . . I'm done! I'm done with the whole family. They can have their Jesus and I'll have myself and when I need any Jesus I'll take him out of a bottle. . . .

I'm awfully lonely. That's the reason I wrote this letter full of nothing.

I think of nothing but you, dear. I'm only going to stay about two days when I come there for I won't have much money . . . and I never sponge on friends. I only want to see you, please, and no strangers.

A.

Goldman to Sperry, New York, August 17, 1912:

Dearest Almeda—I want you to have a letter waiting when you get home and to know that you cannot be lonely because I am thinking of you.

When I say that love and not money should be the glue between people, not filthy false morality peddled by the vicious beasts they call religious guides, I do not mean "worship"! Worship will make you blind to the faults of those you love and that is the end of any possible equality. If people love each other truly, but never blindly, they can tell each other hard truths, and I have to tell you one now, 'Meda. You write about not caring what others think of you, and not caring a jot about the men you have sex with for money, but you count them on your fingers in shame. You have earned what you eat, 'Meda, and the respect of your comrades, and yet you torment yourself with self-abasement. My dear, sweet girl, you tell yourself lies and carry with you bitter pills of guilt like cheap romances procured on the same street corner. . . .

Your visit could not come at a better time as I feel much rested after my time in Ossining with my dush, tho his fretting about his writing almost destroyed the calm. He is almost done though now, and I can tell you it is a book of truthfulness that will shake convention. And not just the world outside, the world of our inward-looking comrades who care nothing for the beautiful, honest sensitivity in its pages.

Do not fear, I will have you to myself in New York, 'Meda dearest, though Ben and Sasha were so hoping to meet you as I have not tired of telling them of your wit and how you have bewitched me. I feel something so strong between us, Meda, a current of sympathy; it pulls me toward you and promises pleasures perhaps.

Em. x

Sperry to Goldman, New Kensington, August 24, 1912:

Dearest: —

It is so very, very sweet of you to address me with such endearing terms.... I note where you say that love should not mean worship as that smacks of too much slavishness for you. I discuss that matter because I naturally wanted to find just what your definition of the term meant.

In speaking of having known intimately more men that I can count on my fingers I meant that it appalled me to think that a woman would do such a thing for mercenary reasons. You will agree with me that it is a most horrible thing and appalling. I believe that it is nobody's business if a woman has loved a hundred men . . .

Certainly I do not mind a criticism from you. You could not criticize if I were not worth it. Now, is that subtle flattery? . . . I will never mind criticism from you because I love you and believe you to be a thoroly sincere person and also I learn things from your criticism . . .

I have been very sick this week. Fred and I had a terrific quarrel and also a "terrific" reconciliation and also I got drunk. When I say drunk I mean drunk since I cannot touch one drop of liquor without drinking a couple of quarts. . . . Fred and I beat each other and I am all over bruises. We are both sorry and are going to try over. We are both hulks of humanity who were started out wrong in life . . .

If it is agreeable to you I would like to come to you the night of September 2nd arriving at the New York terminal at 8.08 A.M. Let me know what time to meet you and where.

Lovingly, lovingly,
Almeda

. . . I do not regard men like Berkman and Reitman as strangers; they are brothers.

Sperry to Goldman, New Kensington, August 24?, 1912:

Dearest: —.

Of course there is something in telepathy. And between two such electric natures as ours. I tell you, Emma, if you are good to me I will never be weak again. It is just because I don't want things very badly that

I let things slide but, when I do want anything and want it badly I am ruthless. But I think that I have said enuf wild things to you—I'd better save some until I see you.

Lovingly,
Almeda.

Goldman to Sperry (postcard), September 5 to 24?, 1912:

Ah, Almeda! Let me give you a gift as you have given me so many, and I blush at the memory of your many generosities! Ask anything of me and I will raise heaven and earth to give you what you want. I love you but you are cruel, leaving me so soon. Your Em. X

Sperry to Goldman, New Kensington, between September 5 and 24, 1912:

Dear heart: You said you would give me a gift. May I tell you what I want? I want that picture of yours that hangs in the office above Ben's desk. If this is too much to ask for, never mind. The picture I have of you is out of a newspaper and is no good. If it is Ben's picture, ask him if I cannot have it. Ah God! He couldn't be so cruel to refuse me, could he, since he has the real you before his eyes every day.

Lovingly,
A.

Goldman to Sperry, New York, September 12, 1912:

'Meda mine: I cannot get you out of my mind, and my body is blotched with purple prints of your clever fingers.

You have turned the banal into the exotic, my dear. Sweet wine and cigarettes will never taste the same again—I can see you reclining with one in each hand, laughing at my stories and shyness, and then being quiet suddenly as you put them both down . . . You know I hate jealousy of any kind, but I am maddened with thoughts of your soft mouth on the cigarettes I left for you. I hope you are satisfied, you temptress! You have made me mad with envy over a cigarette!

Can I persuade you to join me in the country—there will be nothing to do but entertain one another, sleep, and take energizing walks. Tell me, 'Meda, will you come? Several comrades you met might also join us. Hutch has certainly spoken of little other than your wit and fierce beauty since the evening he interrupted us, and begs me to ask you to write—will you?

I have not slept well these past days and you know why—I keep looking at my arms, legs, belly . . . and wondering: what new flesh is this that holds the memory of another's so long?

Your Em. x

Ben says to tell you that he will need persuading to part with that picture of mine . . .

Sperry to Goldman, New Kensington?, September 19, 1912?:

Dear, I cannot write much today. I, too, wish that I could spend a week with you in the country. I am with you in spirit, at any rate. Just before you sink into slumber, dear heart, I rest in your arms. I browse amongst the roots of your hair—I kiss your body with biting kisses—I inhale the sweet, pungent odor of you and you plead with me for relief.

No, I won't write to "Hutch," especially after reading his book. My soul is not to be vivisected for the benefit of the general public. Besides, if he wants me he knows my address. He is an observer—he does not know emotion altho he strives for it desperately; he has a subtle mind but it is not half so subtle as my own and he does not need to think that I am like a ripe fruit, ready to be plucked at his will. This is terrible—I alternate between longing for him and repulsing him but you must never tell him.

Lovingly

A.

Sperry to Goldman, New Kensington?, September 23, 1912?:

Dearest: I have been flitting about from one thing to another today, in vain endeavour to quell my terrible longing for you. But my work is done and now that I have sat down to think, I am instantly seized with a fire that races over my body in recurrent waves. My last thots at night are of you. I dream of you during my slumbers and that hellish alarm clock is losing some of its terrors for me for my first waking thots are of you. . . .

Nell Davis has moved away—the only woman of real intelligence I ever met in this town . . . She would let me go to see her but she never called on me; her husband wouldn't let her on account of my reputation . . . Nell don't know that I know her husband used to be a pimp in a whorehouse. There is no worse stickler for propriety than a reformed pimp nor no worse stickler for prohibition than a reformed drunk and he is both . . .

How I wish I were with you on the farm! You are so sweet in the morning—your eyes are like violets and you seem to forget, for a time, the sorrows of the world. And your bosom—ah, your sweet bosom, unconfined.

Lovingly, Almeda.

Do not write to me, dear, if it takes any of your strength from your lectures.

Goldman to Sperry, Ossining, between September 15 and 30, 1912:

Dearest, my lectures go so slowly even out here with no distractions. Words are like stubborn teeth and rotten to the core when I do get them out! I worry too much about their reception—when I was younger and more vigorous, I just said whatever came into my head, and damn the consequences; now, I worry about damage to the cause, and how this or that green-eyed comrade might laugh to see me falter.

Sasha is miserable at his work with a dark humor that I know only too well, and that cannot be shaken. How I wish you were here to enliven our sorry dinners with tales of New Kensington and that good-for-nothing Fred, 'Meda. And Ben writes rarely and then of mostly bureaucratic matters . . . Almeda, I need you to teach me how not to care so much about one man's attentions. I want so much to embrace love's freedom—I know it to be the only way—but I have always seen my soul so clearly reflected in each man's eyes, though I know how freeing love's generosity truly is.

Ah! Sometimes I wish I were more like you, with your wild and savage ways. I know that what you really want is to have me for yourself, though you would say otherwise. And yet you were the one who put on your hat and walked through the door though I begged you to stay. I can still taste your salt skin and when I close my eyes I lose myself again in your open lips.

Emmy. x

Sperry to Goldman, New Kensington, between September 5 and 24, 1912:

Dearest: It is a good thing that I came away when I did . . . If I had only had courage enuf to kill myself when you reached the climax then—then I would have known happiness for then, at that moment, I would have had complete possession of you. Now you see the yearning I'm possessed with—the yearning to possess you at all times and it is impossible. What greater heaven—what greater hell? . . . At this moment I am listening to the rythm of the pulse coming thru your throat. I am surg along with your life blood coursing thru the secret places of your body. I wish to escape from you but I am harried from place to place in my thots. I cannot escape from the rythmic spurt of your love juice. . . .

I pray for death for I have had the greatest thing in the world. To yearn for a thing with great intensity is to suffer but to kill the yearning with satisfaction is deadly. Sweet yearning! Maddening yearning—revolutionary yearning.

I am in pain, dear heart, I am in pain but you have enriched me—you have enriched me—at this moment I feel you open your mouth in sweet irritation so you see, dear heart, I can now possess you at any time . . . and can even spill wine upon you in mad abandon and hear you moan with the shock of it and hear you moan at the cruelty of my dalliance.

At times my hatred of you is greater than my love. I hate you that your interests are myriad. I hate you for my own cowardice in not killing you, that your life is not mine to keep or mine to take. I can give to no other person what I have given to you, my dear, my dear!—my dear whose succulence is sweet and who drips with honey.

Now I am prostrat upon the ground and the rain is beating down upon me and dark clouds loom above and around me. I am desolate. I am alone.

Almeda

Goldman to Sperry, Ossining, September 26, 1912:

Dearest Almeda: Your passion warms my heart, and you know how deeply I felt the newness of our time together. You know too that I have long been outraged at the treatment of the "invert" and have said so publicly despite the sneering disapproval of comrades. And now I have felt the freedom of loving fully in another way, and truly, 'Meda, I feel my life transformed.

What we feel is natural as the movement of the planets, and I feel no shame in our love; I believe all have such tendencies, particularly when young. But my loving, kind friend—you go too far in your desire to possess me utterly. That privilege is denied to all pretenders! I fear you go mad with wanting me for yourself, and the proof is in your letter indeed: all jealousy finally turns to hatred and yours has taken you there so very quickly.

You must hold off from drinking night and day, 'Meda, for it does you no good, even though I know you do it to get away from the stuffy atmosphere of the closed house in the closed small town you call home—your very own Doll's House!

With loving hope, Emma.

Sperry to Goldman, New Kensington?, September 5 to 30, 1912:

After reading your letter today my spirit was no longer supine and it is a new Almeda . . . that begs you to forget a letter written in a moment of madness in which she used the word possession in connection with yourself. It is thru "sin" that we rise to great spiritual heights. I knew I was doing wrong at the time but I have been punished. How well you understand me dear heart; the same thing made me suffer that made you suffer and that [made] me so crazy that I wished to kill myself and even spoke of hatred. It is a terrible thing that I must be constantly begging forgiveness from you.

I am not drinking today, dearest, and you are helping me give it up. I feel more and more that I don't need the stuff. . . . Fred and I had a terrible scene when I got home. I was so wretched I asked him to get his supper at a restaurant and it infuriated him and he made me get it anyway so I poured whiskey into myself. I hope I never do it again for I feel that I always want to have possession of my [?] mind so that I can love you more and more every day. I am quite well now. I have great resiliency when I am loved and forgiven. . . .

I resent your saying my atmosphere is stuffy—it is no longer stuffy since I have lived near you a whole week and since you have held me in your arms. . . .

Almeda.

Sperry to Goldman, New Kensington?, between September 5 and 30, 1912:

Dearest: I received a letter from you today. . . . I feel like a spent summer from my terrible emotions of the last few days. I feel that you are rigt in all you say and that I have done you [an?] irreparable injury. It may be true that some day I may lose these tendencies but I do not know that I have any desire to [lose?] them as they are natural and not acquired. For the life of me I do not understand why people look askance at those tendencies which by the way, have been directed towards but two women. However, I will never offend you again unless you entertain thoughts of return and you are too nearly normal for that.

Goldman to Sperry, New York, October 3, 1912:

Dearest 'Meda:

On Sunday I start my lectures in the city and I am impatient to get going on them. With the election coming up—and the people being damned if they do damned if they don't—I am talking most about the bankrupt practice they call politics. The socialists who put all their faith in democracy! And who have their false hopes dashed when disappointed—I am sick to death of their dismissal of Anarchism and mocking of its advocates. We are hoping for a big audience because I have decided to speak in English and Yiddish. I have never understood comrades' resistance to spreading the word in whatever tongues we can, as though Yiddish or Russian were somehow purer—such absurd nostalgia for countries that never did them any favors!

I hope your efforts to keep away from whiskey and cigarettes are proving fruitful, dear. You know I like a drink as much as any woman—but there is no point in striving to defeat the masters of authority and tyranny in one sphere only to worship them in one's inner life. Small wonder your "darling Fred" doesn't know if he's coming or going—I have little sympathy with a man who resents women's liberty as he does, but you blow hot and cold with vitriol and compassion when your appetites are given free rein, 'Meda. For all his faults, he has been patient with you in his way, and perhaps you should be with him too.

'Meda, you misunderstand me: I long to return to your arms—as well you know!—it is true that I am not a woman whose love for other women is strongest in her. I can't help feeling that a man and a woman were meant to be together, my sweet, even though I have wanted you so badly I shake at the thought of it. In time our lust will fade and we will be as two sisters again—Ah! I wish you could be here to share the energy of the people, particularly for my lectures on modern drama, which I know you adore so much. Write and tell me how you are, and how you long for me, dear sweet 'Meda.

Your Emmy x

Sperry to Goldman, Pittsburgh?, October 11, 1912:

Dearest Heart:—

I have tried to keep from writing you lately, first, because I know that you are fatigued enough lecturing, without being bothered by others and second, because there is nothing in my head but inane things.

I have walked around about forty thousand drinks since the last time I wrote you. I simple cut it off short I have not been smoking so much, either and have developed quite an appetite—everything "tastes" good. . . .

Dearest, I am glad that you said to me what you did about patient understanding and about bringing out better things in Fred. You speak the truth. Fred is like a barometer—and I am the atmosphere which controls him. . . .

I feel pretty well balanced tonight. Of course, I have an ache for you but it is a sad ache, not a passionate ache. I do not believe in allowing passion to [?] one's head for then it is not love but lust.

There has been quite a stir in Pittsburg lately with the "Moral Efficiency Commission." They are sticking their puking mugs in everybody's business....

I kiss your dear hands.

A

Sperry to Goldman, Pittsburgh, October 17, 1912:

Dearest: I wonder what has dried me up so suddenly that I am unable to pour my heart out to you? ...

Dearest, I destroyed you in a dream last night. You were a rose—a great, yellow rose with a pink centre—but the petals were folded one upon the other so tightly. I prayed to them to yield to me and held the rose close to my lips so that my warm breath might persuade them to open. Slowly, slowly they opened, revealing great beauty—but the pink, virginal centre of the flower would not unfold until the tears gushed from my eyes when it opened suddenly, revealing in its centre a crystal drop—dew. I sucked the dew and bit out the heart of the flower. The petals dropped to the ground one by one. I crushed them with my heel and their odor wafted after me as I walked away.

Almeda.

Sperry to Goldman, New Kensington?, October 18, 1912:

Honey-bug:—

You are quite close to me tonight, for some reason. Lately, I have held out to you imploring arms but you do not seem to respond. I am feeling so well, dearest, that I am beginning to perceive how it is that some people can degenerate into beings that live merely to eat. I am still not drinking and feel quite tame—so tame, please notice, that I do not even feel like swearing....

Oct 21st

I am reading Hutch's book again and am enjoying it; the first time I read it, it gave me the horrors, especially when one day a drop of water came thru the ceiling and hit me on the nose. I immediately got drunk until the walls were alive with creeping things ...

You know that I could love Hutch Hapgood but I have had a revulsion against him for there is a compromising savor to his writings. "A tragic limitation to the social rebel?" Yes, but only when the social rebel allows himself to be swayed by bandages of lethargy.

Dearest, could you send me a couple of copies of Berkman's book? I have every afternoon free and my cold is almost better and while I am out selling the book I will be away from cigarettes . . .

Lovingly
A.

Sperry to Goldman, New Kensington, October 21, 1912:

Don't you ever show this to anybody

Do you know, dear, that sometimes I feel quite cruel towards you? When I do not hear from you I wish I were a giant with thirty league boots. I would stride to where you are, grab you up with my big paws and dump you down in the middle of this community and whenever you would try to escape I would just push you back into it again just to let dispair creep into your heart. I would like to strike you in the mouth. I think, "She is at the tail end of a blind alley anyhow. To hell with other people—damn the swine! they do not understand any part of her and she is giving, giving, giving giving herself to them. She will die in extreme poverty, if she does not die in harness. . . ."

Oct 22

And then sometimes I think, "Perhaps she is just studying me—all my personalities for the good of her cause—studying this peculiar product of our civilization. Her cause is first. But if I were really assured of this fact I would carve her heart out. Mark how the blood spurts! But by carving her heart out, Almeda, you would only acknowledge your weakness and you do love to kiss her hands, Almeda, and lay your head on her wonderful bosom. . . .

Bah, you, you! don't you think I'd send you away if I did not need you? Canaille! I am the gnome who sits at the top of your intelligence.
The gnome is gone. I am covered with sweat. I am ill.

Sperry to Goldman, New Kensington?, between March 1912 and September 1913:

O horrible, horrible fear that you have become indifferent to me. O, horrible midnight vision of you—so unsatisfying—gazing past me into the beyond. See, the walls begin to creep upon me—old hags with dead faces and living, clutching claws approach. They scourge me and I escape into the air but the sky is falling and only a tunnel is left to hurry back along into the house and the roof of the tunnel is sinking, sinking.

I hurry back into the house.—ah! you are there. I seize a knife. O, glittering edge, how beautiful you are! I long to cut something soft and white like your soft white bosom. So! The blood spurts. How beautiful you are, crimson flood.

Your gaze is arrested, horrible vision. How you are looking at me. I have compelled you to look at me. I am the Present. I but I am hell-fire when you gaze past me indifferently. I am hell-fire and I drag you back to me for there are many things in me you have not fathomed.

Horrible vision, peering into the future, you must pay attention to me or I will become mad and plunge the knife in deeper for if you no longer love me the future does not want you nor will I permit you to love anyone else if you do not love me for I will blind your eyes and leave you to rot.

Almeda.

Goldman to Sperry, New York, October 24?, 1912:

Almeda! You must stop your ravings, or stop writing altogether! It pains me to the core to receive your violent outpourings—I could not open your last letter from sorrow and anger and had Sasha open it for me and read it aloud. (Poor dush, I think you quite shocked him.) Whatever your passion for me I had hoped your faith in Anarchism, in our common cause, would win out. I thought that even if you were pulled along by too many Masters that you would know I could not be; and now your madness threatens to pull me under with you.

You have betrayed me, Almeda. You pretended unfettered love and the cause above all else, and I allowed myself to be seduced by your words as well as your mouth. You say you admire and respect me, but your canting demands say the opposite. I am a lover of openness, and cannot tolerate your desire to tie me to you in a dance of morbid singleness.

'Meda, we have enjoyed each other so much! But I fear this will never be enough for you 'Meda, and that grieves me. It hurts me to think you would misunderstand me in service to your own desires. I feel I cannot give freely of myself to you, cannot come back to you, unless I promise you everything. I have tried and tried to tell you that I can't be all yours, all anyone's. You doubt my loyalty when I am unable to write, but I have told you again and again that I love you and that you are always in my heart. Your lack of belief in me hurts more than the knife you say you will plunge into my white flesh, and I see now that the only "loyalty" you could "trust" would be one that proved loving you was the best, the only thing, the final thing in my life. Would you really want me to be yours for fear you would kill me otherwise? Do you not care for me at all? Do your worst then, 'Meda, it doesn't scare me: I have faced worse villains, you vicious child!

Don't you remember how free we felt that day, hiding from the rain and pretending not to be at home, and when we talked and touched and your openness — oh — don't you remember? I am weeping hot tears of sadness and shame at what your love has become and I entreat you to return to yourself . . .

Emma.

Sperry to Goldman, New Kensington?, between March 1912 and September 1913:

Dearest: Don't be sad anymore. I am tip top today. I am so volatile, dear, and each one of my personalities takes complete possession of me at the time it enters my mind. Sometimes there seems to be a force other than myself, which seems to drive me.

I am not worth your being sad.

I never thought I would do anything mean to you — of all people. However that was "yesterday." But we are living today.

I love you utterly

A

It is hard to be my friend isn't it? O Jesus! Well, I'm no hypocrite with you, anyway.

> I wish you were looking into
> my eyes just now.
> A.

Goldman to Sperry, New York, between October 27 and November 1, 1912:

Dearest Almeda: Now that my rage has burned and gone, I can be more measured in my thoughts. I am glad that you are in my life, and our comrades could learn much from your fearlessness. I am sad that I cannot return your love in the way that you surely want, but I am happy to have you as my dear friend, and share a passion for life and each other when we can. I feel your gaze and your touch as a searing heat that pulls me to you, and know our shared love to be entirely natural. But as you know, I cannot abide jealousy in any form, from anyone.

'Meda, would you be able to secure a hall in New Kensington for me to lecture in? I have long wanted to visit your hell, and to shock the sensibilities of those townspeople who scorn you and to support the socialists and comrades who work tirelessly without hope. We will give them a show and revive the memory of the Homestead heroes!

> In loving comradeship, Emmy, x

Can you be sure of a large audience, or else it may not be worth the journey.

Sperry to Goldman, New Kensington, November 1, 1912:

Dearest:—

. . . If you come here I will have a leaflet about you put in the mailbox or door-way of every house from Oakmont (that's full of swells) up to Braeburn, on this side of the river and from Pringdale to Natrona on the other side of the river and of course put notices in the paper and if I don't fill the hall then it is not my fault.

I've been sick again. I caught a cold and last Saturday night I was unhappy about you and miserable and I went down to! Pittsburg and got on a street car and rode street cars until 1.30 in the morning and then went to a hotel and stayed there until Sunday evening and had it out with the devil; it was the only way I could have any privacy. I thought I was going to pipe out and if I was going to pipe out it would be by myself....

Thank you for being so nice and kind to me. Don't mind me when I have bats in my belfry.

Lovingly, Almeda

Goldman to Sperry, New York, between November 1 and 5?, 1912:

Meda:

There is a little madness in all of us, dear heart! But I worry about your health and your nerves, and wait anxiously for you to return to your sweet-tempered caustic self! We can talk about all this and much else besides when we are together again with the time to get used to each other's ways. In the meantime, you must promise me not to exhaust yourself...

What do you think the crowd would best like to hear me lecture on? Syndicalism perhaps, the horrors of false moralism? Or would there be interest in Sasha's book?

Are you sure to be able to secure large numbers for the audience? — I hate to press but have been at times in halls outside larger towns where comrades had not got the word out, and these were sorry evenings.

Em.

Sperry to Goldman, New Kensington, November ?, 1912:

Dearest: —

Thank you for being so very nice to me when I do not deserve it. Yes, please give us a lecture on Syndicalism if I can procure a hall. We certainly need it.... On second thought, tho, I think it would be better to announce a Berkman lecture together with a discussion of syndicalism....

The circulars will be well distributed. I will personally hand them to the working-men as they leave the shops and will have them put in all the dwellings around here....

Berkman's book is the work of a genius. It has made me realise also... the sincerity of a true revolutionary is as near to another truth as it is possible in a universe where all things are relative. I have a deep affection for him and a wholesome awe. I have a wonderful, deep and lasting affection for him and it is a greater affection than the ordinary love between a man and a woman. I cannot explain—it is an impersonal affection and yet I feel at a oneness with him. I have gulped the book whole, I have nibbled at it, I have played with it as a cat does with a mouse and again and again I have returned to it to pick out some little expression that appealed to me. Fred says that all I have done since reading it is to stare into nothingness. . . .

Lovingly, A

Sperry to Goldman (telegram), New Kensington, November 7, 1912:

NEW KENSINGTON PA 7

EMMA GOLDMAN

55 WEST 28 ST NEW YORK

HAVE SECURED HALL FOR TUESDAY NOVEMBER TWENTY SIXTH

A

Goldman to Sperry, New York, November 9, 1912:

'Meda mine: Imagine my surprise when I opened your package—such a crazy gift, and so like you! My goodness, I wasn't sure if I should use it as a plate, wear it, or hang on the door nail? Ben says I am ample enough already but he is just sulking.

Thank you, 'Meda, for all the hard work you are doing to ensure my visit goes smoothly. I am a little worried about the advertising, which you have not told me about—you really must make sure it goes out in time. And you must tell me about the tickets: shall I send them to you now or bring them along with me when I come?

A dear friend will be coming with me to New Kensington—she is a trusted comrade. Ben is not coming with me this time, and I do need someone along to ensure I get off at the right station! Perhaps you would like to come with me on part of my lecture tour after New Kensington as my friend must go back to New York. Oh do say yes, Almeda? It will give us time together and I miss your sweet devotion.

Emmy x.

Sperry to Goldman, New Kensington, November 14, 1912:

Dearest: That was a crazy gift but I reckon I have some strange ideas. I wanted you to eat off it at least once.

I just went up to see about that ad; it is all right—is fixed just like the front of enclosed circular. There are a couple of little mistakes in the circulars but it is pretty good work for the P. F. Press; their printer is the dumbest I ever saw. I hope you like it and wont kick about the price.... I wish I had made the price of admission 25c for I don't see how you will make out with all this expense unless you sell a lot of books or take up a collection... About the tickets—sure send them along. I may not sell many but will try and there are a couple of friends of mine who want a batch....

I don't think I can go to New Castle and those places as first, I have no money 2nd; my clothes are on the bum [turn?] and 3rd Fred wouldn't want to get his own meals and couldn't buy any as he has spent all his money on an awful spree. Between Fred . . . and that dumb printer I am about all in. Of course you know how delighted I would be to be near you a number of days both to be near your own dear self and to learn at the lectures.

I shall be delighted to meet your friend as it will be a great comfort for me to meet a kindred spirit. There are so few of them....

Emma, what do you think of the God damn cowards in this world?

Lovingly, A

Goldman to Sperry, New York, November 24?, 1912:

Ah 'Meda:— my heart breaks that you can't—won't—travel with me. Damn Fred and his appetites! I set off tomorrow and can already see your dear face—wisps of smoke curling up and around as you wait for us to get off the bus.

Your Em. X

Goldman to Sperry, New Castle, November 28?, 1912:

Dear Almeda: I can't write very much now, since I have had to adapt my lectures to smaller audiences than I expected this entire trip. Really: I do feel that comrades could do more to show their support for those who put their entire lives on the line for the cause.

It is a good thing you are not with me, since your demanding petulance would simply make things worse. First you make a scene after my lecture—pouting and snapping at everyone because I wouldn't leave everyone else alone and focus only on you. Then I arrive in New Castle—exhausted, dirty, and with a hot head—to find a rose of the bunch we gave you as thanks for all your work sent back to me with its petals all pulled off the stem. You are too much, Meda!

I could see the wounded anger in your eyes, but I am first and foremost an Anarchist and only after a friend, Meda. I have given up plenty of comfort in my life—children and a home to call my own—and you think I will give up the cause for your dubious love? You are surely even crazier than I thought. I wonder about your commitment to revolution, Meda, because you seem to take your eye off the prize at each and every opportunity.
I will put the fallen petals in a book and hope that some of their sweetness returns along with your senses.

Emma.

Sperry to Goldman, New Kensington, November? 1912:

Dear Emmy: You win! I am haunted by your eyes and sad mouth. . . . I kiss them—and how I looked into them with a defiant stare. . . .

I walk the streets with my head [. . . ?] feeling proud. All the rest of these people are a mirage—only my Emma is true. . . .

I am happy.

A.

Sperry to Goldman, New Kensington?, December 12, 1912:

Dearest: I am trying to read Stirner's "Ego and His Own." I don't have to read that book and I'm not going to—he must have had piles his writing is so strained. . . .

Raphael says you must come here again as he has met ever so many people who didn't even know you were here and they are sorry they missed you. I ot to have advertised in the two capitalist papers. Well, a person has to learn. Dearest, when you come anywhere near Pittsburg will you let me know so I can go to see you? Say Cleveland or some place like that. I could go in the morning and come home at night. I've simply got to see you before you start out west. I wont annoy you, dear. I only want to look at you. . . .

I didn't tell you I am in a family way, did I? Talk about neuralgia and vomiting. Yoi! It is strange I had to wait until after I was thirty to start to get "knocked up." I wish it were Sash Berkman's baby. I'd have it. He is a man.

Lovingly
Almeda.

Goldman to Sperry, New York, December 15, 1912:

Dear 'Meda: I gave almost the same lecture on syndicalism in Brooklyn last night only to ten times the audience! The thunderous applause made it hard to speak, and I was carried out of the hall on the shoulders of the working men who had given up their evening to hear a poor Russian woman speak to them of the general strike.

Darling 'Meda, you are with child! A glorious thing it is when a radical is to become a mother—it gives me hope that the Cause will carry on and not be forgotten when we are all worm fodder.

It is true that you have wounded me, but once I love it is hard to push me away, and I would rather pull you into my arms and hold you fast than lose you. And perhaps I would not only hold you fast, sweet Meda.

Your Emmy.

Sperry to Goldman, New Kensington?, December? 1912?:

Dear Heart; I have read your letter to me—so unworthy—your letter wherein you offer me the refuge of your arms—and it has taken away from me the desire to kill myself. For a week or more I have lain stupidly around with that desire in my heart—I could hardly see or hear and would forget everything. But everything is well now—I do not feel so alone.

You do not know how grateful I am for your great goodness and you do not know how the tears gushed to my eyes when I read your letter. I had a sense of your presencse and I laid my head on your bosom and listen to the rythm of your heart-beats.

Life is so wonderful when you hold out your arms to me of your own volition ... Dearest one, no one can ever hurt me again. Ah, dearest one, I part your hair strand by strand and kiss the partings.

My love-juices are flowing. I am so grateful—so grateful.

Great-heart-of-the-world! You are part of my soul.

A.

Sperry to Goldman, New Kensington?, December 20, 1912?:

Dearest: Nothing to do this evening—nothing to read. I long for some-one to talk to who has some gray matter. Have been reading "God and the State" but it bored me. . . .

I once saw a strike-breaker hit a little baby on the head; the baby was in its father's arms and ever since then I think that it is not a crime to kill a strike-breaker—coldly and deliberately or to kill the man or men who employ him. But I had to see that in order to come to that conclusion. So now I think it is a worse crime to offend the sensibilities of a loved one (as I offended yours not long ago) than it is to murder. So one learns more from life than from books.

Since I committed that crime against you I seem to have become more mature and more thoughtful of others. Patient understanding is what you have given me and I cannot express my gratitude—Immutable one! . . .

The doctor operated on me again today. He says I ot not to allow myself to have such revulsion of the soul "under the present system."

I wish Hapgood were here now—he and I alone. I wish he had Sash Berkman's uncompromising spirit. I'd like to tell Hutch what I did to you and see what he says about it.

One cannot have everything one wants in one person can he, Emma? I like Berkman's soul but his body does not appeal to me in the least and Hutch's does. I tell you everything I think don't I, dearest? Almost everything . . . .

I have rooted jealousy out of me, Emma. Rooted it!

Lovingly
Almeda

Goldman to Sperry, New York, Christmas card, December 20?, 1912:

Season's Greetings—come to the Mother Earth Ball or join us the week after! Emmy x.

Goldman to Sperry, New York, December 22 to 25?, 1912:

'Meda, you do make me laugh! Berkman's soul and Hapgood's arms: what a creature let loose on the world that would be! Dearly though I love him and always will, I despair of my Sasha's disapproval of bodily pleasures. You should see him at a dance, 'Meda, it's like his mouth has been stuffed with lemons and iron weights have been strung to his ankles!

I can forgive anyone anything if they make me laugh, 'Meda, and you have a talent for it, I must say. But your passions exhaust me sometimes and if I ever give you flowers again and you fly into a rage: no need to send one back, just gnaw at it at your leisure and destroy it that way, dearest!

I hope you are eating and drinking well, because we need strong brave men for the cause not slender weaklings. Ah! I wish I were stronger, though: I have another cold and must be well before the new lecture tour. Perhaps there will be some rest in the next few weeks.

I wish all good things for you in the coming year, my sweet, bruised friend.

Your Emmy.

Sperry to Goldman, New Kensington?, December 23, 1912?:

Dearest: I have just received your card and am filled with a great peace. I am a little remorseful for wanting to hear from you so badly—you may have been very tired when you sent it—perhaps it was an effort for you to merely address the envelope—you never spare yourself and we "all" expect too much from you. The postman was late this morning—I thot that he had passed and I was wistful—wistful. I will never again have anger for you nor ever feel impatient again for I have lived a thousand years in the last two weeks.

Tell me, Emma, why is it that when a person knows he has been as bad as he can be—why is it that he picks out the one he loves the most to hurt. And why did I have to show you the savage part of me and want to even beat you! I hope you got your fill of the primitive. . . .

It is a good thing that one half of me is decent. I wish I had had a mother like you. You are my mother. Fred said that day I sent the rose back—you know I woke up screaming—"O, will you never be anything else but a child? If I know Em, she wont pay any attention to it." Then I went back to sleep for Fred always knows. . . .

I reckon I must love you more than I ever loved anybody because I used to do everything I felt like doing without stopping to consider others. You are the first person who ever "got my goat." I reckon its because I believe in you. If I didn't I'd kill you.

Almeda.

Sperry to Goldman, New Kensington?, December 24–25, 1912:

Christmas Eve

Honeybug: . . . Certainly I am not going to propagate a weakling. I dont know how the deuce it happened but it is a good lesson on carelessness.

Christmas Day

Don't feel so very well today. Was at the doctor's again yesterday—third operation. Am all done. Fred went to a shooting match. If I felt well I would have gone along and made some money. Always have to place my bets on the first few shots as it tires my arm to hold a gun too long.

I am so sorry you have a cold. You must wear spats on rainy or slushy days. I was thinking about that the day I touched your ankle at the Colonial. Low cut skirts are foolish on a rainy day—ones skirts get wet at the bottom and make ones ankles wet. . . .

I shall have all the things you wish for me in the coming year if you keep on loving me—you sweet dear. If you were here I would kiss your hands—not from servility—I am servile to no one!—but because they are such sweet little ducks of hands. I would do more than that—I am famished to rest my head on your bosom.

Lovingly, A.

Goldman to Sperry (postcard), New York, between December 25 and 31, 1912:

Dearest: The loss of a child must surely be the worst pain. You must be strong even though you feel wretched. Come and stay with us in New York and we will take your mind from your troubles. Your Emmy x.

Sperry to Goldman, New Kensington?, January 5, 1913?:

Dearest: As you well know I have been bad again. I had no business to write to Reitman that way even if I do believe it. However, I can not stand insults and he has insulted me more than I have him. I am the one woman of all your friends that he should not have spoken to lasciviously. And his manner of sending that bill—well it is of no moment now—my anger is like the flash in the pan and is always making me do things against my better nature—and such terrible things.

As a comrade I love Mr. Reitman but as an individual I beg of him never to come in contact with me again either in writing or any other way. However, both he and I (terribly self-centered, intolerant, and wicked as I am) can both try to make ourselves at one with evolution. We are all "good," I reckon as the elements within us permit us to be. . . . Not long ago I degraded myself to the level of a beast thru jealously. I have risen beyond that and there are more things that I must rise beyond. . . .

I have been thinking, my dearest one—my real woman—perhaps I have not the moral right to encroach upon your time—so necessary to the cause—by writing to you because as long as I write I shall pour out my inner soul to you and make you suffer. I do not want you to ever suffer on my account any more and I do not ever want to detract your attentions from more important things than myself. I will do as you say about it. Of course if I cease writing to you it will be like parting with half of my soul but you are very real to me at all times—even when I do not write. . . .

S'long! Almeda.

Goldman to Sperry, New York, January 7?, 1913:

Almeda: I received your letter, and am frankly outraged at your lack of remorse. You are right you had no business writing that letter: Ben has shown it to me, and the foul language of accusation is extraordinary—even for you. He most certainly will not reply to your letter, but I feel I must, if only because you have once again betrayed my trust in you.

Ben has been most generous in all his dealings with you—meeting you at the station in New York on more than one occasion, sending you anarchist materials for distribution without asking for money in advance because of our friendship, and—this one you do not know—advising me not to break our ties because of your violent jealously when I was ready to. And now you call him a common pimp and a lout, a sexual pervert and a "villainous scab"! It really is too much, 'Meda. As my tour manager and a devoted anarchist, Ben's concern to call in money owed is political, not personal, and—as always—you mix the two together and create a goddam mess.

I thought you came to see me and Hutch, and you end up in the wrestling ring with poor Ben. And now you threaten not to write again as though out of concern for my work. Why must you cause discord wherever you go, 'Meda?

Em.

Sperry to Goldman, New Kensington?, January? 1913:

My dear Emma: I am amused at Reitman going to you with his troubles. Enclosed find the letter Reitman sent me acknowledging receipt of $2.50 and saying that it cleared my whole Berkman account, besides enclosing bill. What was I to infer?

I don't think I used any worse language to Reitman than he has used to me; he asked Hutch Hapgood to suck one of my breasts while he sucked the other so I could have two orgasms at the same time and that was after I had had the most divine of conversations with Hutch. He also asked me how many men there are in this town that I had not fucked yet. I let all that pass until I received that bill. I now admit that my anger was unjustified. Dearest, if you want to know just how much Reitman has hurt me from the first day I met him just go out on the streets awhile, as

I foolishly did when I was about twenty-one, and go with strange men for money. For a woman of your knowledge you are strangely innocent.

I ask for no forgiveness of the language I used towards him but I do ask forgiveness for my anger. He has received from me just what he has given me—no more—no less. He tackled the wrong woman when he tackled me. I have had a deep horror of him ever since he met me at the N.Y. station. I understood him thoroly as soon as he grabbed my arm as we walked along the street. I used the same kind of language he did. Please ask him that, for the sake of the Cause, if he ever goes to meet another sin-laden woman who is beginning to see a glimmer of light—please ask him for humanities sake, for his own sake and the woman's sake—not to begin "fuck" talk. Please ask him to remember that he stands by your side as representing anarchism.

I have shown you the secret places of my soul thinking if I did so without reservation that it would help the cause along. I would not care if you told my story to the public or even use my name from the platform. And there are depths I have not told you for I have not had time.

And now, dearest, I am going to say good-bye—for your sake to save you suffering. I suppose I am a poisonous weed—fatal to myself and everyone around me.

With deep respect, Almeda.

. . . I'll send you that $4.50 I owe you, personally, next Saturday a week. I've got some coming.

Goldman to Sperry, New York, January 1913:

Almeda, I can't believe you continue in your insistent accusations against Ben. It sounds as though you think him greedy for your "hard earned" cash so he can spend it on a new hat! And now you also paint a picture of my naïveté to boot—as though the many failings of my dear, loyal, vain hobo had escaped my notice. Honestly, 'Meda, if you think he would pimp you, what do you think of me?

It seems your violent fantasies have turned from me to him in the blink of an eye. Can you not imagine the memories it brings back for Ben when someone says they'll rip his balls from his belly and feed them to him for sport? Meda, I am filled with such unhappiness at my sweethearts at each other's throats like children—can't you just apologize and start again. Ben really is a treasure, if only you knew him better.

Your Emma

Sperry to Goldman, New Kensington?, January? 1913:

Dearest: Forgive me for referring to that matter again. I never dreamed of Ben's wanting any lousy money for himself—he is the soul of generosity— I only got blind with rage at his manner of presenting that bill—it seemed to impugn my honesty. I merely used whorehouse vituperation on him and said what I said because I could not think of anything worse. As for doing what I threatened to do—why that would be ridiculous because everyone knows what he has suffered for the cause. And he is not a pimp because pimps don't work and he does. But I'll never apologise to him until he treats me with respect.

Ben tried to make me feel the great honor you had done me in allowing me to visit you. "Why, people would even come from Europe to meet her if she'd let them!" Emmy, I don't care what kings of intellect you've entertained . . . I would like to win your respect but fear it is impossible. I'll try again and again. I have not filled Newt's place and it is horrible to be broke all the time. I could fill his place in a minute by the mere use of the telephone but some way or other I cannot—ever since you looked into my eyes that way and I must say I missed the bunch of money he usually gave me at Christmas. . . .

Timidly I breathe the fragrance of your hair. Look up that I might see your eyes, dear heart. Ah! your love for me is tinged with a deep sadness. Mine too, is tinged with sadness and a terrible regret.

Almeda.

Goldman to Sperry, New Kensington?, January 15 to 30, 1913:

Thank you 'Meda: It must have been hard for you to send that note to Ben. He was so chastened it took him a whole day to even mention it to me, curse his eyes. Your visit at the end of the month may not be a good idea, sweet girl. There are so many comrades taking over my precious space, and I cannot be distracted further by your hands-lips-lashes.

Love Emmy x

Sperry to Goldman, New Kensington?, January? 1913:

Honeybug—don't you want me to come to see you on the 24th. Why, I would be willing to go as far as San Francisco just to speak with you for a half hour; to me, it would be well worth the effort. But if I thot it would disturb the tenor of your thots and make you garble your lectures I would not come for, honeybug, there are greater things than love and one of them is the cause you work for and your faithfulness to it is the foundation of my love for you. . . .

A.

. . . Fred is awfully good to me now since my mother is ill.

Sperry to Goldman, New Kensington?, January 12, 1913?:

Dearest: I went to see my mother last week; her neck is about as thin as your wrist. It is marvellous to me how she clings to life . . . All passions have left her and only love remains. I pour my heart out to her now and I never used to. She listens to me calmly and said, "Almeda, if you would learn self-control, you could do anything you wanted." . . .

My mother seems all spirit now. My mother, too, used to have an unreasonable fury the moment she grew impatient and woe betide the poor kid who did not keep away from the reach of her arm. . . . My mother worked very hard to "educate" us and worked very hard at preserving, cooking and such things, but somehow she failed us at crucial periods of our lives. She taught us nothing of sex and would not expend any money towards painting lessons for my sisters nor violin lessons for myself. . . .

Last night I dreamed you were in a grave and I was a worm battening upon your flesh. I started eating your soft, white shoulder and once in awhile would sting your lips but there was no response. I peered under your eyelids and looked into the pellucid blue of the iris—your eyes were as compassionate and benevolent as ever but as baffling in death as in life. I shrivelled in ecstacy at the mystery of your eyes.

Lovingly
(but I don't deserve to be
allowed to write that)
Almeda.

Goldman to Sperry, New York, January 15 to 30?, 1913:

Dearest 'Meda: The 24th until the end of the month I will be sharing my space with more comrades than there are ticks in the bedding! I'd rather you came to see me when I'm on tour—perhaps you could join me in Cleveland and then there would only be my lectures and time to prepare; we wouldn't be pulled upon from every direction from people wanting a piece of E.G.

Forgive me: if you do come, you must promise not to make a scene or return to the old jealousy that you say you have put to bed. Our time together means so much to me—you know I love you!—but I cannot promise to be yours alone, and your stories of worms and death make me worry that you are returning to your earlier madness. Lately, my feelings for you have become as for a treasured friend in whose touch I find comfort and rest.

I am sorry that your mother is ill. It is hard enough to deal with illness and death in those we love, but if family relationships are strained it is even worse.

Your Emmy x

Sperry to Goldman, New Kensington, between March 1912 and September 1913:

Dearest: . . .

I got your letter. O, you lovely bruised purple grape—you crushed pineapple—you smotherd crab-apple-blossom—your beautiful odor of rotten apples. Will I come to Cleveland? Would I go to Kanchatka? Would I go to Kalamazoo? Sure—only don't notice my clothes. I have a friend in Boston whose husband is leading a teamster's strike. She has to hunt work and needs shoes—her feet are out—she has three kids. I am sending her mine—I gave $4.50 for them—the other ones are half-soled and old.

Never mind about not feeling as I do. I find restraint to be purifying. Realization is hell for it is satisfying and degenerating.

Love. A.

Sperry to Goldman, New Kensington?, January? 1913:

Dear Heart—dear heart. Forgive me. I have been having a feeling of revenge in my heart against someone lately and I thot you could not love me anymore.

Dear heart, I am ill. My most gracious mother is dying. Perhaps I shall not be able to see you in Cleveland. I shall try, tho.

Lovingly
Almeda.

Sperry to Goldman, New Kensington?, January? 13?, 1913?:

Dearest Emma: I feel rather embittered at not getting to see you—the fates do seem to resent my love for you.

My mother's death was not so shocking to me—I was very glad for her sake since she has suffered so. But I am completely unnerved at the actions of some of my Christian sisters. Hardly had my mother's body been cold than they started to steal her clothing and other stuff. . . .

They all gave me hell, Emmy, for being your friend and for smoking cigarettes. . . .

And another thing that has made me sad and prevented my coming to see you—Fred got into some awful trouble and it took all our money. It is too disgraceful to tell you about—it has taken the last ounce of my strength—and my affection. . . .

I may possibly see you in Chicago. But in the event that I do not—will you let me see you for a day—only a day—next summer—only I want you all to myself for that day. Oh! I know I'm selfish. . . . If I can make it to Chicago I only just want to lay my head upon your bosom—just an instant.

A strange girl! Yes! I know.

A.

Goldman to Sperry, New York, January 15 to 30, 1913:

My very dear, Almeda: I am sorry to hear about your mother, and about your family's nasty treatment of you. Don't they know that you are the only member of the family with an open heart? Here are some of your favourite "wicked" cigarettes 'Meda—I hope you enjoy smoking them in your brother's face and corrupt his wife!

Sweet Almeda—you sound so alone and so desperate; I am worried for you. Fred's antics never cease to amaze me, and now he has once again put you in a situation of penury. I am of course also devastated I won't see you in Cleveland—I have such a longing to see you—and I just hold out a hope for Chicago or the summer (which is too far away, dearest, but better than nothing).

Love Emmy x

Sperry to Goldman, New Kensington?, January? 1913:

Dearest: I am smoking one of your cigarettes; they are dandy but I'm surprised that you cater to one of my vices.

Thank you for the nice things you have said to me lately. Hon, I thot that I had lost you and the light of the world had gone out for me. I no longer cared to live—the inside of my head was even cold. . . . I did nothing but cry and tear things like rags, newspapers and handkerchiefs and I had the back of my hands bitten purple. I wanted to tear you limb from limb and wanted to take your entrails and string them in a long string. O, what makes me so vicious?

Sperry to Goldman, April 7, 1912 [this is clearly wrongly dated because Sperry's mother died in early 1913; it is probably from the end of January/early February 1913]:

Dearest: I hope you'll forgive the letter I sent you the other day. I have been a perfect fiend since my disappointment at not meeting you but I believe I have recovered my poise. . . . It is so sweet of you to say you had a longing to see me. I, too, have a longing to see you and it seems more terrible every day. I am better, dear, but I drank, drank since my mother died, until today. . . .

It is strange: I tried to obliterate you from my memory but I reckon you are in my mind to stay and I am compelled to tell you everything about myself so as to be honest with you. I have a new "sweetheart"—need the money—besides, I need diversion or would go mad—I need music, the theatre—money-money-money—and I will not work. I hope you can be my friend, knowing this, but if you cannot, I will have to accept it as I do everything else lately, with apathy—with apathy.

I wish I could lay my head in your lap. . . .

Lovingly, A.

Goldman to Sperry (postcard), Cleveland, February to March 1913:

Dear Almeda: my tour so far has seemed interminable and no one seems interested in the Cause. They only come to see me for the sport, it seems, and I am sick of being the "High Priestess of Anarchy" for the ignorant mob. I am reminded of how much more fun it would be if you were here with me in Cleveland. All money down the drain in Toledo; write to me of New Kensington life in St. Louis!

Love, Em

Sperry to Goldman, New Kensington?, March? 9?, 1913:

Dearest: Just a line to greet you upon your arrival in St. Louis. I am so sorry that your tour is dragging. It is surprising to me that you lost money in Toledo; in a town of that size you should have won out. I do not think the comrades were active enuf in advertising the meeting. What is wrong with Americans anyway?

Last night a boy of sixteen lost the fingers and thumb of one hand in a press at the Aluminum; this is nothing new and it happens every week. And yet people like that spider of a Slayton want us to wait on the vote—it makes my gorge rise and also makes me ashamed of my depression of a couple of days ago.

I have, in a measure, recovered from my disappointment at not meeting you. I reckon one must always bow to the inevitable and fall back on the grey-matter that Hutch talks so much about. So I will just imagine that I am with you, with my head cuddled on your bosom and now I put my arms around you and give you a long, long kiss. Such liberties I do take—away from you.

I am smiling at you now, whimsically and wistfully.

My Honeybug. Mine!

A.

Sperry to Goldman, New Kensington, May 1913:

Dearest Honeybug. Am going to the country tomorrow so address me there when you are in the mood to write. Reckon I can stand it in the country as they don't nag like sister does out there. Anyway I've given the old lady to understand that I'm radical and she must accept me as I am. She'll be darn glad to get me back as I can do her hoeing for her and she can stay out of the sun. . . .

Aren't you glad I'm well, Honeybug? Do you love me, Honeybug?

A.

Sperry to Goldman, Parnassus, May 13, 1913?:

Dearest: I am out in the country and am wondering if there is not any mail at my place in New Kensington—from you. I s'pose I've wounded your feelings too deeply in some letter I wrote when not myself and spose you are very busy.

I am having to store my furniture this month and then come out here the rest of the summer. . . . I wonder how long I'll be good like this? Just until I get some strength back, perhaps. If only you were here to love that would be different.

I don't smoke here—it would hurt this lady's feelings and she knew my mother. . . .

Did you get my picture?

I have an article in the Free Press I am going to send you to criticize . . .

Honeybug, my head always rests upon your bosom even if I have lost you. . . .

Lovingly, Almeda.

Goldman to Sperry, Los Angeles, May 22 to 25, 1913:

Dearest 'Meda: I know I have been lax in writing lately. The tour has taken the last strength I have, and I have been ill and fretful. Ben has been in a terrible mad state for at least two weeks and we had hoped to put the vigilante demons to rest once and for all when we arrived in San Diego. But we were arrested and put on a train before we even had a chance because the station was surrounded. But at least here in Los Angeles comrades have given us a hero's welcome and the support for our lecture did both of us good. We go to San Francisco soon, and after that all over. I hope perhaps to make a little money with the drama lectures, but I never count on such things. I shan't be back in New York until September and am not sure when I will be able to write again.

Love Emmy.

Sperry to Goldman, New Kensington, July 1913:

Dear Emmy: If the doctrine of eternal recurrence be true and Nietzsche has "absolutely no reason to renounce the hope for a Dionysian future of music" then, in two milleniums there will be another Almeda sitting on her behind listening.

Don't you dare ever try destroy me, Emmy, nor ever forget me. I've got a hell of a beating in my ear.

I wonder if that Nietzsche ever went dippy over a woman.

Nietzsche's mind is more interesting than yours. I'm glad you're alive tho — because one can't kiss a dead person.

Love
A.

Goldman to Sperry, Seattle, August 9 to 17, 1913:

Dearest Almeda: Seattle looks set to be a great success—people are clamoring for radical opinion and literature here, and it finally seems that the message of giving of oneself rather than trying to amass a pitiful handful of beans may be getting through! I have had my old leg trouble and so haven't been able to help with advertising, but I have a radical army here of young and trusted friends.

I think you are right that Nietzsche never "went dippy" over a woman, and I wish the same could be said of my friend Almeda, who continues to imagine me dead or dying. Your last letter sounded like you were back on the whiskey, dear, with your thoughts returning to betrayal—kisses have to be freely given, and perhaps you would prefer me dead because then I couldn't complain about your haranguing me!

It is true that I have been lonely these last months on the tour, because each week is a new set of people, a new set of hopes and disappointments. But I wouldn't exchange this life for the world.

Your friend, Em.

Sperry to Goldman, New Kensington, August 1913?:

Dearest Emmy: Thank you for writing to me. I wish I were in Seattle now. I would distribute handbills too.

When I come away from the post office without a letter from you I say, "It's darn good for you, Almeda—you don't deserve a letter." You are a wonderful woman, Emmy, to use some of your energy to write to me and I feel guilty for harrowing you so but you see I am human, Emmy, and terribly lonely just now and you are the only person I have much love for. You have been so kind to me and so understanding that I hope and hope that I can prove my appreciation by giving my life for you—it is not worth much but it is all I have.

I am full of nothingness. I love peace, love and truth and will not work for them so the best thing I can do is to see you once more and then drink laudanum for I am no good. Whiskey has lost its charm, "raising hell" has lost its charm. When I go to get drunk I see your eyes looking at me. . . .

I wish I were there with you so that I could do my puny best for you—after all there is nothing else worth doing. . . . Christ knows there are no riches in it for you—only loneliness. I don't see how you can stand your loneliness, changes of cooks, hotels, the constant travelling, the constant speaking and the meaness of the people with whom you come in contact. But your ideal drives you on in spite of lack of support from friends, in spite of bitter loneliness, in spite of myriad discomforts. No I won't commit suicide. Coward! Coward! Almeda. I will woo you all over again. I'll write impressions—it may take me a little while—it may take me years but, Emmy, if I write from my heart and tell the truth I know you will love me from something more than pity.

Emmy, honeybug, I have been reading Brieux and have been struck with his play about syphilis. Why, it is the simple truth only what I will write about will be greater than what he has written—he doesn't tell it all.

We've all been bad to you, Emmy. It's because we think there is no limit to your strength and we dump all our confessions and troubles on yur dear shoulders. Oh, it is ghastly! All the time we are torturing you . . .

My life is always full of cheer when I hear from you.

Don't be lonely anymore dearest. Truly, there are lots of us who would die for you. The only trouble is that we are not all Emmas. Oh, Emmy, if I only had something big to give you. I had nothing to give you even on your birthday and I cried. . . .

I don't care a damn what anyone wrote or thought if you didn't love me and I don't care who knows it. I'm never going to be bad again. I'll bet I did come near losing you this time.

> Love and love and love
> A.

Sperry to Goldman, East Pittsburgh, September 2, 1913:

Dear Emmy: the librarian at Braddock has bought me a volume of Nietzsche's Ecce Homo. I say, Emmy, please interpret Nietzsche for simple minded dubs like me—he's got me turned inside out and I'm sweatin' like the devil besides spinnin' around like a top and I don't know whether I'm comin' or goin'. All due respect to Nietzsche! I, a mountebank and poseur say this.

I have met "Gerty" and have found her to be like all people who write for money or a capitalist newspaper—compromising. I'm going to keep up the acquaintance to have someone to argue with. She is very quick witted.

> Dear honeybug!
> A.

Goldman to Sperry, New York, September 15, 1913:

Dearest Almeda: my sweet lonesome girl. I have returned home to New York and have a new lease of life that has made some things—including my relationship to you—clear as a bell. We cannot keep this friendship up, 'Meda—it will never be enough for you to have part of me, and you will never trust that I hold you in my heart. I have tried so hard to be patient, and I wanted so much for our friendship to come out of the terrible night and into a calm dawn. You tell me all the time you are no longer jealous, but I do not believe you. You are smart as a whip, 'Meda, and know what I want to hear. You have been a sweet sweet treasure in my life, but I cannot carry the weight of your longing with me any more. Ben has persuaded me that someone with the taste for drink that you have will always be pulled back into the madness it brings, and your desires for me will always turn grasping in the end.

You have wounded me so severely 'Meda, and I have done the same to you. But I no longer have time or taste for the uncertainty of your trust, and I need comrades around me who will take me as I am. I have loved your eyes, hands, and fingers, 'Meda, as you know, and I hope for another life for you—free of me, free of Fred, free of loneliness and harm. You have the potential for greatness, as Nietzsche himself would have known—it is just that you have no idea what to do with your talents and numb yourself with wine and more.

Tenderly, Emma.

I am sending back your letters separately to do with as you will. Don't doubt my passion for you was real, 'Meda—you will see I read these with dirty fingers more than once.

Please burn my letters to you, and do not write to me, 'Meda—respect at least this request from one you say you love.

Conclusion

From Passion to Panache

I began this book by introducing the reader to the passionate reception of Emma Goldman: her person, her life, her politics, and her writing. The feminist critical archive has cleaved to Goldman with a fervour that mirrors her own. We have been seduced by a Goldman who refuses to bend to authority, who routs out hypocrisy wherever she finds it, and who embraces life with the most impressive lustiness. As Kathy Ferguson—a writer who has been so important for my own work on this project—notes, Goldman has inspired each new generation of feminist thinkers and activists, many of whom describe their heroine as "changing their lives" (2011b, 288–89). While Goldman's contemporaries recognised the "'vigor and passion of her personality'" (Hapgood, in Stansell 2000, 143), later interlocutors have been enthralled by her vision and by the aptness of her analyses for our times as well as her own. Thus, for Christine Stansell, Goldman is an "oracle" (2000, 132), while for Ferguson she is "that relatively rare kind of thinker and performer that political theorist George Shulman calls a prophet" (2011b, 286). A central feature of Goldman's significance, however, is her own refusal to be a prophet of doom, even if she embraces this role in other ways. Indeed, part of the transhistorical appeal of Goldman's person and politics is her enthusiasm, often rendered through the misattributed phrase "If I can't dance, I don't want to be part of your revolution" (or variants thereof). The phrase remains apt, of course, insofar as it references Goldman's insistence that joy and anarchist activism should not be understood as antithetical to one another.

In this conclusion, I want to think with and through Goldman's passionate politics not as an antidote to the politics of ambivalence I have been tracing throughout this project but as that which underwrites her efforts to make revolutionary meaning out of the scraps of life she seized. While Goldman's ongoing struggles to promote and live sexual freedom always fell short of the ideals that she set herself, her enthusiasm for life and anarchism always brought her back from despair and catapulted her into the fray again. That same passion has, as we have seen, inspired her critical audience, even while the contradictions in her thinking and action have also frustrated them. And her larger-than-life presence bursts forth in both her own time and ours to challenge authority rather than submit to false promises and prophets. Passion might well seem at first glance to run counter to the importance of ambivalence I have claimed to be productive throughout this project. It might suggest a more purposeful singularity and the drive to see something through to the end. And, indeed, these qualities of Goldman's are certainly character-ised by passion. But so too, Goldman's passion enables her to hold contradic-tions together without having to resolve them, and to continue to explore the space of political struggle as the privileged site of her utopian dream despite frequent disappointments in politics and love.

In her autobiography, *Living My Life*, which brims with intertwined pas-sion and politics at a variety of levels, Goldman tells the inaugural story of being chided by comrades, including her beloved "Sasha" (Berkman), when dancing at radical community events in New York City: "At the dances I was one of the most untiring and gayest. One evening a cousin of Sasha . . . took me aside. With a grave face . . . he whispered to me that it did not behoove an agitator to dance. Certainly not with such reckless abandon, anyway. . . . My frivolity would only hurt the Cause" (Goldman 1931b, 56). While "furi-ous at the impudent interference of the boy," and insistent that an anarchism "which stood for freedom from conventions and prejudice" should not be one that denied "life and joy" (56), Goldman is nevertheless conflicted in her response. She clings to her right to express herself fully, while taking her com-rades' (including Berkman's) reproaches to heart and dancing "no more that evening" (56). Her contemporaries were captivated and frustrated in equal measure by the "vigor and passion" of the Goldman of Hutchins Hapgood's memory, since she embodied both a zealous political desire and commitment, and an infuriating refusal to bend in the face of disagreement or stumbling blocks. In her infamous attack on her erstwhile mentor Johann Most, for example, Goldman displays perhaps most directly—and to my mind rather gloriously—her willingness to respond with undiluted passion to political detractors. On hearing of Most's public criticism of Berkman (who had been arrested after his failed attempt at the political assassination of Henry Clay Frick) and his refutation of the "propaganda by deed" he had previously advocated, Goldman purchases a horsewhip (105): "When [Most] got up and faced the audience, I rose and declared in a loud voice: 'I came to demand proof of your insinuations against Alexander Berkman.' There was instant silence. Most mumbled something about 'hysterical woman,' but he said nothing else. I then pulled out my whip and leaped towards him. Repeatedly I lashed him across the face and neck, then broke the whip over my knee and threw the pieces at him" (105). Clearly, Goldman was not someone that you wanted to cross, particularly in a moment of devastation such as the incarceration of her beloved Sasha.

Goldman's passion was not restricted to the vehemence with which she opposed what she saw as political conservatism either. She fell hook, line, and sinker for those men (and women) who turned her head. In her autobiography, Goldman represents her relationships with lovers in detail, and in particular provides a compelling account of how overwhelmed by love and lust for Ben Reitman she is. Noting that there is, from the start, an aura of suspicion about his motives and political purity that makes her friends wary of her attachment, Goldman reports that she was nevertheless "caught in the torrent of an elemental passion I had never dreamed any man could rouse in me. I responded shamelessly to its primitive call, its naked beauty, its ecstatic joy" (1931b, 420). It is important to remember that it is Goldman herself who makes the choice to represent these political and personal loves as all-consuming in her autobiography. It is Goldman who fuses "passion and vision" (Ferguson 2011b, 286) at the centre of *Living My Life*, and who folds together her many political and relationship disappointments as well as enchantments for her audience.[1] She was, in other words, quite conscious of her decision to foreground her passionate relationships to others and to the world, but was nevertheless disappointed and angry at the critical response to the book (as well as its failure to deliver the hoped-for revenue) that "readily dismissed" it as the outpourings of "an emotional woman" rather than a political actor of significance (Drinnon and Drinnon 1975, 123). Anna Maria Drinnon and Richard Drinnon note that Goldman was exasperated by the "masculine consensus" (123) that "'EG never acted as a result of having thought out her action. She acted by impulse'" (Kirchwey, in Drinnon and Drinnon 1975, 123), and yet she both encouraged and resisted the framing of her work as pure passion.[2]

These conflicts over the location and significance of passion in Goldman's life and work at the time—between her and others, and between the competing parts of her own worldview—are mirrored in the critical archive. At the most positive end of the spectrum are Kate Rogness and Christina Foust (2011), who argue that Goldman's contributions to political thinking through the concept of "passion" help resolve the false tension between "rights and virtues" that have guided historians of that era. For these two scholars, Goldman's passion enables her to provide a heartfelt critique of the consequences of women's exchange of freedom for dubious economic, social, and moral advantages and informs her "vision of free love . . . as the [basis] for women's public agency" (2011, 154). Rogness and Foust believe Goldman's analyses of the connections between women's reproduction and nationalism, or between sexual freedom and revolution, rely on both a passionate invocation of the personal costs for women of going along with the status quo and a passionate call (that expects a response) to invest in other ways of relating. At the other end of the spectrum we have Vivian Gornick, who considers Goldman's primary contribution to political thinking to be her "hot defiance" of authority (2011a, 4). While affirming Goldman's "eloquent . . . defense of causes . . . that a majority of her fellow anarchists derided as trivializing" (2), Gornick nevertheless reads Goldman's "impassioned faith" as profoundly individualistic, as "lodged in the nervous system," concluding that a "radical politic for her was, in fact, the history of one's own hurt, thwarted, humiliated feelings at the hands of institutional authority" (4). Gornick's failure to connect Goldman's fervency to a broader set of revolutionary claims has the perverse effect of resuturing her to the domestic and frivolous in ways Rogness and Faust would argue she used passion precisely to resist. Don Herzog takes Goldman's passion in a rather different, albeit similarly dismissive, direction, arguing that her true devotion is reserved for "her one and only, anarchism" (2007, 315). For Herzog this emotional attachment means that Goldman is never only disappointed with the waxing or waning of social movements but *betrayed* as a lover would be. While Herzog uses this line of argument to diminish the contributions of both anarchism in general and Goldman in particular,

Lori Jo Marso pertinently notes that in so doing he represents Goldman as a "hysteric" (2008, 124). Commenting on the same debate, Ferguson makes an important distinction between infatuation and love in Goldman's politics, insisting that the latter "sustained her resolve" rather than blinding her to the failures of either lovers or revolutions: "When she eventually did, in both cases, admit the bitter defeat of her cherished dreams, she gathered up her considerable resolve and tried again" (2011c, 753).

This rather delicate balance between wanting to celebrate Goldman's passion while simultaneously being wary of its overassociation with gendered and sexualised dismissals of women's thinking and action frames Penny Weiss, Loretta Kensinger, and Berenice Carroll's intervention in their introductory essay to the landmark collection *Feminist Interpretations of Emma Goldman* (2007, 3–18). These authors want to defend Goldman's position in the history of anarchist as well as feminist thought by claiming her as a theorist *and* activist, and they grapple with ways that representations of her as "merely passionate" problematically enable the lack of seriousness with which she is often read (or written off). They rightly observe that "when applied to women's intellectual work, and specifically that of Goldman, references to 'fervor' and 'commitment' have been used to dismiss and depreciate" (9).[3] These are indeed wise words of caution, which raise questions about the value of thinking with Goldman through the concept of passion at all. The danger of reading her in this way is that she is returned to her body and feelings once more, and her revolutionary thinking dismissed in preference to a focus on her character. But so too there are dangers that arise from ignoring Goldman's passion, of reproducing for ourselves that association of emotion with the private and trivial rather than challenging the same. As Weiss, Kensinger, and Carroll conclude, while passion is double-edged in reading Goldman, even the most dismissive of readers have not managed to dampen either her own or subsequent generations' enthusiasm for her embodied mode of thinking and action (9).

In considering Goldman's passion myself, it is its methodological resonance that most captivates me. Running counter to critical distain, Goldman's passion is not only an orientation towards her cherished object, a way of fetishising it or keeping it close to her own heart. It is a *mode of politics* that seeks to generate a break from conservative or false feeling and create new value appropriate to a new world. It is the motor for bringing a new world into being, one whose contours cannot yet be known, but that we have to have faith in or else slip below the surface of capitalism's miserable tide. Since passion cannot be constrained by form or structure, and is resistant to any authority that seeks to bind it, it chimes with my own concern to prioritise struggle over resolution throughout this project. Thus I agree with Rogness and Foust that passion is a wholly appropriate vehicle for Goldman to centre sexual freedom and women's participation in revolutionary politics. For Goldman, as discussed at some length in chapter 1, women are at a considerable disadvantage in their ability to connect to revolutionary politics, since they are affectively sutured to consumerist attitudes and mean-spirited economic evaluation. With no ability to thrive within the strictures of marriage, capitalism, and religious morality, women feign rather than experience real emotional lives of their own. For Goldman, if we centre women as *feeling political subjects*, we expose the nature of political authority both within and outside of the state (including within revolutionary movements), and the techniques through which that authority is legitimated: namely, a qualitative/quantitative split, a mind/body dualism, and a public/private divide. And as I have argued elsewhere, Goldman emphasises the pleasures "of investing in a different set of—revolutionary—values, as if by sheer force of repetition she could transform women's mood" (Hemmings 2012b, 532).

A generous reading of Goldman would thus interpret her trenchant critiques of women's bourgeois femininity as *willing them* to relinquish their flat reproductive habits and to throw themselves into passionate relationships to others. Sara Ahmed's (2014) recent book on "will" tracks the importance of following the willful soul where she leads us. Ahmed's reading considers the stakes in designating some subjects and not others as willful, and the deconstructive value of considering their claims as part of a genealogy of alternate value. Certainly, Goldman could be included in any history of "willful subjects." Obstinate to the end, she consciously refused to recognise external authority as more important than her own set of anarchist values in shaping her personal or political actions. And so too she willed others to see the generative value of that other genealogy and its proffered relations to others, hoping by sheer enthusiastic force of will to inspire others to relinquish bankrupt investments for a more enriching revolutionary feeling. In this sense, then, Goldman's passion can be read as a means of articulating a counterpolitics as a place of intense feeling and reimagined relationships. Passion is not something that roots you to a narrow sphere of gendered domestic concern but has an expansive power "to transform the humdrum certainties of capitalist accounting and inaugurate a different set of attachments in the world" (Hemmings 2012b, 542).[4] Passion, as embodied and expressed by Goldman's willful person, *underwrites* rather than undermines her struggles to generate revolutionary space from within ambivalence. It allows her to survive and thrive, and live to fight another day.

In prefigurative vein, Goldman sought to inhabit the passionate politics she advocated, and commentators have noted that she achieved this in part through her own love of theatricality (Falk 2002; Wexler 1992). We might recall that Goldman was offered a place in vaudeville, and no doubt anyone who witnessed her ability to think on her feet and read the crowd would have understood why. For Stansell, Goldman's "showmanship" was partly what cemented her relationship with Ben Reitman, who crafted opportunities for her to display her theatrical talents while on tour (2000, 138).[5] Similarly, Wexler explores the different ways in which Goldman self-consciously constructed herself "as a public figure," framing her performances as part of a long-standing "female performing tradition" (1992, 42).[6] In the introduction to this book, I reflected on Goldman's knowing occupation of her position as "E.G.," as the familiar but exceptional figure that allowed people to identify with her, and that provided her with considerable political opportunity. For Candace Falk, the "gusto and eloquence with which she challenged convention became her hallmark. . . . People flocked to hear her lash out against hypocrisy wherever she found it" (2002, 12). According to Falk, Goldman's performance and her high-profile personal life—repeatedly reported on in the papers, as we have seen in previous chapters—were particularly appealing to her audience, since they "created immediacy to her message" (17). But this strategy is not without its own risks either. Martha Watson (1999), for example, highlights the dangers of Goldman's hyperbolic self-representation, suggesting that her larger-than-life persona was as likely to *prevent* audience identification as to foster it. And, indeed, her passionate self-representation could be off-putting even to those who broadly agreed with her political aims. Goldman's integration of the personal into the political, while clearly demonstrating her message in its medium, also risks making her into public property in ways that are not always within her own control. Thus, while "the political stage offered her an opportunity to play the role of one who was above conflict" (Falk 2002, 17), it also made Goldman's dilemmas and difficulties into a frequent object of analysis. We have seen in the previous chapter how Goldman's own femininity and embodiment were subject to intense scrutiny, and her postexile marriage was represented either as straightforward capitulation or as evidence of a more conservative orientation than had previously been allowed. Goldman's very public insistence on the importance of doing things differently meant that any whiff of hypocrisy on her own part was likely to be seized upon as part of a more general ridicule of anarchist ideas, and with a gleeful dismissal of Goldman's own politics and person. Her legitimate struggles became weapons in the hands of unsympathetic detractors.

We have also seen that feminists, in their disappointment at Goldman's hyperbolic attachment to men in general and Ben Reitman in particular, have found it hard to reconcile the Goldman who flouted convention with the one who begged for male attention (Falk 2005; Frankel 1996). As might be expected, Goldman struggled with balancing her public face with her intimate life too, and she experienced profound disappointment (and even rage) at her own as well as others' failures to match up to the great ideal. Goldman's letters to lovers, comrades, and friends reveal a character who was well aware of the demands made upon her, and who was often exasperated by her lack of privacy and the persistent claims made upon her by the movement and her participation in it. In a tone typical of much of her correspondence with him, Goldman writes to Berkman:

> I feel as if I were in a Swamp and try as much as I may I can not get out. Why can I not emancipate from them, why am I cursed with the inability to say no although my whole being rebels against the everlasting Yes, which people so easily abuse and misuse? Just say Yes, once and every body seems to have a mortgage on you. . . . I fear I am for ever doomed to remain public properly and to have my life worn out through the care for the lives of others. . . . I am tired, tired tired. (1904)[7]

As discussed at some length in chapter 3, to ignore the ways in which sexual freedom and passion are, for Goldman, sites of intense negotiation and struggle is to understate the extent to which Goldman and others operated in the midst of profound changes in sexual and gendered politics, as remains the case today. For feminists to read these struggles through their own disappointment seems to me to fall far wide of the mark. Such disappointment fails rather spectacularly to recognise the inherent risks of foregrounding passion as a revolutionary methodology, as though the terrain of knowledge and politics would not be thoroughly fragmented by bringing passion into its heart.

I am not, however, entirely convinced that "passion" is a term that can carry the burden of all the work that we want it to in reading Goldman's archive. It clearly does accurately describe some of her modes of performance and many aspects of her political methodology, and it clearly fuels her struggles to reinvent herself and the world. It is at once a way of highlighting Goldman's fusion of the personal and the political in critiquing existing structures of authority, and her sense of prefigurative sexual freedom as central to her vision of a better world, particularly for women. But so too it points to the unbearable demands of the "prophet's role," in that the fusion of her political vision and its methodology risks exposing Goldman to "failure and rejection" (Ferguson 2011b, 288) each time she goes on the road, develops a new argument, or makes herself vulnerable to others. In that sense, any celebration of this way of understanding Goldman's contributions to political thinking and action needs to fold in the question of gendered and sexual risk.[8] Further, the concept of passion does not, to my mind, quite capture the particular relentlessness with which Goldman always managed to pick herself back up off the floor when her hopes had been dashed, the way she was able to reinhabit the *performance of her passion* even if she was not in the mood, and even though she knew that the cycle of elation and despair would continue in the same way. Passion does not, I think, quite get at the character of Goldman's struggles to resist compromise, while always failing in her attempts to remain above the fray, or to weather the storm of other people's expectations and disappointments. To rest with passion alone threatens to frame Goldman in terms of an authenticity that she herself would probably have laughed away and produces an overidentification in a reader or audience that itself too easily slips into feelings of betrayal. Instead, I want to consider the significance of Watson's (1999) insight that Goldman was in fact such an arresting and flamboyant character that to some extent identification with her was—and still is—bound to be foreclosed. Goldman's struggles are perhaps attractive precisely to the extent that they are not—and perhaps cannot be—ours, whatever our fantasies of being rescued from our humdrum ordinariness.

We need, I think, another term to describe Goldman's conflicted *relationship* to passion, her lifelong attempts to negotiate the intimate and the political together, her consistent failure and success in carrying that burden of representation, and her ability to renew her energies and herself against all the odds. We need something that gets at the ways she inhabited her ambivalence, as well as her certainty about sexual politics and transformation, without thinking of this in terms of falling short of an impossible set of ideals. Falk ends her discussion of Goldman's theatrical strategies, her demonstrations of life's highs and lows, by suggesting that "Goldman played her part in history with *panache*" (2002, 23, my emphasis). I have been caught by this description of Goldman's way of being in the world, reminded of course of

Edmond Rostand's (1897) fearless and doomed hero Cyrano de Bergerac, whose character embraced the term as a final assertion of force of personality over worldly recognition. In what follows I explore panache as a helpful way of describing Goldman's style of life and politics, a way of thinking through "her person" both as a figure of saturated representation and as a live wire that courses through time and place to engender a political frisson in the present. How might the idea of panache help us read Goldman's political complexity without wanting to resolve the productive tensions in her work and life that I have been focusing on throughout this book? What does thinking about Goldman through *panache* enable in terms of strategies for life and politics?

LOSING BATTLES WITH PANACHE

Edmond Rostand's hero Cyrano de Bergerac bursts onto the stage in 1897 in a year that saw Goldman at the beginning of two decades of lecturing across America. That year, Goldman spoke on free speech and free love, women's emancipation, Jews in America, prostitution, the relationship between anarchism and communism, workers' rights, and her vision of anarchism's ideal (among other topics). She argued with socialists, supported anarchist editors subject to censorship, and spoke to audiences of thousands.[9] Performed first on December 27, 1897 (Citti 1897, 50),[10] *Cyrano de Bergerac* presents us with Rostand's charismatic seventeenth-century character who battles his way through the play, consistently refusing convention, authority, and ordinary recognition in preference to autonomy of thought and action, true creativity, and—above all—risking everything for love. De Bergerac swaggers across the pages of Rostand's text, confronting those he despises, protecting those he loves, revelling in continual fights (verbal or actual), and losing his last battle against death with superhuman determination to engage his enemies to his final breath. In the scene of his ultimate demise, fatally wounded yet still honouring his weekly rendezvous with his one true love, Roxanne, de Bergerac's gaze finally moves away from his muse as he enters the one battle he cannot win. It is the final scene of act 5, and a dying de Bergerac pulls himself out of the chair he has been slumped in so he can face death head-on:

He raises his sword.

What are you saying? . . . It's pointless? . . . I know!
But one doesn't only fight in the hope of success!
No! No! It's far more beautiful when it's pointless!
Who do I now find myself surrounded by?—a throng of thousands?

Ah! I recognize you, all my old enemies!
Falsehood?

                                        He cuts thin air with his sword.

Wait just a minute!—Ha! Ha! Compromise, Prejudice, Cowardice!...

                                        He cuts the air.

You want to make a deal?
Never, never!—Ah! there you are, Foolishness, you rogue!
—How well I know that you'll floor me in the end!
Never mind: I fight! I fight! I fight! (1897, 272)[11]

De Bergerac lashes wildly this way and that in a vain attempt to vanquish his lifelong foes, knowing that they will win but relishing the losing battle. Superficial judgment, stupidity, fear, deceit: he greets them as familiar old friends, only this time he also knows that they will get the better of him. Despite being overcome, de Bergerac insists there is something he carries with him to the next life, something spotless and pure: and that is (Roxanne leans in, straining to hear him) ... "his panache" (272).

Rostand's play ends here, and so we have to read back from de Bergerac's claim that he takes panache with him into the next world in order to piece together its features, its force, its capacity to turn a grim and painful death into a last heroic go at life. What are its contours? How do we understand panache, and how might we read Rostand in a way that makes sense of Falk's choice of the term to describe Goldman? Panache, as embodied in Rostand's flawed hero, minimally requires certain characteristics, values, and affects. First, a hero with panache must possess valiance, or even bravado, in the face of danger. De Bergerac, we may recall, bests more than a hundred men in one battle and runs through enemy lines every evening to deliver letters to Roxanne, impervious to the peril this puts him in. Second, there must be a valuing of truth and honour over worldly recognition, the loss of which is a higher marker of esteem than its possession. Thus, de Bergerac embraces poverty over reward in order to preserve his autonomy, and never has a moment's regret at this choice. Third, and very important, the one with panache must enjoy life to the full, their cup brimming over with comradeship, creative accomplishment, food, and drink. There are no half measures here, only a full embracing of the pleasures of the world (but not its censorious modes). In related vein, and fourth, the hero of panache *self-styles* in the face of hostile external representation and puts two fingers up to the authorities that deem them to be brash, ugly, or inappropriate. So, de Bergerac is of course famously subject to mockery for his large nose, but he also creates himself as Roxanne's lover through narrative, overcoming social belittling and internalised shame through this act of self-creation for the eyes and ears of his loved one. And finally, to inhabit panache, love must and should be the only thing worth fighting and dying for, as de Bergerac well knows, and that *losing battle* (for it will inevitably disappoint) is ultimately the only one worth engaging in.[12] Panache, we might say, emerges in a retrospective reading as quite the opposite of a capitalist attitude, then: it shies away from accumulation and advancement; balks at strategic loyalty; is fiercely antiauthoritarian and proud. So too, of course, these characterisations point to the tension at the heart of de Bergerac's panache: he refuses and has no truck with fools, but he is blind to the faults in those he loves and centres pride as well as loyalty. Thus, de Bergerac might be said to be a hero who prefers unrequited love and death to the risk of making a fool of himself in front of Roxanne, a woman he imagines could never love him in the flesh because of his notoriously large nose. He idealises her, but he also fails to trust her, such that she is finally his foil as well as his muse. He is stubborn and fiercely independent in ways that make him the object of admiration, certainly, but that also means he has few real peers. De Bergerac is passionate and foolish, insightful and pigheaded, heroic and absurd in turn. De Bergerac's panache is indeed the stuff of flawed, exquisite myth.

I hope that as I have been tracing the contours of de Bergerac's panache, the potential overlaps with Goldman's genre of heroism have also been resonant for my reader.[13] She faces similar demons and fights them off for her vision of a revolutionary future whose contours are as yet unknown, and she privileges love as the best weapon against malaise, of course. Goldman was a fan of Rostand's work and wrote about his *Chantecler* (1910) in *The Social Significance of the Modern Drama* (1914b). She described Rostand in glowing terms, as remaining "aloof from mediocrity" (138), and *Chantecler* as a lesson in rising above "the meanness of our conventional lies, the petty jealousies of the human breed in relation to each other" (141). Goldman identifies with the abused and somewhat naive—if brave—rooster of the title, whose "passion teaches him to understand life and the frailties of his fellow creatures," and from whom we learn that it is the "struggle for, rather than the attainment of, the ideal, which must forever inspire the sincere, honest idealist" (143). While Goldman never wrote about *Cyrano de Bergerac* directly, her sympathy for Rostand's flawed hero Chantecler identifies themes common to both pieces of work, linking passion and struggle to the "great ideal" and foregrounding the importance of the development of alternative values in creating a revolutionary sensibility.

In act 2, scene 8, of *Cyrano de Bergerac*, we are given one of the fullest accounts of de Bergerac's spirited refusal of convention and determination to live his life in his own way. He mocks the idea that he should be looking for a powerful patron, fawn to a figure of authority to receive paltry favours, write poetry with financial backing in mind, smile without feeling it, bow and scrape to others, receive praise from people whose opinion he does not value, or seek to secure his position through influence (1897, 125–26). Each act of poetic bad faith is interrupted and underlined by de Bergerac's emphatic "no, thank you" (*non, merci*), and he concludes his list of worthless pursuits with the trio Gérard Depardieu so memorably incanted with rising fervor (Rappeneau 1990): "Non, merci! non, merci! non, merci!" (126). Without a break in the verse he continues:

> . . . But . . . singing,
> Dreaming, laughing, passing by, being alone, being free,
> Possessing a steady gaze and true, a full voice,
> Tipping his hat when it pleases him,
> Fighting for a yes, or a no, - or writing a verse!
> Working without thought for glory or fortune,
> . . .
> Never writing except what comes from oneself . . .
> Being satisfied with flowers, fruit or even leaves,
> As long as they are plucked from your own garden!
> And if it comes to pass that you are at all celebrated, by chance,
> Feeling no obligation to offer up anything to Cesar,
> Keeping brief success close to your chest,
> Disdaining the lure of being a creeping parasite,
> Perhaps you might not climb as high as the oak or the lime,
> You may not get far, perhaps, but at least you got there alone! (126)[14]

De Bergerac recognises no authority but his own integrity, and he indeed does not trust even temporary external recognition if and when it comes.

For Goldman, too, a human life should be "a true mirror of nature, a conscious following of the only real necessity, the inner natural necessity . . . no longer held in subjugation to . . . an arbitrary power" (1927?, 9). It is, for Goldman as for de Bergerac, only "emancipation from authority" (Goldman 1940, 12) that brings real freedom, and more specifically the "freedom to do something . . . the liberty to be, to do; in short, the liberty of actual and active opportunity" (14). The social, moral, and political sanctions placed upon human activity and meaning start early within the family for Goldman, within which we are "compelled to battle against the internal and external use of force: You shall! you must! this is right! that is wrong! that is false!" (1906a, 10–11). In my mind's eye, I can hear and see Goldman striding around the stage insisting repeatedly "non, merci!" at the very suggestion that she could be compelled or cajoled into doting on false prophets, or at the very idea that she would seek sanction from a higher authority when things get tough. For both de Bergerac and Goldman, the cost of antiauthoritarianism is not to be measured against the difficulties of external social pressures, as though life and its value were a zero-sum game. One can only be true to one authority—oneself—and such conviction is surely the wellspring of panache.

Liberated from the false gods of worldly recognition, the warrior, the poet, and the activist are free to develop a real creativity of human experience, one unsullied by the social strictures that bind and stifle. Goldman remarks that this is the very reason that she is an anarchist: "because I fervently believe in the creative and constructive quality of man himself, because I believe in the free, untrammeled expression of individual and social life" (1927?, 13). For Rostand's de Bergerac, poetry is the language of love as well as freedom, a medium through which to give voice to inner truth, as we have seen (1897, 126). And we might recall Goldman's enthusiasm for theatre, her cherishing of the ways in which it opens up a democratic space, and its ability to prefiguratively represent an alternative vision.[15] Goldman's valuing of creativity as just as important as other social or political practices rests on her understanding of its relationship to individuality and self-fashioning, much as it does for de Bergerac. In her discussion of Walt Whitman's work, for example, Goldman praises his refusal of convention, which she believes derives from his ability to see directly, without recourse to received interpretation and hierarchy of value: "Whitman saw . . . the naked human soul stripped of all pretense, bombast, falsehood and hypocrisy. It is this quivering, yearning, feeling, suffering human soul Whitman represented" (n.d. [1991b]). In Whitman's genius, Goldman sees "resistance as well as adaptability, and in spite of his universal interests and sympathies he remained an individualist, a heretic, a rebel: in a word, himself" (n.d. [1991b]). As Elena Loizidou (2011) indicates in her careful reading of the relationship between art and politics, Goldman's belief in the importance of an "art of existence" for politics is one driver of her antiauthoritarian self-making.

Rostand's tale is of a seventeenth-century hero, of course, represented in the late nineteenth century as an emblem of a romantic idealism he sees as lost in the modern world. Goldman's embrace of the nineteenth-century Whitman resonates similarly as she insists that we "need Walt Whitman now more than ever. We need his indomitable courage, his beautiful comradeship, his stirring song, that we may not falter in our efforts to build the new life out of the ruins of the old" (n.d. [1991b]). Antiauthoritarianism and antihierarchy are thus, for Goldman and for de Bergerac, the only way to access true expressiveness of action and creativity. For de Bergerac, refusal of external authority is intimately linked to a profound antimaterialism, since it requires placing no value on the things of this world, the empty prizes of capitulation: the play ends with its faithfuls living in poverty or convents; only those who invest in worldly value gain its spoils. For Goldman, a true sign of Whitman's pure independence is the fact that he "was too deeply engrossed in his inner wealth to notice his outer poverty. He was too busily engaged in his creative work to have inclination or time for material achievements" (n.d. [1991b]). And so too my tale is of a twentieth-century heroine who has captured the imagination of repeated generations of feminist and queer theorists, and whose life and writings exemplify the importance of sexual freedom as a window onto a better world. Mine is not a relationship of identification with Goldman; it is a relationship of wonder.

For Goldman as for de Bergerac, continued reduction of life and work to capitalist modes and false value is the result of both bankrupt hierarchies and individual lack of courage. Thus, in her draft lecture "Why I Am an Anarchist," Goldman expresses regret: "Our daily lives have lost all directness, all authenticity; we are full of lies and conformity; we do not express ourselves in our social life, when we walk, when we speak, when we work at our trade; how then shall we suddenly learn to do so when we retire into our studies and lock the door? . . . When people seize life rightly they will make their daily work expressive" (1927?, 10). Living life to the full, meeting people head-on, claiming life in all its misery and glory: Is this how to inhabit panache? De Guiche—de Bergerac's supercilious rival for Roxanne's bodily affections, who is made a duke during the course of the play—certainly thinks so. In visiting Roxanne (who is still in mourning for Christian/Cyrano), and asking for her forgiveness for his past aggression, le Duc listens to de Bergerac's old friend le Bret describing his terrible poverty and isolation. Contrary to the expectation set up by the dialogue, le Duc cautions le Bret "not to pity [de Bergerac] too much: he has lived without allegiance to others, free in his thought as much as in his actions" (Rostand 1897, 252).[16] Despite having all worldly advantages—"I have everything; he has nothing" (*j'ai tout; il n'a rien*)—le Duc admits to feeling not exactly regret "but a vague discomfort" (*une gêne obscure*) with the empty trappings of success, which trail dead leaves behind him like Roxanne's mourning robes (252–53). In le Duc's melancholic admission, Rostand anticipates the dual critique of a dominant social order that Goldman articulates so forcefully. First, that "the living, vital truth of social and economic well-being will become a reality only through the zeal, courage ... [and] non-compromising determination of intelligent minorities, and not through the mass" (Goldman 1910, 78). Only those who resist the "ordinary standards of value" can hope to be truly free. Second, this mode of resistance is likely to lead to penury, or social exclusion, and thus involves considerable risk: "It means giving up their little material achievements" (1933a, 4) in the process of going against the rule of law. It may involve imprisonment, poverty, or isolation, but for Goldman, "unless you are willing to pay the price, unless you are willing to plunge into the very depths, you will never be able to remount to the heights of life" (4). As though responding affirmatively to le Duc in de Bergerac's stead, Goldman responds to the question "Has My Life Been Worth While?" with the following moving statement: "Measured by the ordinary standards of value, my life may be considered wasted. I have nothing in social privilege, wealth, or power—that holy alliance commonly called success—to show for my struggle of forty-three years. But then I had never aspired to those treasures . . . station—power—wealth—how inadequate they have proved! How useless and insecure!" (1933b). For this anarchist coming towards the end of her life, like de Bergerac at the end of his, there are no soft rewards to cushion getting older or getting sick. There is only the knowledge that one has lived one's life at full tilt, and spat right in the eye of authority and the fates.

Panache requires passion, but it also wears danger like a hat at a jaunty angle. Both Goldman and de Bergerac know that one of those dangers is that of external representation. Le Duc may come around to de Bergerac's point of view towards the end of the play, but many others do not, and many actively wish him harm indeed. Goldman suffered all her politically active life with representations of her as foolish or perverse in the media, as we have seen in previous chapters. De Bergerac and Goldman are also subject, of course, to intense physical scrutiny as part of the attempt to belittle them, though in very different ways. De Bergerac's large nose is a source of private mockery, since none would dare mention it in his company (except Christian, to comic effect in act 2, scene 10), and he is known as much for this "tragic flaw" as he is for his acts of heroism and artistic accomplishments. Goldman's face and body are the object of considerable curiosity too, as journalists seek to identify the mismatch between her politics and person, or uncover the physical evidence for her deviance. Panache, then, involves not only the level of self-styling that both de Bergerac and Goldman are pleased to take on but also an ability to recover from the externally imposed representations that seek to frame them. To some extent we might say that Goldman survives representation better than Rostand's hero, since de Bergerac is unable to overcome his (and others') reduction of his person to his appendage, and hence unable to declare his love to Roxanne directly. In this his own self-styling (in letters and love notes) is as a man without the physical characteristic that is in fact a central feature of his transcendence. But perhaps it is precisely the carrying of flaws and contradictions and not their resolution that is the hallmark of panache.

In essence, we might say that panache allows a range of incommensurable positions to be held in tension precisely because of the life force of its subject. While passion as a mode of politics offers the possibility of *overcoming* worldly obstacles, panache describes the courageous way that certain unusual individuals can embrace a losing battle, carry themselves with style, and challenge limits to human endeavour and creativity wherever they find them. Thus de Bergerac has been aptly described as "stumbling towards ecstasy" (Zeck 1999), acting enthusiastically in ways that can only secure his separation from Roxanne, but which we nevertheless marvel at. Goldman, in contrast, takes on anarchism as "a living force in the affairs of our life," embracing the struggle to live as an anarchist although knowing this cannot succeed while there is not yet Anarchy, with a capital *A* (1910, 63). Their foolish, brave actions cannot, and do not, change the circumstances under which they operate: anarchism is, after all, the great failed social movement of the last 150 years, and romantic heroes who sacrifice all for love and honour live on only in our memories and imaginations. Yet the embodied hope and possibility represented by both de Bergerac and Goldman pulse with life; the panache with which they take up their various lost causes inspires the awe that is surely necessary to imagine ourselves other than we already are.

In considering Emma Goldman throughout this project, I have endeavoured to introduce her as a complex character, writer, thinker, and activist for whom anarchism offered a different way of being in the world. Goldman was not prepared to wait for a revolution in order to live a different life: she wanted to live it now. She mobilised passion as a way in and a way out of social critique and as a way of challenging false separations between public and private, sexual and social, familial and national interests. Goldman held extraordinarily high—in fact, often impossible—ideals, but held herself and others up to them nevertheless. When she fell short, she became frustrated and angry, blamed herself and others (often others), but managed to pick herself back up off the floor to continue the struggle another day. The contradictions that we see in Goldman are fruitful ones, I think, and might be thought of as more resonant for us contemporarily than her ideals in many ways. Her combination of resistance to male dominance and profound ambivalence about women is a dilemma that is still very central today: Goldman could not separate them, and nor I think should we. Our negotiations of misogyny (our own and others') take place in a difficult contemporary context of gender equality discourse that makes facing our own demons as hard as it ever was. Goldman's focus on the links between sexual servitude and the nationalist agendas of capitalist, militarist, and religious interests clearly chimes with problems we face today. But more helpful, perhaps, are the ways in which Goldman's own difficulties in negotiating the tricky relationships between and among race and racism, migration and colonialism resonate with our own. Goldman's framing of sexual freedom as the key to revolutionary transformation is, as we have seen, a source of critical delight and unease in equal measure. But without an embrace of Goldman's ambivalence (and our own), we miss the vision of transnational solidarity that sexual freedom has the capacity to offer.

We cannot be disappointed with Goldman when she falters as she wrestles with the contradictions that were and are the stuff of a lived political life. As Julie A. Window pertinently observes, Goldman's "acceptance of uncertainty . . . gave [her] the room to construct herself, to take political agency, to be a punk force of will" (1996, 27). Goldman could not care less whether we approve of her choices, and does not ask us to identify with her. She is not interested in critical or political adoration or disdain, and could not give two hoots about who might feel attached to or betrayed by her. She does want us to be inspired, however, to take our own lives and political spheres as objects of engaged attention and become the architects of our own destiny: on our own and with others. She wants to fuel our imagination not to act in accordance with the parts of her philosophy that we can isolate as infallible but to generate our own ways of intervening and living. There is no doubt this must be a creative endeavour, one filled with passion and risk, driven by a vision (however impossible) of a better life for all. Will it falter, will we get it wrong, and will those who want things to stay the same ridicule such efforts? No doubt. But will it be worth it? That is up to us.

Notes

INTRODUCTION

1. One of these was my own article specifically on Goldman and sexual politics (Hemmings 2014b), while the other three reference her as part of other arguments. In more general terms, the same period also saw publication of a popular biography of Goldman (Gornick 2011a), an intellectual biography framing her within the tradition of American political theory (Chalberg 1991), and an analysis of her two-volume autobiography (Nicholson 2010). In addition, a range of articles across disciplinary sites engage centrally or tangentially with Goldman, and some less well-known or hard-to-obtain pieces of her oeuvre are being republished (e.g., "What I Believe," in Loizidou 2013).

2. A notable strand of thought here is "post-anarchism," which seeks to harness modern anarchist insights for understanding contemporary networks and power relations (beyond socialist or conservative alternatives) but which "rejects the epistemological foundations of 'classical' anarchist theories" (Springer 2012, 1618). Rouselle and Evren's *Post-anarchism: A Reader* (2011) brings together the main thinkers in this subfield. For a useful critique of post-anarchist presumptions about the "essentialism" of classical anarchism, see Allan Antliff's essay "Anarchy, Power and Poststructuralism" (2007).

3. I first raise the question of intimacy in secondary readings of Goldman in my article "Considering Emma" (Hemmings 2013). I extend this early reflection here with more sustained attention to Goldman's own awareness of others' readings of her.

4. Frankel (1996) charts representations of Goldman both at the time of her activism (in the media and among her peers) and through the twentieth century, helpfully identifying the growing feminist interest in her from the 1970s onwards.

5. Candace Falk is the director of the Emma Goldman Papers Project and has brought together the fullest archive of Goldman's work, her correspondence, published and unpublished writings, and ephemera. She is also the main editor of the three volumes of Goldman's writings while in America, *Emma Goldman: A Documentary History of the American Years*.

6. At the height of her popularity in America, Goldman commanded audiences in the thousands (Porter 2004–5). Falk notes Goldman's knowledge of the unusualness of (young) women speakers in the public sphere as part of her appeal, and the ways in which she used this to her advantage (Falk 2003, 13; 2005, 9). Similarly, Judy Greenway (2009b) notes that the association of anarchism with free love was also likely to result in large audiences coming to gawp at the prurient other. When Goldman returns to America in the 1930s the attendance at her talks of only several hundred is clearly framed as a mark of her failure (*New Haven Register* 1934).

7. As if to underline the point, note that both of my articles engaging this question have the same subtitle: "Emma Goldman's Passion."

8. In considering questions of gender, race, and sexuality as a question of "objects" and our vexed relationship to them, I have been strongly influenced by Robyn Wiegman's work in *Object Lessons* (2012). Wiegman's approach engages the desires that queer feminist critics have for their cherished objects, a process that invests them with magical properties they can never deliver on. In my own project, I am more concerned with charting a history of the ambivalence one needs to suppress in order to continue those desiring attachments.

9. The reader may have noticed that I alternate between describing this project and the theoretical and political terrain I am engaged with as "feminist," "feminist and queer," "queer and feminist," or "queer feminist" (among other juxtapositions). My use of these terms is also ambivalent, precisely because it is not always (ever?) entirely clear which subjects and objects are being denoted in this difference. Further, many scholars see themselves as both queer and feminist but nevertheless would want both terms included (rather than the one subsumed under the other). My difficulty in separating them out is a historiographic as well as definitional problem, in that the separation can often denote supersession as well as difference. My use of both is thus also intended to highlight in the text as far as possible that I think of "queer" and "feminist" as by turns indistinguishable, and as taking place in the same sphere, rather than as generationally divided (see also Hemmings 2016). In a more descriptive vein, we might say that feminist thinking is more prevalent in my first chapter on femininity and its discontents, while queer theory is more central to the third chapter on sexual freedom and the historical imagination. But even this is not fully accurate.

10. My thanks to one of the readers of the proposal and first draft of this project for insisting on the importance of the different archives that structure my inquiry. And I am grateful to both readers for their identification of the question of "political ambivalence" as the central feature of the project (which had somehow remained buried).

11. Much of the research for this project involved immersion in the *Emma Goldman Papers: A Microfilm Edition* (1991). This resource is the fullest collection of Goldman's published and unpublished work, letters to and from her, and federal government as well as news media commentary on her life and work. Where reference is made to materials from this source, the original date of publication provides the in-text citation, and the bibliographical reference locates the reel number. Additional sources—e.g., third-party correspondence and hard-to-find secondary criticism—were consulted at the Emma Goldman Papers Project at UC Berkeley.

12. It is Falk who describes Goldman's personal and political mode as one of "panache" (2002, 23). In this book's conclusion I explore the potential of considering panache as a political attitude well suited to a politics of ambivalence.

13. Farhand Rouhami (2012) and Martha Ackelsberg (2012) foreground the importance of prefiguration as part of anarchist revolutionary practice and frame it as the art of living now the future you are working to bring into being.

14. This term recurred in discussions at the two-day workshop "Anarchism and (Homo)sexuality" that took place at the London School of Economics in December 2014. My thanks to all the participants of that workshop for their intellectual enthusiasm, and particularly to my workshop co-organizer, Richard Cleminson.

15. There are of course a range of biographies and web-based introductions to her life and work, many of which are included in this book's reference list, and many articles or longer theoretical texts provide a "snapshot" of Goldman's life as part of their introduction. Such snapshots are never neutral, presenting us with a picture of a vibrant Goldman (Shulman 1982), an emotion-fuelled Goldman (Gornick 2011a), a hysterical Goldman (Herzog 2007), or a politically complex Goldman (Marso 2003) in ways that reflect the main arguments about the value of her thinking. The fullest *intellectual* biographical account of Goldman's years in America comes from Falk's extensive introductions to the three volumes of *Emma Goldman: A Documentary History of the American Years* (2003, 2005, 2012b).

16. Falk is unusual in remaining critical of what she sees as Goldman's flattening out of the differences between Russian and American repression in her critique of the Bolsheviks (2005, 15).

17. When Goldman was finally able to return—for a lecture tour in 1934—her expectations exceeded what her adopted home could deliver, of course. The press is filled with accounts of her ageing body and attitude, as well as the reduced crowds for an anarchist whose heyday is cast as long past.

18. In relation to the production/reproduction nexus, it is of course Friedrich Engels (1884) who is the early socialist reference point for consideration of women's labour as labour.

19. I began this work of challenging the ways sexuality is forced to carry the burden of a cultural/material opposition in theory and politics in chapter 3 of *Why Stories Matter* (2011) and have early reflections on Goldman's value in rethinking sexual history in my more recent piece for *Feminist Review* (2014b).

20. While none of Goldman's lectures on homosexuality remain, we know she was

one of the few anarchists who defended Oscar Wilde (Cook 1979a; Liesegang 2012, 89), and she viewed male homosexuality as a site of creativity and unnecessary oppression (Goldman 1931b, 269; Marso 2003, 318).

21. John D'Emilio's foundational work "Capitalism and Gay Identity" very importantly challenges any easy separation of gay and lesbian identity developments from the emergence of modern capitalism, as he explores ways in which the "expansion of capital and the spread of wage labor" are "most directly linked to the appearance of a collective gay life" (1983, 102).

22. Stefan Dudink (2011) and Eric Fassin (2011) provide useful accounts of the controversial Amsterdam conference I am obliquely referring to here.

23. I use the term "postcolonial" here rather than "critical race" or "decolonial" in order to foreground the question of radical historical methodology. It is postcolonial critics such as Gayatri Spivak (1999) and Antoinette Burton (1999, 2001) who have focused most particularly on the vexed question of authenticity in the "recovery" of the past.

24. I am influenced here by Joan Scott's (1996) other work on paradox as at the heart of any feminist project because of the pull to and away from identities formed in dominant discourse.

25. The contemporary work on queer temporality is consistently indebted to Ann Cvetkovich's landmark book *An Archive of Feelings* (2003), in which the author challenges not only the contents of lesbian history but also its conventional methods. Jackie Stacey's (2013a) account of queer temporality as part of how she situates her reading of Peggy Shaw in "Must" is particularly helpful in outlining the main strands of this body of thought.

26. Most famously, Julia Kristeva's (1981) work "Women's Time" suggests the importance of the embodied and the political in thinking genealogy and generation. Kristeva's rather grand "matriarchal" alternative has been complicated by many thinkers, among them Barbara Taylor (1992), who counters and extends Kristeva's view through thinking different modes of feminist temporality as simultaneous "impulses" rather than drawn-out teleological shifts.

27. Lisa Baraitser's reflection is one of three for the *European Journal of Women's Studies* on Passerini's methodology in connecting feminist politics, history, and memory (Baraitser 2012; Peto 2012; Pravadelli 2012).

28. I borrow my use of the term "queer feminist" from Wiegman (2014), enjoying its challenge to that teleology and the way it opens up the possibility of being both at once.

29. Of course, juxtaposing fraudulent spiritual mediums and queer feminist history here references Sarah Waters's narrative genius in *Affinity* (1999). Spiritualism and feminism have a long connection in fact; Elizabeth Lowry (2015) suggests we see this link as a radical interruption of attempts to control sexuality, gender, and race in a period of transformation.

30. Arabella Kurtz and J. M. Coetzee (2015) discuss the problem of narrative coherence and truth in their recent exchange. For both writers "the truth" is unknowable,

but a narrative resonance one can live with is imperative for any coherence (in analysis or in fiction).

31. The following section on psychoanalytic method is adapted from my article "Considering Emma" (2013, 339–40), which introduces the significance of these approaches.

32. Maria Sturken shifts away from memory tout court and towards what she terms "technologies of memory" (1997, 10), a framing that allows her to focus on "the stakes held by individuals and institutions in attributing meaning to the past" (9). For Sturken, memory and forgetting are thus always "questions of political intent" (9).

33. See also issue 100 of *Feminist Review*, which celebrated the journal's birthday with responses to and engagements with Avtar Brah's original article (Gedalof and Puwar 2012). Here affective attachment to Brah as the longest-standing member of the journal's editorial collective produces an active space of feminist engagement and challenge.

34. As Betty Bergland argues, Goldman's autobiography also refuses a separation between public and private spaces as sites of knowledge and politics (1994, 150).

35. Jacqueline Rose makes a similar point about letters for women—revolutionary and otherwise—in her recent book *Women in Dark Times* (2014), exploring the letters of Rosa Luxemburg, Marilyn Monroe, and Charlotte Salomon as part of how we need to engage women as complex resistant subjects.

36. In a different register, Cheryl McEwan suggests in "Building a Post-colonial Archive" (2003) that we should not look to store endless additional stories in stale institutional contexts but should instead seek to weave subaltern memories into cloth—so that they are useful and colorful and combine with all the other threads.

37. The archive can be visited at http://www.archivesandcreativepractice.com/zoe-leonard-cheryl-dunye/ and consists of a series of staged images of Richards's life, including butch-femme relationships.

CHAPTER ONE. WOMEN AND REVOLUTION

1. In 1939, the Los Angeles Liberation Committee published a seventieth birthday commemorative pamphlet for Goldman, which declares on its front cover "Emma Goldman, 70, Holds Fast to Anarchy" (LALC 1939, 1), underlining her commitment to anarchist struggle.

2. As a web supplement to her book *Emma Goldman: Political Thinking in the Streets* (2011b), Ferguson provides information on radical women contemporaries of Goldman largely obscured by history, lists of now defunct radical journals, and instances of violence against labour activists. I should also note here that Ferguson's book has been an important text in the development of my own project. Her book is one of the few full-length engagements with Goldman as a thinker as well as activist or autobiographer, and Ferguson negotiates the sticky terrain of scholarly criticism on Goldman with enviable aplomb. See "A Companion Website to the Book" on the website of the Political Science Department, University of Hawai'i: http://www.politicalscience.hawaii.edu/emmagoldman/index.html.

3. In "Anarchism and Feminism: A Historical Survey" (1996), Sharif Gemie traces anarchist privileging of the power of the state or bosses over that of "the patriarch"; in "Mirbeau and the Politics of Misogyny" (2001), he explores the overassociation of women with their oppressive position (i.e., as duplicitous or artificial). The combined force of both anarchist positions is that amelioration of women's subordination is not considered urgent.

4. Part of *Strike!* special issue on feminism; http://strikemag.org/portfolio/the -feminist-issue/.

5. Readers will note that some references to Goldman's work from the *Emma Goldman Papers* (1991) have question marks next to the date. This indicates a degree of uncertainty in the dating within the archive and qualifies the year, month, or day that it immediately follows. I retain this form throughout the book.

6. In her recent intellectual biography of Goldman, *Tongue of Fire*, Donna M. Kowal discusses Goldman's contributions to the "sex question" alongside those of Voltairine de Cleyre, Florence Finch Kelly, Kate Cooper Austin, and Lucy Parsons, as part of the development of what she terms an "anarchist-feminist counterpublic" (2016, 4).

7. Despite her opposition to the war, Goldman assures her audience in the late 1920s that no one can now "dare to insist that [woman's] only place is in the home, to waste her substance as domestic drudge or sex commodity" (1926a), and "'no one dares doubt that she has the capacity for public work'" (*Edmonton Journal* 1927).

8. While delighted that birth control had become less controversial by the 1930s such that "'the principle is admitted correct by the majority of Episcopalian Bishops meeting in New York'" (*Montreal Daily Herald* 1935?), Goldman did not remain central to the movement once she had left America. In part this is because of the single-issue focus of birth control activism, as well as because of an argument with Margaret and William Sanger over the former's unwillingness to go to prison for the cause (Sanger 1916).

9. It would be a mistake to read Goldman's views as an endorsement of prostitution, however. Goldman's point here is that marriage and prostitution are two sides of the same poisoned coin, with the strictures of marriage and women's dependence producing rather than providing an alternative to prostitution (Goldman 1909e).

10. Janet Day is helpful in distinguishing between individuality and individualism in Goldman's work: individualism is linked to individual greed, while individuality refers to "potentiality realized" (2007, 110).

11. Candace Falk insists that Goldman's ambivalence around "the majority"—she supported strikes and the organised labour movement—was increasingly resolved through her life as she witnessed the "undifferentiated power of the masses" (2003, 37) in the First World War and in the Russian Revolution. Falk notes that throughout her exile "Goldman trusted only the free association of individuals in an environment that supported radical thinking" (37).

12. Alderson cites Marcuse's definition of "false needs" as "those which are superimposed upon the individual by particular social interests in his repression: the needs which perpetuate toil, aggressiveness, misery, and injustice. . . . Most of the prevailing

needs to relax, to have fun, to love and hate what others love and hate, belong to this category of false needs" (in Alderson 2016, 98).

13. Goldman supported Francisco Ferrer's radical pedagogy (1909a) and wrote against the constraints of normative school structures (1898a). This commitment dovetails with Goldman's more general support of freedom for children, who she believed were stultified from the start by external pressures (1906a). In an interesting twist, Goldman imagined America itself as a youth, "cruel and thoughtless" certainly, but not "stagnant" like Europe (G. Cohn 1926; see also Goldman 1926c). This metaphorisation allows her to continue to believe that America can change, can become a more open, egalitarian society. The anarchist tradition of alternative models of schooling and learning is continued in the edited volume *Anarchist Pedagogies* (Haworth 2012).

14. I return to this discussion in the context of Goldman's understanding of nationalism and propagation in the next chapter.

15. Here she is drawing on Fourier (1772–1837), who "saw passionate attraction as germinal to the egalitarian, extra-familial bonds he envisioned. It was Fourier . . . who first perceived the connection, popular with subsequent sex radicals, between sexual monogamy and the acquisitive mentality fostered by private property" (Snitow, Stansell, and Thompson 1983, 14).

16. For Haaland (1993), Goldman's attachment to both psychoanalysis and sexology keeps her locked into sexual and gendered norms (especially heterosexism), whereas for Ferguson, Goldman is able to integrate Freud into her "toolbox" of many influences, including Stirner, Engels, Bakunin, and Nietzsche (2011b, 165ff.).

17. Dubois and Gordon (1983) situate late nineteenth-century and early twentieth-century free love arguments historically (in relation to the 1920s) and consider the difficulties for women of entering into arrangements they endorsed politically but resisted emotionally. Similar arguments about the potential costs of free love for women can be found in Ellen Trimberger's (1983) account of Greenwich Village up to the 1920s and Ginger Frost's (2009) careful charting of free love practices in Edwardian England.

18. Connections between anarchism and feminism or queer mobilisation are common contemporarily, drawing on their common interest in both challenging authority and emphasising process as well as (or over) outcome. Bice Maiguashca (2014) highlights these links but also the limits feminists can encounter to these overlaps, while Benjamin Shepard (2010) suggests that the attachment to "play" as politically significant is something anarchist and queer activists share. The volume *Quiet Rumours* by Dark Star Collective (originally published in 1984), a collection of anarchist-feminist reflections, went into its third edition in 2012, and the anthology *Queering Anarchism* came out the same year (Daring et al. 2012). The edited volume *Anarchism and Sexuality* includes several pieces on queer theory or practice and anarchism (Heckert and Cleminson 2011a) and an interview with Judith Butler on anarchism and its influence on queer thinking (Heckert 2011).

19. For both these theorists, this typical anarchist oversight is part of why anarchist

feminism more generally did not remain potent in Latin America in the early twentieth century.

20. Ben Reitman was a medical doctor and birth control activist as well as an anarchist. He had been a hobo and was by all accounts a wild character who appealed to Goldman's sense of the extraordinary (Gurstein 2002; Poirier 1988; Stansell 2000, 295). He was Goldman's tour manager at the heyday of her lectures in America, and their tumultuous relationship only really came to an end once Goldman was deported (Goldman 1931b, 1931c).

21. I discuss Goldman's letters to Reitman more fully in the next chapter. For a selection of these letters—in all their smutty, self-promoting, and self-abasing glory—see Falk, Pateman, and Moran (2005, 353–54, 368–71, 422–24, 438–42, 464–67).

22. The letters probably did function as pornography, as a reminder to their intended recipient to hasten desire for the next encounter. As Stansell notes, they may have functioned as pornography for a broader circle of readers as well, since American free love circles included a culture of people reading each other's letters, refusing to be secretive, and generating "a lively discourse of sexual conversation and revelation" (2000, 274).

23. Poirier's work is unusual in this regard: it charts the complex nature of Reitman's relationships with women and positions these as legitimate ways of engaging sexual freedom.

24. Again Gurstein goes further, considering it none of our business what Goldman did in her private life and dismissing the importance of a "tortured love affair" as compared to "going to prison or being deported for one's ideas" (2002, 68). To my mind, however, this is a rather absurd distinction to maintain, given Goldman's insistence on the centrality of sexual politics to women's misery and social transformation.

25. This argument was initially proposed in Hemmings (2013) and is developed here and in the final sections of this chapter in terms of its implications for integrating Goldman into a history of feminist theory and politics.

26. Angela McRobbie's book *The Aftermath of Feminism* (2009) constitutes a strong analysis and critique of this story. Various commentators have emphasised the ways in which feminism's work continues to be necessary and is in fact very much alive (e.g., Dean 2010; Walby 2011).

27. Conventionally, this is termed "the reserve army of labour" (Beechey 1977; Bruegel 1979). Floya Anthias (1980) provides an early critique of the raced and classed presumptions that attend the development of this concept (presuming a white, middle-class woman whose labour is not essential for the maintenance of the family). It is this discourse of "reserve" that is currently being mobilised in order to shame women for "taking men's jobs" in a UK context at the time of writing, however.

28. For gender gaps in education and health as well as pay, see Hausmann, Tyson, and Zahidi 2007 (http://www3.weforum.org/docs/WEF_GenderGap_Report_2012 .pdf); and for enduring pay gaps in the United Kingdom, see "Equal Pay," Fawcett Society, November 7, 2013, https://www.fawcettsociety.org.uk/close-gender-pay-gap/.

29. These positions have of course been extended in numerous directions, most aptly here in terms of the critique of "culture" as a carrier of naturalised inequality (Narayan 1998; Volpp 2001).

30. After raids on sex work premises in London's Soho in December 2013 in the name of clamping down on trafficking, migrant sex workers were detained despite insisting they had not been trafficked. See the Sex Worker Open University Statement, published as a press release on December 6, 2013: http://www.thefword.org.uk /blog/2013/12/swou_statement_Soho; and other commentary on the hypocrisy of police "protection" for sex workers: Paula Nicol, "Guest Post: The Soho Raids Were Not about Trafficking," Feministing, December 2013, http://feministing.com/2013 /12/11/guest-post-the-soho-raids-were-not-about-trafficking/; Mitzi Poesener, "Guest Post: What Motivated the Raids on Sex Workers in Soho," Feministing, December 10, 2013, http://feministing.com/2013/12/10/guest-post-what-motivated-the-raids-on -sex-workers-in-soho/.

31. The UK press has been filled with discussions about contemporary feminist movements, most notably UK Feminista, which focuses on issues of sexual violence against women and targets mainstream porn and prostitution: http://ukfeminista .org.uk. In addition, feminist and mainstream media discussion of intersectionality has been vibrant following Julie Burchill's article "Don't You Dare Tell Me to Check My Privilege," published on February 22, 2014, in *The Spectator* (http://www .spectator.co.uk/features/9141292/dont-you-dare-tell-me-to-check-my-privilege/), which compares it to a "bitch fight" on a talk show. The response of blackfeminists .org group was to organise a "conversation" on intersectionality the following May: http://www.blackfeminists.org/2014/05/07/a-conversation-on-intersectionality -critical-race-theory/.

32. Most notably, Goldman was devastated by the swift transition from revolution into state control and violence that she saw after the Russian Revolution and was an early detractor of the social fantasy she saw as corrupt to its core (1925b). For Carroll (2007), this disappointment resulted in Goldman's changing understanding of revolution and her increased willingness to change her ideas where necessary. Goldman was, as Ferguson points out, able to "gather up her considerable resolve" (2011c, 753) and move forward following both personal and political disappointments in ways that are too hastily identified as eclectic (e.g., Herzog 2007). Falk remains uncomfortable with Goldman's flattening out of the differences between American and Russian repression, however (2005, 15).

33. At a rather wonderful evening event in conversation with Sylvie Tissot, Christine Delphy (Eloit 2017) responded to a doubtful question about veiling as a feminist practice in the following way: feminism should not be thought of as a club for the liberated, she insisted, but a club for those acknowledging their oppression and hoping to express solidarity with others in the same position with a view to challenging it.

34. Similar issues have of course been raised with respect to the white hegemony of dominant strands of feminism that have led a variety of "postfeminists" to use that distance to mark other kinds of political and intellectual attachments (Dean 2012).

35. Jane Flax helpfully suggests we ask not how to liberate women but "why" are women, which would allow us to "shift the focus of inquiry from who is woman really . . . [to] analyzing what produces women and what functions as 'woman'" (2004, 907).

36. This resonates with a queer argument, following Teresa de Lauretis (1988, 1991), that gender can be reframed as "play" from which tension and pleasure may be derived, and too with Judith Butler's (1990, 1993) important insights into the "gap" between gender as fiction and fact that supports ethical consideration of gay male, butch-femme, queer, and trans subjectivities as other than pathologised.

CHAPTER TWO. RACE AND INTERNATIONALISM

1. Perhaps Goldman's most notorious stereotyping comes in her characterisations from her autobiography of black prisoners on Blackwell's Island, whom she represents as both privileged and sly (1931b, 138). I discuss these depictions later in the chapter.

2. A range of recent publications have stressed the importance of diaspora and exile as central to strategy and the development of a transnational anarchist sensibility. Constance Bantman (2013) and Petro Di Paola (2013) explore the importance of French and Italian anarchists in London, respectively, while Timothy Messer-Kruse (2012) emphasises the importance of transatlantic networks in the aftermath of the Haymarket tragedy. The movement of people (as well as politics) across borders made it harder to recognise individual insurgents too, of course, as they would often have left the country by the time their presence became known to the authorities.

3. Sian Byrne and Lucien Van der Walt note similarly that anarchism was "global and transnational," with mobility among radicals meaning that this radical movement was "enriched" by exile (2015, 99).

4. Adapting Arjun Appadurai (1996), we might think of the movements of anarchist revolutionary thought as a kind of politico-"scape" that had an unprecedented ability to change dominant geopolitical landscapes at the time.

5. As Ferguson (2011b) suggests, the lack of a sense of anarchism's dominance on the Left also serves to erase our knowledge of the systematic violence required to eradicate its hold over labour movements both before and after the First World War by both the Left and the state.

6. This would also be the position of a range of post-anarchist thinkers such as Todd May (1994) and Saul Newman (2007): namely, that anarchism provides a philosophical as well as (or even in preference to) a political point of social intervention. In this body of work "post-anarchism" references both the time after anarchism's heyday and the importance of poststructuralist philosophical traditions that both rely on and complement modern anarchist thinking. Evren's and Cohn's focus is more firmly on the importance of a transnational (rather than a European continental) approach (to both sources and perspectives), however, and I find this more persuasive in terms of my historiographic interest in challenging what we think we already know about the

(multiple) histories we inherit. See Rouselle and Evren's collection *Post-anarchism: A Reader* (2011) for a useful collection referencing both approaches.

7. Arturo Escobar (2004) writes that in the context of what others have described as "global coloniality" there is heightened marginalisation and suppression of alternate knowledges and cultures. For Escobar, then, this is where we need to begin in order to challenge knowledge production as part of historical memory.

8. Emma Goldman, "Address to the Jury," delivered during her anticonscription trial, New York City, July 9, 1917; text found at http://sunsite.berkeley.edu/goldman/Writings/Speeches/170709.html.

9. Loretta Kensinger (2007) notes that this antinationalism made Goldman extremely cautious with respect to the imagination of a Jewish state in Palestine. Interestingly, Judith Butler (2011) critiques Goldman for that same scepticism that would also make conceiving of a Palestinian homeland problematic.

10. Goldman was fond of repeating the story of William Buwalda, a soldier who attended a lecture of hers on patriotism and was placed under military arrest (Goldman 1931b, 428). Meeting him for a second time after he was pardoned by Roosevelt, Goldman describes his "fine, open face, intelligent eyes, and firm mouth" that she reads as "indicative of an independent character" (444) and tells him that "'now that you are free from your military shackles, we can shake hands without fear'" (446).

11. Enrique Álvarez (2012) also critiques the aggressive revolutionary masculinities that were lauded during the Spanish Civil War. Goldman would have taken pleasure in the variety of masculinities identified and discussed by Richard Cleminson within the *Revista Blanca* (2012). She was well aware that nonaggressive masculinities were likely to be framed as homosexual as well as dissident, resulting in a policing of modes of masculinity as central to the Spanish anarchist revolutionary imagination.

12. While Goldman was a champion of homosexual rights and understood homosexual identity as offering a specific gendered as well as sexual challenge to the tyranny of the majority, she remained ambivalent about homosexuality in her personal life. As we will see in the next chapter, she made unpleasant remarks about effeminacy in men on more than one occasion and also mocked what she read as the masculinity and brittleness of lesbianism.

13. By the time Goldman was writing her autobiography in the 1930s, however, she had changed her view, stating that birth control "was unquestionably an important issue, but by no mean the most vital one" (1931b, 591). Her change of position may have been because of the increasing acceptance of birth control by that time (and her location in Europe); it may also reflect the increasing distance of the birth control movement from broader social issues.

14. See chapter 1 for a fuller discussion of this epistemological issue, with particular reference to Goldman's chapter "Minorities versus Majorities," in which she links the preference for murderous majoritarianism to quantification (1910, 69–78).

15. I return to the issue of racialisation of sexual freedom in the Goldman archive in the next chapter.

16. Stansell further contextualises this bourgeois "loss of confidence" in terms of the concomitant "celebration of sports and martial vigor as antidotes to the plague of effeminacy, in a vogue for bodybuilding (and its companion religion, Muscular Christianity), and . . . in the cult of the 'strenuous life' and of 'roughing it' in wild, restorative places with 'primitive' men—Indians, cowboys, native guides" (2000, 31).

17. The context for this political declaration in volume 2 of Goldman's *Living My Life* is the ongoing arguments she and Reitman had with Margaret Sanger over her willingness (or lack thereof) to go to jail for her belief in and support of birth control, and her general lack of support for anarchist birth control activists (1931b, 590–91). Already here, then, Goldman sees the relative conservatism of what she would no doubt have viewed as a bourgeois desire for recognition.

18. Indeed, this might also partially account for Gilroy's interest in cosmopolitanism (see particularly 2005) but also his return to the limits of urging a "post-racial" perspective in continued contexts of race-bound oppression. See Jacob Breslow's (2017) reflection on this shift in Gilroy's thought in the context of the Black Lives Matter movement in the United States.

19. As Falk makes plain, "United efforts for social change, even among urban cosmopolitans attracted to the transformative possibilities of the New Woman and the New Negro, were marred by intense racial segregation," such that "anarchism had few, if any, followers among African Americans" (2012b, 16).

20. Alyosxa Tudor (2017) theorises "migratism" as the conflation of discriminations produced by migration and/or racism; Goldman's parallelism and displacing of racist exclusion in her Blackwell's Island account of hierarchically organised difference is a good example of this.

21. Falk also discusses this disagreement (2012b, 42).

22. In her chapter on Goldman and the African American experience—"How Could She Miss Race?" (Ferguson 2011b)—Ferguson gently mocks critical amazement over Goldman's omission, framing it instead as a question of political precision and sustained argumentation.

23. Reitman was tarred, feathered, branded, and sodomised by the crowd that formed in violent protest against the International Workers of the World (IWW).

24. In this article, Lumsden reads images across a selection of anarchist and socialist journals between 1903 and 1917, complementing her earlier work on *Mother Earth* (2007). Her argument is that—irrespective of the text itself—graphic images brought the radical message alive but also threatened to alienate potential "converts" through stereotyping.

25. As Ferguson (2011b) notes in a related vein, Goldman's rejection of the necessity of a distinct theory of racism is also carried by the accusation of reformism of African American political movements. It provides a political alibi for ignoring the prejudice that accompanied conflation and metaphorisation.

26. Wexler is the most explicit about this identification, noting that she felt close to Goldman because "my grandparents were also Russian Jews" (1992, 38).

27. As Nathaniel Hong argues, anarchism was characterised as "the beast," as "a

is *primarily* concerned to track the pernicious impact of sexual oppression for women, she is also concerned about the limitations it places on men's capacities for real sexual feeling at the same time.

7. As Ferguson points out, and as discussed in chapter 1, to think of Goldman as *ahead* of her own time is to do great injustice to the range of dissenting voices in America and Europe in the first half of the twentieth century (2011b, 251).

8. Davis explored these ideas at the "Anarchism and (Homo)sexuality: Comparative Perspectives" workshop at the London School of Economics (December 4–5, 2015), co-organised by me and Richard Cleminson. The workshop brought together academics and activists working with anarchist negotiations of (homo)sexuality currently to think through the importance of methodology in approaching the sexual archive.

9. Or, as Davis inquires: "What is the connection between love and revolution? Judging by the contemporary 'common sense' understanding of these terms, the answer would appear to be 'very little'" (2011, 103).

10. Parker reads letters between Marx and Engels as homosocial exchanges, the erotic nature of which is denied precisely through the appeal to the reproduction/production opposition at the heart of their emerging analysis of capitalism (1993, 5). If sex belongs to the private sphere, then bonds between workers can be purged of erotic content and solidarity can be sexless.

11. For what would contemporary Marxist criticism, including its variant post-Marxist forms, be without its grown-up boy subjects suspiciously certain of the "problem" of identity politics as residing elsewhere.

12. Firestone's contributions to feminist queer analysis of the political economy of sexuality have been recognised in Mandy Merck and Stella Sandford's (2010) volume of critical essays on her work.

13. In a broader psychoanalytic vein Goldman would have had sympathy with, Marcuse (1955) similarly seeks to separate sex from its commodification within capitalist processes that he believes repress real desire, and makes the influential proposition that "un-repressing" sex will challenge the very fabric of our social order. Sabsay (2016) might be said to be working in this tradition by extending the critique of the limits of sexual identity to the rights-based framework that has replaced "un-repression" in some ways. For Sabsay, it is precisely in the psychic struggles with the ambivalence of desire that the possibilities for reimagining sexual freedom reside.

14. This early gay liberation emphasis on homosexual difference from a production/reproduction dyad is extended in Lee Edelman's *No Future* (2004), of course, in which the political significance of nongenerational queer thinking and being is promoted and embraced. It further resonates with the important work on queer temporalities discussed briefly in my introduction, in which it is argued that to take queerness seriously is to interrupt historical narratives of sexual and gendered progress and loss (see Freeman 2010; Love 2007; Wiegman 2014).

15. Sex difference, as Christine Delphy (1980) pertinently notes, is a representation of that naturalisation of labour.

16. Danae Clark (1991) uses the term "commodity lesbianism" to express her concern at the increasing market governance of lesbian social life, and Alan Sears (2005) introduces a distinction between gay-identified and queer subjects as in part hinging on the absence or presence of the critique of such commodification.

17. Scholars such as Anthony Giddens (1992) and Elizabeth Beck-Gernsheim (1998) argue that changes in patterns of kinship over the twentieth century—as women enter the workforce in the West in greater numbers and as a result of legislative and cultural shifts brought about by feminist and lesbian and gay social movements—have altered the nature of ties between sexuality and the economy. Within political theory, Nancy Fraser (1996, 1997) has most famously suggested that such shifts have resulted in a need for an alternative mode of social justice—recognition—for marginal sexual subjects, whose oppression or exclusion is no longer central to the functioning of the (productive) economy. In a less optimistic reading, however, this autonomy from the doubled security of family and employment leads to an excessive burden of individual responsibility and privileges youth, wealth, and attractiveness in both love and work (Bauman 2003; Skeggs 2004). My own intervention into these debates stresses the undervaluing of psychic investment in sexual norms in such pragmatist accounts (Hemmings 2012c).

18. Donna Haraway (1991) has suggested that to take colonial histories seriously challenges how we think about gender and the relationship between production and reproduction in the first place, and she explores the idea of a "race/gender" system as equally apt for analytic and descriptive purposes as the more familiar "sex/gender" system proposed by Gayle Rubin in "The Traffic in Women" (1975).

19. This link between commodification of gay identities and global economic power relations is made particularly clear in work on China over the last decade. As both Lisa Rofel (2007, 2010) and David Eng (2010) have argued, the take-up of nonfamilial, nonheterosexual desires in identity form can act to legitimate the entry of postsocialist subjects into international capitalism. Indeed, the increasing role that sexual rights in identity mode have had over the last thirty or so years cements the association of homosexuality in particular—though less so other forms of nonfamilial sexual liberty—with global capitalism, and capitalism with social democracy as against cultural tyranny.

20. As Joseph Massad (2007) and Evelyn Blackwood (2008) have both indicated, non-Western forms of sexual alterity or deviance from the dominant norm remain obscured as part of the underdeveloped past of sexual politics, risking their erasure both from the present and from the historical record.

21. Robyn Wiegman and Elizabeth A. Wilson (2015) explore the limits that an assumption that queer theory or practice is inherently transgressive, "anti-normative," or freeing places on this body of thought. Wiegman (2015) further explores the ways in which that transgression tends to be bonded with identity in her reading of the critical desire for Eve Sedgwick to have been speaking and writing from a "lesbian" subject position in her own article for the special issue.

22. I am reminded here of the importance for queer theory of Diana Fuss's collection *Inside/Out* (1991), in which she highlights the work that the "inside" needs to do to keep on expelling the "outside" from its heart. That dynamic is a kind of vomiting

out of what is (sexually) intolerable and is marked by the affects of nausea or disgust that Parker picks up on.

23. See the important work by Sarah Bracke (2012) and Jin Haritaworn (2010, 2012) that seeks to trace the epistemological and political continuities (and differences) between "women's rights" and "gay rights" as modes of racist othering historically and contemporarily.

24. Eric Fassin (2010, 2011) in particular has explored the importance of a broader conception of "sexual democracy" for holding together the variety of sexual identities and practices that underwrite contemporary fantasies of "the modern." And indeed, Puar's (2006) essay on homonationalism suggests very clearly that this is a subset of heteronormativity, rather than a defining feature of queer life.

25. Thus, while D'Emilio (1983) certainly stresses that capitalism's authorship of modern sexuality should not be understood as wholly determined, because of the community possibilities created that do not remain static or merely responsive, the teleology he charts can nevertheless appear cast in stone.

26. Quite a range of theorists have explored Goldman's interest in and take-up of Friedrich Nietzsche in this respect. The work tends to read his influence in Deleuzian vein as a post-anarchist challenge to understanding Goldman's ideas of nature as essentialist (Bertalen 2011; Blake 1997; Morgan 2009) or as an indicator of her foregrounding of passion and play as part of an anarchist method with a history (Rossdale 2015). Unusually, Ferguson (2007) uses Nietzsche as a way of reading Goldman's passion as "the passion," and thus as evidence of her profound spirituality outside of an organised religious adherence. Allan Antliff (2007) has a somewhat different position, reading postanarchist theorists' preference for Nietzsche as part of how they "clean up" the supposed essentialism of earlier anarchist thought as a citational and genealogical erasure of the complexity of that same body of theory.

27. It is rather difficult to single out individual feminist or queer theorists who critique biological essentialism, since this is such a major strand in the field. Because citation is partly a way of identifying one's own reading history, I will just highlight the importance for my own thinking about antiessentialism of Elizabeth Spelman's *Inessential Woman* (1988). Published earlier than many of the texts more usually credited with the poststructuralist critique of sexual and gendered essence, Spelman's piece focused particularly on "race," essentialism, and exclusion.

28. Yet Lumsden's views on this issue should be taken with a few grains of salt, I think. Lumsden is so strongly attached to Goldman's biological determinism that she expresses surprise that Goldman was so active in the birth control movement, which she views as a challenge to the supremacy of the natural reproductive body (Lumsden 2007, 45). Birth control was of course central to Goldman's views about sexual freedom.

29. As Hexe quips, though not specifically in relation to Goldman: "Anarchism has always been a little queer, and anarchists have always been nerds for sexual freedom and choice" (2012, 233).

30. As discussed at length in chapter 2, here "race" would refer to a universal human race that Goldman believed would be the basis of a revolutionary transnational empathy.

31. Goldman was moved by the generosity she experienced from women and girls working in the brothel she rented a room in when anarchist comrades would no longer house her after Berkman's arrest for the attempted assassination of Henry Clay Frick in 1892 (1931b, 104–5).

32. Positions on the "sex wars" are many and various, but perhaps most helpful is Lisa Duggan's introductory article to the coauthored collection *Sex Wars: Sexual Dissent and Political Culture* (2006, 15–28), since it provides a careful overview of these debates.

33. Heather Tapley's engaging article "Mapping the Hobosexual" (2012) explores the sexualised and racialised representations of the itinerant homeless community (of which Reitman was a part). Her innovative queer reading foregrounds the importance of same-sex attachments in "riding the rails" as both economically and community driven.

34. In her article "Emma Goldman, Ben Reitman, and Reitman's Wives: A Study in Relationships" (1988), Suzanne Poirier tries to provide a different vantage point that centres Reitman himself, but largely we have little texture to Reitman in the secondary literature.

35. As Anthony Ince explains: "Anarchist prefigurative politics resides in the contestations and practices of everyday life, producing a revolutionary imagination that is rooted in process and becoming" (2012, 1653).

36. In imagining a postdeath conversation between Goldman and Berkman in Utopia, Ruth Kinna (2014) has Berkman correct misunderstandings of Goldman's free love as follows: "'You never said that the love you had in mind was only for straights, or that it was constrained by nature—motherhood, witchery, nurturing. Only that love was natural and that human nature, driven by defiant passion, is fluid, plastic, responsive to new conditions and that it can be changed.'" "'That's true,'" Goldman replies.

37. I discuss Goldman's ambivalent relationship to eugenics in the previous chapter. While Goldman actually advocated "race suicide," her positioning of mothers as "incessant breeders" and a lack of clarity on the meaning of "race" here make for an uncomfortable reification of motherhood. Questions of race purity aside, Goldman's position here might still raise concerns about her representation of mothers as pure conduits for a politicised future.

38. On a visit to San Francisco, Goldman recounts meeting Abe and Mary Isaak (the founders of *Firebrand*) and being profoundly moved by the application of their anarchist principles to the organisation of their household. She writes that the "comradeship between the parents and the complete freedom of every member of the household were novel things to me. In no other anarchist family had I seen children enjoy such liberty. . . . To him [Abe] and Mary that was just what freedom meant: equality of the sexes in all their needs, physical, intellectual, and emotional" (1931b, 224).

39. As Greenway notes of Elspeth Probyn's animation of the queer theorist, desire is "'a method of doing things, of getting places'" (2009b, 154).

40. No doubt Goldman rather enjoyed the whiff of scandal, but as Marjorie Garber notes, she was "unquestionably a champion of homosexuality in principle and of Oscar Wilde in particular" (1995, 76).

41. Goldman's defence of both Wilde and Whitman should also be read in the context of the renewal of the Comstock Act, which censored sexually explicit material and was used to prevent mailing of radical journals—including *Mother Earth*—identified as such (often because of a positive view of sexual freedom or birth control). As Falk notes (2005, 20), the act was specifically used to curb the widespread circulation of anarchist materials; the *Masses* was taken to trial on this basis, and although the editors were never convicted, the halting of business forced the journal to close (Lumsden 2010, 238).

42. My favourite among these is Goldman's correspondence with Agnes Smedley between 1924 and 1926. The letters between them show Smedley to be Goldman's intimate and good friend: they share advice about political and personal dilemmas, tease and encourage one another, and reference the difficulties of being women in a context of male dominance (themes Smedley extends in her autobiography *Daughter of Earth* [1929]). The tone of equals in the letters is no doubt due to Smedley's comparable revolutionary zeal—she worked for Indian independence and Chinese socialism throughout her lifetime, and she was hounded out of the United States after the Second World War as part of the process of the House Un-American Activities Committee. As Ruth Price (2005) explores, Smedley did in fact turn out to be a Soviet spy, despite Left investment in countering conservative insistence on this story.

43. This somewhat ambiguous comment is made in an unpublished outline for her autobiography and does not make it into the final version. It is traces such as these, however, whose frayed edges ask to be pulled on to unravel another sexual history for figures such as Goldman and others.

44. Almeda Sperry's letters to Goldman were read in *Emma Goldman Papers: A Microfilm Edition* (1991). All quotations are taken from Sperry 1912–1913, reels 6, 7, and 68. Original letters are housed at the Boston University Libraries Special Collections. Many of the original letters from Sperry are undated or only partially dated. Their ordering in *Emma Goldman Papers* provides dates with question marks or a likely range where there is insufficient information.

45. Sperry's letters have occasional deliberate or accidental spelling and grammar errors. I leave all originals as they are, and have avoided using *sic* in the text to preserve the letters' rhythm.

46. Misdated 1902 in Sperry's original.

47. The weather in early September 1912 is reported to have been very cool and dull with above average rainfall, but perhaps they would not have minded.

48. This is also the sentiment in Dale Sheldon's (2009) "Gay History Wiki: A History Discovered," published at http://gayhistory.wikidot.com/almeda-sperry.

CHAPTER FOUR. A LONGING FOR LETTERS

1. Almeda Sperry's letters to Goldman were read in the *Emma Goldman Papers: A Microfilm Edition* (Goldman 1991). All quotations are taken from Sperry 1912–1913, reels 6, 7, and 68. Original letters are housed at the Boston University Libraries Special Collections.

CONCLUSION

1. C. Brid Nicholson (2010) critiques Goldman's *Living My Life* as a constructed text rather than a window on the truth of her experience. Yet of course this is precisely the nature of autobiography, as numerous feminist scholars have pointed out (e.g., Gilmore 1994), and Goldman's was no exception (Falk 2005, 3). Maria Tamboukou remarks that in preparing for her writing, Goldman asked friends to send her letters they had received to prompt her memory (2012, 3), and Candace Falk revels in the fact that "the book is a self-conscious re-creation of the drama of her life, a self-portrait that is, at once, didactic and inspirational" (2002, 22).

2. Goldman and Berkman exchange a series of letters on this issue, in which Goldman laments that the reviews focus too strongly on her depictions of her love life over other aspects of the work, while Berkman reminds her that this aspect of her life—her belief in sexual freedom as fundamental to revolutionary possibility—has indeed been central. Berkman further uses this opportunity to suggest that women are indeed more oriented towards sex and love than men, reassuring Goldman that "by sex here I mean everything, affection, love, passion, all together. And I believe also that with most women in public life . . . it is the strong urge of sex that is the mainspring of all activity. . . . But I do not think the same is true of men—at least not to the same extent" (1931, 167). On the one hand, Berkman's position has elements of dismissal of women's capacity for rational public action; on the other, it interestingly inverts the assumption that the sex urge is strongest in men. Goldman's response makes clear that she takes issue with the puritanism that she believes underwrites such reviews and with their failure to recognise her "lacerating struggles every time I had to decide between my love for a man and my ideas" (Goldman 1931a, 168).

3. Weiss, Kensinger, and Carroll are thinking here particularly of Martha Solomon's hostile reduction of that commitment to an "'ideological sincerity [that] does not obscure the weaknesses in her presentation of her ideas' (1987, 50)" (2007, 9).

4. Alice Wexler notes the gendered nature of the political significance of passion, in her reprint of Goldman's engagement with Mary Wollstonecraft. For both Wollstonecraft and Goldman, the ability to express a "grand passion" gives men greater opportunities to expand their personal (and hence political and intellectual) horizons (1981, 118).

5. As discussed in the introduction, Goldman engaged in a range of theatrical "tricks" to entertain as well as educate her audience, chaining herself to her podium or stuffing rags in her mouth to highlight the limits of free speech for anarchists, rousing the audience to anger and empathy (Falk 2002, 12–15).

6. It is certainly true that Goldman made full use of the shifts in women's role, ma-

nipulating and challenging expectations of her femininity as part of the "development of her specific political aesthetic" (Adrian 2007, 217).

7. Goldman also writes to Margaret Sanger, Agnes Smedley, Max Nettlau, James Colton, and others of the impossibility of meeting others' expectations, of her inability to find the space she needs for personal autonomy, and—most frequently of all—of her constant exhaustion and sickness.

8. We may remember that for Stansell, for example, Goldman's belief in sexual freedom as both revolutionary methodology and outcome makes her particularly vulnerable to abuse by men "on the make" such as Ben Reitman (2000, 294), although this view of Reitman is also a contested one.

9. "Emma Goldman: A Guide to Her Life and Documentary Sources" (1995), http://www.lib.berkeley.edu/goldman/pdfs/goldman_chronology1869-1800.pdf.

10. Ann Bugliani notes that the first production of Rostand's play in Paris received no fewer than forty curtain calls (2003, 55).

11. Translations from the 1990 Librairie Générale edition are my own; the French original is reproduced here in the notes:

Il lève son épée

Que dites-vous? . . . C'est inutile? . . . Je le sais!
Mais on ne se bat pas dans l'espoir du succès!
No! non! C'est bien plus beau lorsque c'est inutile!
Qu'est-ce que c'est que tous ceux-là?—Vous êtes mille?
Ah! Je vous reconnais, tous mes vieux ennemis!
Le Monsonge?

Il Frappe de son épée le vide.

Tiens, tiens!—Ha! ha! Les Compromis,
Les Préjugés, les Lâchetés! . . .

Il frappe.

Que je pactise?
Jamais, jamais!—Ah! Te voilà, toi, la Sottise!
—Je sais bien qu'à la fin vous me metrrez à bas;
N'importe: je me bats! je me bats! je me bats!

12. Slavoj Žižek shares Rostand's love of lost causes, writing that it defines the "limit of common sense" and "involves a Leap of Faith." He notes further that "in a time of crisis and ruptures, skeptical empirical wisdom itself . . . cannot provide the answers" (2009, 2).

13. Ferguson (2011c) writes on Goldman's different articulations of gendered subordination and freedom as a question of genre rather than incommensurable positions. Her position resonates with my sense of Goldman as inhabiting styles of persuasion as part of her revolutionary methodology and fits with an understanding of passion as *a part* of panache.

14. The original French is as follows:

... Mais ... chanter,
Rêver, rire, passer, être seul, être libre,
Avoir l'œil qui regarde bien, la voix qui vibre,
Mettre, quand il vous plaît, son feutre de travers,
Pour un oui, pour un non, se battre, - ou faire un vers!
Travailler sans souci de gloire ou de fortune,
...
N'écrire jamais rien qui de soi ne sortît,
...
Sois satisfair des fleurs, des fruits, même des feuilles,
Si c'est dans ton jardin à toi que tu les cueilles!
Puis, s'il advient d'un peu triompher, par hazard,
Ne pas être obligé d'en rien rendre à César,
Vis-à-vis de soi-même en garder la mérite,
Bref, dédaignant d'être le lierre parasite,
Lors même qu'on n'est pas le chêne ou le tilleul,
Ne pas monter bien haut, peut-être, mais tout seul!

15. Goldman's main theatrical interests were in realist plays, with Ibsen and Strindberg among her favourites. Interestingly, Ferguson identifies Goldman's concentration on this over other forms of representation—such as film or modernist poetry, for example—as part of her romantic attachment to creativity as "unmediated" and as accessible to all (2011c, 742).

16. "Ne le plaignez pas trop: il a vécu sans pactes, / Libre dans sa pensée autant que dans ses actes."

References

PRIMARY SOURCES

Berkman, Alexander. 1912. *Prison Memoirs of an Anarchist.* New York: Mother Earth Press.

———. [1931] 1975. "Letter to Emma Goldman, 22 December." In *Nowhere at Home: Letters from Exile of Emma Goldman and Alexander Berkman*, edited by Richard Drinnon and Anna Maria Drinnon, 167–68. New York: Schocken Books.

Berkman, Alexander, and Emma Goldman. 1919. *Deportation: Its Meaning and Menace.* New York: M. E. Fitzgerald.

Bly, Nellie. [1893] 2003. "Nellie Bly Again: She Interviews Emma Goldman and Other Anarchists." In *Emma Goldman: A Documentary History of the American Years.* Vol. 1, *Made for America, 1890–1901*, edited by Candace Falk, Barry Pateman, and Jessica M. Moran, 155–60. Berkeley: University of California Press. Originally published in *New York World*, September 17.

Brooklyn Eagle. [1916] 1991. "Some Civitas Members Wanted to Be 'Thrilled.' So Emma Goldman Was Asked to Address Them." January 16. In *Emma Goldman Papers*, reel 48.

Bruno, Guido. [1917] 1991. "Emma Goldman — Fighter and Idealist." *Pearson's Magazine* 38, no. 2 (August): 61. In *Emma Goldman Papers*, reel 48.

Chicago Daily Journal. [1908] 2005. "'Reds' Leader Flays Police." March 17. In *Emma Goldman: A Documentary History of the American Years.* Vol. 2, *Making Speech Free*

1902–1909, edited by Candace Falk, Barry Pateman, and Jessica M. Moran, 290–94. Berkeley: University of California Press.

Chicago Inter Ocean. [1908] 2005. "Emma Goldman Clashes with Police on Meeting." March 8. In *Emma Goldman . . . Making Speech Free 1902–1909*, 284–87.

Cohn, Gene. [1926] 1991. "Emma Goldman, Former Queen of Agitation, Found to Be Tamed . . ." *Stanford Advocate*, November 12. In *Emma Goldman Papers*, reel 51.

Colton, James. [1936] 1991. "Letter to Emma Goldman." [August?]. In *Emma Goldman Papers*, reel 38.

Edmonton Journal. [1927] 1991. "Contented Woman Stumbling Block in Path of Progress Is Belief of Emma Goldman." March 14. In *Emma Goldman Papers*, reel 51.

Ellis, Havelock. [1924] 1991. "Letter to Emma Goldman." December 14. In *Emma Goldman Papers*, reel 14.

Emma Goldman Papers: A Microfilm Edition. Chadwyck Healey Inc., Berkeley University Library.

Emma Goldman Scrapbook. 1933. "I Wonder What's Become of . . ." Magazine Section, May 7. In *Emma Goldman Papers*, reel 52.

Globe and Commerce. [1911?] 1991. "Labor's Seeress Predicts a Commune If M'Namaras Die." [October?]. In *Emma Goldman Papers*, reel 47.

Goldman, Emma. [1894] 2003. "My Year in Stripes." In *Emma Goldman . . . Made for America, 1890–1901*, 194–202. Originally published in *New York World*, August 18.

———. [1897a] 1991. "Marriage." *Firebrand* (Portland), July 18. In *Emma Goldman Papers*, reel 47.

———. [1897b] 1991. "What Is There in Anarchy for Women?" *St. Louis Dispatch*, October 24. In *Emma Goldman Papers*, reel 47.

———. [1897–98] 2003. "Letters from a Tour." In *Emma Goldman . . . Made for America, 1890–1901*, 300–317. Originally published in *Sturmvogel*, between December 15, 1897, and February 15, 1898.

———. [1898a] 2003. "Letter to the *Detroit Sentinel*." In *Emma Goldman . . . Made for America, 1890–1901*, 340–43. Originally published in *Detroit Sentinel*, July 25.

———. [1898b] 2003. "The New Woman." Transcript of lecture originally presented to Free Society, February 13. In *Emma Goldman . . . Made for America, 1890–1901*, 322–23.

———. [1899] 1991. "An Anarchist Propagandist." *Oakland Enquirer*, July 15. In *Emma Goldman Papers*, reel 47.

———. [1900] 2003. "The Effect of War on the Workers." Transcript of address in *Freedom* 14 (March–April): 10–11. In *Emma Goldman . . . Made for America, 1890–1901*, 384–88.

———. [1901] 2003. "Emma Goldman Defines Her Position." In *Emma Goldman . . . Made for America, 1890–1901*, 478–80. Originally published in "Letter" to *Lucifer, The Lightbearer*. New York, November 11.

———. [1904] 2005. "Letter to Alexander Berkman." New York, January 18. In *Emma Goldman . . . Making Speech Free 1902–1909*, 129–31.

———. [1906a] 1991. "The Child and Its Enemies." *Mother Earth* 1, no. 2 (April): 7–14. In *Emma Goldman Papers*, reel 47.

———. [1906b] 1991. "The Tragedy of Women's Emancipation." *Mother Earth* 1, no. 1 (March): 9–18. In *Emma Goldman Papers*, reel 47.

———. [1907] 2005. "The International Anarchist Congress." In *Emma Goldman . . . Making Speech Free 1902–1909*, 234–45. Originally published in *Mother Earth* 2 (October): 307–19.

———. [1908a] 2005. "Letter to Ben Reitman." Rochester, June 29. In *Emma Goldman . . . Making Speech Free 1902–1909*, 334.

———. 1908b. *Patriotism: A Menace to Liberty*. New York: Mother Earth Publishing Association. In *Emma Goldman Papers*, reel 47.

———. [1909a] 2003. "Francisco Ferrer." In *Emma Goldman . . . Making Speech Free 1902–1909*, 461–63. Originally published in *Mother Earth* 4 (November): 275–77.

———. [1909b] 2005. "Letter to Ben Reitman." New York, June. In *Emma Goldman . . . Making Speech Free 1902–1909*, 440–42.

———. [1909c] 2005. "Letter to Ben Reitman." New York, December 13. In *Emma Goldman . . . Making Speech Free 1902–1909*, 464–65.

———. [1909d] 2005. "A New Declaration of Independence." In *Emma Goldman . . . Making Speech Free 1902–1909*, 450–51. Originally published in *Mother Earth* 4 (July): 137–38.

———. 1909e. *The White Slave Traffic*. New York: Mother Earth Publishing Association.

———. [1909f] 1991. "A Woman without a Country." *Mother Earth* 4, no. 3 (May): 81–82. In *Emma Goldman Papers*, reel 47.

———. 1910. *Anarchism and Other Essays*. New York: Mother Earth Publishing Association.

———. 1911. *Marriage and Love*. New York: Mother Earth Publishing Association. In *Emma Goldman Papers*, reel 47.

———. [1912a] 1991. "Suffrage Dealt Blow by Women of Titanic." *Denver Post*, April 21. In *Emma Goldman Papers*, reel 47.

———. [1912b] 1991. "Woman Center of Social Storm Which Is Sweeping Us Along." *Denver Post*, April 28. In *Emma Goldman Papers*, reel 47.

———. [1912?] 1991. "Cause and Possible Cure of Jealousy." In *Emma Goldman Papers*, reel 54.

———. [1913] 1991. *Victims of Morality and the Failure of Christianity*. New York: Mother Earth Publishing Association. In *Emma Goldman Papers*, reel 48.

———. [1914a] 1991. "Our War Letter Box." *Spur* (London), November. In *Emma Goldman Papers*, reel 48.

———. 1914b. *The Social Significance of the Modern Drama*. Boston, MA: The Gorham Press.

———. [1914c] 1991. "To Our Comrades and Friends." *Mother Earth* 9, no. 8 (October): 241–42. In *Emma Goldman Papers*, reel 48.

———. [1914d] 1991. "Woman Suffrage." *Woman Rebel* 1, no. 4 (June): 27. In *Emma Goldman Papers*, reel 48.

———. [1915] 1991. "Preparedness, the Road to Universal Slaughter." *Mother Earth* 10, no. 10 (December): 331–38. In *Emma Goldman Papers*, reel 48.

———. 1916a. "Letter to Van Valkenburgh." New York, March 18. In *Emma Goldman Papers*, reel 48.

———. [1916b] 1991. "My Arrest and Preliminary Hearing." *Mother Earth* 11, no. 1 (March): 426–30. In *Emma Goldman Papers*, reel 48.

———. [1916c] 1991. "The Social Aspects of Birth Control." *Mother Earth* 11, no. 2 (April): 468–75. In *Emma Goldman Papers*, reel 48.

———. 1917a. "Promoters of the War Mania." *Mother Earth* 12, no. 1 (March): 5–11.

———. [1917b] 1991. "Speech Before the No Conscription League." Hunts Point Palace, New York, June 14. In *Emma Goldman Papers*, reel 48.

———. [1917c] 1991. "We Don't Believe in Conscription." Speech given at Harlem River Casino, 127th Street, May 18, government transcript. In *Emma Goldman Papers*, reel 48.

———. 1917d. "The Woman Suffrage Chameleon." *Mother Earth* 12, no. 3 (May): 78–81.

———. [1920] 1991. "What I Believe." Abridged edition. *Spur* (London) 6, no. 9 (May): 52–53. In *Emma Goldman Papers*, reel 49.

———. [1923?] 1991. "Letter to Magnus Hirschfeld." Berlin, January. In *Emma Goldman Papers*, reel 13.

———. [1924] 1991. "Vladimir Ilyich Ulyanov Lenin." February, draft obituary. In *Emma Goldman Papers*, reel 49.

———. [1925a] 1991. "Letter to Edward Carpenter." Bristol, October 29. In *Emma Goldman Papers*, reel 15.

———. 1925b. *My Disillusionment in Russia*. London: C. W. Daniel Company.

———. [1925?] 1991. "Heroic Women of the Russian Revolution." Draft. In *Emma Goldman Papers*, reel 50.

———. [1926a] 1991. "Feminism's Fight Not Vain, Emma Goldman's Conclusion." *Rochester Times-Union*, November 16. In *Emma Goldman Papers*, reel 51.

———. [1926b] 1991. "My Attitude to Marriage." Draft. In *Emma Goldman Papers*, reel 51.

———. [1926c] 1991. "Young America Beckons Emma Goldman, Declares Idealist, in Article Written by Herself." *Stamford Advocate*, November. In *Emma Goldman Papers*, reel 51.

———. [1927] 1975. "Letter to Ben Capes." July 8. In *Nowhere at Home: Letters from Exile of Emma Goldman and Alexander Berkman*, edited by Richard Drinnon and Anna Maria Drinnon, 196. New York: Schocken Books.

———. [1927?] 1991. "Why I Am an Anarchist." Draft lecture. In *Emma Goldman Papers*, reel 51.

———. [between 1927 and 1930] 1991. "The Passing of the Family." Draft lecture. In *Emma Goldman Papers*, reel 51.

———. [1928?a] 1991. "Anarchism and What It Really Stands For." Draft. In *Emma Goldman Papers*, reel 51.

———. [1928?b] 1991. "Anarcho Syndicalism." Fragment of draft. In *Emma Goldman Papers*, reel 51.

———. 1929. "An Unexpected Dash through Spain." *The Road to Freedom* 5, no. 8 (April): 1–2.

———. [1929?] 1991. "Outline for Living My Life." Fragment. In *Emma Goldman Papers*, reel 54.

———. [1931a] 1975. "Letter to Alexander Berkman." December 25. In *Nowhere at Home . . .* , 168–69.

———. [1931b] 1970. *Living My Life: Volume One.* New York: Dover.

———. [1931c] 1970. *Living My Life: Volume Two.* New York: Dover.

———. [1932] 1991. "Letter to James Colton." March 1. In *Emma Goldman Papers*, reel 26.

———. 1933a. "An Anarchist Looks at Life." Speech at Foyles Twenty-Ninth Literary Luncheon, Grosvenor House, London, March 1.

———. [1933b] 1991. "Has My Life Been Worth While?" *[Daily] Express*, January 30. In *Emma Goldman Papers*, reel 52.

———. [1934?] 1991. "The Tragedy of the Modern Woman." Fragment. In *Emma Goldman Papers*, reel 54.

———. [1935] 2006. "Letter to Max Nettlau." February 8. In *Vision on Fire: Emma Goldman on the Spanish Revolution*, edited by David Porter, 254. Edinburgh: AK Press.

———. [1935?a] 1991. "August Strindberg." Fragment. In *Emma Goldman Papers*, reel 54.

———. [1935?b] 1991. "Sexuality, Motherhood, and Birth Control." Fragment. In *Emma Goldman Papers*, reel 54.

———. [1936] 1991. "Letter to James Colton." August 5. In *Emma Goldman Papers*, reel 38.

———. [1940] 1991. *The Place of the Individual in Society.* Chicago: Free Society Forum. Pamphlet. In *Emma Goldman Papers*, reel 53.

———. [n.d.] 1991a. "The Continental Feminist Movement." Draft of leaflet/pamphlet. In *Emma Goldman Papers*, reel 49.

———. [n.d.] 1991b. "Walt Whitman." In *Emma Goldman Papers*, reel 54.

Los Angeles Liberation Committee. [1939] 1991. *70th Birthday Commemorative Edition.* Pamphlet. In *Emma Goldman Papers*, reel 53.

Los Angeles Record. [1916] 1991. "Emma Goldman Enthusiastic Agitator of Birth Control." June 1. In *Emma Goldman Papers*, reel 48.

Los Angeles Times. 1925. "The Wild-Eyed Emma." March 16.

Montreal Daily Herald. [1935?] 1991. "Progress Catching Up with Red Emma." [March?] In *Emma Goldman Papers*, reel 53.

NEA *Service.* [1926] 1991. "Emma's Love Views." November 12. In *Emma Goldman Papers*, reel 51.

New Haven Register. [1934] 1991. "Small Crowd at Goldman Lecture Here." [February 18?]. In *Emma Goldman Papers*, reel 52.

New York Herald. [1916a] 1991. "Birth Control Speech Startles." March 2. In *Emma Goldman Papers*, reel 48.

———. [1916b] 1991. "Emma Goldman Is Held for Her Talk on 'Birth Control.'" February 29. In *Emma Goldman Papers*, reel 48.

New York Sun. 1901. "Talk with Emma Goldman." January 6.

New York World. [1892] 2003. "Anarchy's Den." July 28. In *Emma Goldman . . . Made for America, 1890–1901*, 111–15.

———. 1901. "Story of the Arrest of Anarchist Queen." September 11.

Philadelphia North American. 1901. "A Character Study of Emma Goldman." April 11.

Phrenological Journal and Science of Health. [1895] 2003. "Character in Unconventional People." In *Emma Goldman . . . Made for America, 1890–1901*, 214–16.

Providence Evening Bulletin. [1897] 2003. "Anarchy: Emma Goldman Held Forth on Olneyville Square Last Night." September 4. In *Emma Goldman . . . Made for America, 1890–1901*, 282–84.

Reynold's News. [1932] 1991. "An Evening with Red Emma." [London]. October 30. In *Emma Goldman Papers*, reel 52.

Rochester Times-Union. [1924] 1991. "Miss Goldman 'Home' after 15-Year Exile." February 1. In *Emma Goldman Papers*, reel 52.

———. [1926] 1991. "Emma Goldman, Marries, Has Not Changed Views." November 13. In *Emma Goldman Papers*, reel 51.

San Francisco Cell. [1898] 2003. "Emma Goldman, Anarchist." April 27. In *Emma Goldman . . . Made for America, 1890–1901*, 331–33.

Sanger, William. [1916] 1991. "Letter to Emma Goldman." March 14. In *Emma Goldman Papers*, reel 9.

Spain and the World. [1937] 1991. "Emma Goldman's Impressions: The Spanish Woman Not Sufficiently Emancipated." January 8. In *Emma Goldman Papers*, reel 53.

The Spectator. [1927] 1991. "Emma Goldman Pays Visit to Hamilton." May 10. In *Emma Goldman Papers*, reel 51.

Sperry, Almeda. [1912–13] 1991. "Letters to Emma Goldman." In *Emma Goldman Papers*, reels 6, 7, and 68.

Spokesman-Review. [1908] 2005. "Goldman Traces Anarchy to 1776." May 31. In *Emma Goldman . . . Making Speech Free 1902–1909*, 323–27.

St. Louis Post-Dispatch. [1897] 2003. "Anarchy: Emma Goldman Held Forth on Olneyville Square Last Night." October 24. In *Emma Goldman . . . Made for America, 1890–1901*, 289–92.

———. 1908. "Emma Goldman Says Anarchism Will Mean Absolute Equality and Freedom for Women with No Dual Moral Code." November 1.

Sunday Chronicle. [1935] 1991. "Most Dangerous Woman—A Nice Old Lady." November 24. In *Emma Goldman Papers*, reel 53.

Thompson, Charles Willis. [1909] 2005. "An Interview with Emma Goldman." In *Emma Goldman . . . Making Speech Free 1902–1909*, 431–37. Originally published in *New York Times Magazine*, May 20.

The Toronto Daily Star. [1935] 1991. "Scorns Religion for Crushing Sex." March 18. In *Emma Goldman Papers*, reel 53.

The Toronto Star. [1926] 1991. "Emma Goldman in Canada, Puts O.K. on Flapper." November 6. In *Emma Goldman Papers*, reel 51.

The Toronto Star Weekly. [1926] 1991. "Toronto's Anarchist Guest." December 31. In *Emma Goldman Papers*, reel 51.

The Toronto Telegram. [1926] 1991. "Prohibition a Failure." December 1. In *Emma Goldman Papers*, reel 51.

The World. [1920] 1991. "Women Don't Want Special Comforts." January 19. In *Emma Goldman Papers*, reel 49.

SECONDARY SOURCES

Ackelsberg, Martha. 2001. *Free Women of Spain: Anarchism and the Struggle for the Emancipation of Women*. Edinburgh: AK Press.

———. 2012. "Preface." In *Queering Anarchism: Addressing and Undressing Power and Desire*, edited by C. B. Daring, J. Rogue, Deric Shannon, and Abbey Volcano, 1–4. Edinburgh: AK Press.

Adrian, Lynne. 2007. "Emma Goldman and the Spirit of Artful Living: Philosophy and Politics in the Classical American Period." In *Feminist Interpretations of Emma Goldman*, edited by Penny A. Weiss and Loretta Kensinger, 217–26. University Park: Penn State University Press.

Agustín, Laura María. 2007. *Sex at the Margins: Migration, Labour Markets and the Rescue Industry*. London: Zed Books.

Ahmed, Sara. 2004. "Affective Economies." *Social Text* 22 (2): 117–39.

———. 2014. *Willful Subjects*. Durham, NC: Duke University Press.

Alaimo, Stacy. 2000. "Emma Goldman's *Mother Earth* and the Nature of the Left." In *Undomesticated Ground: Recasting Nature as Feminist Space*, 87–107. Ithaca, NY: Cornell University Press.

Alderson, David. 2016. *Sex, Needs and Queer Culture: From Liberation to the Postgay*. London: Zed Books.

Alexander, Jenny. 2011. "Alexander Berkman: Sexual Dissidence in the First Wave Anarchist Movement and Its Subsequent Narratives." In *Anarchism and Sexuality: Ethics, Relationships and Power*, edited by Jamie Heckert and Richard Cleminson, 25–44. London: Routledge.

Alexander, Sally, and Barbara Taylor, eds. 2012. *History and Psyche: Culture, Psychoanalysis and the Past*. London: Palgrave.

Altman, Dennis. 1996. "Rupture or Continuity? The Internationalization of Gay Identities." *Social Text* 48: 77–94.

Álvarez, Enrique. 2012. "Man Un/made: Male Homosocial and Homosexual Desire in Anarchist Culture of the Spanish Civil War." *Journal of Iberian and Latin-American Studies* 18 (1): 17–32.

Anderson, Benedict. 2005. *Under Three Flags: Anarchism and the Anti-colonial Imagination*. London: Verso.

Andrijasevic, Rutvica, Carrie Hamilton, and Clare Hemmings, eds. 2014. "Revolutions." *Feminist Review*, no. 106.

Anim-Addo, Joan. 2008. *Imoinda: Or She Who Will Lose Her Name—A Play for Twelve Voices in Three Acts*. London: Mango Press.

Anthias, Floya. 1980. "Women and the Reserve Army of Labour: A Critique of Veronica Beechey." *Capital and Class* 4 (1): 50–63.

Antliff, Allan. 2007. "Anarchy, Power, and Poststructuralism." *SubStance* 36 (2): 56–66.

Appadurai, Arjun. 1996. "Disjuncture and Difference in the Global Cultural Economy." In *Modernity at Large: Cultural Dimensions of Globalization*, 27–47. Minneapolis: University of Minnesota Press.

Arondekar, Anjali. 2009. *For the Record: On Sexuality and the Colonial Archive in India*. Durham, NC: Duke University Press.

Ascher, Carol, Louise DeSalvo, and Sara Ruddick. [1984] 1993. "Introduction." In *Between Women: Biographers, Novelists, Critics, Teachers and Artists Write about Their Work on Women*, edited by Carol Ascher, Louise DeSalvo, and Sara Ruddick, xix–xxv. New York: Routledge.

Bantman, Constance. 2013. *The French Anarchists in London, 1880–1914: Exile and Transnationalism in the First Globalisation*. Liverpool: Liverpool University Press.

Baraitser, Lisa. 2012. "Delay: On Temporality in Luisa Passerini's *Autobiography of a Generation: Italy, 1968*." *European Journal of Women's Studies* 19 (3): 380–85.

Bauman, Zygmunt. 2003. *Liquid Love*. Cambridge: Polity Press.

Beck-Gernsheim, Elizabeth. 1998. "On the Way to a Post-familial Family: From a Community of Needs to Elective Affinities." *Theory, Culture and Society* 15 (3–4): 53–70.

Beechey, Veronica. 1977. "Some Notes on Female Wage Labour in Capitalist Production. *Capital & Class* 1 (3): 45–66.

Benjamin, Walter. [1940] 1969. "Theses on the Philosophy of History." In *Illuminations*, edited and introduced by Hannah Arendt, trans. Harry Zohn, 253–65. New York: Schocken Books.

Bergland, Betty. 1994. "Postmodernism and the Autobiographical Subject: Reconstructing the 'Other.'" In *Autobiography and Postmodernism*, edited by Kathleen M. Ashley, Leigh Gilmore, and Gerlad Peters, 130–66. Boston: University of Massachusetts Press.

Berlant, Lauren. 2007. "Nearly Utopian, Nearly Normal: Post-Fordist Affect in La *Promesse* and *Rosetta*." *Public Culture* 19 (2): 273–301.

———. 2011. *Cruel Optimism*. Durham, NC: Duke University Press.

Bertalen, Hilton. 2011. "When Theories Meet: Emma Goldman and 'Post-anarchism.'" In *Post-anarchism: A Reader*, edited by Duane Rousselle and Süreyyya Evren, 208–30. London: Pluto Press.

Blackwood, Evelyn. 2008. "Transnational Discourses and Circuits of Queer Knowledge in Indonesia." *GLQ: A Journal of Lesbian and Gay Studies* 14 (4): 481–507.

Blake, Linnie. 1997. "A Jew, a Red, a Whore, a Bomber: Becoming Emma Goldman, Rhizomatic Intellectual." *Angelaki* 2 (3): 31–54.

Bland, Lucy, and Laura Doan, eds. 1998a. *Sexology in Culture: Labelling Bodies and Desires*. London: Wiley.

———. 1998b. *Sexology Uncensored: The Documents of Sexual Science*. Chicago: University of Chicago Press.

Bracke, Sarah. 2012. "From 'Saving Women' to 'Saving Gays': Rescue Narratives and Their Discontinuities." *European Journal of Women's Studies* 19 (2): 237–52.

Brah, Avtar. 1999. "Scent of Memory: Strangers, Our Own, and Others." *Feminist Review* 61: 4–26.

Brah, Avtar, and Ann Phoenix. 2004. "Ain't I a Woman? Revisiting Intersectionality." *Journal of International Women's Studies* 5 (3): 75–86.

Breslow, Jacob. 2017. "The Theory and Practice of Childhood: Interrogating Child-hood as a Technology of Power." PhD diss., Gender Institute, London School of Economics.

Brettschneider, Maria. 2013. "Emma Said It in 1910; Now We're Going to Say It Again: Firebrand Emma Goldman Continues to Spark Our Imaginations, Activism, and Political Theorizing." *New Political Science* 35 (4): 648–52.

Brown, Gavin. 2012. "Homonormativity: A Metropolitan Concept That Denigrates 'Ordinary' Gay Lives." *Journal of Homosexuality* 59 (7): 1065–72.

Browne, Victoria. 2014. "Explorations in Feminist Historiography: Rhetoric, Affect, and 'What Really Happened' in Feminism's Recent Past." *Subjectivity* 7 (2): 210–18.

Bruegel, Irene. 1979. "Women as a Reserve Army of Labour: A Note on Recent British Experience." *Feminist Review* 3: 12–23.

Bugliani, Ann. 2003. "Man Shall Not Live by Bread Alone: The Biblical Subtext in *Cyrano de Bergerac*." *Renascence* 56 (1): 55–62.

Burton, Antoinette. 1999. *Gender, Sexuality and Colonial Modernities*. New York: Routledge.

———. 2001. "Thinking beyond the Boundaries: Empire, Feminism and the Domain of History." *Social History* 26 (1): 60–71.

Butler, Judith. 1990. *Gender Trouble: Feminism and the Subversion of Identity*. New York: Routledge.

———. 1993. *Bodies That Matter: On the Discursive Limits of Sex*. New York: Routledge.

———. 1997. "Merely Cultural." *Social Text* 52/53: 265–77.

———. 2008. "Sexual Politics, Torture and Secular Time." *British Journal of Sociology* 59 (1): 1–23.

———. 2011. "Queer Anarchism and Anarchists against the Wall." Lecture presented at the conference "Anarchist Developments in Cultural Studies," New School, New York, May 5. Accessed September 1, 2015. http://www.egs.edu/faculty/judith -butler/videos/queer-anarchism/.

Byrne, Sian, and Lucien Van der Walt. 2015. "Worlds of Western Anarchism and Syndicalism: Class Struggle, Violence and Anti-imperialism." *Canadian Journal of History* 50 (1): 98–123.

Carroll, Berenice A. 2007. "Emma Goldman and the Theory of Revolution." In *Feminist Interpretations of Emma Goldman*, edited by Penny A. Weiss and Loretta Kensinger, 137–75. University Park: Penn State University Press.

Chalberg, John C. [1991] 2008. *Emma Goldman: American Individualist*. New York: Pearson Longman.

Citti, Pierre. [1897] 1990. "Préface." In Edmond Rostand, *Cyrano de Bergerac: Comédies Héroique en Cinq Actes et en Vers*, 5–29. Paris: Le Livre de Poche.

Clark, Danae. 1991. "Commodity Lesbianism." *Camera Obscura* 9 (1): 181–201.

Cleminson, Richard. 1998. "Anarchism and Feminism." *Women's History Review* 7 (1): 135–38.

———. 2012. "The Construction of Masculinity in the Spanish Labour Movement: A Study of the *Revista Blanca* (1923–36)." *International Journal of Iberian Studies* 24 (3): 201–17.

Coetzee, J. M. 1986. *Foe*. London: Secker and Warburg.

Cohn, Jesse. 2010. "Sex and the Anarchist Unconscious: A Brief History." *Sexualities* 13 (4): 413–31.

———. 2014. *Underground Passages: Anarchist Resistance Culture, 1848–2011*. Edinburgh: AK Press.

Connell, Raewyn. 1995. *Masculinities*. Cambridge: Polity Press.

Connell, Raewyn, and James Messerschmidt. 2005. "Hegemonic Masculinity: Rethinking the Concept." *Gender and Society* 19 (6): 829–59.

Conrad, Ryan. 2012. "Gay Marriage and Queer Love." In *Queering Anarchism: Addressing and Undressing Power and Desire*, edited by C. B. Daring, J. Rogue, Deric Shannon, and Abbey Volcano, 19–24. Edinburgh: AK Press.

Cook, Blanche Wiesen. 1979a. "Female Support Networks and Political Activism: Lillian Wald, Crystal Eastman, Emma Goldman." In *A Heritage of Her Own: Towards a New Social History of American Women*, edited by Nancy F. Cott and Elizabeth H. Pleck, 412–44. New York: Simon and Schuster.

———. 1979b. "The Historical Denial of Lesbianism." *Radical History Review* 20: 60–65.

———. [1984] 1993. "Biographer and Subject: A Critical Connection." In *Between Women: Biographers, Novelists, Critics, Teachers and Artists Write about Their Work on Women*, edited by Carol Ascher, Louise DeSalvo, and Sara Ruddick, 397–411. New York: Routledge.

Crenshaw, Kimberlé. 1991. "Mapping the Margins: Intersectionality, Identity Politics, and Violence against Women of Color." *Stanford Law Review* 43 (6): 1241–99.

———. 2011. "The Curious Resurrection of First Wave Feminism in the U.S. Elections: An Intersectional Critique of the Rhetoric of Solidarity and Betrayal." In *Sexuality, Gender and Power: Intersectional and Transnational Perspectives*, edited by Anna G. Jónasdóttir, Valerie Bryson, and Kathleeen B. Jones, 227–42. New York: Routledge.

Curtis, Debra. 2004. "Commodities and Sexual Subjectivities: A Look at Capitalism and Its Desires." *Cultural Anthropology* 19 (1): 95–121.

Cvetkovich, Ann. 2003. *An Archive of Feelings: Trauma, Sexuality and Lesbian Public Cultures*. Durham, NC: Duke University Press.

———. 2012. *Depression: A Public Feeling*. Durham, NC: Duke University Press.

Daring, C. B., J. Rogue, Deric Shannon, and Abbey Volcano, eds. 2012. *Queering Anarchism: Addressing and Undressing Power and Desire*. Edinburgh: AK Press.

Dark Star Collective, eds. [1984] 2012. *Quiet Rumours: An Anarcha-Feminist Reader*. 3rd ed. Edinburgh: AK Press.

Davis, Kathy. 2007. "Transnational Knowledges, Transnational Practices." In *The Making of "Our Bodies, Ourselves": How Feminism Travels across Borders*, 197–212. Durham, NC: Duke University Press.

Davis, Laurence. 2011. "Love and Revolution in Ursula Le Guin's *Four Ways to Forgiveness*." In *Anarchism and Sexuality: Ethics, Relationships and Power*, edited by Jamie Heckert and Richard Cleminson, 103–30. London: Routledge.

———. 2014. "Untitled Presentation on Love and Revolution." Presented at the

"Anarchism and Sexuality" Workshop, London School of Economics, London, December 4–5.

Day, Janet E. 2007. "The 'Individual' in Goldman's Anarchist Theory." In *Feminist Interpretations of Emma Goldman*, edited by Penny A. Weiss and Loretta Kensinger, 109–36. University Park: Penn State University Press.

Dean, Jonathan. 2009. "Who's Afraid of Third Wave Feminism? On the Uses of the 'Third Wave' in British Feminist Politics." *International Feminist Journal of Politics* 11 (3): 334–52.

———. 2010. *Rethinking Contemporary Feminist Politics*. London: Palgrave Macmillan.

———. 2012. "On the March or on the Margins? Affirmations and Erasures of Feminist Activism in the UK." *European Journal of Women's Studies* 19 (3): 315–29.

de Lauretis, Teresa. 1988. "Sexual Indifference and Lesbian Representation." *Theatre Journal* 40 (2): 155–77.

———. 1991. "Film and the Visible." In *How Do I Look? Queer Film and Video*, edited by Bad Object-Choices, 223–76. Seattle: Bay Press.

———. 1994. *The Practice of Love: Lesbian Sexuality and Perverse Desire*. Bloomington: Indiana University Press.

Delphy, Christine. 1980. "The Main Enemy." *Feminist Issues* 1 (1): 23–40.

———. 2016. "Feminism in Transnational Times: A Conversation with Christine Delphy." Gender Institute Public Lecture Series, London School of Economics, February 10.

D'Emilio, John. 1983. "Capitalism and Gay Identity." In *Powers of Desire: The Politics of Sexuality*, edited by Ann Bar Snitow, Christine Stansell, and Sharon Thompson, 100–113. New York: Monthly Review Press.

D'Emilio, John, and Estelle B. Freedman. 1988. "Introduction." In *Intimate Matters: A History of Sexuality in America*, xi–xx. New York: Harper and Row.

Department of Economic and Social Affairs. 2010. *The World's Women 2010: Trends and Statistics*. New York: United Nations.

Di Paola, Petro. 2013. *The Knights Errant of Anarchy: London and the Italian Anarchist Diaspora (1880–1917)*. Liverpool: Liverpool University Press.

Doan, Laura. 2013. *Disturbing Practices: History, Sexuality and Women's Experience of Modern War*. Chicago: University of Chicago Press.

Drinnon, Richard, and Anna Maria Drinnon, eds. 1975. *Nowhere at Home: Letters from Exile of Emma Goldman and Alexander Berkman*. New York: Schocken Books.

Dubois, Ellen Carol, and Linda Gordon. 1983. "Seeking Ecstasy on the Battlefield: Danger and Pleasure in Nineteenth-Century Feminist Thought." *Feminist Studies* 9 (1): 7–26.

Dudink, Stefan. 2011. "Homosexuality, Race, and the Rhetoric of Nationalism." *History of the Present* 1 (2): 259–64.

Duggan, Lisa. 2003. *The Twilight of Equality: Neoliberalism, Cultural Politics, and the Attack on Democracy*. Boston: Beacon Press.

———. 2006. "Contextualizing the Sex Wars." In *Sex Wars: Sexual Dissent and Political Culture*, edited by Lisa Duggan and Nan D. Hunter, 15–28. New York: Taylor and Francis.

Dunye, Cheryl, dir. 1996. *The Watermelon Woman*. New York: First Run Features.

Edelman, Lee. 2004. *No Future: Queer Theory and the Death Drive*. Durham, NC: Duke University Press.

Elam, J. Daniel. 2013. "The 'Arch Priestess of Anarchy' Visits Lahore: Violence, Love, and the Worldliness of Revolutionary Texts." *Postcolonial Studies* 16 (2): 140–54.

Eloit, Ilana. 2017. "Feminism in Transnational Times: A Conversation with Christine Delphy." Edited transcript of Christine Delphy and Sylvie Tissot's Public Talk at the London School of Economics, February 10, 2016. *Feminist Review* 117 (forthcoming).

Eng, David. 2010. "The Queer Space of China: Expressive Desire in Stanley Kwan's *Lan Yu*." *Positions* 18 (2): 459–87.

Engels, Friedrich. [1884] 1942. *The Origin of the Family: Private Property and the State*. London: Lawrence and Wishart.

Escobar, Arturo. 2004. "Beyond the Third World: Imperial Globality, Global Coloniality and Anti-globalisation Social Movements." *Third World Quarterly* 25 (1): 207–30.

Evren, Süreyyya. 2012. "There Ain't No Black in the Anarchism Flag! Race, Ethnicity and Anarchism." In *The Continuum Companion to Anarchism*, edited by Ruth Kinna, 311–27. New York: Continuum.

Faderman, Lillian. 1991. *Odd Girls and Twilight Lovers: A History of Lesbian Life in Twentieth-Century America*. New York: Columbia University Press.

———. 2000. *To Believe in Women: What Lesbians Have Done for America—A History*. Boston: Mariner Books.

Falk, Candace. 2002. "Emma Goldman: Passion, Politics, and the Theatrics of Free Expression." *Women's History Review* 11 (1): 11–26.

———. 2003. "Forging Her Place: An Introduction." In *Emma Goldman: A Documentary History of the American Years*. Vol. 1, *Made for America, 1890–1901*, edited by Candace Falk, Barry Pateman, and Jessica M. Moran, 1–84. Berkeley: University of California Press.

———. 2005. "Raising Her Voices: An Introduction." In *Emma Goldman: A Documentary History of the American Years*. Vol. 2, *Making Speech Free 1902–1909*, edited by Candace Falk, Barry Pateman, and Jessica M. Moran, 1–80. Berkeley: University of California Press.

———. 2007. "Let Icons Be Bygones! Emma Goldman: The Grand Expositor." In *Feminist Interpretations of Emma Goldman*, edited by Penny A. Weiss and Loretta Kensinger, 41–69. University Park: Penn State University Press.

———, ed. 2012a. *Emma Goldman: A Documentary History of the American Years*. Vol. 3, *Light and Shadows, 1910–1916*. Stanford, CA: Stanford University Press.

———. 2012b. "Into the Spotlight: An Introductory Essay." In *Emma Goldman: A Documentary History of the American Years*. Vol. 3, *Light and Shadows, 1910–1916*, edited by Candace Falk and Barry Pateman, 1–171. Stanford, CA: Stanford University Press.

Falk, Candace, Barry Pateman, and Jessica M. Moran, eds. 2003. *Emma Goldman: A Documentary History of the American Years*. Vol. 1, *Made for America, 1890–1901*. Berkeley: University of California Press.

———. 2005. *Emma Goldman: A Documentary History of the American Years*. Vol. 2, *Making Speech Free 1902–1909*. Berkeley: University of California Press.

Fanon, Frantz. 1991. "The Fact of Blackness." In *Black Skin, White Masks,* 77–99. London: Pluto Press.

Fassin, Eric. 2010. "National Identities and Transnational Intimacies: Sexual Democracy and the Politics of Immigration in Europe." *Public Culture* 22 (3): 507–29.

———. 2011. "From Criticism to Critique." *History of the Present* 1 (2): 265–74.

Felman, Shoshana. 1977. "To Open the Question." In "Literature and Psychoanalysis: The Question of Reading: Otherwise." *Yale French Studies,* nos. 55/56: 5–10.

Felski, Rita. 2002. "Telling Time in Feminist Theory." *Tulsa Studies in Women's Literature* 21 (1): 21–28.

Ferguson, Kathy. 2007. "Religion, Faith, and Politics: Reading Goldman through Nietzsche." In *Feminist Interpretations of Emma Goldman,* edited by Penny A. Weiss and Loretta Kensinger, 91–107. University Park: Penn State University Press.

———. 2008. "Discourses of Danger: Locating Emma Goldman." *Political Theory* 36 (5): 735–61.

———. 2011a. "Becoming Anarchism, Feminism, Indigeneity." *Affinities: Theory, Culture Action* 5 (2): 96–109.

———. 2011b. *Emma Goldman: Political Thinking in the Streets.* Lanham, MD: Rowman and Littlefield.

———. 2011c. "Gender and Genre in Emma Goldman." *Signs* 36 (3): 733–57.

Firestone, Shulamith. 1970. *The Dialectic of Sex: The Case for Feminist Revolution.* New York: William Morrow.

Flax, Jane. 2004. "What Is the Subject? Review Essay on Psychoanalysis and Feminism in Postcolonial Time." *Signs* 29 (3): 905–23.

Floyd, Dell. 1913. *Women as World Builders: Studies in Modern Feminism.* Chicago: Forbes.

Fogg, Ally. 2010. "Emma Goldman: A Thoroughly Modern Anarchist." *Guardian,* October 6.

Foucault, Michel. 1972. *The Archaeology of Knowledge and the Discourse on Language.* New York: Pantheon.

———. 1980. *Language, Counter-memory, Practice: Selected Essays and Interviews.* Ithaca, NY: Cornell University Press.

Frankel, Oz. 1996. "Whatever Happened to 'Red Emma'? Emma Goldman, from Alien Rebel to American Icon." *Journal of American History* 83 (3): 903–42.

Fraser, Nancy. 1996. *Justice Interruptus: Critical Reflections on the "Postsocialist" Condition.* New York: Routledge.

———. 1997. "Heterosexism, Misrecognition, and Capitalism: A Response to Judith Butler." *Social Text* 52/53: 279–89.

———. 2013. "How Feminism Became Capitalism's Handmaiden—and How to Reclaim It." *Guardian,* October 14.

Freccero, Carla. 2012. "Ideological Fantasies." *GLQ: A Journal of Lesbian and Gay Studies* 18 (1): 47–69.

Freedman, Estelle B. 1998. "'The Burning of Letters Continues': Elusive Identities and the Historical Construction of Sexuality." *Journal of Women's History* 9 (4): 181–200.

Freeman, Elizabeth. 2010. *Time Binds: Queer Temporalities, Queer Histories.* Durham, NC: Duke University Press.

Freud, Sigmund. [1931] 1991. "Female Sexuality." In *On Sexuality: Three Essays on the Theory of Sexuality and Other Works*, 367–92. Harmondsworth: Penguin.

———. 1933. "Femininity." In *New Introductory Lectures on Psychoanalysis*, 145–69. London: Hogarth Press.

Frost, Ginger. 2009. "'Love Is Always Free': Anarchism, Free Unions, and Utopianism in Edwardian England." *Anarchist Studies* 17 (1): 73–94.

Fuss, Diana, ed. 1991. *Inside/Out: Lesbian Theories, Gay Theories*. London: Routledge.

Garber, Majorie. 1995. *Vice Versa: Bisexuality and the Eroticism of Everyday Life*. New York: Simon and Schuster.

Gedalof, Irene, and Nirmal Puwar, eds. 2012. "Recalling 'The Scent of Memory.'" *Feminist Review*, no. 100.

Gemie, Sharif. 1996. "Anarchism and Feminism: A Historical Survey." *Women's History Review* 5 (3): 417–44.

———. 2001. "Mirbeau and the Politics of Misogyny." *European Studies* 31 (121): 71–98.

Giddens, Anthony. 1992. *The Transformation of Intimacy: Sexuality, Love and Eroticism in Modern Societies*. Cambridge: Polity Press.

Gilman, Sander. 1992. "Black Bodies, White Bodies: Toward an Iconography of Female Sexuality in Late Nineteenth Century Art, Medicine and Literature." In *Race, Culture and Difference*, edited by James Donald and Ali Rattansi, 223–57. London: Sage.

Gilmore, Leigh. 1994. *Autobiographics: A Feminist Theory of Women's Self-Representation*. Ithaca, NY: Cornell University Press.

Gilroy, Paul. 1998. "Race Ends Here." *Ethnic and Racial Studies* 21 (5): 838–47.

———. 2000. *Against Race: Imagining Political Culture beyond the Color Line*. Cambridge, MA: Harvard University Press.

———. 2004. *After Empire: Melancholia or Convivial Culture*. London: Routledge.

———. 2005. "A New Cosmopolitanism." *Interventions* 7 (3): 287–92.

Gordon, Avery. 2008. *Ghostly Matters: Haunting and the Sociological Imagination*. Minneapolis: University of Minnesota Press.

———. 2011. "Some Thoughts on Haunting and Futurity." *Borderlands* 10 (2): 1–21.

Gordon, Linda. 1979. "Birth Control and Social Revolution." In *A Heritage of Her Own: Towards a New Social History of American Women*, edited by Nancy F. Cott and Elizabeth H. Pleck, 445–75. New York: Simon and Schuster.

Gornick, Vivian. 2011a. *Emma Goldman: Revolution as a Way of Life*. New Haven, CT: Yale University Press.

———. 2011b. "Goldman Occupies Wall Street." *Nation*, December 26.

Greenland, Cyril. 2002. "Dangerous Women, Dangerous Ideas." *Canadian Journal of Human Sexuality* 11 (3–4): 179–85.

Greenway, Judy. 2009a. "Sex Bombs: Anticipating a Free Society." *Anarchist Studies* 17 (1): 106–13.

———. 2009b. "Speaking Desire: Anarchism and Free Love as Utopian Performance in Fin de Siècle Britain." In *Anarchism and Utopianism*, edited by Laurence Davis and Ruth Kinna, 153–70. Manchester: Manchester University Press.

———. 2011. "Preface: Sexual Anarchy, Anarchophobia and Dangerous Desires." In

Anarchism and Sexuality: Ethics, Relationships and Power, edited by Jamie Heckert and Richard Cleminson, xiv–xviii. London: Routledge.

Gregg, Melissa, and Gregory Selgworth. 2010. *The Affect Theory Reader*. Durham, NC: Duke University Press.

Grosz, Elizabeth. 1995. *Space, Time and Perversion: Essays on the Politics of Bodies*. New York: Routledge.

———. 2004. *The Nick of Time: Politics, Evolution and the Untimely*. Durham, NC: Duke University Press.

Gurstein, Rochelle. 2002. "Emma Goldman and the Tragedy of Modern Love." *Salmagundi*, nos. 135/136: 67–89.

Haaland, Bonnie. 1993. *Emma Goldman: Sexuality and the Impurity of the State*. Montreal: Black Rose Books.

Haraway, Donna J. 1991. "'Gender' for a Marxist Dictionary: The Sexual Politics of a Word." In *Simians, Cyborgs and Women*, 127–48. London: Free Association Press.

Hardt, Michael. 1999. "Affective Labor." *Boundary 2* 26 (2): 89–100.

Haritaworn, Jin. 2010. *Queer Lovers and Hateful Others: Regenerating Violent Times and Places*. Chicago: Pluto Press.

———. 2012. "Women's Rights, Gay Rights and Anti-Muslim Racism in Europe: Introduction." *European Journal of Women's Studies* 19 (1): 73–78.

Hartman, Saidiya. 2002. "The Time of Slavery." *South Atlantic Quarterly* 101 (4): 757–77.

———. 2008. "Venus in Two Acts." *Small Axe 26* 2 (2): 1–14.

Hausmann, Ricardo, Laura D. Tyson, and Saadia Zahidi. 2007. *The Global Gender Gap Report 2007*. Geneva, Switzerland: World Economic Forum.

Haworth, Robert H., ed. 2012. *Anarchist Pedagogies: Collective Actions, Theories, and Critical Reflections on Education*. Oakland, CA: PM Press.

Heckert, Jamie, ed. 2010. "Relating Differently." *Sexualities* 13 (4).

———. 2011. "On Anarchism: An Interview with Judith Butler." In *Anarchism and Sexuality: Ethics, Relationships and Power*, edited by Jamie Heckert and Richard Cleminson, 93–99. London: Routledge.

———. 2012. "Anarchy without Opposition." In *Queering Anarchism: Addressing and Undressing Power and Desire*, edited by C. B. Daring, J. Rogue, Deric Shannon, and Abbey Volcano, 63–75. Edinburgh: AK Press.

Heckert, Jamie, and Richard Cleminson, eds. 2011a. *Anarchism and Sexuality: Ethics, Relationships and Power*. London: Routledge.

———. 2011b. "Ethics, Relationships and Power: An Introduction." In *Anarchism and Sexuality: Ethics, Relationships and Power*, edited by Jamie Heckert and Richard Cleminson, 1–22. London: Routledge.

Hemmings, Clare. 2005. "Invoking Affect: Cultural Theory and the Ontological Turn." *Cultural Studies* 19 (5): 548–67.

———. 2011. *Why Stories Matter: The Political Grammar of Feminist Theory*. Durham, NC: Duke University Press.

———. 2012a. "Affective Solidarity: Feminist Reflexivity and Political Transformation." *Feminist Theory* 13 (2): 147–61.

————. 2012b. "In the Mood for Revolution: Emma Goldman's Passion." *New Literary History* 43 (3): 527–45.

————. 2012c. "Sexuality, Subjectivity . . . and Political Economy?" *Subjectivity* 5 (2): 121–39.

————. 2013. "Considering Emma." *European Journal of Women's Studies* 20 (4): 334–46.

————. 2014a. "The Materials of Reparation." *Feminist Theory* 15 (1): 27–30.

————. 2014b. "Sexual Freedom and the Promise of Revolution: Emma Goldman's Passion." *Feminist Review*, no. 106: 43–59.

————. 2016. "Is 'Gender Studies' Singular? Stories of Queer/Feminist Difference and Displacement." *differences* 27 (2): 79–102.

Hennessy, Rosemary. 2000. *Profit and Pleasure: Sexual Identities in Late Capitalism.* New York: Routledge.

————. 2014. "Thinking Sex Materially: Marxist, Socialist and Related Feminist Approaches." In *The Handbook of Feminist Theory*, edited by Mary Evans, Clare Hemmings, Marsha Henry, Hazel Johnstone, Sumi Madhok, Ania Plomien, and Sadie Wearing, 308–26. London: Sage.

Herzog, Don. 2007. "Romantic Anarchism and Pedestrian Liberalism." *Political Theory* 35 (3): 313–33.

Hexe. 2012. "Anarchy, BDSM and Consent-Based Culture." In *Queering Anarchism: Addressing and Undressing Power and Desire*, edited by C. B. Daring, J. Rogue, Deric Shannon, and Abbey Volcano, 231–36. Edinburgh: AK Press.

Himmelweit, Susan, and Ania Plomien. 2014. "Feminist Perspectives on Care: Theory, Practice and Policy." In *The Sage Handbook of Feminist Theory*, edited by Mary Evans, Clare Hemmings, Marsha Henry, Hazel Johnstone, Sumi Madhok, Ania Plomien, and Sadie Wearing, 446–64. London: Sage.

Hirsch, Marianne, and Leo Spitzer. 2013. "First Person Plural: Notes on Voice and Collaboration." In *Writing Otherwise: Experiments in Cultural Criticism*, edited by Jackie Stacey and Janet Woolf, 190–202. Manchester: Manchester University Press.

Hochschild, Arlie. 1989. *The Managed Heart: Commercialization of Human Feeling.* Berkeley: University of California Press.

Hong, Nathaniel. 1992. "Constructing the Anarchist Beast in American Periodical Literature, 1880–1903." *Critical Studies in Mass Communication* 9 (1): 110–30.

Hustak, Carla. 2012. "Saving Civilization from the '"Green-Eyed" Monster': Emma Goldman and the Sex Reform Campaign against Jealousy, 1900–1930." *Journal of Transnational American Studies* 4 (1): 1–29.

Hutchison, Elizabeth Quay. 2001. "From 'La Mujer Esclava' to 'La Mujer Limón': Anarchism and the Politics of Sexuality in Early-Twentieth-Century Chile." *Hispanic American Historical Review* 81 (3–4): 519–53.

Ince, Anthony. 2012. "In the Shell of the Old: Anarchist Geographies of Territorialisation." *Antipode* 44 (5): 1645–66.

Irigaray, Luce. 1973. "Psychoanalytic Theory: Another Look." In *This Sex Which Is Not One*, 34–67. Ithaca, NY: Cornell University Press.

Jackson, Peter. 2009. "Capitalism and Global Queering." *GLQ: A Journal of Lesbian and Gay Studies* 15 (3): 357–95.

Jacobus, Mary. 1995. "Freud's Mnemonic: Screen Memories and Feminist Nostalgia." In *First Things: The Maternal Imaginary in Literature, Art, and Psychoanalysis*, 1–22. New York: Routledge.

Jolly, Margaretta. 2008. *In Love and Struggle: Letters in Contemporary Feminism*. New York: Columbia University Press.

Katz, Jonathan Ned. [1976] 1992. "1912: Almeda Sperry to Emma Goldman—'I am a savage, Emma, a wild, wild savage.'" In *Gay American History: Lesbians and Gay Men in the USA—A Documentary History*, edited by Jonathan Ned Katz, 523–30. New York: Penguin.

Kennedy, Kathleen. 1999. "Liberty with Strings: The Case of Emma Goldman." In *Disloyal Mothers and Scurrilous Citizens: Women and Subversion during World War I*, 39–53. Bloomington: Indiana University Press.

Kensinger, Loretta. 2007. "Speaking with Red Emma: The Feminist Theory of Emma Goldman." In *Feminist Interpretations of Emma Goldman*, edited by Penny A. Weiss and Loretta Kensinger, 255–82. University Park: Penn State University Press.

Khanna, Ranjana. 2003. *Dark Continents: Psychoanalysis and Colonialism*. Durham, NC: Duke University Press.

———. 2012. "Touching, Unbelonging, and the Absence of Affect." *Feminist Theory* 13 (2): 213–32.

Kilkey, Majella, Diane Perrons, and Ania Plomien. 2013. *Gender, Migration and Domestic Work: Masculinities, Male Labour and Fathering in the UK and USA*. Basingstoke: Palgrave Macmillan.

Kinna, Ruth. 2014. "An Anarchist Guide to . . . Feminism: The Emma Goldman Angle." *Strike! Magazine* (Spring): 22–23.

Kissack, Terence. 2008. *Free Comrades: Anarchism and Homosexuality in the United States 1895–1917*. Oakland, CA: AK Press.

Kowal, Donna M. 2016. *Tongue of Fire: Emma Goldman, Public Womanhood, and the Sex Question*. Albany: State University of New York Press.

Kristeva, Julia. 1981. "Women's Time." Translated by Alice Jardine and Harry Blake. *Signs* 7 (1): 13–35.

Kurtz, Arabella, and J. M. Coetzee. 2015. *The Good Story: Exchanges on Truth, Fiction and Psychotherapy*. London: Harvill Secker.

Lacan, Jacques. 1991. *The Four Fundamental Concepts of Psycho-analysis*. Harmondsworth: Penguin.

Levine, Cathy. 2012. "The Tyranny of Tyranny." In *Quiet Rumours: An Anarcha-Feminist Anthology*, edited by Dark Star Collective, 77–80. Edinburgh: AK Press.

Liesegang, Jerimarie. 2012. "Tyranny of the State and Trans Liberation." In *Queering Anarchism: Addressing and Undressing Power and Desire*, edited by C. B. Daring, J. Rogue, Deric Shannon, and Abbey Volcano, 87–99. Edinburgh: AK Press.

Loizidou, Elena. 2011. "This Is What Democracy Looks Like." In *How Not to Be Governed: Readings and Interpretations from a Critical Anarchist Left*, edited by James Martel and Jimmy Casas Klausen, 167–87. New York: Lexington Books.

———, ed. 2013. *Disobedience: Concept and Practice*. New York: Routledge.

Lorde, Audre. [1973] 1993. "The Uses of the Erotic: The Erotic as Power." In *The Les-*

bian and Gay Studies Reader, edited by Henry Abelove, Michèle Aina Barale, and David M. Halperin, 339–43. New York: Routledge.

Love, Heather. 2007. *Feeling Backward: Loss and the Politics of Queer History.* Cambridge, MA: Harvard University Press.

Lowry, Elizabeth. 2015. "Spiritual (R)evolution and the Turning of Tables: Abolition, Feminism and the Rhetoric of Social Reform in the Antebellum Public Sphere." *Journal for the Study of Radicalism* 9 (2): 1–16.

Lumby, Catharine. 2011. "Past the Post in Feminist Media Studies." *Feminist Media Studies* 11 (1): 95–100.

Lumsden, Linda L. 2007. "Anarchy Meets Feminism: A Gender Analysis of Emma Goldman's *Mother Earth* 1906–1917." *American Journalism* 24 (3): 31–54.

———. 2010. "Striking Images: Visual Rhetoric and Social Identity in the Radical Press, 1903–1917." *Visual Communication Quarterly* 17 (4): 225–40.

Maiguashca, Bice. 2014. "'They're Talkin' bout a Revolution': Feminism, Anarchism and the Politics of Social Change in the Global Justice Movement." *Feminist Review,* no. 106: 78–94.

Marcus, Jane. [1984] 1993. "Invisible Mending." In *Between Women: Biographers, Novelists, Critics, Teachers and Artists Write about Their Work on Women,* edited by Carol Ascher, Louise DeSalvo, and Sara Ruddick, 381–95. New York: Routledge.

Marcuse, Herbert. [1955] 1987. *Eros and Civilization.* London: Routledge.

Marso, Lori Jo. 2003. "A Feminist Search for Love: Emma Goldman on the Politics of Marriage, Love, Sexuality and the Feminine." *Feminist Theory* 4 (3): 305–20.

———. 2008. "The Perversions of Bored Liberals: Response to Herzog." *Political Theory* 36 (1): 123–28.

Massad, Joseph. 2007. *Desiring Arabs.* Chicago: University of Chicago Press.

Massumi, Brian. 2002. *Parables for the Virtual: Movement, Affect, Sensation.* Durham, NC: Duke University Press.

May, Todd. 1994. *The Political Philosophy of Poststructuralist Anarchism.* University Park: Pennsylvania State University Press.

McClintock, Anne. 1995. *Imperial Leather: Race, Gender and Sexuality in the Colonial Context.* New York: Routledge.

McEwan, Cheryl. 2003. "Building a Post-colonial Archive? Gender, Collective Memory and Citizenship in Post-apartheid South Africa." *Journal of Southern African Studies* 29 (3): 739–57.

McKenzie, Jonathan, and Craig Stalbaum. 2007. "Manufacturing Consensus: Goldman, Kropotkin, and the Order of an Anarchist Canon." In *Feminist Interpretations of Emma Goldman,* edited by Penny A. Weiss and Loretta Kensinger, 197–216. University Park: Penn State University Press.

McRobbie, Angela. 2004. "Postfeminism and Popular Culture." *Feminist Media Studies* 4 (3): 255–64.

———. 2009. *The Aftermath of Feminism: Gender, Culture and Social Change.* London: Sage.

Merck, Mandy, and Stella Sandford, eds. 2010. *Further Adventures of the Dialectic of Sex: Critical Essays on Shulamith Firestone.* London: Palgrave Macmillan.

Messer-Kruse, Timothy. 2012. *The Haymarket Conspiracy: Transatlantic Networks*. Chicago: University of Illinois Press.

Mieli, Mario. 1980. *Homosexuality and Liberation*. London: Gay Men's Press.

Mitchell, Juliet. 1974. *Psychoanalysis and Feminism*. New York: Pantheon.

Mohanty, Chandra Talpade. 1988. "Under Western Eyes: Feminist Scholarship and Colonial Discourses." *Feminist Review*, no. 30: 61–88.

Molyneux, Maxine. 1986. "No God, No Boss, No Husband: Anarchist Feminism in Nineteenth-Century Argentina." *Latin American Perspectives* 13 (1): 119–45.

Morgan, Kevin. 2009. "Herald of the Future: Emma Goldman, Friedrich Nietzsche and the Anarchist as Superman." *Anarchist Studies* 17 (2): 55–80.

Mulvey, Laura. 1989. *Visual and Other Pleasures*. Basingstoke: Macmillan.

Narayan, Uma. 1998. "Essence of Culture and a Sense of History: A Feminist Critique of Cultural Essentialism." *Hypatia* 13 (2): 86–106.

Newman, Saul. 2007. "Anarchism, Poststructuralism and the Future of Radical Politics." *SubStance* 36 (2): 3–19.

Nicholson, C. Brid. 2010. *Emma Goldman: Still Dangerous*. Montreal: Black Rose Books.

Ostman, Heather. 2009. "'The Most Dangerous Woman in America': Emma Goldman and the Rhetoric of Motherhood in *Living My Life*." *Prose Studies: History, Theory, Criticism* 31 (1): 55–73.

Parker, Andrew. 1993. "Unthinking Sex: Marx, Engels and the Scene of Writing." In *Fear of a Queer Planet: Queer Politics and Social Theory*, edited by Michael Warner, 19–41. Minneapolis: University of Minnesota Press.

Passerini, Luisa. 1992. "A Memory for Women's History: Problems of Method and Interpretation." *Social Science History* 16 (4): 669–92.

———. 1996. *Autobiography of a Generation: Italy, 1968*. Hanover, NH: Wesleyan University Press.

Perrons, Diane. 2012. "'Global' Financial Crisis, Earnings Inequalities and Gender: Towards a More Sustainable Model of Development." *Comparative Sociology* 11 (2): 202–26.

Peto, Andrea. 2012. "Collective Life Story as a Lonely but Necessary Experiment." *European Journal of Women's Studies* 19 (3): 376–79.

Phillips, Adam. 1996. "Freud and the Uses of Forgetting." In *On Flirtation: Psychoanalytic Essays on the Uncommitted Life*, 22–38. Cambridge, MA: Harvard University Press.

———. 2005. "The Forgetting Museum." *Index on Censorship* 34 (2): 34–37.

———. 2012. "Keeping Our Distance." In *History and Psyche: Culture, Psychoanalysis and the Past*, edited by Sally Alexander and Barbara Taylor, 211–17. London: Palgrave.

Poirier, Suzanne. 1988. "Emma Goldman, Ben Reitman, and Reitman's Wives: A Study in Relationships." *Women's Studies* 14 (3): 277–97.

Porter, David, ed. [1983] 2006. *Vision on Fire: Emma Goldman on the Spanish Revolution*. Edinburgh: AK Press.

———. 2004–5. Review of Emma Goldman, *A Documentary History of the American Years*, vol. 1, *Made for America, 1890–1901*. *Social Anarchism* 37. Accessed September 1, 2015. http://www.socialanarchism.org/mod/magazine/display/131/index.php.

Pravadelli, Veronica. 2012. "Responses to Luisa Passerini's *Autobiography of a Generation: Italy, 1968.*" *European Journal of Women's Studies* 19 (3): 371–76.

Presley, Sharon. 2000. "No Authority but Oneself: The Anarchist Feminist Philosophy of Autonomy and Freedom." *Social Anarchism* 27. Accessed May 4, 2009. http://library.nothingness.org/articles/SA/en/display/338.

———. 2004–5. Review of Emma Goldman, *A Documentary History of the American Years*, vol. 2, *Making Speech Free, 1902–1909*. *Social Anarchism* 37. Accessed September 1, 2015. http://www.socialanarchism.org/mod/magazine/display/132/index.php.

Price, Ruth. 2005. *The Lives of Agnes Smedley.* Oxford: Oxford University Press.

Prichard, Alex. 2010. "Proudhon's Anti-feminism." Paper presented at the sixtieth annual conference of the Political Studies Association, Edinburgh, April 1.

———. 2013. *Justice, Order and Anarchy: The International Political Theory of Joseph-Pierre Proudhon.* London: Routledge.

Proulx, Annie. 2016. *Barkskins: A Novel.* New York: Simon and Schuster.

Prügl, Elisabeth. 2012. "'If Lehman Brothers Had Been Lehman Sisters . . .': Gender and Myth in the Aftermath of the Financial Crisis." *International Political Sociology* 6 (1): 21–35.

Puar, Jasbir K. 2006. "Mapping U.S. Homonormativities." *Gender, Place and Culture* 13 (1): 67–88.

———. 2007. *Terrorist Assemblages: Homonationalism in Queer Times.* Durham, NC: Duke University Press.

Radstone, Susannah, and Bill Schwarz. 2010. "Introduction: Mapping Memory." In *Memory: Histories, Theories, Debates*, edited by Susannah Radstone and Bill Schwarz, 1–9. New York: Fordham University Press.

Ramnath, Maia. 2011. *Decolonizing Anarchism: An Anti-authoritarian History of India's Liberation Struggle.* Edinburgh: AK Press.

Rappeneau, Jean-Paul. 1990. *Cyrano de Bergerac.* France/Hungary: Union Générale Cinématographique.

Redding, Arthur. 1995. "The Dream Life of Political Violence: Georges Sorel, Emma Goldman, and the Modern Imagination." *Modernism/Modernity* 2 (2): 1–16.

Reizenbaum, Marilyn. 2005. "Yiddish Modernisms: Red Emma Goldman." *Modern Fiction Studies* 51 (2): 456–81.

Rhys, Jean. 1966. *Wide Sargasso Sea.* London: André Deutsch.

Riviere, Joan. 1986. "Womanliness as Masquerade." In *Formations of Fantasy*, edited by Victor Burgin, James Donald, and Cora Kaplan, 35–44. London: Methuen.

Robbins, Timothy. 2015. "Emma Goldman Reading Walt Whitman: Aesthetics, Agitation, and the Anarchist Ideal." *Texas Studies in Literature and Language* 57 (1): 80–105.

Rofel, Lisa. 2007. *Desiring China: Experiments in Neoliberalism, Sexuality, and Public Culture.* Durham, NC: Duke University Press.

———. 2010. "The Traffic in Money Boys." *Positions* 18 (2): 425–58.

———. 2012. Queer *Positions*, Queerying Asian Studies." *positions* 20 (1): 183–93.

Rogness, Kate, and Christina Foust. 2011. "Beyond Rights and Virtues as Foundation for Women's Agency: Emma Goldman's Rhetoric of Free Love." *Western Journal of Communication* 75 (2): 148–67.

Roof, Judith. 1996. *Come as You Are: Sexuality and Narrative.* New York: Columbia University Press.

Rose, Jacqueline. 1983. "Femininity and Its Discontents." *Feminist Review*, no. 14: 5–21.

———. 1996. *States of Fantasy.* Oxford: Clarendon Press.

———. 1998. "Negativity in the Work of Melanie Klein." In *Reading Melanie Klein*, edited by L. Stonebridge and J. Phillips, 126–59. New York: Routledge.

———. 2014. *Women in Dark Times.* London: Bloomsbury Press.

Rosenberg, Jordana, and Amy Villarejo, eds. 2012. "Queer Studies and the Crises of Capitalism." Special issue, *GLQ: A Journal of Lesbian and Gay Studies* 18 (1).

Rosenfeld, Kathryn. 2004–5. "Who the Hell Wants to Be Reasonable?" *Social Anarchism* 37. Accessed September 1, 2015. http://www.socialanarchism.org/mod/magazine/display/135/index.php.

Rossdale, Chris. 2015. "Dancing Ourselves to Death: The Subject of Emma Goldman's Nietzschean Anarchism." *Globalizations* 12 (1): 116–33.

Rostand, Edmond. [1897] 1990. *Cyrano de Bergerac: Comédie Héroique en Cinq Actes et en Vers.* Paris: Le Livre de Poche Classique.

———. 1910. *Chantecler: Pièce en Quatre Actes, en Vers.* Paris: Charpentier et Fasquelle.

Rouhami, Farhand. 2012. "Lessons from Queertopia." In *Queering Anarchism: Addressing and Undressing Power and Desire*, edited by C. B. Daring, J. Rogue, Deric Shannon, and Abbey Volcano, 77–86. Edinburgh: AK Press.

Rouselle, Duane, and Süreyyya Evren, eds. 2011. *Post-anarchism: A Reader.* London: Pluto Press.

Rubin, Gayle. 1975. "The Traffic in Women: Notes on the 'Political Economy' of Sex." In *Toward an Anthropology of Women*, edited by Rayna Reiter, 157–210. New York: Monthly Review Press.

———. 1984. "Thinking Sex: Notes for a Radical Theory of the Politics of Sexuality." In *The Lesbian and Gay Studies Reader*, edited by Henry Abelove, Michele Aina Barale, and David Halperin, 3–44. New York: Routledge, 2003.

Sabsay, Leticia. 2012. "The Emergence of the Other Sexual Citizen: Orientalism and the Modernisation of Sexuality." *Citizenship Studies* 16 (5–6): 605–23.

———. 2014. "Sexual Citizenship and Cultural Imperialism." In *Routledge Handbook of Global Citizenship Studies*, edited by Engin F. Isin and Peter Nyers, 96–109. London: Routledge.

———. 2016. *The Political Imaginary of Sexual Freedom: Subjectivity and Power in the New Sexual Democratic Turn.* London: Palgrave Macmillan.

Scharff, Christina. 2011a. "Disarticulating Feminism: Individualization, Neoliberalism and the Othering of 'Muslim Women.'" *European Journal of Women's Studies* 18 (2): 119–34.

———. 2011b. "'It Is a Colour Thing and a Status Thing, Rather Than a Gender Thing': Negotiating Difference in Talk about Feminism." *Feminism and Psychology* 21 (4): 458–76.

———. 2012. *Repudiating Feminism: Young Women in a Neoliberal World*. London: Ashgate.

Scott, David. 2008. "Introduction: On the Archaeologies of Black Memory." *Small Axe* 26 12 (2): v–xvi.

Scott, Joan. 1996. *Only Paradoxes to Offer: French Feminism and the Rights of Man*. Cambridge, MA: Harvard University Press.

———. 1999. *Gender and the Politics of History*. New York: Columbia University Press.

———. 2007. *The Politics of the Veil*. Princeton, NJ: Princeton University Press.

———. 2011. *The Fantasy of Feminist History*. Durham, NC: Duke University Press.

———. 2012. "The Incommensurability of Psychoanalysis and History." *History and Theory* 51 (1): 63–83.

Sears, Alan. 2005. "Queer Anti-capitalism: What's Left of Lesbian and Gay Liberation?" *Science and Society* 69 (1): 92–112.

Sedgwick, Eve Kosofsky. 1985. *Between Men: English Literature and Male Homosocial Desire*. New York: Columbia University Press.

———. 1990. "Introduction: Axiomatic." In *The Epistemology of the Closet*, 1–63. Berkeley: University of California Press.

———. 2003. *Touching Feeling: Affect, Pedagogy, Performativity*. Durham, NC: Duke University Press.

Seidman, Steven. 1993. "Identity and Politics in a 'Postmodern' Gay Culture: Some Historical and Conceptual Notes." In *Fear of a Queer Planet: Queer Politics and Social Theory*, edited by Michael Warner, 105–42. Minneapolis: University of Minnesota Press.

Serisier, Tanya. 2012. "Theoretical Stories" [Review of Clare Hemmings, *Why Stories Matter: The Political Grammar of Feminist Theory* (Duke University Press, 2011), and Janet Halley and Andrew Parker, eds., *After Sex? On Writing since Queer Theory* (Duke University Press, 2011)]. *Cultural Studies Review* 18 (1): 247–55.

Shaffer, Kerwin. 2011. "Contesting Internationalists: Transnational Anarchism, Anti-imperialism and US Expansion in the Caribbean, 1890s–1920s." *Estudios Interdisciplinarios de América Latina y el Caribe* 22 (2): 11–38.

Shantz, Judith. 2004. "A Marriage of Convenience: Anarchism, Marriage and Borders." *Feminism and Psychology* 14 (1): 181–86.

Shepard, Benjamin. 2010. "Bridging the Divide between Queer Theory and Anarchism." *Sexualities* 13 (4): 511–27.

Shulman, Alix Kates. [1982] 2007. "Dancing in the Revolution: Emma Goldman's Feminism." In *Feminist Interpretations of Emma Goldman*, edited by Penny A. Weiss and Loretta Kensinger, 241–53. University Park: Penn State University Press.

———. 1984. "Living Our Life." In *Between Women: Biographers, Novelists, Critics, Teachers and Artists Write about Their Work on Women*, edited by Carol Ascher, Louise DeSalvo, and Sara Ruddick, 1–13. Boston: Beacon Press.

Silvestri, Vito N. 1969. "Emma Goldman: Enduring Voice of Anarchism." *Today's Speech* 17 (3): 20–25.

Simic, Zora. 2010. "'Door Bitches of Club Feminism'? Academia and Feminist Competency." *Feminist Review*, no. 95: 75–91.

Skeggs, Beverley. 2004. *Class, Self, Culture*. London: Routledge.

Smedley, Agnes. [1929] 1987. *Daughter of Earth*. New York: Feminist Press.

Snitow, Ann Barr, Christine Stansell, and Sharon Thompson. 1983. "Introduction." In *Powers of Desire: The Politics of Sexuality*, edited by Ann Barr Snitow, Christine Stansell, and Sharon Thompson, 9–50. New York: Monthly Review Press.

Solomon, Martha. 1988. "Ideology as Rhetorical Constraint: The Anarchist Agitation of 'Red Emma' Goldman." *Quarterly Journal of Speech* 74 (2): 184–200.

Spelman, Elizabeth V. 1988. *Inessential Woman: Problems of Exclusion in Feminist Thought*. Boston: Beacon Press.

Spivak, Gayatri Chakravorty. [1988] 1994. "Can the Subaltern Speak?" In *Colonial Discourse and Post-colonial Theory*, edited by Patricia Williams and Laura Chrisman, 66–111. New York: Columbia University Press.

———. 1999. "History." In *A Critique of Postcolonial Reason: Toward a History of the Vanishing Present*, 198–311. Cambridge, MA: Harvard University Press.

Springer, Simon. 2012. "Anarchism! What Geography Still Ought to Be." *Antipode* 44 (5): 1605–24.

Stacey, Jackie. 2013a. "Embodying Queer Temporalities: The Future Perfect of Peggy Shaw's Butch Noir." Paper presented at seminar series "Queer Now and Then," University of Manchester, November 16.

———. 2013b. "On Being Open to Others: Cosmopolitanism and the Psychoanalysis of Groups." In *Writing Otherwise: Experiments in Cultural Criticism*, edited by Jackie Stacey and Janet Woolf, 45–60. Manchester: Manchester University Press.

Stansell, Christine, ed. [2000] 2009. *American Moderns: Bohemian New York and the Creation of a New Century*. Princeton, NJ: Princeton University Press.

Sturken, Maria. 1997. "Introduction." In *Tangled Memories: The Vietnam War, the AIDS Epidemic, and the Politics of Remembering*, 1–18. Berkeley: University of California Press.

Tamboukou, Maria. 2012. "Archive Pleasures, or Whose Time Is It?" *Qualitative Social Research* 12 (3): 1–19.

Tapley, Heather. 2012. "Mapping the Hobosexual: A Queer Materialism." *Sexualities* 15 (3–4): 373–90.

Taylor, Barbara. 1992. "Mary Wollstonecraft and the Wild Wish of Early Feminism." *History Workshop Journal* 33 (1): 197–219.

Trimberger, Ellen Kay. 1983. "Feminism, Men, and Modern Love: Greenwich Village, 1900–1925." In *Powers of Desire: The Politics of Sexuality*, edited by Ann Barr Snitow, Christine Stansell, and Sharon Thompson, 131–52. New York: Monthly Review Press.

Tronto, Joan. 2002. "The 'Nanny' Question in Feminism." *Hypatia* 17 (2): 34–51.

Tudor, Alyosxa. 2017. "Dimensions of Transnationalism." *Feminist Review*, no. 117 (forthcoming).

Turcato, Davide. 2007. "Italian Anarchism as a Transnational Movement, 1885–1915." *International Review of Social History* 52 (3): 407–44.

UNAIDS. 2012. *Impact of the Global Economic Crisis on Women, Girls and Gender Equality*. UN Issues Brief. New York: United Nations.

Vicinus, Martha. 1994. "Lesbian History: All Theory and No Facts or All Facts and No Theory?" *Radical History Review*, no. 60: 57–75.

Volpp, Leti. 2001. "Feminism versus Multiculturalism." *Columbia Law Review* 101 (5): 1181–218.

Walby, Sylvia. 2011. *The Future of Feminism.* Cambridge: Polity Press.

Ward, John William. [1970] 1999. "Introduction." In Alexander Berkman, *Prison Memoirs of an Anarchist*, xi–xxviii. New York: New York Review of Books.

Waters, Sarah. 1999. *Affinity.* London: Virago.

Watson, Martha. 1999. "Emma Goldman as a Liberated Woman: A Feminist Writes an Anarchist Life." In *Lives of Their Own: Rhetorical Dimensions in Autobiographies of Women Activists*, 31–46. Columbia: University of Southern California Press.

Weed, Elizabeth. 2014. "The Lure of the Postcritical." Paper presented at Les quarante vies du Centre d'études féminines et d'études de genre, fortieth anniversary conference, Université Paris 8, May 26–27.

Weeks, Kathi. 2007. "Life within and against Work: Affective Labor, Feminist Critique, and Post-Fordist Politics." *Ephemera: Theory and Politics in Organization* 7 (1): 233–49.

———. 2011. *The Problem with Work: Feminism, Marxism, Anti-work Politics, and Post-work Imaginaries.* Durham, NC: Duke University Press.

Wehling, Jason. 2007. "Anarchy in Interpretation: The Life of Emma Goldman." In *Feminist Interpretations of Emma Goldman*, edited by Penny A. Weiss and Loretta Kensinger, 19–37. University Park: Penn State University Press.

Weiss, Penny A., and Loretta Kensinger, eds. 2007. *Feminist Interpretations of Emma Goldman.* University Park: Penn State University Press.

Weiss, Penny A., and Loretta Kensinger, with Berenice A. Carroll. 2007. "Digging for Gold(man): What We Found." In *Feminist Interpretations of Emma Goldman*, edited by Penny A. Weiss and Loretta Kensinger, 3–18. University Park: Penn State University Press.

Wetzsteon, Ross. 2002. *Republic of Dreams: Greenwich Village, the American Bohemia 1910–1960.* New York: Simon and Schuster.

Wexler, Alice. 1981. "Emma Goldman on Mary Wollstonecraft." *Feminist Studies* 7 (1): 113–33.

———. 1984. *Emma Goldman: An Intimate Life.* London: Virago.

———. 1992. "The Anxiety of Biography." In *The Challenge of Feminist Biography: Writing the Lives of Modern American Women*, edited by Sara Alpern, Joyce Antler, Elisabeth Israels Perry, and Ingrid Winter Scobie, 34–50. Chicago: University of Illinois Press.

Wiegman, Robyn. 2012. *Object Lessons.* Durham, NC: Duke University Press.

———. 2014. "The Times We're In: Queer Feminist Criticism and the Reparative 'Turn.'" *Feminist Theory* 15 (1): 4–25.

———. 2015. "Eve's Triangles, or Queer Studies beside Itself." *differences* 26 (1): 48–73.

Wiegman, Robyn, and Elizabeth A. Wilson. 2015. "Introduction: Antinormativity's Queer Conventions." *differences* 26 (1): 1–25.

Williams, Rachel, and Michele Andrisin Wittig. 1997. "'I'm Not a Feminist, But . . .': Factors Contributing to the Discrepancy between Pro-feminist Orientation and Feminist Social Identity." *Sex Roles* 37 (11–12): 885–904.

Window, Julie A. 1996. "Emma Goldman: Queen of the Anarchists, Anti–Role Model." *H2S04*, no. 6: 26–27.

Wittig, Monique. [1980] 1992. *The Straight Mind and Other Essays*. Boston: Beacon Press.

Womankind. 2009. *Who Pays the Price? The Impact of the Global Economic Recession on Women in Developing Countries*. London: Womankind.

Wright, Michelle M. 2015. *Physics of Blackness: Beyond the Middle Passage Epistemology*. Minneapolis: Minnesota University Press.

Young-Bruehl, Elisabeth. 1998. *Subject to Biography: Psychoanalysis, Feminism and Writing Women's Lives*. Cambridge, MA: Harvard University Press.

Yuval-Davis, Nira. 2006. "Intersectionality and Feminist Politics." *European Journal of Women's Studies* 13 (3): 193–209.

Zeck, Jeanne-Marie. 1999. "Stumbling toward Ecstasy: 'Cyrano De Bergerac' as Comedy in Martin's 'Roxanne' and Well's [sic] 'The Truth about Cats and Dogs.'" *Literature/Film Quarterly* 7 (3): 218–22.

Zinn, Howard. 2012. "Preface: Emma." In *Three Plays: The Political Theatre of Howard Zinn—Emma, Marx in Soho, and Daughter of Venus*. Boston: Beacon Press.

Žižek, Slavoj. 2009. *In Defense of Lost Causes*. London: Verso.

Index

Note: Entries include material covered in Sperry's (real-life) letters to Goldman but not in Goldman's (fictional) letters to Sperry.

Antliff, Allan, 253n26
archives: consulted in research, 238n5, 239n11, 255n44; critical, 2, 6–7, 12–14, 16; imaginative, 8–9, 35–36, 129, 131–32, 165–216; living, 8–9, 239n14; subjective, 2, 6–7, 30–32; theoretical, 2, 7, 13–14
Arondekar, Anjali, 21
austerity, 66–67, 123, 244n27
autobiography, 218–20, 241n34, 256n1

Bakunin, Mikhail, 40, 200
Beck-Gernsheim, Elizabeth, 252n17
Behn, Aphra, 33
Benjamin, Walter, 85
Bergland, Betty, 241n34
Berkman, Alexander, 9–10, 120–21, 218, 224, 256n2; exile of, 116, 250n39; homosexual attachments of, 131, 158, 250n5; imprisonment of, 9, 131, 219, 250n5, 254n31; Sperry on, 195–96, 199–200
Berlant, Lauren, 30, 52, 123–24, 145
biographies of Goldman, 239n15, 242n6
birth control, 42–43, 53–54, 90–96, 126, 242n8, 247n13
bisexuality, 161, 164
Blackwood, Evelyn, 252n20
Blake, Linnie, 132, 148
Bly, Nelly, 249n30
Bracke, Sarah, 253n23
Brady, Ed, 155
Brah, Avtar, 30, 104, 241n33
Breslow, Jacob, 248n18
Brettschneider, Maria, 1, 21
Brieux, Eugène, 215
Brown, Gavin, 143
Bruno, Guido, 110
Bryant, Louise, 42, 134
Butler, Judith, 1, 127, 138, 243n18, 246n36, 247n9, 250n2
Buwalda, William, 247n10
Byrne, Sian, 246n3

Capes, Ben, 107
Carroll, Berenice, 52, 221, 245n32

Chalberg, John, 10, 249n37
China, 252n19
Clark, Danae, 252n16
Cleminson, Richard, 134, 247n11
Clinton, Hillary, 68
Coetzee, J. M., 33, 240n30
Cohn, Gene, 117–18
Cohn, Jesse, 83, 85–86, 247n6
colonialism, 84, 86–87, 139–41, 151, 247n7, 252n18. See also racism
Colton, James, 116–23, 257n7
Comstock Act, 255n41
Connell, Raewyn, 76
Cook, Blanche Wiesen, 21, 58, 157, 160, 164
creativity, 51, 145–46, 158, 230, 258n15
Crenshaw, Kimberlé, 68, 104
Curtis, Debra, 142
Cvetkovich, Ann, 157, 240n25
Cyrano de Bergerac, 226–33, 257n10
Czolgosz, Leon, 5, 9, 90

dance, 218
Davis, Kathy, 75
Davis, Laurence, 135, 251nn8–9
Day, Janet, 147, 242n10
Dean, Jonathan, 74–75
de Cleyre, Voltairine, 41
Defoe, Daniel, 33
de Lauretis, Teresa, 246n36
Deleuze, Gilles, 58, 148
Delphy, Christine, 245n33, 251n15
D'Emilio, John, 21, 139–40, 240n21, 253n25
disappointment, 86, 123–24, 220–21, 224–25, 245n32, 250n39
disgust, 253n22
Doan, Laura, 22, 131
Dodge Luhan, Mabel, 41–42
Drinnon, Anna Maria and Richard, 4, 97, 220
Dubois, Ellen, 56, 107, 134, 243n17
Duggan, Lisa, 142–43, 254n32
Dunye, Cheryl, 34–35, 241n37

Eastman, Crystal, 41, 134
Eastman, Max, 41, 62
Edelman, Lee, 251n14
education, 243n13
Elam, J. Daniel, 84
Ellis, Havelock, 159
Eng, David, 144, 252n19
Engels, Friedrich, 55, 239n18, 251n10
equality, 54, 60–61, 66–70, 244n28
Escobar, Arturo, 247n7
Espinosa, Magno, 41
essentialism. *See* heterosexism, Goldman's; nature
eugenics, 53–54, 90–96
Evren, Süreyyya, 84–85, 247n6
exile, 83, 116, 246nn2–3, 249n37, 250n39. *See also* migration

Faderman, Lillian, 157, 161, 164
Falk, Candace, 238n5; on autobiography, 256n1; on bisexuality, 161; criticisms of Goldman, 56, 149, 239n16; on Goldman's name, 4–5; on Goldman's public appearances, 3, 223, 238n6; on Goldman's relationship with Reitman, 153; on metaphor, 54; on minorities vs. majorities, 242n11; on panache, 225; on racism, 97, 103, 248n19, 249n29
Fanon, Frantz, 106, 249n28
Fassin, Eric, 253n24
Felman, Shoshana, 28
femininity, 10–12, 37–65, 76–79, 112–15, 117, 256n6; and lesbianism, 159–60; and respectability, 48–49, 74
feminist and/or queer, as terms, 24–25, 238n9, 240n28. *See also* antifeminism
Ferguson, Kathy, 1, 221, 241n2, 251n7; on Goldman's inconsistencies, 62, 245n32, 257n13; on Goldman's influences, 243n16, 253n26; on intersectionality, 58; on love, 217; on racism, 80–81, 95, 97–98, 122, 248n22, 248n25; on sexual instinct, 154–55; on violence, 23, 246n5

Ferrer, Francisco, 23, 243n13
Firestone, Shulamith, 127, 137, 251n12
Fitzgerald, Eleanor, 159
Flax, Jane, 246n35
Floyd, Dell, 134
Fogg, Ally, 1
Foucault, Michel, 23, 131
Fourier, Charles, 243n15
Foust, Christina, 58, 87, 220, 222
Frankel, Oz, 58, 238n4, 249n37
Fraser, Nancy, 69, 129, 250n2, 252n17
Freccero, Carla, 139–40, 144–45, 150n2
free love. *See* sexual freedom
Freeman, Estelle, 21
Freud, Sigmund, 55, 76, 243n16
Frost, Ginger, 134, 243n17
Fuss, Diana, 252n22

Garber, Marjorie, 161, 164, 255n40
Gemie, Sharif, 242n3
Giddens, Anthony, 252n17
Gilman, Sander, 111
Gilroy, Paul, 96, 124, 248n18
Gordon, Avery, 33
Gordon, Linda, 48, 56, 107, 134, 243n17
Gornick, Vivian, 1, 220
Greenland, Cyril, 4, 87
Greenway, Judy, 56, 159, 238n6, 254n39
Grosz, Elizabeth, 24
Gurstein, Rochelle, 244n24

Haaland, Bonnie, 16, 147, 164, 243n16
Hapgood, Hutchins, 184, 190–91, 200, 204, 219
Haraway, Donna, 252n18
Haritaworn, Jim, 253n23
Hartman, Saidiya, 30, 34
Heckert, Jamie, 4, 134
Hennessy, Rosemary, 135–36, 139–40, 142, 144
Herzog, Don, 220–21
heterosexism, Goldman's, 16, 56, 61–62, 147
Hexe, 1, 253n29

Hirschfeld, Magnus, 157–59
history: and affect, 2–11, 19–22, 25–31, 131, 238n8; and letter-writing, 30–33; and loss, 32–35, 85–86, 252n20; and psychoanalysis, 26–28; radical, 21–25, 85–86, 128–31, 139, 157; speculative, 30, 34–35. *See also* temporality
hobos, 151, 254n33
homonationalism, 141, 253n24
homonormativity, 142–43, 253n24
homosexuality, 56–57, 131, 135–36, 137–42, 240n21, 250n5; Goldman's ambivalence about, 128, 130, 156–66, 247n12; Goldman's support for, 38, 57–58, 90, 138, 239n20, 247n11. *See also* lesbianism; Sperry, Almeda
homosociality, 137, 251n10
Hong, Nathaniel, 248n27
Hoover, J. Edgar, 116
Hustak, Carla, 92, 95
Hutchinson, Elizabeth Quay, 59

Ibsen, Henrik, 42, 258n15
identity, 15–17, 22, 127–31, 139–44, 252n19, 252n21
Ince, Anthony, 254n35
India, 84
individualism, 10, 51–52, 115, 242n10, 249n37
individuality, 51–52, 55–56, 145–46, 242n10, 249n37
internationalism, 13–14, 80–124, 246n4, 247n6
intersectionality, 57–58, 103–6, 245n31
intersubjectivity, 70–73, 83–84
intimacy, 2–4, 237n3. *See also* kinship, universal
Isaak, Abe and Mary, 254n38

Jackson, Peter, 143
Jewishness, 103–8, 114, 247n9
Jolly, Margaretta, 31

Katz, Jonathan Ned, 163
Kennan, Ellen, 159

Kensinger, Loretta, 1–2, 58–59, 77, 158, 221, 247n9
Kersner, Jacob, 116
Khanna, Ranjana, 27
Kinna, Ruth, 41, 254n36
kinship, universal, 93–96, 105, 118–23, 126, 155, 254n38
Kowal, Donna M., 58, 242n6
Kristeva, Julia, 240n26
Kropotkin, Peter, 40, 52
Kurtz, Arabella, 240n30

labour: affective, 136; domestic, 12, 59–61; productive, 15, 125–26, 135–37, 250n3; reproductive, 38–65, 90–95, 101, 125–28, 132–38, 154–56, 239n18, 252n17; reserve army of, 42, 244n27
Landauer, Martin, 40
Lenin, Vladimir, 90
Leonard, Zoe, 34–35, 241n37
lesbianism, 35, 73, 138, 157, 159–61, 164. *See also* homosexuality; Sperry, Almeda
letter-writing, 30–32, 62, 83, 87, 241n35, 244n22; Goldman and Colton, 119–23; Goldman and Reitman, 62, 152–53, 244n21; Goldman and Smedley, 255n42; Goldman and Sperry, 35–36, 131–32, 161–215, 255nn44–45; Marx and Engels, 251n10
Loizidou, Elena, 4, 230
love, 45–46, 56, 118, 126, 133, 219
Lumsden, Linda, 59, 81, 106, 147, 248n24, 253n28

Maiguashca, Bice, 1, 243n18
Marcus, Jane, 22
Marcuse, Herbert, 52, 128, 242n12, 250n1, 251n13
marriage, 45–50, 52, 100–101, 150, 242n9; Goldman's, 9–10, 87–88, 109–10, 116–23, 250n40
Marso, Lori Jo, 62, 164, 220–21
Marx, Karl, 251n10
Marxism, 85, 136, 143, 145, 250n3, 251n11

masculinity, 88–92, 160, 247n11, 248n16, 250n6
Massad, Joseph, 252n20
materialism, 15, 129, 135–45
May, Todd, 246n6
McEwan, Cheryl, 241n36
McKinley, William, 5, 9
McRobbie, Angela, 74, 244n26
Merck, Mandy, 251n12
methodology, 17–30, 54–55, 130–31, 221–25, 250n4
Michel, Louise, 159–60
Mieli, Mario, 137–38
migration, 13–14, 87–88, 103–4, 245n30, 248n20. *See also* exile
militarism, 15, 45–48, 67, 88–91, 100, 105
minorities vs. majorities, 51–52, 102, 242n11
Mirbeau, Octave, 40, 240n3
Molyneux, Maxine, 43, 59
Most, Johann, 219
Mulvey, Laura, 78
Muslim veiling, 66–67, 245n33

names, Goldman's, 3–5
nationalism, 43, 68, 81, 115–16, 124, 127
nature, 129–30, 145–56, 158, 253nn26–27
Nettlau, Max, 53, 155, 257n7
Newman, Saul, 246n6
Nicholson, C. Brid, 160–61, 164, 256n1
Nietzsche, Friedrich, 213, 215, 253n26

Occupy movement, 85
O'Hare, Kate, 159
Oroonoko, 33
Ostman, Heather, 155

Palestine, 247n9
panache, 225–35, 239n12
Parker, Andrew, 135–36, 142, 144–45, 250n3, 251n10
Passerini, Luisa, 24
passion, 3, 133–35, 144, 217–35, 253n26, 256n4

performances, Goldman's, 3, 49, 87, 98, 110, 223, 238n6, 239n17, 256n5
Phillips, Adam, 27–28
Phoenix, Ann, 104
phrenology, 111
physical appearance, Goldman's, 9, 110–14, 117, 239n17, 249nn33–34
Poirier, Suzanne, 62, 244n23, 254n34
Porter, David, 41, 58
postcolonialism, 22, 33–34, 66, 240n23, 241n36
Presley, Sharon, 4
Price, Ruth, 255n42
Prichard, Alex, 41
prison, 43, 98–100, 131, 158–59, 250n5
prostitution, 45–46, 67, 148–51, 242n9, 245n30, 254n31; Sperry's experiences of, 161–63, 179, 185, 204–5
Proudhon, Pierre-Joseph, 40–41, 46
Proulx, Annie, 249n36
psychoanalysis, 26–28, 77–78, 243n16, 251n13
Puar, Jasbir K., 127, 141, 144, 253n24
public/private divide, 38–41, 44, 57–60, 64–65, 118, 135–36, 241n34

quality vs. quantity, 50–56, 68–70, 91–95
queer and/or feminist, as terms, 24–25, 238n9, 240n28

racism, 80–115, 123–24, 248n18, 248n25, 249n28, 253n23. *See also* anti-Semitism; colonialism; violence: racial
Radstone, Susannah, 27
Ramnath, Maia, 86
Reclaim the Night, 68
Reitman, Ben, 62, 102, 151–53, 219, 244n20, 248n23, 254n34; quarrel with Sperry, 203–6
Reizenbaum, Marilyn, 103
representation, 4–5, 39, 108–19, 173, 248n24, 249n30, 249n35
reproductive labour. *See* labour: reproductive

Rhys, Jean, 33
rights, 127–29, 141, 251n13, 252n19, 253n23
Riviere, Joan, 78
Robinson Crusoe, 33
Rofel, Lisa, 141, 143, 252n19
Rogness, Kate, 58, 87, 220, 222
Roosevelt, Theodore, 47, 169
Rose, Jacqueline, 27–28, 241n35
Rosenfeld, Kathryn, 4
Rossdale, Chris, 153
Rostand, Edmond, 226–33, 257n10
Rouhami, Farhand, 239n13
Rubin, Gayle, 127, 252n18
Russia, 9, 90, 245n32, 250n39

Sabsay, Leticia, 127, 141, 251n13
Sanford, Stella, 251n12
Sanger, Margaret, 42, 101, 134, 159, 248n17, 257n7
Scharff, Christina, 73–74
Schwarz, Bill, 27
Scott, Joan, 2, 22, 28, 66, 240n24
Sears, Alan, 252n16
Sedgwick, Eve, 68–69, 136–37, 250n4, 252n21
Seidman, Steven, 142
sexual freedom, 15–17, 54–57, 61–63, 70, 92, 126–67, 243n17, 251n13
Shepard, Benjamin, 243n18
Shulman, Alix Kates, 58, 61, 64, 147, 163
Simic, Zora, 73–74
slavery, 33–34, 99–101, 107
Smedley, Agnes, 255n42, 257n7
Solomon, Martha, 49, 149–50, 256n3
sorrow, 120–21
Spelman, Elizabeth, 253n27
Sperry, Almeda, 35–36, 130–32, 161–215, 255nn44–45
spiritualism, 240n29
Spitzer, Leo, 26
Spivak, Gayatri, 22
Stacey, Jackie, 240n25

Stansell, Christine: on feminist history, 40, 59; on Goldman's charisma, 3, 217, 223; on Goldman's letters, 31; on racism, 97; on sexual freedom, 92, 134, 147, 244n22, 248n16
Stirner, Max, 198
Strindberg, August, 55, 258n15
Sturken, Maria, 241n32
subject/object divide, 71–72
suffragism, 11, 38, 43–44, 49–50, 67
Swinton, John, 99

Tamboukou, Maria, 63, 256n1
Tapley, Heather, 254n33
Taylor, Barbara, 240n26
temporality, 15, 22–24, 240nn25–26, 251n14. See also anarchism: as prefigurative; history
theatre, 135–36, 162, 214, 226–33, 249n37, 257n10, 258n15. See also performances, Goldman's
Thompson, Charles, 114
Trimberger, Ellen, 243n17
Tudor, Alyosxa, 104, 248n20

Van der Walt, Lucien, 246n3
Van Valkenburgh, Warren Starr, 4
Vicinus, Martha, 32, 131
violence: racial, 34, 80–82, 97, 101–3, 106–8, 115 (see also slavery); sexual, 67, 115, 245n31, 248n23, 249n29; state, 23, 246n5

Ward, John, 4
Watermelon Woman, The, 34–35
Watson, Martha, 223, 225
Weeks, Kathi, 136
Wehling, Jason, 2
Weiss, Penny, 221
Wells, H. G., 42
West, Rebecca, 42
Wexler, Alice, 2–3, 10, 58, 64, 103, 248n26, 256n4

Whitman, Walt, 19, 158, 230–31
Wide Sargasso Sea, 33
Wiegman, Robyn, 24, 104, 238n8, 240n28, 252n21
Wilde, Oscar, 157–58
Wilson, Charlotte, 43
Wilson, Elizabeth A., 252n21
Window, Julie A., 234
Wittig, Monique, 138

Wollstonecraft, Mary, 19, 256n4
Wright, Michelle, 96

Young-Bruehl, Elisabeth, 25–26
young women and feminism, 73–75
Yuval-Davis, Nira, 104

Zinn, Howard, 161
Žižek, Slavoj, 257n12